Harry Byrd
and
the Changing Face of
Virginia Politics
1945 – 1966

Harry Byrd

and the Changing Face of
Virginia Politics
1945-1966

J. Harvie Wilkinson III

The University Press of Virginia
Charlottesville

THE UNIVERSITY PRESS
OF VIRGINIA
Copyright © 1968
by the Rector and Visitors
of the University of Virginia

First published 1968
Second printing 1969

Standard Book
Number: 8139–0239–8
Library of Congress
Catalog Card Number: 68–22731
Printed in
the United States of America

To My Father

Acknowledgments

A BOOK is so often the product of many minds that one
person might well blush to be termed its author. My
acknowledgments, bibliography, and footnotes fall far short of
expressing my total indebtedness. To those people in Virginia
and elsewhere who assisted the project, limited space compels
me to extend a collective and too impersonal thanks.

I owe much to Yale University and its Scholar of the House
Program under the direction of Professor Frederick M. Watkins for relieving me of academic commitments during my
senior year to permit concentration on the completion of the
manuscript of this book. Of particular help was my adviser,
William Lilley, with whom I spent many a productive (and
embattled) hour. Professor C. Vann Woodward of the History
Department of Yale University and Professor Fred I. Green-
stein of the Political Science Department of Wesleyan University read the manuscript, suggested needed refinements of
style and subject matter, and rescued me from mistakes of fact
and interpretation.

Only the generous assistance of members of the Virginia
press made the book possible. Reporters, columnists, and editors were always willing to share knowledge of the workings
of Virginia politics with me. James Latimer, Charles
McDowell, Jr., Virginius Dabney, and former state Senator
FitzGerald Bemiss read the manuscript with an eye for proper
emphasis and nuance.

Over seventy-five interviews were conducted during the course of the study. Interviewees included courthouse officials, state office holders, members of the press and academic communities, municipal reformers, appointive officials, Negroes, union leaders, and Republicans. They were often persons whose opinions were not available in manuscript or published sources. In most cases I promised not to give the names of those interviewed, but their contribution to my understanding of Virginia politics was invaluable. Throughout the book, the symbol "°" will be used to indicate that an interview was the source of the statement or quotation involved.

Several Virginians greatly aided particular sections of the book. My special thanks go to state Senator Joseph C. Hutcheson for his hospitality in Brunswick County and his contributions to Chapter 1, to George Kelley of the Norfolk *Virginian-Pilot* for illuminating the politics of the Hampton Roads area, and to Horace Edwards, Edwin E. Holm, and Alan S. Donnahoe for insights on topics discussed in Chapters 4, 6, and 11, respectively. Books by Benjamin Muse and Robbins L. Gates and source materials given me by W. Gibson Harris, Jr., eased my task considerably in the chapter on massive resistance. Map II in that chapter is based on materials and maps in Mr. Gates's *The Making of Massive Resistance*, published by the University of North Carolina Press in 1962. Assistance was often given by many whose views differed from my own, and for the deficiencies of the final product all, save the author, stand acquitted.

The illustrations, including the frontispiece, are reproduced by courtesy of Richmond Newspapers.

To Betty Cox and Sue Rasberry go my thanks for typing the manuscript and to JoAnn Daugherty and Mary Page Winberg for other valuable clerical assistance. The staffs of the Virginia State Library, Sterling Memorial Library at Yale, the Richmond Public Library, and the Alderman Library at the University of Virginia maintained good humor in the face of extreme provocation. On occasion Dean Morris and his comrades at the file room for Richmond Newspapers broke the monotony of clippings and microfilm with festive diversions which were most welcome. The staff of the University Press of Virginia was most helpful during the later revisions and final preparation of the manuscript.

Finally, I would like to thank Mr. Lewis F. Powell, Jr., and Mr. Virginius Dabney for inspiring and sustaining my interest in the politics of Virginia and the nation for almost as long as I can remember. Much of the credit for whatever merit the book may possess goes to them and to my father, who has encouraged the project in every conceivable way from the dreaming stage through the fourth revision.

J. HARVIE WILKINSON III

Richmond, February 1968

Contents

Illustrations

Maps

Text Tables

Part I
Harry Byrd's Virginia

Introduction

W AS the Byrd organization a wonderful "one-hoss shay,"
sturdily constructed for many a decade only to collapse
in a heap in the mid-nineteen-sixties? Was it some form of
political chameleon, always changing with the changing times?
Or was it instead the stern sea cliff, forever beating back the
challenging surf?

Until recently, many adhered to the last view, so indubita-
bly did Virginia's immediate past belong to the Byrd machine
and to Harry Flood Byrd. Although devotees claimed for its
principles eternal truth, and enemies saw it as the agent of
permanent evil, the Byrd organization was never a transcen-
dental force somehow ordained to carry on forever in Virginia's
political life. It emerged as an understandable response to a
particular period in Virginia history whose pages have already
been turned. Its origins trace to Virginia in the "dark days" of
Reconstruction, during which many leaders of the Byrd organization spent their boyhood.

Throughout Reconstruction, Virginia struggled to mitigate
her poverty and pay the remnant of a staggering Civil War
debt. The debt issue dominated the state's politics for many
years after the war, for by 1870 the debt, with interest,
amounted to about $45,000,000. Interest payments at 6 per
cent reached $2,700,000 annually, a sum larger than the tax
income of the Old Dominion in many a prewar year. During

the 1870's control of the state government rested in the hands of Carpetbagger Republicans and Conservatives, who spoke generally for business, railroad, and urban interests and who advocated, in the name of state honor, full repayment of the debt, even if repayment meant shutting down the public school system to satisfy out-of-state creditors. Bitterly opposed to this position were the Readjusters, who came to power in 1882. They promised to scale down the debt and allot a greater proportion of the state's revenues to public schools.[1]

Harry Byrd was born in 1887 in a state scarred by poverty and committed more to repaying past obligations than maintaining present services. Byrd's boyhood experiences paralleled to some extent the hardships of the state. When he was fifteen, he left high school to try to salvage his father's bankrupt weekly newspaper, now a thriving daily, the Winchester *Evening Star*. He there learned the difficulties of struggling out of debt. With the newspaper's credit exhausted, the young publisher arranged to have only enough newsprint delivered each morning to meet that afternoon's needs. He paid cash for each delivery.[2] By the time he was twenty, he had converted the newspaper deficit into an annual profit. He began then to lease and buy apple orchards around Winchester, an activity which led to his ownership of the largest one-family apple-growing, packing, and processing enterprise in the world.

Abhorrence of public debt and cash-drawer frugality were the hallmarks of the Byrd era in Virginia. Many analysts have traced these attitudes to Byrd's early struggle to save the family newspaper and to his awareness of the debt Virginia strove to pay off while he grew up. Byrd first gained prominence on the state political scene in 1923 when he led a fight against a proposed $50,000,000 bond issue for highway construction. Although many of the state's urban, business, and industrial leaders favored the bonds, Virginia farmers feared that their lands

---

[1] C. V. Woodward, *Origins of the New South, 1877–1913* (Baton Rouge, La.: Louisiana State University Press, 1951), pp. 4–5, 92–98; W. E. Hemphill, M. W. Schlegel, and S. E. Engelberg, *Cavalier Commonwealth* (New York: McGraw-Hill, 1957), pp. 372–81.

[2] Hemphill *et al.*, pp. 423–24.

would bear the brunt of new state taxes, and they opposed all proposals for new bonds for highway construction.[3] The bond issue was decisively defeated in a popular referendum, and Byrd's famous "pay-as-you-go" fiscal policy was instituted instead. Revenue from gasoline taxes and motor vehicle licenses was reserved for highway construction, and pavement was laid down only as fast as that revenue permitted. Virginia avoided any trace of public debt.

The machine did not, however, emerge simultaneously with the rise of pay-as-you-go and Harry Byrd. It existed long before Byrd. Its founder, Thomas Staples Martin, was neither a farmer nor an aristocrat, but a shrewd railroad lawyer. Martin in 1893 won an upset election to the United States Senate over Fitzhugh Lee, former governor of Virginia and nephew of the great Confederate general. Martin served in the Senate and headed the "regular" Democratic organization from 1894 until his death in 1919. During this period the organization acquired characteristics which persisted throughout Byrd's lifetime.

Among the organization's early achievements was the Virginia constitution of 1902, which drastically reduced the state's electorate through such devices as a poll tax and a literacy test and which formally provided for racially segregated schools. As a result of the new constitutional provisions, the number of Negroes qualified to vote shrank from 147,000 to 21,000, and the number of votes cast in Virginia in the presidential election of 1904 was only slightly more than half the total cast four years earlier.[4] In spite of the diminished electorate Martin and his lieutenants were constantly forced to conclude alliances both with "independent" Democrats led by Carter Glass and with the powerful Anti-Saloon League, headed by Bishop James Cannon, Jr.[5] Only in 1917, when the organization split, did an insurgent candidate, Westmoreland Davis, upset its supremacy.

[3] Richmond *Times-Dispatch*, Oct. 21, 1966.

[4] James Reichley, *States in Crisis* (Chapel Hill, N.C.: University of North Carolina Press, 1964), pp. 7–9.

[5] See Virginius Dabney, *Dry Messiah* (New York: Alfred A. Knopf, 1949), for an insightful account of the politics of this period.

After Martin's death in 1919 state politics came under a brief period of collective leadership. Byrd first emerged on the state scene during these years. His father, Richard Evelyn Byrd, had been speaker of the House of Delegates and a trusted aide of Senator Martin. Byrd also learned politics from "Uncle Hal," a congressman from Appomattox County and another leader in the old Martin organization. Even with these powerful connections Byrd entered his race for governor as something of an insurgent. Bishop Cannon had decided to swing the Democratic nomination in 1925 to his pet spokesman, G. Walter Mapp, and he strongly advised Byrd not to run. But Cannon's warning angered Byrd, and the youthful state senator, who had originally intended to run in 1929, pushed his timetable up four years and decisively defeated Mapp and a Republican opponent to become Virginia's chief executive at the age of thirty-eight.[6]

Though Byrd has long been labeled a conservative, he did not always fit that mold. As governor of Virginia from 1926 to 1930, he was more often termed a progressive, and his administration is generally conceded to have been one of the most fruitful in Virginia's history. Under his "Program of Progress" he converted a million-dollar deficit into a handsome surplus. He sponsored strict legislation which made lynching a state offense and all members of a lynch mob subject to murder charges. He also implemented voting and tax reforms to attract new residents and industry to Virginia, abolished the state tax on land, and promoted rural electrification, conservation, and the tourist trade.[7]

Byrd never neglected Virginia's farmers. He had championed the farmers' cause in 1923 by defeating the bond issue. As governor he continued to act in their behalf. In his 1926 message to the General Assembly on taxation Byrd noted that

agriculture in Virginia is bearing a heavier burden of taxation, in terms of net income, than any other industry is bearing. The state would be quickly rewarded by a readjustment of our tax burden in

[6] Richmond *Times-Dispatch*, Oct. 21, 1966.
[7] Reichley, p. 9; Hemphill *et al.*, pp. 426–27.

order to give reasonable relief to agriculture. . . . I favor the removal of the State tax on land and tangible personal property which . . . will do much to accelerate the slowly returning prosperity of the Virginia farmer and will also help the householder and wage earner.[8]

Byrd's most significant reform, however, was a complete reorganization of Virginia's state government. Frequently referring to Wilson's maxim of simplified and visible government, Byrd consolidated nearly one hundred bureaus, boards, and departments, previously independent of the governor, into fourteen departments directly subject to the governor's control.[9] The number of statewide elective officers was reduced from seven to three. Byrd's reforms were initially praised by liberals and progressives everywhere, but critics in Virginia later viewed his measures as little more than a device for machine control. Although the form of Byrd's politics in the early years may have been progressive, their substance became increasingly conservative. Byrd's genius was in establishing reins of control which he and his lieutenants held long after he left the governor's chair in 1930.

Byrd was the only major innovator in Virginia for years. His daring and his early passion for reform were never equaled by the many who followed him. A Virginia-born newspaperman, Cabell Phillips, has claimed that the Byrd organization produced "leaders and functionaries of uniform honesty and competence, but few who have risen above the dead level of mediocrity. It has given Virginia 'good' government . . . but it has been uninspired, unimaginative government." [10] Although Phillips' evaluation was in several instances cruelly unjust, there have been some who would lay the blame for unimaginative government on Byrd's doorstep. When Byrd, who became United States senator from Virginia in 1933, issued orders not to run, those who defied his wishes went unsupported. Since

[8] *Message to General Assembly on Taxation,* Feb. 2, 1926.
[9] Hemphill *et al.,* pp. 426–27; Byrd, *Address to General Assembly on Subject of Simplification of Government in Virginia,* Feb. 3, 1926 (Richmond, 1926).
[10] "New Rumblings in the Old Dominion," *New York Times Magazine,* June 19, 1949, p. 10.

Byrd generally gave his "go-ahead nod" only to those whose ideas closely paralleled his own, a deadening conformity was always in danger of developing. Yet for decades Virginians felt the Byrd banner the best possible standard to which to conform.

This attitude prevailed especially in the years between Byrd's governorship and World War II when the organization was rarely challenged. The only break in its hegemony occurred in 1937, when James H. Price, then lieutenant governor, decided to seek the governorship. Price, a man far more in sympathy with the New Deal and the national Democratic administration than was Senator Byrd, did anything but delight the organization with his announcement. Inasmuch as he had constructed a formidable network of friendships and alliances throughout the state, the organization soon realized that it would be difficult to defeat him and finally supported him to avoid embarrassment. When Price became governor, however, the organization, through its control of the state legislature, successfully delayed or killed most of his program.[11]

It was not until after World War II that many suspected the Byrd machine might be something less than immortal. Then cracks and fissures began to appear and majorities grew slimmer. By 1967 a major upheaval had occurred. The story of that upheaval and the causes and consequences of the Byrd machine's demise are the subject of this study.

[11] V. O. Key, Jr., *Southern Politics* (New York: Alfred A. Knopf, 1949), p. 23.

Chapter 1

The Byrd Organization
on the Local Level
Brunswick Courthouse

THE county courthouse will go down in history as the symbol of Byrd's political rule in the Old Dominion. For forty
years and more courthouse crowds from almost every county in
Virginia faithfully supported Harry Flood Byrd and the subsequent procession of Byrd loyalists to the governor's chair. Nowhere was this support more devoted than in the Southside,
that sprawling stretch of rural Virginia from Nansemond to
Patrick County (see Map I). This stanchly conservative area
was for years a prolific source of votes for Harry Byrd and it
contributed to the organization some of its most colorful and
distinguished spokesmen. If Byrd's word was law throughout
most of Virginia, it was nothing short of gospel throughout the
Southside.

There is romance to the Southside. Here were the lordly
plantations which graced Virginia before the Civil War. Here
also the Johnny Rebs fought the final stages of that war—at
Petersburg, where rawboned men last-ditched against the
hated Yankee, and at Appomattox, where Lee surrendered and
the lost cause lies forever enshrined. Today the region boasts of
Smithfield hams, peanuts, and dark-green tobacco fields
stretching sleepily in the summer sun.

Beneath the haze of history and rural rhapsody lies another
Southside; this one not so pleasant. To one native Virginian the
region appeared "a bleak country of red clay and scrub pine; of

somnolent small towns; of marginal, worked-out farms; of much poverty, ignorance, and prejudice."[1] It was long an area of one-room schools, of unrelieved ruralism where lack of industry and opportunity chased the most ambitious away and where the past languished in a stagnant and provincial present. (See Table 1 for a statistical picture of the Southside at mid-century.)

Table 1   Southside Virginia (1950)

	Southside (all residents)	Southside nonwhites	State
Population	612,724	246,640	3,318,680
Rural farm population	40.8%	—	22.1%
Nonwhite population	40.3%	—	22.2%
Median school years completed—persons 25 yrs. and over *	7.1	5.2	8.5
Median income—families and unrelated individuals	$1,474	$1,061	$2,172

Source: U.S. Bureau of the Census, *Population*, *1950*, II, 46, *Virginia*.
*The figures for income and education in the Southside were compiled by taking the median of the median levels of income, education, etc., of the twenty-five counties and six independent cities of the area (see Map I).

The race problem has plagued the Southside as no other section of Virginia. Slaves outnumbered whites in the antebellum years,[2] and Southampton County witnessed Nat Turner's slave insurrection in 1831. The Southside suffered dearly at the hands of history: in 1865 the region was desolate; plantations were plundered and slaves freed without compensation to owners. For many years after the Civil War this region was the center of Negro political power; in 1888 it elected Representative John M. Langston, the only Negro ever to represent Vir-

[1] Cabel Phillips, "Virginia—The State and the State of Mind," *New York Times Magazine*, July 28, 1957, p. 49.
[2] Hemphill *et al.*, p. 231.

Virginia's Independent Cities

Map Key	City	Congressional District (1960)
1	Alexandria	10
2	Bristol	9
3	Buena Vista	7
4	Charlottesville	8
5	Chesapeake	2
6	Clifton Forge	6
7	Colonial Heights	3
8	Covington	6
9	Danville	5
10	Fairfax	10
11	Falls Church	10
12	Franklin	4
13	Fredericksburg	8
14	Galax	5
15	Hampton	1
16	Harrisonburg	7
17	Hopewell	4
18	Lynchburg	6
19	Martinsville	5
20	Newport News	1
21	Norfolk	2
22	Norton	9
23	Petersburg	4
24	Portsmouth	2
25	Radford	6
26	Richmond	3
27	Roanoke	6
28	South Boston	5
29	Staunton	7
30	Suffolk	4
31	Virginia Beach	1
32	Waynesboro	7
33	Williamsburg	1
34	Winchester	7
35	Lexington	7

KEY

☐ Regional Areas

⬚ Congressional Districts

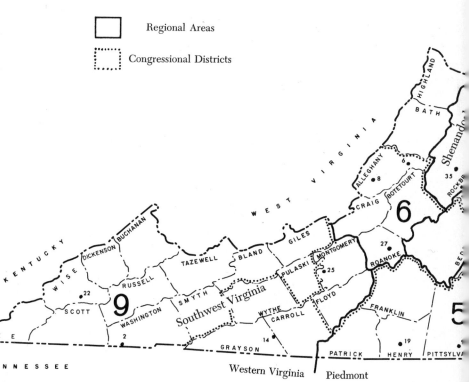

Map   I. Virginia: Regional Areas,* Congressional Districts
(1960),† Counties,‡ and Independent Cities §

Notes to Map I

* The Southside defies exact geographical designation. Topography, population characteristics,
congressional districting lines, and political history have determined the area shown here.
† Taken from the *Congressional District Data Book* (*Districts of the 88th Congress*), p. 511.
‡ Norfolk and Princess Anne counties were eliminated in 1963.
§ The independent cities include those incorporated through 1966, although they are listed
in their 1960 congressional districts.

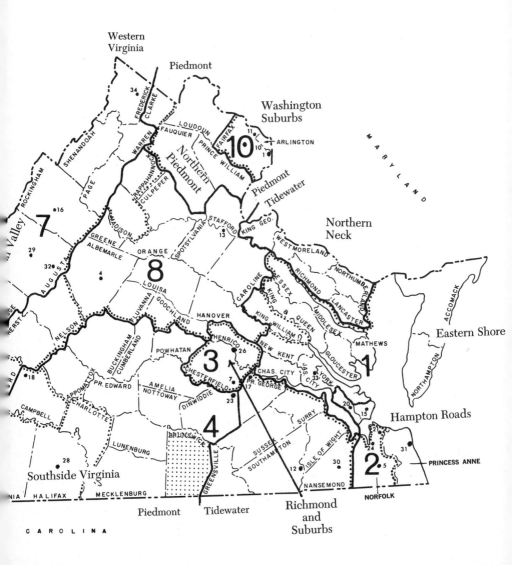

ginia in Congress. By 1950, despite vast migrations to the cities
of both North and South, Negroes still comprised over 40 per
cent of the Southside's population, almost twice the proportion
in the state as a whole. Under a rigid caste system Negroes in
1950 averaged barely three-fifths the income of southside
whites and only slightly more than five years of education.
Although they comprised over two-fifths of the area's population, Negroes constituted well under one-fifth of the registered
voters.[3] Yet violence between the races was not condoned:
Virginia's Southside, of all rural black belts in the South, offered the Negro the most genuine protection and paternalistic
concern.[4]

In the Southside the word was Byrd. It would be ridiculous
to assume that the Southside was the only stronghold of Virginia's famous machine. From the Shenandoah Valley to the Eastern Shore, from the northern Piedmont to the North Carolina
border, through vast tracts of rural Virginia, the Byrd organization reigned supreme. But nowhere was the supremacy more
imposing than in the Southside. In election after election it
provided pro-Byrd margins of large proportions (see Table 2).

Snuggled away in central southside Virginia, Brunswick
County (see Map 1) competed with its neighbors at each
election for the privilege of providing swollen majorities for
Senator Byrd and his associates (see Table 2). Here, as in most
Virginia counties, the courthouse in the county seat of Lawrenceville was the hub of political activity and general community life.[5] Four massive white columns dominated the entrance
to the old colonial courthouse, and the deep-red brick of the
courthouse itself was matched by the adjacent clerk's office and
county jail. The courthouse square with its lush grass, plentiful

[3] See official voter registration lists, 1950–1960, State Board of Elections,
Richmond, Va.
[4] Key has stated that "Virginia's white citizens in and out of the machine
have demonstrated a relatively acute sense of responsibility toward the Negro
—an attitude that may account in part for the fact that its race relations are
perhaps the most harmonious in the South" (p. 32).
[5] Much of the description of Brunswick County, Lawrenceville, and W.
Emory Elmore's role in political affairs results from the author's visit and
interviews there, Aug. 1–3, 1966.

Table 2 Southside and Brunswick County Support of the Byrd Organization

Year	Office	Candidates *	Statewide vote	Southside vote	Southside's proportion of total state vote	Brunswick vote
			%	%	%	%
1946 P	Senator	*Byrd*	63.5	71.0 †	20.6	69.8
		Hutchinson	36.5	29.0		30.2
1952 P	Senator	*Byrd*	62.7	68.7	19.7	72.1
		Miller	37.3	31.3		27.9
1953	Governor	*Stanley*	54.8	70.4	15.8	83.3
		Dalton	45.2	29.6		16.7
1957	Governor	*Almond*	63.2	79.3	16.6	84.9
		Dalton	36.8	20.7		15.1
1961 P	Governor	*Harrison*	56.7	71.4	20.1	86.6
		Stephens	43.3	28.6		13.4

* Names of organization candidates are in italics.
P Primary.
† Unless otherwise stated, all election data given in tables and text are based on official election returns issued by the State Board of Elections, Richmond.

shade, and ever-present sparrows typified the summer leisure and charm of rural Virginia. A fitting touch of history in the square was on the statue of a lone Confederate soldier dedicated to the "Confederate Heroes of Brunswick County, 1861–65." Across Main Street from the courthouse stood the shopping center of Lawrenceville—a short row of grocery, drug, and 5-and-10-cent stores serving more as centers for town gossip than as places of purchase. Every half-hour the chiming clock of the Farmers and Merchants Bank interrupted for a moment the monotony of small-town talk and commerce.

A visitor to Lawrenceville in the late forties and early fifties might have noticed a small, elderly man passing frequently through the double-screen door of the courthouse. This gentleman was W. Emory Elmore, county clerk in Brunswick since 1920 and a well-known figure to practically everyone in Lawrenceville and the surrounding area. To his fellows he was a genuinely affable and Christian man—interested alike in the community's church life [6] and golf course. His good nature at times overextended itself: when on the putting green, he conceded opponents' shots which even the great Sam Snead would have found difficult. No single man had more respect in Brunswick County than Elmore. When he died in 1955 his townsmen hung his portrait on the wall of the old county courtroom.

Emory Elmore also liked politics. To him politics and Harry Flood Byrd were a way of life—an absorbing hobby and a sacred duty. For twenty-seven years he served as chairman of the county Democratic committee; [7] for twenty-seven years and more he worked religiously for Byrd and the disciples of his political creed. When E. R. ("Ebbie") Combs went to Richmond to captain the Virginia operations of the Byrd organization, Elmore was a trusted local lieutenant. Even more important, he was known in Brunswick to be a close friend of

[6] The courthouse and the church were the two main foci of life in a small rural community such as Brunswick. The political powers in the community were often leaders in the community's church life as well.

[7] E. R. Bell and W. L. Heartwell, Jr., *Brunswick Story* (Lawrenceville, Va.: Brunswick Times-Gazette, 1957), p. 71.

the Senator himself, one of those allowed in the back room of
Byrd's Washington office and Virginia hotel suites. In Brunswick County he had the inside word, was far more "in the
know" than any local paper. Small wonder, then, that gubernatorial aspirants came to Brunswick as much as two years before
election day to pay their respects to W. Emory Elmore.

There will always be a certain mystique surrounding the
manner in which the organization picked its candidates for
governor. Legend (and certain liberal critics) had it that Senator Byrd dictated the choice while the courthouse crowds
stepped obediently in line. Others claimed that a consensus
naturally developed around the man to be "anointed." Three
prime ingredients, however, were evident in the selection process, although there will never be a way to determine precisely
how much influence each factor had in any given election.
Elmore and his counterparts throughout the state had a definite voice in the selection, and word of their individual preferences filtered up to Senator Byrd. The Senator weighed the
various sentiments and consulted members of his high command throughout the state. From the infomal give and take of
courthouse preferences, the Senator's own wishes, and the
choice of the Senator's closest advisers, a preferred candidate
usually emerged and proceeded to an almost certain victory in
the forthcoming Democratic primary and general election.[8]

In Brunswick County, Elmore organized the local election
effort for the organization candidate. The campaign process
there has been described as a "team effort" with the names and
numbers of the players known long in advance. Campaign
leaders generally included most of the county officials—men
who, like Elmore, had held elective county office for many
years without serious opposition. The average elective official
in Brunswick served for slightly over a decade.[9] Almost 80 per
cent of incumbents either retired, died, or moved on to other

8 Most observers of Virginia politics support this general view of the selection
process. See especially Key, p. 23, and Benjamin Muse, *Virginia's Massive
Resistance* (Bloomington, Ind.: Indiana University Press, 1961), pp. 41–42.

9 See *Reports of the Secretary of the Commonwealth to the Governor and
General Assembly of Virginia,* 1925[–1966] (Richmond: Division of Purchase
and Printing, 1925[–1966]).

office; rarely were they defeated. County offices, moreover, were frequently hereditary, and it was not unusual to find that half of the officials incumbent at any one time had fathers and grandfathers who had also enjoyed long Brunswick County political careers. Elmore's campaign team constituted, therefore, a small, secure, hereditary aristocracy in prime position to influence the county's vote.

Five of these officials, known as constitutional officers, were responsible for the daily functions of county government.[10] Besides Elmore, who as clerk kept the official records of the county, there were, in 1950, the two law enforcement officers, Sheriff H. E. Valentine and J. C. ("Joe") Hutcheson, the amiable commonwealth's attorney who went to the state Senate in 1958; the county treasurer, J. Haskins Rogers; and the commissioner of revenue, W. S. Moseley, whose father had occupied the same post for forty-two years.

These constitutional officers were generally aided in any important campaign by the members of the Board of Supervisors. The Board was the official governing body of the county, and each of its five members represented for a four-year term one of the county's five magisterial districts.[11] The campaign team further enlisted the enthusiastic support of the county's representative to the Virginia General Assembly. A background potentate in all these proceedings was often the judge of the circuit court, who with his abundant appointive powers in the county could encourage backing for the organization's candidate.[12]

Each of the various officials in Brunswick could be relied upon to support the organization candidate with unflagging regularity. The antiorganization official was rarer than rain in the Sahara. Research and interviews with nine leading Brunswick officials in 1966 revealed eighty-two instances of support

[10] Constitutional officers are so named because their election in each county is provided for in the Virginia constitution, Art. VII, Sec. 110.

[11] A magisterial district was a subdivision of a county. Meherrin, Powellton, Red Oak, Sturgeon, and Totaro formed the five magisterial subdivisions of Brunswick.

[12] See Appendix I for an outline of the structure of county government in Virginia.

for regular Byrd organization candidates in critical campaigns from 1945 to 1966, three instances of support for candidates in the organization's moderate wing, and not a single instance of support for an antiorganization figure. The occasional Democratic primary fight between two organization loyalists might produce a minor split among Brunswick officials, as in 1949 and 1953, but even then one of the candidates was clearly more acceptable and commanded the preponderance of official support. At any rate, supporting an antiorganization leader over a Byrd man was unthinkable.

Similar courthouse support for the Byrd organization throughout the state caused observers to look for an arm-twisting device enabling the state hierarchy to keep its local lieutenants in line. What has been overlooked, however, was the remarkable similarity of viewpoint among organization members, which, in the long run, unified them far more effectively and fundamentally than any pressure or patronage tactics ever could have. "As for this so-called iniquitous [Byrd] machine," said John Stewart Battle in his 1949 gubernatorial campaign, "it is nothing more or less than a loosely knit group of Virginians . . . who usually think alike, who are interested in the welfare of the commonwealth, who are supremely interested in giving Virginia good government and good public servants, and they usually act together." [13] "It's like a club," said Governor J. Lindsay Almond, Jr., in 1958, "except it has no bylaws, constitution or dues. It's a loosely knit association, you might say, between men who share the philosophy of Senator Byrd." [14]

Brunswick County shared this philosophy. With its many small tobacco farms and independent merchants, its high percentage of Negroes, its relatively low levels of income and education, and its many native Virginians (see Table 3), Brunswick bred among its white citizens a fierce conservatism based partly on race and partly on a rugged individualism which an expanded federal government might easily undermine. Every elective official interviewed in Brunswick de-

[13] Quoted in Benjamin Muse, "The Durability of Harry Flood Byrd," *Reporter,* Oct. 3, 1957, pp. 27–28.

[14] *Time,* Sept. 22, 1958, p. 16.

Table 3   Brunswick County (1950 and 1960)

	1950		1960	
	Brunswick	Virginia	Brunswick	Virginia
Population	20,136	3,318,680	17,779	3,966,949
Nonwhite population	57.8%	22.2%	58.7%	20.8%
Rural farm population	66.3%	22.1%	45.2%	10.0%
Rural nonfarm population	33.7%	30.9%	54.8%	34.2%
Native population	—	—	91.2%	69.2%
Median school years completed—persons 25 years and over *	6.8	8.5	7.4	9.9
Median income—families and unrelated individuals *	$1,278	$2,172	$1,943	$4,043

Source: U.S. Bureau of the Census, *Population, 1950*, II, 46, *Virginia*, and *Population, 1960*, I, 48, *Virginia*.

* Negroes in Brunswick had a considerably lower educational level (5.5 school years completed for persons 25 years and over) and median income ($966) than did the county as a whole. The figures given are for 1950.

scribed himself as a "stanch conservative" or "Virginia Democrat," two terms which in southside Virginia meant virtually the same thing. To the courthouse crowd in Brunswick federal spending was "water in a bucket full of holes" and federal funds "a night stick to beat the states with." ° States seeking federal assistance were as the "greedy monkey reaching in for the coconut, then finding the trap door slam shut on his arm." ° To the white man in the street in Brunswick, Supreme Court decisions and wild federal spending marked the inevitable path to liberalism and all the unknown socialistic horrors beyond.

Dissatisfaction with "wild federal spending" combined with

° Throughout the book, this symbol (°) will be used to show that a personal interview or interviews was the source of the quotation or opinion involved. Over 75 interviews were conducted during 1966–67, and in most cases interviewees were promised anonymity (see Acknowledgments).

an even greater resentment over the civil rights decisions which have come from Washington since World War II. Race relations in Brunswick, while hardly blissful, have heretofore been relatively calm. Virginia's Southside has, for the most part, been free from the racial flare-ups of the urban North and the poisonous racial strife of the deep South. The attitude throughout Brunswick remained one of benevolent paternalism toward the Negro in his place at the bottom of the caste system [15] and stubborn resistance to his drive for equality.° Segregation served as a guiding principle for many whites in the county, and the Byrd policy of massive resistance to school integration found widespread support.° Such county leaders as Walter B. Moseley, Sr., the outspoken former chairman of the Board of Supervisors, had "nothing against the colored folks. Many of them are my friends. But I do believe in separation of the races, the whites here and the Negroes there, not together." [16] Another veteran county official, who spent his "boyhood on the farm with Negroes," stoutly believed that the "colored folks have lower moral standards" and attacked integration as leading to intermarriage and lower moral standards for the white race.°

Conservative as it is, Brunswick has historically been Democratic. The Republican party must atone for history before enlisting the loyalties of southside Virginians. On its shoulders lay the onus of Civil War and Reconstruction, and its image lingered as the party of "Wall Street, big bankers, and high tariffs" while the Democratic party represented the "man on the street, the farmer, the low-tariff boys." ° Until 1964 old Democratic ties carried Brunswick County and most of southside Virginia for even the most liberal Democratic presidential nominees. Although Virginia went Republican in 1952, 1956, and 1960, Brunswick County remained faithful; when Virginia returned to

[15] Negro voting power in Brunswick, for instance, was negligible before repeal of the poll tax in 1964. Fifty-two per cent of Brunswick's white adults but only 8 per cent of its Negro adults were registered to vote in 1950. By 1960 81 per cent of the eligible whites were registered but only 16 per cent of the eligible Negroes (see official voter registration lists at State Board of Elections, Richmond, Va.).

[16] Richmond *Times-Dispatch*, Aug. 7, 1966.

the Democratic fold in 1964, Brunswick ironically went Republican for the first time in recent history (see Table 4).

There has been an interesting sideshow in Brunswick and throughout southside Virginia to the traditional two-party circus of American politics. When the Democratic nominee for

Table 4 Presidential Voting in Brunswick County (1948–1964)

Year	Candidates *	Brunswick	State
		%	%†
1948	Truman (D)	48.7	48.2
	Dewey (R)	10.5	41.3
	Thurmond (States' Rights)	40.8	10.4
1952	Stevenson (D)	59.8	43.5
	Eisenhower (R)	40.2	56.5
1956	Stevenson (D)	43.1	38.4
	Eisenhower (R)	25.3	55.4
	Andrews (States' Rights)	31.6	6.2
1960	Kennedy (D)	66.3	47.0
	Nixon (R)	31.6	52.4
	Coiner (Conservative)	2.1	.5
1964	Johnson (D)	42.4	53.7
	Goldwater (R)	57.6	46.3

* Several minor candidates are not included in this tabulation.

† Percentages are rounded off to the nearest tenth and thus do not always total exactly 100.

President was intolerably liberal, Brunswick conservatives flocked to third-party candidates. Stalwart segregationist Strom Thurmond drew 895 votes from Brunswick in 1948, almost four times as many as the Republican presidential nominee, and T. Coleman Andrews, running on the States' Rights ticket in 1956, outpolled Dwight D. Eisenhower. This same phenomenon occurred on the state level in the gubernatorial race of 1965, when the Conservative party candidate William Story drew more votes in Brunswick than the Republican and Democratic candidates combined.

Whatever the sporadic successes of third-party candidates, Democrats of all varieties generally found Brunswick County congenial political territory. When the candidate was a Democrat of the Harry Byrd variety, the outcome of the election was a foregone conclusion. Campaign gatherings with Emory Elmore seldom discussed the prospects of an organization victory but rather the size of the majority. The traditional chore of getting out the vote was stressed, for voter turnouts in Virginia

Table 5   Voter Turnout in Brunswick County in Major Democratic Primaries (1949–1961)

Year	Office	Adult population voting in Brunswick	Adult population voting in Virginia
		%	%
1949	Governor	18.3	15.6
1952	Senator	21.4	17.0
1953	Governor	15.5	11.3
1961	Governor	31.3	15.2

have always been notoriously low. Generally Brunswick's electorate responded to campaign appeals with better turnouts than did those of the state as a whole (see Table 5), for the organization demanded a hefty vote from its white southside supporters to counteract the more liberal tips of the Virginia triangle—Norfolk-Portsmouth, northern Virginia, and the "Fightin' Ninth" District in the Southwest. (When one realizes that most of Brunswick County's 60 per cent Negro population never voted, the turnout of Brunswick whites noted in Table 5 becomes even more remarkable.) The campaign team in Brunswick was further warned not to concentrate solely on the county seat of Lawrenceville, but to push the candidate in every recess of the far-flung county. The Byrd organization always fared better in the counties than the cities, and it prospered most in the rural parts of a rural area. Smoky Ordinary, Dromgoole, Rock Store, and the county's other nooks and crannies handed the organization even more overwhelming majorities than did the county seat of Lawrenceville (see Table 6), where whatever minuscule liberal or Republican organization the county possessed was likely to exist.

Table 6 Patterns of Voting within Brunswick County

Year	Office	Candidates *	Bruns-wick vote	Lawrence-ville vote	Vote outside Lawrence-ville
			%	%	%
1946 ᴾ	Senator	*Byrd*	69.8	64.3	74.0
		Hutchinson	30.2	35.7	26.0
1949 ᴾ	Governor	*Battle*	41.5	35.5	45.3
		Miller	19.3	25.7	15.2
		Edwards	30.2	31.0	29.7
		Arnold	9.0	7.8	9.8
1952 ᴾ	Senator	*Byrd*	72.1	66.8	75.4
		Miller	27.9	33.2	24.6
1953 ᴾ	Governor	*Stanley*	73.2	69.3	75.6
		Fenwick	26.8	30.7	24.4
1953	Governor	*Stanley*	83.3	75.3	89.1
		Dalton	16.7	24.7	10.9

Source: Based on Brunswick County election returns, clerk's office, Lawrenceville, Va.
ᴾ A primary.
* The stanchest Byrd organization candidate is italicized.

Political gatherings for the entire county flourished only so long as they offered a social attraction as well. Barbecues with steaming Brunswick stew and after-dinner stump oratory often attracted from 500 to 1,000 persons in certain southside counties. Candidate appearances also featured a handshaking tour near the courthouse, followed by impassioned eloquence before a small but sympathetic courtroom crowd. Large fans hanging from high ceilings to break the heat of a July afternoon, light-green courtroom walls broken only by faded pictures of county fathers and former circuit judges, Harry Byrd grimly warning of a grasping federal government—such was a classic snapshot which would soon take its place beside the New England town meeting and presidential whistle stop in the gallery of fond political memories.

Chapter 2

The Byrd Organization
on the State Level

For outsiders, the politics of the South unfortunately call to mind the circus figures and colorful demagogues who blustered and strutted across the South's political stage for well over half a century. There were "Cotton Ed" Smith with his flowery orations on stainless southern womanhood, Huey Long who roused the rednecks across the Louisiana bayous, "Ma" and "Pa" Ferguson with their Texas-sized scandals, and such politicos of the present day as George Wallace, James O. Eastland, and Orval Faubus, each with his own brand of political showmanship. The leaders of Virginia's Byrd organization, however, stood apart both from the typical southern stumper and from the newer Kennedy-Lindsay types who have glamorized contemporary politics. They were, in one respect, a unique political breed living in a unique political world. To many a friend and foe, Harry Flood Byrd, John Stewart Battle, A. Willis Robertson, Albertis S. Harrison, Jr., and the rest of Virginia's ruling oligarchy appeared as antebellum aristocrats —either that honest, gracious, and sincere or that outmoded and reactionary. If the Byrd political organization was the county courthouse, the Byrd political leader was the country gentleman.

The trail to political leadership in the Byrd organization was well marked, and the young political aspirant seldom deviated from the conventional path. A point of view similar to that of

Senator Byrd was obviously a first prerequisite for political success. In commencing his apprenticeship, the young conservative first aimed at some county office, generally commonwealth's attorney.[1] His local base consolidated, the future leader journeyed next to the state Senate to make those organizational contacts so indispensable in a statewide race. After demonstrating his devotion to organization policy in the state legislature, he gained greater public exposure with a position on the statewide ticket, either as lieutenant governor or attorney general. If all these hurdles could be successfully cleared, he might take the last triumphant step and become governor of the Commonwealth of Virginia. This was the path to the governor's mansion, and the practice of Virginia politics over the past forty years showed only minor variations.

Yet this path was not always easy. Political pyramids grow small indeed at the top, and the shape of the Byrd organization was not exceptional. Victory demanded an intense campaign for the favor of Senator Byrd, his associates in the ruling oligarchy, and the courthouse rings around the state. If this support was gained, the electorate's ratification was one of the more certain things in American politics.

Studies of political leadership in the Old Dominion provide essential clues to the Byrd organization's most ingrained characteristics. Almost every familiar figure of the organization (Byrd, Tuck, Smith, Combs, Robertson, Harrison, Stanley, and others) had a rural background. Virginia's metropolitan areas seldom launched successful statewide candidates. Not a single governor or United States senator in Virginia from 1946 to 1965 had a metropolitan upbringing,[2] but four of the six governors

---

[1] In the courthouse scheme of things, the offices of clerk and commonwealth's attorney were generally most important politically. Clerks were primarily local powers who stayed in office year after year and influenced county politics. Commonwealth's attorney, however, was a post often held by those seeking eventual advancement to the statewide scene.

[2] Virginia's major metropolitan areas were Newport News-Hampton, Norfolk-Portsmouth, Richmond, Roanoke, and Washington's Virginia suburbs. One governor, J. Lindsay Almond, Jr. (1958–62), spent his adult life in a metropolitan area (Roanoke) but nonetheless had a distinctly rural background (Orange

serving from 1946 to the present came from southside Virginia.[3] The six had spent an average apprenticeship of twenty-three years in lower elective and appointive positions before their inaugurations as governors.[4] During the apprentice years the organization sternly impressed upon all aspirants the importance of basic conformity to conservative policies. Deviates and incompetents were weeded out long before they reached the top. Political leaders in Virginia were neither business nor professional leaders, neither rabble rousers nor "erratic" reformers, who suddenly decided to jump into politics with crusading zeal. Most of the statewide and courthouse professionals who manned the Byrd organization had enjoyed or looked forward to almost a lifetime of public service, and most of them had a strong vested interest in the welfare of the organization which gave them their jobs.

William Munford Tuck was peculiarly suited to thrive on the courthouse politics of the Byrd organization. More roughhewn than most of its leaders, Bill Tuck was nonetheless such a lovable and colorful individual that he ranked as a Virginia political institution of the first order. Born and raised on a tobacco farm in southside Halifax County, Tuck, according to one boyhood friend, became the county's foremost tobacco chewer shortly after his twelfth birthday.[°] He reached the House of Delegates while still in his twenties (in 1924) and entered the governor's mansion in 1946.

Never one to be formal, Governor Tuck was sitting one afternoon on a bench in Capitol Square tossing peanuts to the squirrels and pigeons. Two soldiers, passing through Richmond on their way home, came upon Tuck and thinking him little

County). Another, John S. Battle, lived in the small city of Charlottesville but as a state senator represented the highly rural district of Albemarle, Fluvanna, Greene, and Madison counties and the city of Charlottesville.

[3] They, and their home county or city, were William M. Tuck, 1946–50 (Halifax); Thomas B. Stanley, 1954–58 (Henry); Albertis S. Harrison, 1962–66 (Brunswick); Mills E. Godwin, 1966–   (Suffolk). A fifth, John S. Battle (1950–54), spent much of his boyhood in the southside city of Petersburg.

[4] See Appendix II for a table showing political offices held by the six Virginians before they became governors.

more than an ordinary bum, casually asked him where was the
best place in town for a stiff drink. Tuck chatted with them a
moment and then, remembering their request, took the
shocked strangers into the governor's mansion for the cocktail
hour.[5]

Tuck's political success rested on his remarkable understanding of human relations. He knew just how to make the other
fellow feel good. As governor of Virginia he hobnobbed frequently with cronies in every corner of the state. "Probably
nobody in Virginia is called by his first name by so many of his
fellow citizens as Bill Tuck," a Richmond editor once remarked.[6]

Tuck may also have been the most conservative member of
an organization leadership which specialized in archconserva-
tism. The 235-pound governor was jokingly regarded by his
friends as the Virginia politician "most likely to secede." [7] And
many of Tuck's attacks on Washington rivaled in rancor the
invective hurled by Southerners at Union policy more than a
century ago. Fortunately Tuck's unfailing humor generally sof-
tened the blows. This "jolly warrior of the South" [8] had a
vocabulary all his own when he described Democratic national
leadership as "political rapscallions . . . tormenting minions of
vice and venality . . . political vultures." [9] He pictured opponents as "Washington wastrels" and "union churls" and their
actions as nothing less than "Judas-like betrayals" and "out-
bursts of perfidy." The verbal climax of his career came when
he once declared that an organization opponent had "retracted
like a man in a patch of sneeze weed." [10]

Many took Bill Tuck for a buffoon. In the early years of his

[5] Interview with one of Tuck's associates, Aug. 27, 1966.

[6] Richmond *Times-Dispatch*, Aug. 8, 1945.

[7] Charles Houston, *Virginians in Congress* (Richmond: Richmond Newspapers, 1966), p. 13. This is a reprint of a series of 13 articles on Virginia
congressmen originally published in the Richmond *News Leader*, July 16–Aug.
3, 1965.

[8] *Ibid.*

[9] Benjamin Muse, "Virginia," in *Presidential Nominating Politics in
1952—The South*, ed. Paul T. David, Malcolm Moos, and Ralph M. Goldman
(Baltimore: Johns Hopkins Press, 1954), pp. 19–20.

[10] Houston, *Virginians in Congress*, p. 13.

political life some organization leaders regarded him as a playboy and clown who could never be trusted with the responsibility of high office. One insider reported that Senator Byrd was a bit wary of Tuck until his election as governor.° Tuck's conservative credentials were impeccable, but his behavior frequently was not. In an organization which prided itself on discreet and efficient administration of government and generally disdained the vulgar and spectacular, Tuck was regarded in some quarters as downright dangerous.

But William Munford Tuck came into his own as governor of Virginia and for four years he held center stage. He pleased, angered, amused, and alarmed Virginians with his "shoot-'em-up" conservatism. The Tuck approach seemed to one author "a boisterous summer storm with deafening thunder, blinding lightning, and driving rains from which the land emerged rejuvenated, all sweet, green, smiling, and amazed." [11] Whatever the weather (and the political skies seemed more often stormy than serene), the Tuck years belong to the golden age of Byrd organization hegemony in Virginia. During his term relations between governor and General Assembly struck high notes of harmony; Byrd backers rolled up heavy majorities throughout most of the state, and the organization, though it committed several serious indiscretions, never became embroiled in the magnitude of crisis and dissension which wracked it throughout the 1950's.

The campaign of Roanoke attorney Moss Plunkett against Tuck in the 1945 Democratic gubernatorial primary offers a good illustration of the efforts of antiorganization leaders over the years to topple the Byrd machine. The Tuck-Plunkett contest was not so heated as the Battle-Miller (1949) or Byrd-Miller (1952) combats, but Plunkett did launch a concerted attack on what he considered the failings of the machine.

His campaign alternated between a serious indictment of the Byrd organization for its record in suffrage, education, health, and welfare and almost hysterical harangues about the "machine" for tyrannically abusing democracy in Virginia. Plun-

[11] Guy Friddell, *What Is It about Virginia?* (Richmond: Dietz Press, 1966), p. 64.

kett's formal platform revealed the more sober side of his complaints and contained a sincere but nebulous plan for liberalizing Virginia's public services, abandoning the patronage devices of the Byrd organization, and fostering a more sympathetic attitude toward labor and the poor.[12] Plunkett then ranged the state asserting that the "machine" had hand-picked Tuck for public office and that none of its members dared aspire to office without first receiving the "nod" from the "boss who pulls the potent power strings from his throne rooms in Washington."[13] In Richmond on July 12, 1945, Plunkett charged that the poll tax and democracy "cannot live in the same State. . . . We either have one or the other, and we certainly have not had democracy in Virginia during the reign of the poll-tax machine." Plunkett also championed a civil service program which would "root out any and all forms of coercion, and free the minds of the State employees from the machine terror which has long held many in its grip." A week later in Hopewell he claimed that the complacent Byrd machine "wants things exactly as they are, or as they used to be. It hates change and fears progress. It even becomes alarmed when the Federal government steps in to fulfill some function long neglected by the State and then it screams about 'State's Rights.' But you never hear the machine say anything about the State's wrongs." In a radio address during the campaign windup Plunkett asserted he sensed in Virginia "a spirit of revolt which I believe is akin to that which recently manifested itself in Great Britain."[14]

In Halifax County Bill Tuck's campaign pace seemed glacial, his pronouncements vacuous. As late as July 5 he was quoted as declaring that he would direct his campaign from his front porch in South Boston, that he had no statement to make concerning any planks in his platform for governor, and that he also had no speaking engagements between that date and the primary.[15] "The reverberating silence from his camp is nothing

[12] See Appendix III for the full text of Plunkett's platform.

[13] Richmond *Times-Dispatch*, July 8, 1945.

[14] *Ibid.*, July 13, 22, 31, 1945. The "revolt in Britain" was Clement Atlee's (Labor) victory over Winston Churchill (Conservative).

[15] *Ibid.*, July 23, 1945.

short of thunderous," the *Times-Dispatch* announced.[16] Tuck did have the courage to go on record as favoring an adequate military force to protect the nation when peace returned; he strongly endorsed Thomas Jefferson for something or other, and he repeatedly confessed his liking for rural people and the farmer's way of life.[17] "Our farms constitute the bedrock of the State's progress," he declared. "It is important for Virginia to remain an agricultural State."[18] But Tuck's silence on major issues caused newspapers across the state to wage a united campaign to make him speak. The Norfolk and Richmond papers labeled him the "blank check" and "gumshoe" candidate; the Roanoke *World News* claimed he was "the most uncommitted candidate on record"; and the Roanoke *Times* described him as "silent as the Sphinx."[19] Many candidates had taken a campaign posture of ignoring an opponent, but few had ignored the public as well. Tuck's political lockjaw became so alarming that the organization had to prod him to speak. Finally he endorsed more specific programs designed to appeal primarily to rural areas, such as the abolition of the state's outmoded one- and two-room schools, periodic examinations of school children by public health officials, and better electricity and telephone facilities for farmers.[20] Tossing these tidbits to the voters at least got the papers off his back, and the *Times-Dispatch* remarked that at last "Tuck's front porch has done a fadeout as a piece of campaign furniture."[21]

The revolt in Virginia predicted by Plunkett, to no one's surprise, least of all Tuck's, failed to materialize. Attacks on the Byrd organization failed even to diminish the majority vote for its candidate. Tuck coasted to nomination on the old Byrd formula of a limited electorate and top-heavy majorities supplied by loyal courthouse rings.[22]

[16] July 5, 1945.   [17] *Ibid.*   [18] *Ibid.*, July 19, 1945.
[19] Quoted, *ibid.*, July 20, 1945.   [20] *Ibid.*, July 19, 21, 25, 1945.
[21] July 23, 1945.
[22] Tuck polled 69.9 per cent of the total vote, 76.7 of the county vote, and 58.2 per cent of the city vote. Only 6.2 of the adult population in Virginia voted for Tuck in his handsome 1945 primary victory, causing Key to observe that a "smaller proportion of Virginia's potential electorate votes for governor than does that of any other state of the South" (p. 20). See Appendix XI for a detailed vote analysis of important state elections.

Tuck's inertia during the campaign was understandable in the context of Virginia politics. Having secured Senator Byrd's approval and solidified the loyalties of the courthouse rings, Tuck felt assured of victory. Why should he bother to go through the motions of a public campaign whose outcome had been decided at least several months before? Only in the Old Dominion could one stand, not run for office, but Tuck was to be the last governor to enjoy that luxury.

Although campaign charge and countercharge had little real effect on election outcomes, opponents through the years leveled serious charges at the Byrd leadership. They felt the organization offered Virginians inferior services—that expenditures for education, health, and welfare were meager. Critics also claimed that the organization stayed in power only through devious political stratagems designed to shackle healthy opposition. The poll tax, the State Board of Compensation, and the patronage ring surrounding the circuit judge thus came under heavy fire. The organization's attitude toward labor and the Negro was deemed repressive and venomous, and, lastly, the refusals of prominent Virginia Democrats to support the national party dismayed more "loyal" Democrats. Collectively, these failings constituted a weighty indictment, yet several of the charges rested on shaky foundations.

Politics often appears to the man in the street as a dirty game. The Byrd organization, however, overcame this stigma and won national renown as a paragon of political integrity.[23] One normally hostile critic characterized the organization as "forthright, incorrupt, and almost offensively virtuous" and admitted that bribery in the state legislature, low deals with contractors, and general winking at abuses were virtually "unheard of" among the gentry who ran Virginia's Byrd organization.[24] Antiorganization leaders sought, on occasion, to blemish this reputation and implicate the respectable Byrd leaders in scandal.

[23] Practically every major observer has conceded the honesty and integrity of the Byrd organization. See Key, p. 19, and Muse, "Durability of Byrd," p. 26.

[24] See William Manchester, "The Byrd Machine," *Harper's Magazine*, CCV (Nov. 1952), 80–87.

Their trump card was the State Board of Compensation. The State Compensation Board was charged with determining salaries and expense allowances for all locally elected courthouse officials who performed certain state functions (treasurer, sheriff, commonwealth's attorney, and so forth).[25] In fixing salaries the Board operated within certain general population brackets set by the General Assembly. In fixing office expense allowances, it considered "the work involved in the discharge of duties of the respective officers . . . the efficiency with which the affairs of each office are conducted and such other matters as the Board may deem pertinent and material."[26] In other words, standards for salaries and expense allowances were flexible and members of the Compensation Board exercised considerable discretion.

Opponents of the organization seldom failed to exploit this situation. The chairman of the three-man Compensation Board, they pointed out, was appointed by an organization governor and nearly always possessed a long record of loyalty to the machine. The Compensation Board, they implied, manipulated allowances of local officials on the basis of service and subservience to Senator Byrd's wishes. The dutiful local official on election day would be the happy local official on pay day. If an occasional official with antiorganization views received a high salary, the organization was only buttering him up to swing him to the machine candidate in the next election. Antiorganization men delighted to point out "machine" officials with "bloated" salaries and allowances.

The Compensation Board spent untold hours trying to parry these attacks. Partisans of the organization freely admitted that there were seeming inconsistencies in the pay scales of county officials, but they protested the idea that these inconsistencies resulted from any political machinations on the part of the Compensation Board. Rather, the confusing bramble of official salaries stemmed from multiple factors, none of them relating to devotion to the Byrd organization. Requests for salary raises

[25] This discussion of the State Compensation Board is based to a large extent on an analysis of the Board by the Richmond *News Leader* in editorials, Aug. 8–12, 1955.

[26] *Ibid.*, Aug. 8, 1955.

from local officials themselves and the salary recommendations of the county Board of Supervisors weighed heavily in the Compensation Board's decisions. Some local officials, the Board explained, refused to request high salaries for fear of antagonizing their constituents and the local Boards of Supervisors who shared payment of these salaries with the state. Many devoted officials regarded public service as a duty to be performed at some financial sacrifice. Some would never request a salary increase which might make their office more desirable to prospective opponents. Other important factors jumbled into the complex salary equation were the length of service, the efficiency of the official and, perhaps most significant, the volume of work which he had to perform. Far from admitting dishonesty, the Compensation Board claimed method in its seeming madness and defied critics to prove otherwise.

So many charges were hurled at the Compensation Board in each campaign that the Richmond *News Leader* conducted an exhaustive investigation to discover what part, if any, politics played in the Board's determination of local salaries. Their conclusions were (1) that the salaries and expense allowances approved by the Compensation Board were a mass of inconsistencies; (2) that most of this inconsistency was the result of local considerations, such as the conservatism of a "tight" Board of Supervisors, beyond the Compensation Board's control; (3) that no pattern of political favoritism could be found in the Board's actual operations; (4) that changes in the law were desirable to the end that greater uniformity might be achieved in payments to local officials for state duties performed.[27] The controversy was best summed up by Cabell Phillips when he stated: "The bonds of natural loyalty between the courthouse rings and the State Capitol were reinforced with the iron bars of economic self-interest. There is no evidence that this power has ever been abused. But there is no evidence, either, that it is merely negligible as an influence for discipline or right thinking." [28]

[27] See Appendix IV for a more detailed description of the *News Leader*'s investigation.
[28] Phillips, "New Rumblings," p. 34.

Less dramatic and probably better grounded than the controversy raging over the Compensation Board were charges focused on the patronage opportunities of the circuit judge. Virginia is divided into forty circuits, each of which contains at least one city or county and one circuit judge elected by the General Assembly for an eight-year term.[29] The Byrd organization never lacked comfortable majorities in either house of the General Assembly, and the General Assembly did not elect circuit judges with avowed anti-Byrd sentiments.[30] Moreover, the appointive powers of the circuit judge were formidable. For each county in his circuit, the judge appointed the Board of Reassessors, which appraised real property in the county every six years, the Welfare Board, which administered general relief programs, and the School Trustee Electoral Board, which in most counties named the local school board.[31] He further designated the county court judge and interim holders of county elective offices. Perhaps the most delicate of his appointments was the Electoral Board, which supervised all official elections for the county.

Organization opponents predictably charged that political considerations influenced the circuit judge's appointments. Merit was tossed out the window; devotion to Harry Byrd was the major criterion for a county appointive post. An Electoral Board named by a circuit judge deprived Virginians of unbiased supervision of elections. Antiorganization forces demanded an "immediate divorce of the judiciary from politics by relieving the judges of all political appointments!"[32]

It is as difficult to believe the extreme antiorganization case as to think that only pure altruism dictated the circuit judge's selections. "Virginians are justly proud of their own judiciary," stated Benjamin Muse, certainly no apologist for the organization. "The reputation of the state's unique political organiza-

[29] See A. E. Ragan, "Virginia's Judicial System: Organization and Improvement," *University of Virginia News Letter*, April 15, 1963.

[30] Thus Republicans controlled no appointive posts even where they were strong at the polls. For further discussion, see Chapter 8.

[31] See Virginia State Chamber of Commerce, *Virginia's Government* (Richmond: Whittet and Shepperson, 1964), pp. 84–85, 99–104.

[32] Richmond *Times-Dispatch*, July 12, 1945.

tion for producing able public servants is nowhere better justified than in the men who are chosen to preside over circuit courts or are elevated to the Supreme Court of Appeals." [33] Agreeing with Muse that most circuit judges were "competent and reasonably fair and conscientious men," another informed political observer explained: "It is a generally accepted fact of Virginia political life that circuit judges in the counties are part of the Byrd organization. . . . Some circuit judges are in politics up to their ears, some only up to their navels, and others seem a bit detached. None is venal or corrupt, and most are not overly partisan. It cannot be avoided, however, that the judges are part of the political power structure." [34]

Vacancies in a circuit judgeship occasioned sharp struggles among organization followers interested in the appointment. The resignation of Burr P. Harrison as judge of the 17th judicial circuit (Clarke, Frederick, Shenandoah, and Warren counties and Winchester city) in the fall of 1946 initiated a typical contest between two prominent lawyers.[35] As the General Assembly was not in session at the time, the appointment fell to Tuck. He was beset by letters, telegrams, phone calls, and petitions praising one or another of the two candidates and recounting incidents which "should forever bar" the other "from consideration for a judicial appointment." [36] Prominent citizens, lawyers, and courthouse officials within the circuit and various members of the legislature and judiciary throughout the state took sides in the matter. "My District is very evenly divided and there is a great deal of bitterness in the Judgeship fight," Delegate E. Blackburn Moore wrote to the Governor.

[33] Muse, *Massive Resistance*, p. 122.

[34] James Latimer, "Virginia Politics, 1950–1960," pp. 114–15 (MS). The manuscript consists of notes on Virginia politics by the chief political reporter of the Richmond *Times-Dispatch* in 1961.

[35] See W. M. Tuck, Executive Papers, Box 25, Circuit Court, 17th Judicial District, for the correspondence concerning this judgeship hassle. (The Executive Papers are located in the Archives room of the Virginia State Library in Richmond, Va.)

[36] The letter of Colonel Parker Hitt to Tuck, Oct. 10, 1946, is one of several questioning the competence and capabilities of one or another of the candidates for the judgeship.

"At the present time, with the facts as they are, I am taking a neutral position." [37] (Moore was the most powerful organization spokesman in the circuit.) By mid-October one candidate held a 23 to 18 lead in public endorsements from licensed lawyers in the circuit, with two remaining neutral.[38] Tuck weighed the expression of sentiment, made the appointment, and received the new judge's letter thanking him for "the fulfillment of a life-long ambition" and promising to perform his new duties "in a manner such as will never cause you regret for my appointment." [39]

Through the State Compensation Board and the appointments of the circuit judge the Byrd organization extended its powerful arm into every county and city in Virginia. In small rural communities, especially, this influence was prodigious. "The young lawyer," stated the Washington *Post*, "knows that the road to political success begins not on the hustings but at the circuit judge's Christmas party and he is apt to do nothing disloyal enough to endanger his invitation. . . . Acceptance into local Organization cliques always carried a measure of social as well as political approval and a community's social elite is in many cases indistinguishable from its political leadership." [40] The Byrd organization was undoubtedly "a club of like-minded gentlemen," but the powers of the circuit judge and, to a lesser extent, the State Compensation Board added materially to the club's cohesion.

This cohesive aspect of Virginia politics was a distinctive characteristic, and it sharply differentiated the Old Dominion from many of its sister southern states. The combination of similar political attitudes, a patronage system centering on the circuit judge, and the vast appointive powers of the governor encouraged courthouse crowds in every corner of the state to support the organization's choice in a statewide election. In sharp contrast to states such as Alabama, Florida, and South Carolina, where a fluid factionalism and localism prevailed, Vir-

[37] Letter of Oct. 7, 1946.   [38] H. K. Benham to Tuck, Oct. 15, 1946.
[39] Elliot Marshall to Tuck, Nov. 4, 1946.
[40] Washington *Post*, July 18, 1965.

ginia maintained an orderly, centralized system for the recruit-
ment and development of political leaders.[41] If Virginia never
witnessed a Huey Long or a Gene Talmadge, it was due partly
to the recognition by would-be mavericks that patient allegiance
to the pervasive machine would be more useful than the frothy
phrases of the stump. Where candidates for office in other
southern states won their biggest majorities in their home town
areas on a "friends 'n neighbors" vote, Byrd organization candidates also ran well in sympathetic areas far away from their
home base. Organization men from southside Virginia relied on
heavy majorities from Fauquier, Culpeper, Albemarle, and
other piedmont counties, while the organization's candidates
from the Shenandoah Valley or Piedmont picked up large majorities in the Northern Neck or Southside. Although "friends 'n
neighbors" voting played a part in Virginia elections, the operations of the Byrd organization were far too precise and predictable to allow extraneous considerations of localism or
personality to reverse the outcome of important statewide
campaigns.[42]

It is easy to see why organization opponents concentrated
their attention on the centralizing devices of the Compensation
Board and the circuit judge. Yet their accusations were of
limited campaign value. Old antiorganization leaders took the
term "Byrd machine" literally and often assumed that destruction of its power lay in a conventional antimachine attack.
They insinuated misuse by the organization of patronage, operation of a thriving spoils system, and corrupt management of
the Compensation Board. Their claims were frequently exaggerated and deeply resented by many voters. Byrd and his
followers had gained in Virginia an almost unassailable reputation for honest and frugal management of the state government
and of state finances. It proved difficult to label the Byrd

[41] See Key, pp. 36–57, 82–105, 130–55, for descriptions of localism in the
three above-mentioned states.

[42] Appendix XI indicates the wide range of support throughout the state for
organization candidates and the relative predictability of a county's vote in a
Democratic primary or general election. The organization's strength and cohe-
siveness in Virginia generally meant that Democratic primaries in Virginia had
but two contestants (an organization and an antiorganization candidate).

machine a Virginia version of Tammany Hall. Only when campaigns touched on issues other than graft and corruption was the Byrd organization vulnerable.

The Virginia poll tax was known in politics as a pocketbook issue; everyone understood paying a dollar and a half to vote. Poll tax denunciation long served as a rallying cry for Republicans and antiorganization Democrats: this single issue seemed to many to embody all that was evil in the Byrd machine. They claimed it stunted democracy in Virginia; that it deprived minorities of their rightful say; that it alone kept the Byrd machine in power. These and similar charges dragged on day after day, year after year, but the poll tax remained. When it finally succumbed to a constitutional amendment and the Supreme Court, many people felt that a new day had dawned in Virginia politics. And in a way it had, for if the poll tax had great practical consequence, its symbolic and psychological value was even more important.

Obviously the poll tax discouraged widespread political activity, but it was not solely responsible for the low levels of participation in Virginia elections. The average citizen was simply not excited over elections in which the outcome seemed always so certain. Paying $1.50 to vote in such an election made even less sense. Virginia law further demanded poll tax payment six months prior to the general election, long before political interest even in the primary campaign was aroused. Moreover, a Virginian who had been lax in meeting his poll tax payments and who suddenly wished to resume voting would have to pay for the present and two preceding years a total of $4.50, and whatever additional levy was imposed by local authorities. Frustrated organization opponents believed the poll tax provisions did everything possible to keep potential voters from the polls.[43]

Yet the antiorganization leader frequently had greater troubles with the poll tax as a political issue than he did either with the circuit judge or with the Compensation Board. Voters were apathetic about the franchise in a state where organization

[43] For a discussion of different poll tax provisions throughout the South, see Key, pp. 578–98.

victories were an accepted part of life. Many Virginians also felt that government guided by gentlemen need not be closely watched. There was little scandal or corruption, and Virginians seldom felt the urge to pay their poll tax and "vote the rascals out." Moreover, those who had not paid the poll tax and presumably would benefit most from poll tax repeal were unable to vote for those candidates who espoused it.

The poll tax was also long recognized as a symbol of white supremacy. Virginia first adopted the tax in its constitution of 1902 and its immediate effect was to help cut the number of Negroes qualified to vote from 147,000 to 21,000.[44] That thousands of whites were likewise disfranchised went relatively unnoticed. Many poor whites whom poll tax repeal would ostensibly benefit clamored for its continuation. Any antiorganization spokesman demanding its repeal ran headlong into the formidable problem of overt or latent racism. And if many poor Virginia whites hoped to disfranchise the Negro, many Virginia gentlemen wished to keep illiterates and other "riffraff" from voting. Poll tax repeal might open the gates to both. The Virginia gentleman demanded a limited, stable, and predictable electorate, and many felt the poll tax necessary to assure it.

Less bitter, but ultimately more important than these controversies, were charges that the Byrd organization had shortchanged the Virginia public on essential services—health, education, highways, and welfare. The record in public services was at all times a testimony to the fiscal orthodoxy of a leadership joined in homage to the balanced budget. Deficit financing was felt to be an insidious path for the state to travel; public debt was to be avoided at all costs. Senator Byrd's favorite homily was a comparison of state and family finance; as the family struggled to avoid debt, so must the state do likewise. It was with pride that Virginia's leaders proclaimed it a debt-free state.

Virginia, as you all know [said Tuck in an address to the 1947 special session of the General Assembly], is unalterably committed to the balanced budget and the pay-as-you-go principle. The wis-

[44] Reichley, p. 8.

dom of this policy has been fully demonstrated. As a result, Virginia is one of the few states in the Union which has been able to free itself entirely of debt. . . . The membership [of the General Assembly] should recognize that it is committed to a policy of financing any improvements in governmental services within the principle of the balanced budget. I do not intend that my administration shall launch the Commonwealth upon the treacherous path of deficit spending.[45]

This attitude spared Virginia the follies of extravagant spending, but it also meant inadequate services for many. And to the extent that the state government failed to spend adequately in education, health, and other fields of both state and local concern, the localities were left with correspondingly greater financial burdens and hardships.

Almost as sacred as the balanced budget was Virginia's reputation as a "low-tax state." This reputation, however, confused those critics who rushed to the conclusion that corporations and the wealthy in general enjoyed a privileged tax status while the state did nothing to improve sagging health or educational standards for the public at large. This theory became even more inviting when one considered that business interests in general were solidly behind the organization. In 1949 Key claimed that the machine

enjoys the enthusiastic and almost undivided support of the business community and of the well-to-do generally, a goodly number of whom are fugitives from the New York state income tax. Organization spokesmen in Congress look out for the interests of business, and the state government, although well managed, manifests a continuing interest in the well-being of the well-to-do. The quid pro quo for support of the organization is said to be taxation favorable to corporations, an anti-labor policy, and restraint in the expansion of services, such as education, public health, and welfare.[46]

Business did back the organization, but this support did not stem from a favored tax status. From the beginning business

[45] *Address to the General Assembly and People of Virginia, Jan. 6, 1947* (Richmond: Division of Purchase and Printing, 1947).

[46] Key, pp. 26–27.

was no more than a secondary element in the old Byrd coalition. It was always the courthouse clerk and not the corporation head about whom the organization's inner core revolved. Nevertheless, the urban well-to-do found much to admire in the ruling oligarchy of their state. The Byrd organization was honest and it ran state government in the frugal, economical, and efficient manner one might admire in a private corporation. Although the Byrd leadership was overwhelmingly rural in background, it had a businesslike air: politics was conducted with a minimum of emotion and a maximum of efficiency. Harry Byrd's life had uniquely exemplified the businessman's creed of the self-made man. During his long years in the Senate, Byrd faithfully voiced the businessman's virtues of initiative and economy and bowed before the shrine of free enterprise. He and his colleague, Senator A. Willis Robertson, served on the Finance and Banking and Currency committees —two groups of special interest to the business world. These senators and Howard Smith, their potent counterpart in the House, were more than amenable to helping the business leaders of the state.

Business had only to look south to appreciate its good fortune. There the well-to-do had had to fight long and bitter wars with Huey Long, Theodore Bilbo, and neo-Populist demagogues out to share the corporate wealth. But the Byrd organization was stable, and until the late fifties even kept Virginia out of the volatile racial currents which discouraged new industry from settling in the deep South. Above all, the Byrd organization was entrenched and powerful, and business leaders saw every reason to keep on good terms.

Yet business balked at Tuck's major proposals in the 1948 session of the General Assembly. The Governor wanted to hike the state's corporate income tax from 3 to 5 per cent and raise individual income tax rates to 2 per cent of the first $3,000, 3 per cent of the next $2,000, and 5 per cent on all income above $5,000.[47] Many business leaders immediately screamed that

[47] Tuck, *Address to General Assembly, Jan. 14, 1948* (Richmond, 1948). Previously Virginia's rates had been 1½ per cent on the first $3,000, 2½ per cent on the next $2,000, and 3 per cent on all income over $5,000.

Tuck's proposals would make Virginia a high-tax state. The economy cry greeting the tax reform became so great that Tuck explained he had to "talk, eat and practically sleep" with the legislature to get his proposals passed.[48] After the Tuck tax program was enacted, it was clear that Virginia's corporate income taxes, while not astronomical, did not offer a financial haven for business interests. Comparative tax studies for 1951 showed over thirty states with significantly more lenient corporate income tax rates than Virginia's. Nor did Virginia's individual income tax policy cater to the well-to-do. Seventeen states, for instance, imposed no personal income tax at all in 1951, while twenty others had personal income tax rates more lenient than Virginia's.[49] Moreover, Virginia did not permit deduction of federal income taxes in arriving at the taxable base for paying Virginia state income taxes. The tax structure could hardly be said to favor business or the well-to-do.

Whatever reputation Virginia had as a low-tax state rested mainly on the consistent refusal of organization leaders to enact a general sales tax. For many years taxes were raised by increasing the rates on existing subjects of taxation. The motor fuel tax, the corporate and individual income tax, the numerous state license taxes—all climbed slowly upward while the revenue benefits of the general sales tax remained untapped. A study of state sales taxes in 1955 revealed that thirty-three states relied on this lucrative tax for one-fourth to one-half of their revenue.[50] Virginia continued to tinker with existing forms of taxation, which did not satisfy state needs.

Refusing to abandon a balanced budget or to adopt a state sales tax, the Byrd organization not surprisingly found itself hard-pressed to provide many essential services. Although few Virginians ever questioned the honesty of the organization's management of state funds, many questioned its generosity.

[48] This phrase was attributed to Tuck by a member of his staff.

[49] *The Book of the States, 1952–1953* (Chicago: Council of State Governments, 1954), pp. 205, 208; U.S. Bureau of the Census, *State Government Finances in 1951* (Washington: U.S. Government Printing Office, 1951), pp. 9–10.

[50] T. R. Snavely, "The Sales and Use Tax," *University of Virginia News Letter*, Nov. 15, 1955.

Even admirers of the organization freely conceded that its record in public education was hardly distinguished, and the charge was often made that "Virginia's schools are among the nation's poorest." [51] This is not to say that organization leaders were unconcerned: Colgate Darden, Bill Tuck, John Battle, and others spent many frustrating hours in determined efforts to upgrade the quality of Virginia's schools. But between the established ground rules of the commonwealth's tax and spending policy and the public apathy so prevalent in many localities, education visibly suffered. Teacher salaries were low; state and local school expenditures were relatively meager. In spite of Tuck's promise to abolish them the Old Dominion at mid-century was still plagued with one- and two-room county schools. Antiorganization criticism of Virginia's low rank in education had substance.

The plight of Virginia's schools could not be blamed solely on inability to provide a better school system. Studies of state *effort* in public education always found Virginia low on the list. In 1947–48 Virginia ranked thirty-fourth of the forty-eight states in its effort to support education as measured by the ratio of state and local expenditures on public schools to total personal income.[52] Similar studies for 1950–51 and 1953–54 showed Virginia thirty-fourth and thirty-eighth,[53] respectively. In the latter studies the Old Dominion ranked behind every other southern state save Kentucky in its support of public schools. Since the studies included school expenditure both from state and local sources, Virginia would have ranked even lower had it not been for the fact that a few progressive localities spent heavily for their own school systems. The funds which the Byrd organization provided through the state government were dismally low.

Urban and suburban areas suffered doubly under the organi-

[51] M. W. Fishwick, *Virginia: A New Look at the Old Dominion* (New York: Harper and Brothers, 1959), p. 252.

[52] *Book of the States, 1950–1951*, p. 267.

[53] National Education Association of the United States, *Educational Differences among the States (March 1954)* (Washington: The Association, 1954), p. 22, and its *Rankings of the States (Jan. 1957)* (Washington: The Association, 1957), p. 16, Table 26.

zation's education policy. Not only did their own local taxes provide for most of the improvements in their schools, but urban and suburban centers also furnished a large portion of whatever state revenues for education the organization decided to levy. Approximately two-thirds of the state's general fund—so indispensable for education, health, and other vital state functions—was derived from individual and corporation income taxes, which hit hardest at urban areas.[54] Industrial and corporate growth was primarily an urban phenomenon,[55] and the raising of corporation taxes affected Virginia's metropolitan centers, not the rural, courthouse-controlled counties. Urban incomes were significantly higher than rural ones,[56] and the slightly graduated individual income tax obtained most revenue from the urban and suburban higher income brackets. The sales tax, on the other hand, "spreads the cost of government to all groups of citizens," stated a prominent economist in 1955 in the *University of Virginia News Letter*. "This tax, properly combined with an income tax, is necessary for a balanced and well rounded system." [57] The Byrd organization, however, did not welcome any tax which spread a greater part of the cost of government to its rural strongholds.

State support of education was so pitiful, critics of the Byrd organization contended, that it mattered little how funds were disbursed. The bulk of public school revenue was generally distributed on the basis of a certain amount for each child in average daily attendance in school. The General Assembly in its 1948 session appropriated almost $30,000,000 for the support of public schools in the next school year.[58] Of this sum Vir-

[54] See Virginia State Chamber of Commerce, p. 95, for the percentage of general fund revenue derived from individual and corporate income taxes.

[55] See E. E. Holm, "The Changing Virginia Economy," *Virginia Economic Review*, XIV (Aug. 1962), for a breakdown of Virginia's industrial and corporate concentrations.

[56] L. A. Thompson, "Income Payments by Cities and Counties of Virginia, 1947 & 1945," p. 3, lists county per capita income in 1947 at $837.00 and city per capita income at $1,275. Typescript is available at University of Virginia Bureau of Population and Economic Research.

[57] Snavely, "Sales and Use Tax," p. 3.

[58] Virginia, *Acts of the Assembly, 1948* (Richmond: Division of Purchase and Printing, 1948), pp. 1163–79.

ginia's counties received approximately $24,000,000 and the
cities $6,000,000.[59] The ratio of disbursements to counties and
cities roughly followed the school-age population ratio (510,000
to 153,000).[60] The counties received somewhat more money than
their school-age population justified, primarily because of rural
transportation needs and minimal educational requirements.[61]
No graft and little favoritism occurred in the disbursement of
revenue for public schools; the state gave each locality too
little.

"The amount of public school revenue coming from State
sources is lower [in Virginia] than in any of the other ten
Southern States surveyed by NEA [National Education Association in 1963]," stated the Washington *Post* in a series of
articles on the Byrd organization. "Receiving this minimal aid,
the local cities and counties must decide for themselves
whether to have quality education. In a rich urban district the
answer is 'yes.' In a poor rural county the answer can only be
'no.' "[62] Since the formula for state revenue disbursement gave
almost no credit for local effort or initiative,[63] localities were
under little pressure from the state to provide adequate schooling. This situation produced an alarming disparity in the quality of schools in different areas of the commonwealth. A
wealthy suburban county such as Arlington was able and willing to provide a mean teacher salary of $3,009 in 1948–49, while
Carroll County in southwest Virginia had one of $1,452.[64] In

[59] Virginia, *Report of the Superintendent of Public Instruction, 1948–1949*
(Richmond: Division of Purchase and Printing, 1949), pp. 218–21.
[60] *Ibid.*, pp. 292–97.   [61] See *Acts of Assembly, 1948*, pp. 1163–79.
[62] July 21, 1965.
[63] Under the 1948–49 distribution formula each county and city was encouraged to pay in local taxes for public schools at least 30 per cent of the amount
allocated to it for school operations under the state program. It was permitted
to pay as little as 20 per cent if it proved unable to pay 30 per cent after having
a ratio of assessed to actual value of property assessable for school purposes as
great as the rest of the state. This provision could hardly be termed an
"incentive inducer" as it had no effect on the nine-tenths of Virginia's localities
which provided far more than 30 per cent of the state appropriation through
local taxes (*Acts of Assembly, 1948*, pp. 1165–66).
[64] *Report Supt. Public Instruction, 1948–49*, p. 287.

the counties, the amounts spent per pupil in average daily attendance in 1948–49 varied from $163.74 in Arlington to $58.75 in Dickenson.[65]

More shocking perhaps was the gap in the quality of education between Virginia's counties and cities. Mean teacher salaries for Virginia's cities stood at $2,674, while county salaries were only $1,931.[66] A dual crisis thus developed around Virginia's educational policy. In many rural counties standards of schooling were so pitiful as to blight any hope of a productive and progressive future for the area, and the cities grumbled increasingly at having to shoulder alone the major responsibility for improvement of their schools.[67] It is hardly surprising that the education issue proved in time the Achilles heel of the old Byrd organization and it plagued it incessantly during the two decades after World War II.

Efforts to include highways in the list of poor services provided by the Byrd organization must be viewed with some skepticism. Pay-as-you-go headlined Virginia's highway development ever since Harry Byrd inaugurated the policy in the mid-twenties. Virginians renounced deficit spending and bond issues; instead they constructed highways only as fast as current revenues from gasoline and automobile licensing taxes permitted. This decision drew sharp fire from proponents of bond financing, who contended, with much justification, that the savings to highway users and the industrial development of the state brought about by acceleration of the road improvement program would more than compensate for the interest charges on the bond issues. Key contends that "North Carolina, by floating a bond issue, built roads right and left and paved the way for the development of rural industry. Virginia, with its pay-as-you-go policy, postponed the same kind of development twenty years." [68]

---

[65] *Ibid.*, p. 298.   [66] *Ibid.*, pp. 290–91.

[67] Through local taxes cities provided almost three-fourths of the money needed to improve their schools (*Report Supt. Public Instruction, 1948–49*, pp. 220–21).

[68] Page 27.

Jean Gottmann takes a more balanced view. He terms North Carolina's 1921 bond issue

a bold and impressive investment in highway construction. In the 1920's it brought North Carolina an excellent highway network and the reputation of being the "good road state." Virginia, meanwhile, had established a state highway system in 1918; to develop it, the pay-as-you-go financing policy was adopted in 1923. For some years the construction of highways proceeded more slowly in Virginia than in North Carolina. This lead, which North Carolina assumed in the 1920's, may be partly responsible for the quicker and earlier development of manufactures, particularly of textile mills, in North Carolina. . . . In 1931, the state [North Carolina] took over the county roads and developed the secondary highways. Virginia followed in 1932, again at a somewhat slower pace, endeavoring to avoid indebtedness and paying for the highways through taxes rather than borrowing.

Both states were forced into further highway expansion by the surge of motor traffic after World War II. North Carolina finds now that the primary system which has been its pride has become more obsolete every year and that it is, in 1954, far short of the needs of traffic. . . . Virginia having started slightly later and having constructed her roads at a slower pace, finds herself in a better position today, with wider and more modern major highways, with less congestion along the principal thoroughfares than in North Carolina, and with fewer problems of alignment in the sections of highways which need enlargement.[69]

Another controversy over highway finance, with potentially grave consequences for the Byrd organization, arose. During the depression when the financial burdens of county governments were especially heavy, the State Highway Commission took over the secondary highways under the "Byrd Road Law" of 1932. This act gave the State Department of Highways jurisdiction over all the public roads, landings, and wharves that had previously been under county supervision and in

[69] *Virginia at Mid-Century* (New York: Holt, 1955; now distributed by the University Press of Virginia), pp. 527–28.

effect removed from the counties the responsibility of constructing and maintaining their parts of the highway system.[70] Although counties could vote to remove themselves from the provisions of the act, only two, Arlington and Henrico, eventually did so. Cities, meanwhile, continued to support and maintain their own streets.

Virginia's cities felt that under the Byrd Road Law the organization paid far more attention to rural farm-to-market roads than to city streets. Highway expenditures bore out this point. Whereas the Byrd organization appropriated over $14,000,000 in 1948–49 for construction and maintenance of the secondary road system in the counties, it allotted only $1,200,000 to city streets because they were not covered under the Byrd Road Law.[71] City streets were eligible for state highway funds of $4,000 a mile only if they formed an extension of the state's primary highway system. Otherwise the streets received $300 per mile per year if they met certain difficult specifications. A mere 1,600 miles of city streets were able to meet the specifications by 1949–50.[72] The cities, meanwhile, were paying both local taxes for the support of their own streets and the state gasoline and motor vehicle taxes used in part to support the secondary system in the counties. Although the secondary system was always in bad need of improvement, although some of the secondary roads ran through heavily populated suburban areas, and although urban areas would ultimately benefit from the improvement of rural roads, Virginia's cities remained dissatisfied with the organization's obvious favoritism. "The cities pumped ⅔ of all gasoline taxes into the state treasury and received little more than a pittance in return," complained one important urban leader.° The entire pay-as-you-go system of highway finance was to emerge as a prime source of friction between Virginia's cities and the Byrd

[70] *Ibid.*, p. 136.   [71] *Acts of Assembly, 1948*, p. 1222.
[72] Virginia, *Report of the State Highway Commission, 1949–1950* (Richmond: Division of Purchase and Printing, 1950), pp. 20–22, 55–56. City streets were required to have at least a 40-foot right-of-way and a hard-surface width of not less than 20 feet to qualify for the $300-a-mile payment in 1949–50. During the next 15 years these specifications were gradually relaxed and payments slowly increased.

organization at a time when Byrd forces could ill afford to alienate anyone.

That the state government should in some way promote education and build highways was obvious to all. But public welfare was another question; here the greatest stinginess appeared to some a downright virtue. Key observed that "individualistic farm people—and their representatives—have an inbred hostility toward relief," and the aversion to any "giveaway program" was particularly widespread in Virginia.[73] "Welfare" was always a nasty word in the Byrd vocabulary. The Senator saw the welfare state as "that state of twilight in which the glow of democratic freedoms is fading beyond the horizon, leaving us to be swallowed in the blackness of socialism, or worse." [74] The skeletal sums allotted for public welfare in Virginia's annual budget reflected this view.[75] To avoid inculcating dependence on the public dole, Virginia wrote its welfare checks at the lowest possible levels. Welfare assistance in Virginia exceeded that of several other southern states, but organization leaders raised it only with the greatest reluctance.

The low-tax, low-service attitudes of the Byrd leadership invite comparison with those of the Longs of Louisiana. The leaders of the two organizations, Harry F. Byrd and Huey P. Long, shatter forever any myth of the monolith of southern politics. Byrd and Long were governors in the 1920's, and each extended or fashioned an organization which endured for decades. But there the similarity ends. The Kingfish shot to power on the florid phrases of the stump, galvanizing the agrarian masses as the irresistible political force.[76] The patrician of the Old Dominion reigned over a limited, predictable, almost Tory

[73] Page 377.

[74] "The Threat to the American System," in *The Welfare State and Our National Welfare,* ed. Sheldon Glueck (Cambridge, Mass.: Addison Wesley Press, 1952), p. 76.

[75] In December, 1948, Virginia ranked fortieth in the U.S. in general assistance, fortieth in aid to dependent children, forty-fourth in aid to the blind, and forty-ninth in old age assistance. See *Book of the States, 1950–1951,* pp. 350–53.

[76] Material about Huey Long has been drawn from his *Every Man a King* (New Orleans: National Book Co., 1933) and Key, pp. 156–82.

electorate. He courted respect; he aroused emotion only as a last recourse. Long made political hay by propelling agrarian unrest into headlong clash with business and the well-to-do. But Byrd quietly guided an orderly courthouse-corporation coalition. Long gave his following vastly increased services— hospitals, schoolbooks, bridges, and highways. He plunged the state into debt, waged war on vested interests, and acquired an aura of venality and thuggery. He gratified the long-repressed needs of his volatile following much in the manner of a Latin dictator. Byrd made a fetish of frugality, a deity of the debt-free state. If Virginia provided little, it also asked for little with which to provide.

The Senator from Virginia gloried in the Old Dominion's history. Gentleman Byrd called to mind the Washingtons, Jeffersons, Lees, and Jacksons whom present-day Virginians had come to revere. He was a direct descendant of William Byrd of Westover, who laid out Richmond in 1737. Harry Byrd always carried with him a sense of the past.

Long had a very different sense of the past. He reminded his partisans of past woes, past disappointments, and past injustices. In a classic speech under the Evangeline Oak, the Kingfish evoked history in a most un-Virginian manner:

And it is here under this oak Evangeline waited for her lover, Gabriel, who never came. This oak is an immortal spot, made so by Longfellow's poem, but Evangeline is not the only one who has waited here in disappointment.

Where are the schools that you have waited for your children to have, that have never come? Where are the roads and highways that you sent your money to build, that are no nearer now than ever before?

Where are the institutions to care for the sick and disabled? Evangeline wept bitter tears in her disappointment, but it lasted through only one lifetime. Your tears in this country, around this oak, have lasted for generations. Give me the chance to dry the eyes of those who still weep here! [77]

[77] Key, p. 99.

Harry Byrd and Huey Long stood light years apart. Yet around and between these two poles much of the drama of southern politics has until recently revolved.

William Munford Tuck was inaugurated governor of Virginia on January 16, 1946, but many had forecast this event almost two years earlier. As governor, he had but four years to make his mark, for the Virginia constitution allowed no chief executive to succeed himself. Aside from this limitation, however, the governor was an exceedingly powerful figure. He appointed virtually all state department heads, boards, and commissions and except for the attorney general was the only full-time elected officer of the state. Some governors were far stronger than others, but when basic questions were involved in the customary twenty-two months between legislative sessions, "there . . . [was] but one source for the answers—the Governor." [78]

The governor possessed important legislative powers. He recommended to each session of the General Assembly important measures for the commonwealth, including a biennial budget. The item veto on an appropriation bill and the general veto power (both of which only a two-thirds vote of each house of the General Assembly could override), the power to recommend amendments to bills presented to him if he approved their general purpose but disapproved some part thereof, the authority to call a special session of the General Assembly—all these lay in the governor's hands. [79]

When Tuck arrived at the governor's mansion, he found his formal powers immeasurably enhanced by the organization's grip on the state legislature. If by some miracle, moderate or liberal forces captured the governor's chair, they would be unable to implement any program opposed by an organization

[78] C. O. Lowance, "The Governor of Virginia," *University of Virginia News Letter,* Feb. 15, 1960, p. 2.

[79] G. W. Spicer, "Gubernatorial Leadership in Virginia," *Public Administration Review,* I (Autumn 1941); *Constitution of Virginia,* Art. 5, Sec. 73–76 (as printed in 1966 *General Assembly Manual*).

legislature.[80] Tuck relied on the tightly knit chain of command in both houses of the General Assembly to enact his program and generally keep matters under control.

In the House of Delegates the governor looked to the speaker. This powerful figure controlled the flow of action on the floor, made all committee appointments, referred new bills "to the proper committee," and doubled as chairman of the House Committee on Rules.[81] Elected by the entire House, the speaker invariably embodied the organization's policies. Thomas B. Stanley, G. Alvin Massenburg, and especially E. Blackburn Moore were favorite targets of antiorganization leaders for alleged "slave-driving" tactics and "doghouse discipline." ° Moore, a member of the House since 1933 and speaker since 1950, held a special place in the organization's hierarchy. As a fellow applegrower, hiking companion, and political confidant of Senator Byrd, Moore was a center of concentration for countless Virginians seeking to decipher the Senator's thoughts and plans. The feeling quickly spread that Moore's cackle was "an echo of Byrd's chirp." [82] But this gaunt, russet-faced conservative was a formidable force in his own right. One reporter termed him "a fascinating man to watch because he operates in the classically inscrutable manner of the true old pros" of the Byrd organization.[83] Admitting that Moore presided over the House with presence, humor, and dignity, the Washington *Post* asserted that "in making appointments, he has rewarded his friends and punished the opposition. Legislative committees . . . as a result have reflected the parochial viewpoint of Moore and the Byrd organization." [84] Until the mid-1950's however, there was little need for a strong-armed speaker, so completely did the organization dominate the state legislature.

[80] Such had been the fate of Governor James H. Price (1938–42). See Key, p. 23.
[81] See "Rules of the Virginia House of Delegates," secs. 15, 18, and 37, *Manual of the Senate and the House of Delegates, Session 1966* (Richmond: Department of Purchases and Supply, 1966).
[82] J. Lindsay Almond, Jr., quoted in Norfolk *Virginian-Pilot*, June 8, 1964.
[83] Charles McDowell, as quoted in the Washington *Post*, Feb. 5, 1961.
[84] Feb. 5, 1961.

In the state Senate there was E. R. Combs. A casual observer of that body in the late 1940's or early 1950's might have pointed first to the lieutenant governor, the Senate's president, and next to one of the senators to select the organization power from these men. He would have been wrong. In the inconspicuous office of the clerk of the Senate was the power behind all Virginia thrones. There, at the clerk's desk, sat a courtly, mild-mannered gentleman, respectfully referred to as "Chief" by those who knew. He was a quiet man, of white-haired dignity, who never lost his temper and seldom raised his voice. Yet Combs appropriately came to symbolize the durable, efficient state Democratic organization of Senator Harry Flood Byrd, and he gained wide acceptance as that organization's number two man.[85]

"Ebbie" Combs began his career in the wilds of southwest Virginia when he helped to wrest the Ninth District from Republican control. As early as 1912 he called on the farmers of Russell County and respectfully asked them to elect him clerk of the circuit court over his Republican opponent. As clerk, his path crossed the rising star of Harry Byrd, and the two worked strenuously to defeat the highway bond proposal of 1923. When Byrd ran for governor, Combs managed his campaign in the Ninth District. Governor Byrd brought Combs to Richmond in 1928 and installed him as Virginia's first state comptroller. In 1934 he was named chairman of the State Compensation Board, in 1940 clerk of the Senate. These appointive jobs, many of which Combs held simultaneously, gave little clue to his real importance to the organization through the years.

E. R. Combs was, in a way, the boss of the Byrd machine, though he resembled not at all the stereotyped Tammany ward boss with beer belly, mustache, and fat cigar. It was the special job of Combs, the genteel boss, to keep the organization trim between campaigns, to visit the courthouse squares for a little social politicking with the Emory Elmores and their fellows.° Combs never neglected to call on Senator Byrd between these courthouse tours to discuss upcoming campaigns, the best

[85] Richmond *Times-Dispatch*, Jan. 6, 1957.

means of exploiting various issues, and grass root sentiment around the state. Combs would then go to Richmond to advise the governor on upcoming appointments and inform everyone in the Capitol what the Senator was thinking.° At General Assembly time Combs was again at his clerk's desk in the Senate quietly working away.

In the late 1940's the membership of the Virginia Senate read like an honor roll of hard-core Byrd leaders. Most estimates gave the number of organization devotees in the Senate as thirty, neutrals as nine, and "incorrigible antis" as one.° The loner, Lloyd M. Robinette of Lee County, wrote of his colleagues in despairing terms:

The Senate of Virginia is composed of men who sneer at Roosevelt and everything that he ever stood for, and who praise to the skies the Brickers . . . the Tafts . . . the Moores, the O'Daniels, and the Byrds. You have no conception of the situation existing in the Senate of Virginia today. There is hardly a whisper of liberalism in the whole membership, because they are bound to the chariot wheels of Senator Byrd and his crowd of buccaneers. They very much prefer a Republican in the White House to a Democrat with the slightest liberal leanings.[86]

Robinette was indeed overwhelmed by waves of well-known organization stalwarts: Senators Ben Gunter of Accomack, Garland Gray of Sussex, Albertis Harrison of Brunswick, Dr. J. D. Hagood of Halifax, Charles Moses of Appomattox, Morton Goode of Dinwiddie, John Battle of Charlottesville, Robert Button of Culpeper, Robert Norris of Lancaster, Lloyd Bird of Chesterfield, Robert Vaden of Pittsylvania, and the Senator's own son, Harry Byrd, Jr., of Winchester. These rural senators presented an imposing array of organization strength; they practically monopolized key committee chairmanships and provided the major pool of talent from which future statewide officers emerged.

The Byrd organization exerted maximum effort to ensure its emphatic control over the state legislature. The Virginia consti-

[86] Letter to E. H. McConnell, Feb. 18, 1947 (Martin Hutchinson Papers, Box 8, Alderman Library, University of Virginia).

tution required that "a reapportionment [of the state legisla-
ture] shall be made in the year nineteen hundred and thirty-
two and every ten years thereafter." [87] Although apportionment
was based primarily on population, a convenient rationale existed by which rural Byrd strongholds received dispropor-
tionately large representation. Urban legislators, it was argued,
could communicate with their closely knit constituents with
relative ease, whereas rural representatives were obliged to
travel long distances to confer with voters on the farms. Con-
stituent compactness became a major factor in apportionment,
and this augmented the already overwhelming Byrd forces in
the legislature. In 1956, for example, at the height of the school
integration controversy, the five rural congressional districts in
Virginia received an average of one state representative per
21,336 inhabitants, the three most urban districts an average of
one per 28,531. Four of the five rural districts had given Byrd
over 65 per cent of the vote in his primary race against Francis
Pickens Miller in 1952. None of the urban districts treated him
to comparable support. The Tenth and Second Districts, the
urban areas most hostile to the organization, fared worst in the
apportionment scheme, while Byrd's home district in the Shenandoah Valley (the Seventh) and the sprawling southside
Fourth District were most overrepresented. The organization
did, however, stick to its constituency compactness formula
even when it meant giving the rural, anti-Byrd Ninth District
substantial representation, and its apportionment plans,
though tilted toward rural areas, were far more representative
than those of most other state legislatures. [88]

No organization governor could meet with great obstacles

[87] *Constitution of Virginia*, Art. 4, Sec. 43.

[88] Virginia's index of representativeness in 1955 (87.6) placed it second
among the 50 states in the equitability of representation as determined by a
population standard. This index of representativeness was computed by adding
the minimum population percentages that could elect a majority of the members of each house of the state legislature. In Virginia 43.69 and 43.93 per cent
of the population was required to elect a majority of the House of Delegates
and Senate, respectively. See Paul T. David and Ralph Eisenberg, *Devaluation
of the Urban and Suburban Vote* (Charlottesville: University of Virginia Press,
1961), pp. 4–6. Appendix V gives a more detailed breakdown of the apportionment of the 1956 legislature.

under such a sympathetic and well-organized legislature. Tuck
certainly experienced no insuperable difficulties with the General
Assembly. Much of the legislation of his term represented
the highly necessary but undramatic matters common to all
state legislatures. Within the ground rules of the organization's
"cash and carry" financing, Tuck strove to improve Virginia's
school system: he summoned a special session of the General
Assembly in 1947 to recommend a $6,500,000 appropriation to
increase teachers' salaries. The Governor, however, frequently
cautioned lest new conditions and government services mean
the loss of old virtues:

In abolishing the one-room school, let us not abolish the spirit that
prompted the older boys to arrive early to build the fires and the
girls to sweep the floor. The one-room school, with all its handicaps,
promoted concepts of character and training which remain the
fundamentals of today. Children must not be taught that the government
will do everything for them, and it is incumbent upon the
family to assist the schools in the proper indoctrination of the
pupils. In this duty we, as citizens, have been derelict.[89]

Bill Tuck is best remembered for his big stick with labor. He
angered union leaders with stiff legislation; he assailed them in
the press; he thwarted strikes and blunted expansion—all this
he did in the name of the public interest. If his methods
seemed crude, at least he avoided the pressure group paralysis
which afflicts many political figures.

In his labor wars, particularly, was Tuck's rough and tumble
personality apparent. His rhetoric was often out of keeping
with the gentlemanly tone of the Byrd organization. It seemed
to place Tuck in a neo-Populist mold, better suited to the
roughshod fanfare of the deeper South. Yet if Tuck had a
"Populist personality," he adapted it to conservative ends.
Under the umbrella of Byrd organization politics, most young
and aspiring Virginians became, from some combination of
conviction or ambition, irrevocably conservative. Had Tuck
been raised in northern Alabama or the Piney Woods region of

[89] *Address to General Assembly, Jan. 14, 1948.*

Mississippi, he might have blazed a Populist trail of some note. As it was, he became a dedicated conservative and his antiwelfare, antilabor utterances are classics.

Organized labor was worth far more to Byrd as a perennial whipping boy than as a potential ally. Estimates of CIO voting strength in Virginia at mid-century seldom exceeded 15,000,[90] and most union strength was confined primarily to southwest Virginia and Hampton Roads. During Tuck's term unions across the nation were engaged in strikes and walkouts, and tolerance of the labor movement was generally at a low ebb.[91] Any crackdown on labor by Byrd leaders in Richmond was certain to be gleefully received at the courthouse and on the farm. Key reasoned that "an agrarian culture may be innately hostile toward the labor unionist—he who would have a greater share of the fruits of the earth in return for less sweat,"[92] and antiorganization spokesmen knew all too well of the enthusiasm generated by Byrd's castigation of the CIO. "Unions are not popular here with the farmers," fretted one Byrd opponent, "and you may rest assured that the . . . [organization] plays this up to a fare-you-well in all State campaigns."[93] If antilabor harangues delighted the courthouse, they certainly did not displease most corporation heads. Tuck's labor tactics, however daring on the surface, were in actuality a safe political bet.

The opening guns of the 1946 session of the General Assembly were aimed squarely at labor. The Governor noted in his address to the Assembly that "a movement has been initiated that, unless immediately halted, may result in serious disturbances in our state and local government." This movement involved the attempts of a labor union field agent to unionize employees of the city of Richmond and conduct bargaining negotiations with the city authorities. Tuck denounced this as "an intolerable situation . . . utterly incompatible with sound and orderly government." Unionization of public employees

[90] Key put the figure at 10,000 (p. 32).

[91] See E. F. Goldman, *The Crucial Decade—and After* (New York: Random House, 1960), pp. 20–25.

[92] Key, p. 375.

[93] J. B. Mapp to Martin Hutchinson, Aug. 5, 1949 (Hutchinson Papers, Box 17).

might cause "complete paralysis of necessary governmental activities and functions, thus jeopardizing the safety and welfare of the people." It diverted "the loyalty, allegiance, and obligations of the employee from the people and their government, which are entitled to them, and transfers them to the union. It creates a tendency on the part of the public servant to defy the constituted public authorities and rely upon the threats of strikes by the union to compel the granting of his demands." [94] Tuck so vividly painted the "evils" of unionization among public employees that the General Assembly passed both a resolution declaring it against "public policy" for a public official to bargain collectively with a labor union claiming the right to strike and a law prohibiting reemployment of a public worker for one year if he left his job on strike.[95]

Labor fought back. "Never to my knowledge has any Governor of any State ever delivered such a vicious anti-labor message," said Virginia CIO Director Ernest P. Pugh. "The CIO deplores the Governor's announced policy and feels that he is adopting the same tactics that were adopted by Hitler and Mussolini before the revolutions in their countries." [96] Labor's cries failed to halt Tuck whenever he considered the public interest paramount. If labor disliked the enactments of the 1946 General Assembly, it never forgave Tuck for his activities in the threatened VEPCO strike shortly after the legislature adjourned.

Negotiations between the management and the employees of the Virginia Electric and Power Company had deadlocked by mid-March of 1946. A strike loomed which would cut off electricity in much of Virginia for an indeterminate period. Faced with this crisis, Tuck acted quickly. On March 23 he threatened seizure and operation by the state of all VEPCO facilities in the event of a strike.

Industry . . . [bellowed Tuck], will be brought to a standstill if such a strike develops. It is even more serious than that, however,

[94] *Address to General Assembly, Jan. 21, 1946.*
[95] *Acts of Assembly, 1946,* pp. 561, 1006.
[96] Richmond *Times-Dispatch,* Jan. 22, 1946.

for human health and safety facilities will be paralyzed. Hospitals with their numerous expectant mothers, their seriously ill and their emergency patients, will be left in darkness, and physicians will be without power to carry on and administer to the needs of the suffering and afflicted. Dairies running full force to feed our children, as well as adults, will be shut down. Many homes will be unable to cook a meal or even to so much as toast a biscuit. . . . As Governor of Virginia, I shall not sit idly by and do nothing in the face of such a disaster. If a strike comes, bringing with it these attendant evils, I shall forthwith order these plants, together with all of their properties and equipments, seized by one of the agencies of the Commonwealth which will be instructed to operate them for the protection and benefit of the people.[97]

Yet the April 1 strike deadline neared, and the Governor's threats failed to resolve the deadlock. On Thursday, March 28, Tuck declared "a state of emergency" in Virginia and mobilized the state militia.[98] Still negotiations stalled. Tuck, promising further state action, proceeded to blast the "evil leadership" of the unions and the "wanton and reckless disregard of the rights and safety of others by a truculent and irresponsible labor leader." [99] But labor refused to budge. Finally, on the eve of the threatened walkout, the Governor dramatically called for the induction of 1,600 VEPCO employees into the unorganized state militia. Induction would place the workers under military law, subject to court-martial if they refused to continue in their jobs and work for the state. This last-ditch move was of questionable legality and dubious long-range wisdom, but it helped to bring about a quick settlement of the long-disputed issues in the VEPCO contract, and the threatened strike was narrowly averted.

Labor leaders across the country were outraged at Tuck's behavior. Boyd Payton, president of the Virginia CIO, termed it "the most sinister, damnable, and unprincipled act to date coming from the high command of Byrdism in its move to crush and completely destroy the rights of Virginia's wage

---

[97] *Ibid.*, March 23, 1946.   [98] *Ibid.*, March 29, 1946.
[99] *Ibid.*, March 30, 1946.

earners." Governor Tuck's action, exclaimed AFL Regional Director Paul Smith, "is unprecedented except in the dark days of Alabama when Governor Comer arrested coal miners, put them in chain gangs, and led them back into the coal mines to dig coal. . . . Outside of that I know of no other instance comparable to the action of Governor Tuck except in Fascist Italy and the acts of kings beheading their subjects in the early days of our civilization." Even the Richmond *Times-Dispatch,* noting the embittered union-management relations in VEPCO, said: "It is regrettable that Governor Tuck for all his courage and his laudable desire to prevent a strike and avoid serious hardships to users of VEPCO power and light, has been the chief factor in this deterioration." [100]

The Governor was not fazed by the criticism. He summoned a special session of the General Assembly in January of 1947 and guided through a sympathetic legislature two bills which further infuriated labor. One facilitated state seizure and operation of any utility where such action was deemed necessary to prevent stoppages of vital services threatened by strikes or walkouts.[101] Another was the Virginia right-to-work law, outlawing union membership as a necessary condition for employment.[102] The General Assembly backed the Governor to the hilt, and labor leaders prayed for the end of Tuck's administration.

Labor's partners during this period of complete alienation from the Byrd organization were the loosely organized liberals who formed the antiorganization clique and who unsuccessfully berated the Byrd machine for its poll tax and patronage policies and its failure to provide adequate public services. Antiorganization spokesmen were better off than their union allies only in that they assaulted the organization by choice, while labor leaders were often involuntarily assaulted.

Negroes were little better off in the Byrd scheme of things. The antilynching law passed during Byrd's governorship had assured Negroes that they would be protected from the violence and brutality administered to members of their race in

[100] *Ibid.*   [101] *Acts of Assembly, Extra Session, 1947,* pp. 24–29.
[102] *Ibid.,* pp. 12–13.

other southern states. Although the Negro was never encouraged to vote in Virginia, neither was he categorically denied the franchise. The Byrd organization did, however, set its face against progress for the colored race. Its leaders had a habit of opposing civil rights legislation, and the segregated school system in Virginia might have lasted millenniums had outside pressures not battered it down. Still, Negroes in Virginia were often "allied with the local arms of the Byrd organization, which in turn has protected their right to the suffrage." [103]

Near the center of power and strength in the old Byrd organization one found business interests, professional men, and the press. Although business found much to admire in the tone and flavor of the gentlemanly Byrd organization, tax and spending policy in Virginia was hardly favorable, as has been said earlier, to business, urbanites, or the well-to-do. The Virginia press was also far more sympathetic to the Byrd organization than to those less predictable reformers who sought to supplant it.[104] Occasionally however, it chided the organization for lack of a charitable spirit in public services.

The main power of the Byrd organization resided in the courthouse cliques dotted throughout rural Virginia. In statewide elective and appointive offices, legislative apportionment and committee assignments, campaign platforms, forms and levels of government services and taxation, and attitudes toward labor, civil rights, and welfare, organization policy coincided with the wishes of Brunswick County and its political counterparts throughout the state. In the courthouse complex the Southside enjoyed special influence.

The "high command," as the ruling oligarchy was called, included at mid-century E. R. Combs, Bill Tuck, "Blackie" Moore, Congressman Howard Smith, Sidney Kellam, boss of Princess Anne County, and state Senators Garland Gray and Harry Byrd, Jr. A dozen other men hovered on the periphery of

[103] Key, p. 32. In 1953, for instance, many Negroes supported the gubernatorial bid of the organization's Thomas B. Stanley.

[104] The Washington *Post*, which serves residents of northern Virginia, and the Norfolk *Virginian-Pilot* must be noted as exceptions. Generally, however, the press viewed the organization as more desirable than the "antis" who sought to supplant it.

the ruling circle whose circumference remained purposely clouded. Yet clearly at circle's center stood Harry Byrd.

The Tuck years were the last in which the classic Byrd coalition operated at peak effectiveness and the last in which antiorganization elements were so weak. Tuck was suspect when he entered the governor's mansion; he left it widely respected. He pursued a conservative course vigorously and inevitably made enemies while doing so. He acted frequently with fanfare, always with conviction.

It has been no easy task [he said in his farewell address to the General Assembly], to keep the ship of our state government on an even keel amidst the mountainous waves of false and spurious doctrines which have threatened to carry us onto the rocks of national disaster. When so many are willing to embrace popular evils and run with the winds, without regard for the reefs or the crags, it is the more difficult to chart and steer unwaveringly on the correct course.

At times we may seem to sail alone. So long as we have our compass fixed and men who are prepared to withstand the buffeting of the storm, we need have no fear. Virginia has thrown out the cable tow, knowing that the serene shores of good government offer haven for all who follow in her wake.

In this worthwhile struggle for the supremacy of sound principle, let us never forget: no cause that is right will ever be lost. The Virginia pattern of government will survive.[105]

---

[105] Jan. 11, 1950.

Chapter 3

The Byrd Organization
on the National Level

THE power of the Byrd organization was not confined to the boundaries of Virginia. Although V. O. Key called the Virginia machine a "political museum piece," [1] the organization and its leaders were not archaic misfits in national politics whose influence terminated at the borders of the Old Dominion. For more than three decades Harry Byrd and his Virginia colleagues played significant roles in the battle to determine the direction of national policy. The principles and strategies of the organization, whether in Brunswick, in Richmond, or on the floor of the United States Senate in Washington, demonstrated for the most part a determined and meticulous consistency.

Many delight in describing the United States Congress from 1932 to 1964 as the golden age of the conservative coalition. Southern Democrats and Republicans, so the theory goes, combined against Presidents and northern Democrats to emasculate all proposals for federal spending, civil rights, and national intervention in the affairs of the states. The coalition was pictured by its enemies as a single-minded agrarian conspiracy of the South and West pitted against the needs and aspirations of the urban Northeast, and this coalition was blamed or com-

[1] Page 19.

mended for the course of national politics from Roosevelt to Kennedy.

There were certain limits, however, to the coalition's powers. Neither was it monolithic nor unvaryingly successful. Before 1945 it was an amorphous and erratic political force. In his study of the seven odd-year congressional sessions from 1933 to 1945 Key concluded that "the report of a Southern Democratic–Republican congressional coalition has been not a little exaggerated." Of 598 selected Senate roll calls, he found that on more than half a majority of southern Democratic senators actually disagreed with a majority of Republican senators. On less than 10 per cent of the 598 roll calls did southern Democratic and Republican majorities join in opposition to a majority of the nonsouthern Democrats,[2] and on less than 5 per cent of the roll calls were more than 70 per cent of the southern senators in alliance with Republicans against nonsouthern Democrats.[3]

The lack of a southern Democratic–Republican coalition before 1945 was not the fault of Harry Byrd. While Roosevelt was President, Byrd did more than his part to make one possible. Byrd was the second most "Republican" of the southern Democratic senators of the 1933–45 period: on those roll calls where at least 70 per cent of the southern Democrats opposed a majority of Republicans, Harry Byrd voted with the Republicans 45 per cent of the time.[4]

[2] Unless otherwise stated, a coalition is functionally defined as a majority of Republicans and southern Democrats voting against a majority of nonsouthern Democrats.

[3] *Ibid.*, pp. 355–59. Other investigators also have discovered evidence for a pre-1945 coalition to be thin. One analyst found the coalition untroublesome and indeed almost nonexistent during the early days of the New Deal, cropping up for the first time in 1937–38. This conservative coalition in the late 1930's, however, was not a classic southern Democratic–Republican alliance. Many southern senators continued to support the New Deal while nonsouthern Democrats such as Burke of Nebraska, Gerry of Rhode Island, and Holt of West Virginia joined the conservative alliance against Roosevelt's policies (James T. Patterson, "A Conservative Coalition Forms in Congress, 1933–1939," *Journal of American History*, LII [March 1966], 762).

[4] Key, p. 362.

The Truman administration proved more conducive to the development of a Republican–southern Democratic conservative coalition. The country was no longer charged with the crisis of depression, recession, or world war, and congressional leaders after 1945 were freer to resume their bickering with the executive. Lacking the stature of his predecessor, Truman seemed vulnerable to congressional leaders, many of whom were former colleagues. Whereas Roosevelt had muted the civil rights question, Truman posed as an unflinching champion of Negro rights by desegregating the armed forces and supporting a 1948 Democratic platform calling for poll tax repeal, an antilynching law, and establishment of a Fair Employment Practices Commission. The platform drove many Southerners into the Dixiecrat revolt of 1948 and caused southern members of Congress, some of whom had formerly supported the New Deal, to adopt a more rigid states' rights position.

While the South was balking over civil rights, Republicans were also moving to the right. The 1946 elections were the most successful for the Republicans since the 1920's and the best they would have for many years to come. Republican strength jumped from 190 to 246 in the House and from 38 to 51 in the Senate. Among the new senators were John W. Bricker (R-Ohio), Irving M. Ives (R-N.Y.), William E. Jenner (R-Ind.), William F. Knowland (R-Calif.), George W. Malone (R-Nev.), Joseph R. McCarthy (R-Wis.), Arthur V. Watkins (R-Utah), and John J. Williams (R-Del.). With the exception of Ives, all represented their party's most conservative wing.[5] Most were gravely concerned with the rise of international and internal communism and what they perceived to be a trend toward socialism in the policies of the Truman administration.

Harry Byrd thrived on the congressional conservatism of the postwar period. An anti–New Dealer when Roosevelt was most popular, Byrd welcomed the growing philosophical alliance of southern Democrats and Republicans against the Truman administration and the Fair Deal. As early as 1947 Senators Byrd

[5] *Congress and the Nation, 1945–1964* (Washington: Congressional Quarterly Service, 1965), p. 3.

and Walter George of Georgia were hailed as the "key figures in a new coalition" which consistently saw ten to fifteen southern Democrats allied with Republicans in efforts to defeat Truman's domestic programs.[6] In the Senate the number of Republican–southern Democratic coalitions on significant roll calls for the two sessions of 1949 and 1950 exceeded all the coalitions for the seven sessions studied by Key from 1933 to 1945. The ratio of coalitions to roll calls increased by almost 60 per cent. In the House the average number of coalitions per session tripled between 1933–45 and 1949–50, and the ratio of coalitions to roll calls rose by more than 100 per cent.[7] The Truman Fair Deal bogged down. House and Senate coalitions killed all administration attempts to repeal the Taft-Hartley Act. The FEPC, federal aid to education, and national health insurance proposals were beaten by coalitions in committee or on the floor. The President's housing, rent control, and minimum wage bills passed Congress only in badly mangled form. Truman's reaction was sharp. There were, he remarked, "too many Byrds in the Congress."[8]

Shortly after Truman's retirement Harry Byrd and his Virginia colleagues assumed even greater institutional power in the conservative coalition. By the middle fifties the control of key congressional committees passed to Virginia's senior statesmen. Byrd chaired the Senate Finance Committee by 1955; Howard Smith became chairman of the House Rules Committee that same year; and A. Willis Robertson became chairman of the Senate Banking and Currency Committee by 1959. Between them the Virginia senators had a major voice on almost all taxation, currency, social security, banking, and housing

[6] *United States News,* June 6, 1947, pp. 50–52. Even in the Truman years, however, there were those in both the southern Democratic and Republican camps who veered from the coalition fold. (Senators Kefauver of Tennessee and Pepper of Florida were the Southerners who most obviously spurned the alliance.)

[7] William Lilley, "The Southern Democracy in the Fair Deal, 1949–1950" (MS, Department of American Studies, Yale University, 1962), pp. 5, 6, 15–17.

[8] New York *Times,* May 10, 1949.

measures before Congress. This power was enough to make Capitol Hill listen attentively if not always sympathetically to the two Virginians.

Through their influence over major legislative channels in both houses of Congress, Byrd, Smith, and Robertson continued as powerful figures in the conservative coalitions which functioned effectively throughout the Eisenhower and Kennedy administrations. During the Kennedy years, for example, coalitions won noticeably more than half of the roll calls on which they appeared, though the percentage of victory dropped to 33 per cent after the 1964 elections.[9]

Byrd believed that government at all levels should tighten its belt; his long Senate career represented a sustained attempt to cut federal expenditures and slash executive budgets. Byrd "considers himself the monetary conscience of the Federal Government," read one sketch of the Senator in 1942.[10] "I'm one of the last of the old New Dealers," the Virginian once mused with only the tiniest twinkle of humor. "I campaigned for the New Deal platform in 1932—and I'm still standing on it."[11] The "New Deal platform" for which Byrd campaigned was Roosevelt's 1932 pledge of federal frugality—including a cut of 25 per cent in the cost of federal government. When the President pursued quite a different course, Byrd reacted accordingly. "We have at Washington today," he exclaimed in 1938, "the most costly, the most wasteful, and the most bureaucratic form of government this republic has ever known or has ever been afflicted with."[12] From that statement the Senator never retreated. With each successive administration Byrd's horror at the level of federal spending increased. In April 1947

[9] *Congressional Quarterly Almanac, XXI, 1965* (Washington: Congressional Quarterly Service, 1966), p. 1083. It should be made clear that there is no one standard of measurement which can perfectly test the effectiveness of the conservative coalition. Most measurements so far employed by political scientists have been deficient in that they have failed to test the coalition's considerable effect on bills while in committee and have failed to weigh the relative importance of roll call votes on the floor.

[10] Maxine Block (ed.), *Current Biography 1942* (New York: H. W. Wilson Company, 1942), p. 117.

[11] *Time*, Aug. 17, 1962, p. 12.   [12] *Current Biography 1942*, p. 119.

he pleaded, "If we do not balance the budget now, it may never be balanced until we go over the precipice of financial disaster."[13] The grimness of Byrd's forecasts climbed with the national debt. By 1952 he claimed America was "approaching national bankruptcy . . . suffering under the most cruel taxation in our history" and charged that the "reckless spending of the Truman administration is responsible for a substantial part of this huge burden upon which we will pay interest for many generations to come, and perhaps forever."[14]

The Senator's pet project in these years was his Joint Committee for the Reduction of Nonessential Federal Expenditures —a forum from which he attacked bloated bureaucracies and unfurled rolls of ominous statistics on the economy's health. (When the Republicans took control of Congress in 1947, Byrd offered to resign his chairmanship of this committee, but the GOP insisted he stay on.)[15] "Byrd believes that a dollar should be worth a dollar," wrote *Time* in 1962.[16] And in an age of Keynes, brain truster economists, and a $300 billion national debt, the Byrd dicta of honesty, efficiency, frugality, and simplicity in government seemed irresistible common sense.

"For myself," Byrd explained, "I would vastly prefer to take the Virginia philosophy of government to Washington than to bring the current Washington theories to Virginia."[17] Even enemies conceded his consistency and little doubted that Byrd would have the federal government practice the parsimony of his Virginia machine.[18] Yet there was inconsistency in Byrd's philosophy. He attacked centralization of government in Washington, while his own state machine through such devices as the circuit judge and the Compensation Board achieved one of the most centralized state power structures in the country. He fought for "a simplification of our governmental machinery, the elimination of needless red tape and overlapping

[13] *Congressional Digest*, XXVI (April 1947), 112.
[14] *United States News*, Oct. 31, 1952, pp. 91–94.
[15] *Ibid.*, June 6, 1947, p. 50. [16] Aug. 17, 1962, p. 12.
[17] *United States News*, Oct. 31, 1952, p. 92.
[18] "I don't mind us going to the moon," the Senator once said of the space program, "as long as we pay as we go" (Washington *Post*, July 22, 1965).

activities," [19] at the same time that a Virginia editor claimed that there were "entirely too many employees in the Virginia state government." [20] Byrd urged leaving education in the hands of the states, arguing there was "not a State in the Union which is unable to educate its own children if it is willing to assess taxes to do so." [21] Virginia's schools, meanwhile, were among the nation's poorest. Consistently slashed budgets meant consistently slashed services. Harry Byrd as the "monetary conscience" of government too often let its "conscience of service" wear away.

Byrd represented more in the United States Senate than the budget-balancing arm of the conservative coalition. The Senate, especially in the postwar years, was truly Harry Byrd's milieu, and his presence reinforced the style, the flavor, and the dignity of the upper house. William S. White declared that a Southerner came to the Senate from his state "with the quiet satisfaction of a man rising from his dinner table to stroll contentedly into his sitting room" [22] and the analogy had perhaps its greatest relevance for Harry Byrd. Virginia politics and the United States Senate were ostensibly governed by gentlemanly folkways underneath which, however, lay unique respect for the reality of power. Both the United States Senate and the Old Dominion luxuriated in tradition, in worn splendor, in reverence for propriety, and in a subtle snobbery. The Byrd organization and the Senate ran on seniority: one waited patiently for his elder's nod, and brash upstarts were firmly

[19] *Congressional Digest,* XXVI, 112.

[20] Continuing, Virginius Dabney said, "Various explanations have been advanced, one of them being that the government has been so largely centralized in Richmond that the counties and cities have fewer employees than in many states. In other words, under the rule of the Byrd machine there has been the very sort of centralization at Richmond which that machine decries at Washington. Efforts are being made to whittle the state bureaucracy down to size. Legislation to this end was introduced at the session of 1948, but it was cut to pieces by the machine-dominated General Assembly, and its already limited scope was reduced by at least 50 per cent" ("What We Think of Senator Byrd's Machine," *Saturday Evening Post,* Jan. 7, 1950, p. 31).

[21] *Congressional Digest,* XXVIII (Nov. 1949), 273.

[22] *Citadel* (New York: Harper & Brothers, 1956), p. 72.

pushed aside. The Senate was intimate; its inner club, of which Byrd was a charter member, had much the gentlemanly cliquishness of a county courthouse group in rural Virginia. With the filibuster and its seniority rules the United States Senate resisted mass or majority rule; Virginia with its poll-taxed electorate did the same thing. White wrote that "to have presence in the Institution [Senate] is useful beyond ready explanation, though to be effective it should be graciously used as . . . it is used by Senator Byrd of Virginia, who employs his power by seeming not to employ it at all." [23] Byrd employed his power in the state in much the same manner. The late Douglas Southall Freeman termed his organization the "invisible government" of Virginia.[24] "Some people say I run a political machine in Virginia," said Byrd one day with a chuckle. "All I do is offer a little advice now and then." [25] Such "modest" behavior was also characteristic of Byrd in that most Virginian of all national institutions—the United States Senate.

The Senate was ostensibly a national institution, but its inner workings, in Harry Byrd's heyday, could be provincial. It has been described as an "Old Southern Home" and "the only place in the country where the South did not lose the war." [26] By the 84th Congress, six of the ten most powerful committee chairmen were Southerners, and Southerners dominated the ranking Democratic memberships of those committees whose chairmanships were in nonsouthern hands.[27] Although a "Byrd of Virginia may look with troubled eyes upon the economic heresies of a Sparkman of Alabama," wrote White, "and a Sparkman may somberly return the gaze at what he thinks is the aura of parsimony rising about the seat of the senior Senator from Virginia . . . when all is said and done, all [the

[23] *Ibid.*, p. 70.   [24] Quoted in Latimer, p. 9.
[25] *Wall Street Journal*, April 11, 1952.   [26] White, p. 72.
[27] The six powerful Senate committees with southern chairmen were Agriculture and Forestry, Ellender (La.); Armed Services, Russell (Ga.); Banking and Currency, Fulbright (Ark.); Finance, Byrd (Va.); Foreign Relations, George (Ga.); and Labor and Public Welfare, Hill (Ala.). Southerners also chaired the committees on Government Operations, McClellan (Ark.), and Post Office and Civil Service, Johnston (S.C.).

Southerners] are in the same clan, in a way that goes deeper than political ideas and even political conviction."[28] In some ways Harry Byrd was first a Virginian, secondly a Southerner, and thirdly a United States senator. When the Supreme Court attacked Virginia's and the South's "peculiar institution" in the spring of 1954, Harry Byrd was moved by heritage and by Senate associations to defend the mores of the segregationist South.

Howard Worth Smith guarded the organization's philosophy in the House. Like E. R. Combs in Richmond, Judge Smith shunned the spectacular to concentrate on the exercise of real but background power. As Smith's influence in Congress grew, however, opponents never failed to tack to his name some "crafty, wily, crusty or Victorian" prefix.[29] Judge Smith was an honest gentleman, but he threaded his way through legislative jungles with such resource and skill that he was regarded as foxy.

Smith was a frail, stooped, wisp of a man, once called "a deliberate drag" both personally and politically.[30] He moved, said one writer, as "the praying mantis, that quiet, long-bodied insect that walks on its hind legs with its front claws clasped silently before it, piously, as if in prayer."[31] Long a power in the organization, Judge Smith was known to insiders as Byrd's brains, and his sometimes frosty, sometimes somnolent exterior encased a keen legislative mind. Born on Groundhog Day in 1883 in Fauquier County, Smith by the age of twenty had received a University of Virginia law degree under teachers steeped in the old traditions. He first entered public life as commonwealth's attorney in Alexandria in 1918, became judge of the corporation court in Alexandria in 1922, judge of the 16th circuit court in 1928, and congressman by 1931. His one

[28] Page 74.
[29] See *Time*, Jan. 27, and Feb. 10, 1961, for a number of vivid epithets applied to Judge Smith.
[30] Charles Houston, "Smith and Robertson," *Commonwealth*, XXXIII (Oct. 1966), 28.
[31] Friddell, p. 72.

break with the Byrd organization was most understandable. His brother, William Worth Smith, chose to seek the Democratic gubernatorial nomination in 1933 despite the fact that Senator Byrd was backing George Peery. Although Peery won handsomely, Smith backed his brother so effectively that he carried the Eighth District against the organization's stoutest efforts. "Harry was a little miffed for a time," Smith said of Byrd's reaction to his behavior. "But he got over it." [32] When the time came for Smith's 1934 congressional race, the organization heartily supported him.

Smith's influence in Congress rested on his role in the powerful House Rules Committee. From there he captained the bipartisan conservative alliance which delayed, diluted, or killed liberal legislation in the House at every conceivable opportunity. The Rules Committee served as the major bridge between the floor of the House of Representatives and its vast committee complex. Legislation passing from its original committee to the floor first stopped at the Rules Committee where Smith and his colleagues prescribed the length and manner of debate on the measure. By its power to grant an "open" or "closed" rule, the Committee also decided whether a bill would be subject to amendment on the House floor.[33] Although it was initially designed as a traffic committee to ease and expedite the flow of legislation in the House, the Rules Committee by postponing or refusing to grant a bill a rule bottled up measures which did not win the approval of its conservative majority.

Smith early began to assume a prominent role in the committee. In the late 1930's Democrats Smith and Edward E. Cox of Georgia combined with Republicans led by Joe Martin of Massachusetts to oppose Roosevelt programs.[34] The southern Democratic–Republican alliance in the Rules Committee continued with even greater effect after Cox died in 1952 and Martin was deposed as Republican leader in the House by

[32] Houston, "Smith and Robertson," p. 29.

[33] See J. A. Robinson, "The Role of the Rules Committee in Arranging the Program of the U.S. House of Representatives," *Western Political Quarterly*, XII (Sept. 1959), for an analysis of Rules Committee powers and practices.

[34] Patterson, pp. 757–58.

Charles A. Halleck of Indiana. (Cox and Martin were both reported to have nurtured a "deep affection" for Speaker Sam Rayburn—an affection which occasionally led them astray from strict conservatism. Smith and Halleck did not wander.) [35]

When Smith first became chairman of the committee in 1955, conservative forces held tenuous control. The four Republicans on Rules united with Democrats Smith and William M. Colmer of Mississippi for the six conservative votes on the twelve-man committee, and no bill could clear the committee on a tie vote.

Howard Smith became a favorite whipping boy for the national press and frustrated colleagues as he began to acquire a reputation as a one-man legislative dam. The *New Republic* labeled him "the best-placed and most powerful exponent of reaction in national politics," [36] while *Time* called him "leader of the roadblocking conservative coalition that has dominated the mighty Rules Committee since 1937." [37] Congressman Wright of Texas wrote that "the crusty old Virginian" was a prodigious obstacle to legislative progress in the House,[38] and Richard Bolling, an opponent of Smith's on the Rules Committee, described his behavior in the following terms:

When Smith's position in [Rules] Committee is occasionally imperilled, he resorts to various devices to preserve it. He will let a backlog of needed domestic legislation he opposes accumulate. Then he will let supporters of the accumulated bills know directly or indirectly that they are going to have to choose two or three preferred bills from the backlog for clearance to the floor. Supporters also sense that Judge Smith would be pleased if the bills selected were those that would least damage his nineteenth century world. If the support for a major liberal bill is so great that Rules can't quite manage to keep it in committee pigeonhole, Smith forces modification of it. Its desperate supporters are then grateful. They may win a skirmish and occasionally a battle, but the tide of the legislative war generally continues in favor of Smith and his doughty coalition. Stonewall Jackson would be pleased.[39]

[35] *Time,* Feb. 10, 1961, p. 13.   [36] Feb. 6, 1961, p. 5.
[37] Jan. 27, 1961, p. 14.
[38] Jim Wright, *You and Your Congressman* (New York: Coward-McCann, 1965), pp. 107–16.
[39] *House Out of Order* (New York: Dutton, 1965), p. 80.

Virginia's congressional delegations have usually been as conservative as Byrd and Smith. A study of delegation voting records as late as 1965 reveals that only Mississippi was more conservative than Virginia. Three factors were considered: first, the delegation's support of the Republican–southern Democratic coalition; second, its degree of agreement with President Johnson; and finally, the votes on twelve critical Great Society issues calling for expanded federal activity.[40] Virginia's delegation was significantly more conservative than those of Louisiana, Tennessee, Arkansas, Texas, and Florida. It proved slightly more so than Alabama, South Carolina, North Carolina, and Georgia. Only Mississippi, with its Eastlands, Stennises, and Colmers exceeded it.

This runner-up conservative delegation of 1965 contained five old-line organization veterans—Byrd, Robertson, Tuck, Smith, and Watkins M. Abbitt. Every bit as conservative as these five were John O. Marsh, Jr., an energetic young Democrat from Virginia's Shenandoah Valley District, and David E. Satterfield, III, an earnest and dedicated freshman congressman from Richmond. Holding identical philosophies but different party labels were Virginia's two Republican Congressmen, Richard H. Poff and Joel T. Broyhill. These nine formed the conservative nucleus of the delegation from which moderate-conservative Thomas N. Downing and moderate Porter Hardy, Jr., occasionally strayed.[41]

The delegation's black sheep was W. Pat Jennings from southwest Virginia's "Fightin' Ninth" District. The "Fightin' Ninth" had long been inhabited by poor but rugged mountaineers who declined to leave their native valleys and ridges for jobs in more prosperous urban centers. The highlanders of the Ninth had historically been a rebellious lot: even before the Civil War they were grumbling at the control more genteel and prosperous eastern planters had over state policy. "There's still a frontier swing to the walk, and the thought in Southwest Virginia," wrote Friddell in 1966. "The shade of Daniel Boone

---

[40] Voting records were compiled by the *Congressional Quarterly Almanac, 1965,* pp. 1092–94, 1101, 1104, 1115–17. See Appendix VI for a fuller look at the conservatism of Virginia's 1965 congressional delegation.

[41] See Appendix VI.

lingers there." [42] Key mentions "an ineradicable residue of history . . . in the rebelliousness of the people of the southwestern mountain counties," explaining how, throughout the South, "the voters of the highlands tend to respond when the interests and powers-that-be are baited." [43]

Southwest Virginia's impoverishment doubtless contributed to its antiestablishment attitude. Despite its highland beauty,

Table 7   Southwest Virginia's "Fightin' Ninth" District (1960)

	State	Ninth District *	Rank of Ninth among state's congressional districts
Urban population, %	55.6	19.3	9th
Nonwhite population, %	20.6	2.7	10th
Median years of school completed — persons 25 yrs. and over	9.9	7.5	9th †
Persons 25 yrs. and over with 4 or more yrs. of college, %	8.4	3.1	10th
Median family income	$4,964	$3,370	10th
Median value of owner-occupied dwelling units	$10,800	$5,600	10th
Average farm size (1959), acres	134	100	10th
Farm operator level of living index	80	57	10th

Source: U.S. Bureau of the Census, *Congressional District Data Book* (*Districts of the 88th Congress*), pp. 511–21.
    * The Ninth District in 1960 included the counties of Bland, Buchanan, Dickenson, Giles, Lee, Pulaski, Russell, Scott, Smyth, Tazewell, Washington, and Wise and the cities of Bristol and Norton.
    † Actually it was tied with the Fifth District for ninth place.

the "Fightin' Ninth" was a rural slum, lagging well behind the rest of the state by every conceivable standard of income and education. As Table 7 demonstrates, the Ninth was indisputa-

[42] Page 39.   [43] Key, p. 31.

bly the poorest of Virginia's ten congressional districts, despite the fact it had far fewer Negroes than any other section of the state. Even the low income and educational levels of Negroes in rural Virginia east of the mountains did not reduce the overall living standards of those districts to that of the Ninth.

Subsistence farming had been the major occupation of the Ninth until coal mines were opened in the region early in the century. Mining quickly became a major occupation, and by 1960, of Virginia's 19,277 miners, 16,124 were from the Ninth District.[44] The United Mine Workers early unionized the area and by 1953 had enrolled almost 60 per cent of the region's 17,000 to 20,000 mining force. Chiefly because of the union's efforts, hourly wages for bituminous coal miners in the Appalachian area (including Virginia) rose from 75 cents in 1939 to $2.20 by 1951.[45]

In 1953, however, this economy threatened to collapse. The national market for coal plummeted as railroads, steamship lines, many industrial plants, and domestic users converted to oil. New England markets, formerly served by Virginia mines, now bought from Pennsylvania producers. Technological advances in coal production and nearly exhausted seams further blackened the situation of the miners. Faced with the coming of oil, the advance of automation, the loss of markets, and depleted reserves, many Virginia coal mines shut down. Unemployment in southwest Virginia rose from an estimated 2,000 in January 1953 to 10,000 by September 1954.[46] Median family income, barely $3,000 in the best of times, fell even lower during the mining crisis. The "Fightin' Ninth" was in a very rough predicament.

The Ninth, as might be expected, was little enamored of Byrd conservatism. There was, of course, the historic split between the highlanders and the lowland planters and farmers in rural Virginia east of the Blue Ridge Mountains who now so

[44] U.S. Bureau of the Census, *Congressional District Data Book*, (*Districts of the 88th Congress*), (Washington, 1963), p. 511.

[45] Gottmann, p. 393.

[46] See *ibid.*, pp. 380–98, for a discussion of southwest Virginia's mining crisis.

faithfully supported Senator Byrd and his organization. Moreover the Southwest, in contrast to the Southside, was not
preoccupied with the Negro. Its smaller hillside farms needed
little Negro labor before the Civil War and little needed it a
century later. The Southside's Fourth District, backbone of the
plantation system in pre-Civil War years, still contained by
1960 a 47.9 per cent Negro population, as compared to a 2.7 per
cent Negro population in the Ninth District.[47] The organization's stands against national civil rights measures which so
endeared it to the Southside did not charm the Southwest. The
constant fights between the organization and national Democratic administrations disappointed many persons in this impoverished section who hoped to benefit from the national
relief measures and depressed area bills which Senator Byrd
was striving so fervently to block. It further angered Democrats in the Ninth District that Byrd and Smith deserted Democratic Presidents to ally with Republicans on critical votes, for
the Ninth was one of the few areas in Virginia where two-party
competition was brisk. Southwest Virginians were not delighted
with Virginia's low rank in welfare and other public services.
The United Mine Workers, a powerful political force in the
area, had been alienated by Tuck's strikebreaking activities
and antiunion attitudes.[48] These grievances made the highland
counties of the Southwest the only rural area of Virginia to
oppose the Byrd organization (see Table 8).

During the mining crisis in the early 1950's Pat Jennings,
sheriff of Smyth County and a veteran of World War II, was
busy building his own political network in the Ninth based
primarily on opposition to the precepts of Senator Byrd. In
1954 he ran against Republican incumbent William C. Wampler in a sharply contested congressional campaign and
emerged the victor by a mere 999 votes.[49] If the situation in
southwest Virginia demanded unique representation in Con-

[47] *Congress. Dist. Data Book (88th Cong.)*, p. 512.
[48] The UMW was particularly infuriated when Tuck seized a strip mine in
Buchanan County to assure a graded supply of fuel for home furnaces during
the nationwide coal strike. See Friddell, p. 63.
[49] For an off-year election the Ninth turned out an extraordinarily heavy vote
—nearly 78,000, or some 3,500 above the total cast for President in 1952.

Table 8   Primary Returns in Southwest Virginia

Year	Office	Candidates *	9th's vote	State's vote
			%	%†
1946	Senator	*Byrd*	56.4	63.5
		Hutchinson	43.6	36.5
1949	Governor	*Battle*	32.3	42.8
		Miller	40.0	35.3
		Edwards	25.7	15.0
		Arnold	2.0	7.0
1952	Senator	*Byrd*	46.8	62.7
		Miller	53.2	37.3
1961	Governor	*Harrison*	29.3	56.7
		Stephens	70.7	43.3

* Byrd organization candidates are italicized.

† Percentages are rounded off to the nearest tenth and thus do not always total exactly 100.

gress, Jennings provided it. He ranged far to the left of the Byrd position on questions of federal aid and welfare. He favored aid to Appalachia, rent subsidies, and wars on poverty when his Virginia colleagues were vehemently opposed.[50] He directed his influence against the organization in most races for statewide office. But the real drama in Jennings' congressional life came when he collided with Judge Howard Smith.

In late January of 1961 the Judge faced a full-scale invasion of his Rules Committee by forces of the Kennedy administration who sought to enlarge the committee's membership from twelve to fifteen and to put enough moderate-liberal congressmen in the new seats to override the conservative coalition behind the Judge. At stake was the new administration's domestic program, whose chief features contained the very proposals killed or opposed by Rules the previous year: a minimum wage increase, depressed areas legislation, omnibus housing measures, and a federal aid-to-education program. If Rules blocked these measures again, Kennedy's prestige and

[50] See Appendix VI for the dramatic variance of Jennings' voting record from that of the Virginia delegation as a whole.

the Democratic party's fortunes in the urban Northeast would be seriously endangered. As the floor fight on the enlargement scheme approached, Smith and his potent ally, Republican leader Charles Halleck of Indiana, worked feverishly to gather support. Halleck made opposition to the proposal an official Republican stand by pushing through the twenty-seven-member House Republican Policy Committee a resolution unanimously opposing the "packing" plan. Judge Smith allegedly contacted the National Association of Manufacturers, the American Farm Bureau Federation, the Southern States Industrial Council, the United States Chamber of Commerce, and the American Medical Association urging them to persuade congressmen to oppose the plan. Meanwhile, Sam Rayburn, speaker of the House, and Congressman Richard Bolling were pushing the administration's project. Vice President Johnson, Attorney General Robert F. Kennedy, Interior Secretary Stewart L. Udall, Commerce Secretary Luther H. Hodges, and Special Presidential Assistant Lawrence F. O'Brien joined with the AFL-CIO, civil rights leaders, the National Education Association, Americans for Democratic Action, and other organizations to dilute Smith's influence.[51]

One by one Virginia congressmen announced their adamant opposition to the move to weaken Smith. Jennings, however, remained silent. The Washington *Post* claimed that Jennings was "besieged with telegrams, letters, telephone calls, and personal buttonholing"[52] after it became known he was undecided. Finally, at the end of what Rayburn termed "one of the bitterest fights"[53] he had witnessed in close to half a century in the House, Jennings stood on the winning side of a 217 to 212 vote to increase the membership of the Rules Committee. The Washington *Post* declared that Jennings' vote was "his Declaration of Independence"[54] from the organization. Fellow House member Jim Wright of Texas praised Jennings as a "Rebel in the Old Dominion."[55] But Jennings' position in the Virginia congressional delegation was really that of a one-man

[51] *Congressional Quarterly Almanac, XVII, 1961,* pp. 404–5.
[52] Feb. 1, 1961.   [53] Quoted in Wright, p. 112.   [54] *Ibid.*
[55] *Ibid.,* p. 107.

minority. Seldom could he gaze past the mountains of the "Fightin' Ninth" with any real degree of hope.

Jennings' substantial agreement with the national Democratic administrations over the years obviously placed him in square disagreement with most Virginia Democrats and Senator Byrd. Warfare between the Senator and the national party was incessant, and it became particularly violent during each presidential election. In the months before presidential elections Republicans and Democrats alike generally rush to heal intraparty wounds, patch up former differences, and present to the public an ostensibly united front. Not so did Senator Byrd. He evinced no enthusiasm for Democratic presidential candidates and made no attempt to conceal the differences of principle between himself and the Trumans, Stevensons, Kennedys, and Johnsons bearing the national Democratic standard. Not that the Senator ever went so far as to endorse a Republican or States' Rights candidate. He merely maintained what he termed "golden silence"—a silence which often reduced Democratic presidential hopes in Virginia to zero.[56]

Although Senator Byrd learned in time to keep golden silence with great finesse, the presidential politics of the Byrd organization in 1948 were full of blunders. They hoped to destroy Byrd's arch enemy, Harry S. Truman, but Truman, among other miracles performed that year, eventually captured Virginia's eleven electoral votes. The plot began in February, 1948, when Governor Tuck, with Byrd's approval, announced to the legislature a scheme which would have made any Truman effort to carry Virginia in November useless. Tuck proposed to allow the Virginia state Democratic convention to delegate to a party committee (i.e., Byrd, Combs, Tuck & Co.) the right to instruct the Democratic electors of Virginia for a candidate other than the nominee of the national convention. The state convention or committee could have decided who before or after the election. The bill also could have kept the Democratic national ticket off the Virginia ballot; it would have prevented new parties, like Henry A. Wallace's Progres-

---

[56] Senator Byrd did not actually coin the term "golden silence" until 1960. He had, however, been practicing the concept since 1948.

sives, from getting on the Virginia ballot.[57] Not surprisingly the
measure became known as Tuck's "Anti-Truman Bill." [58] By the
time of the state convention public outrage had forced the
organization to moderate the proposal so as to ensure that
Truman's name would be on the ballot, but the state convention would still have been permitted to nominate a separate
slate of Virginia Democratic candidates whenever the nominee
and platforms of the Democratic national convention proved
unacceptable.[59]

The meeting of the state convention on July 2 did everything
in its power to make certain the decisions of the upcoming
national convention would be acceptable. The organization
passed resolutions endorsing states' rights, blasting Truman's
civil rights program, threatening its own slate of Virginia
Democratic candidates, and instructing its delegates at the
national convention to vote for Dwight D. Eisenhower. Boos
and hoots were heard when Chairman Massenburg refused to
accept cries for division of the resolutions and roll call votes.[60]
The absurdity of the entire convention became more apparent
several days after adjournment when Eisenhower refused to
run, Truman became the Democratic nominee, and the projected Virginia Democratic presidential slate became increasingly impractical. During the ensuing campaign Byrd refused
to support any presidential candidate, and Tuck made his
anti-Truman feelings very, very plain.[61] But Truman carried
Virginia.

The next three presidential elections told a different story.
Senator Byrd's policies, aided by the enormous popularity of
Eisenhower, effectively blocked all attempts of the national

[57] Tuck, *Address to the General Assembly, Feb. 26, 1948.*

[58] Latimer, p. 28.   [59] Richmond *Times-Dispatch,* July 2, 1948.

[60] *Ibid.,* July 3, 1948. State conventions, often run by the organization in a
high-handed manner, needlessly angered the opposition. In the words of one
wrathful delegate Massenburg in 1948 displayed an "intolerant and insolent
refusal to accord the rudimentary rights of democracy to the convention," and
even organization followers fretted that "to deny opportunity for discussion" to
opposition elements would hurt the organization's cause (Harrison Mann to
Massenburg and W. R. Smith to Massenburg, July 8, 1948 [Tuck, Executive
Papers, Box 5]).

[61] Richmond *Times-Dispatch,* Nov. 4, 1948.

Democratic party to win Virginia. The action of the organization in 1952 set the pattern for the next two presidential elections and it merits particular attention.

The southern bloc at national Democratic conventions often exhibited a rather comic futility. Hopelessly outweighed by liberal coalitions of labor chieftains, big city bosses, and civil rights leaders, the Southerners nonetheless frequently insisted on backing some forlorn Dixiecrat, waging a losing battle against the civil rights platform plank, and assuming an embittered minority stance at every available opportunity. When the convention's decision invariably trampled on their resistance, many southern Democrats mumbled something about putting up their own third-party candidates.[62] The Virginia delegation came to the 1952 Democratic convention fully equipped to fight the good (albeit losing) fight. At their own state convention several days earlier Virginia Democrats had been prepared to endorse Senator Richard B. Russell for President. The good Georgian, however, suddenly urged a labor-management conference to revise the Taft-Hartley Act, which Virginia conservatives regarded as inviolable. Virginians quickly soured on his candidacy; Tuck in a heated keynote speech before the convention mentioned the possibility of a bolt from the national party, and the delegation packed for the upcoming national convention in Chicago uninstructed and unenthusiastic about any prospective candidates.[63]

The explosive issue at the national convention did not involve the nominee. Excitement centered instead on the Moody amendment, a proposal stemming from the liberal Harriman forces to exact a definite pledge of loyalty from each delegate to support the decisions of the national convention. To Virginians the pledge was anathema. Not only did it seek to bind them to a candidate with whom many fundamentally disagreed; it also nullified their right to individual action at election time. The caucus of the Virginia delegation on Wednesday, July 23, unanimously voted that "no loyalty pledge be

[62] Strom Thurmond's Dixiecrat candidacy of 1948 was an excellent example.
[63] Richmond *Times-Dispatch*, July 18, 1952.

taken or agreed to by any representative or member of the delegation as provided under the Moody resolution or any amendment thereto or any similar amendment." [64] This adamant refusal to sign anything vaguely resembling a loyalty pledge caused the national convention in its Wednesday afternoon session to suspend Virginia's right to vote. [65]

This insult infuriated the Virginia delegation. Its Thursday morning caucus was charged with crisis. Reporters were excluded, but as Byrd, Governor Battle, Tuck, Combs, Robertson, Massenburg, Kellam, and other veteran organization leaders filed into the caucus room, it was obvious that a critical decision was pending. This decision involved the possibility of a break with the national Democratic party. It has been estimated that about a third of the delegation was inclined to seek a compromise, perhaps giving a loyalty pledge with reservations. Others, probably led by Tuck, proposed that the delegation simply walk out of the convention and go home. The Byrd-Battle plan, which the delegation finally endorsed, "was to stay in the convention, refusing to recognize the Moody resolution, until definitely ousted." [66]

The climax came Thursday night on the convention floor after Governor Battle won what newsmen covering the Virginia delegation called "the great foot race." [67] Battle had asked the chair for a ruling on whether the three state delegations refusing to sign the loyalty pledge were members of the convention. Debate began, and the convention was soon in an uproar. "Where's Jawn going?" asked a delegate, startled by the sight of Battle hurrying toward the speaker's stand. [68] Ex-Governor Tuck, armed with a defiant Dixiecrat manuscript, was also heading in the same direction. [69] Fortunately Battle got there first and delivered a calm, blunt, but reassuring speech:

What, my Democratic friends, we in Virginia object to is the language of this resolution under which it may be construed, as we construe it, that this delegation and the Democrats of Virginia, insofar as we are able to commit them, would be committed to support any future action which might be taken by this convention.

[64] Quoted by Muse in David *et al.* (eds.), p. 24.   [65] *Ibid.*
[66] *Ibid.*, p. 25.   [67] Latimer, p. 49.   [68] Friddell, p. 64.
[69] Latimer, p. 50.

We are unwilling, frankly, to take that pledge. . . .

The great Vice-President of the United States said that this was a nation of free people living in a free country; and we are simply reserving to ourselves the freedom enunciated by Thomas Jefferson —in whose county I happen to live—the great patron saint of this party, who believed in freedom, who believed in freedom of thought and freedom of action, and we are not going to sign any pledge or any commitment which will abridge that freedom which we claim for ourselves and believe you would like for yourselves.[70]

The convention, visibly impressed, voted 650½ to 518 to seat the Virginia delegation and thus narrowly averted a complete parting of the ways of Virginia and her Democratic "brethren."

"Governor Battle received a hero's welcome upon his return to Richmond," wrote Muse. "He was cheered by a crowd estimated at 3,000 in Capitol Square while the band played 'Dixie' and speakers exhausted their superlatives in his praise." [71] The gaiety of this occasion was not to last, however. The November election remained ahead and that election witnessed a strange division in the Byrd organization's usually monolithic front.

By late September the Stevenson bandwagon was rolling along nicely through Democratic officialdom in Virginia. Senator Robertson had announced on July 31 his support of the "straight Democratic ticket," and Governor Battle did the same in late August, praising Stevenson as a "high type, Christian gentleman." A stream of Democratic notables endorsed the Stevenson candidacy, including Congressmen Smith, Stanley, Gary, Hardy, Attorney General Almond, and soon to be Lieutenant Governor Stephens.[72] But no word came from Senator Byrd.

Finally, on October 17, 1952, the patriarch spoke. "Senator Harry F. Byrd," said one editor, "probably will have the largest audience ever enjoyed by a speaker on a purely State-wide radio hook up, when he addresses the people of Virginia . . . on 'the issues' of the presidential campaign. By announcing four days in advance that he will speak on this subject over the radio, the senior Senator from the Old Dominion has roused

[70] Quoted by Muse in David *et al.* (eds.), p. 26.   [71] *Ibid.*, p. 27.
[72] *Ibid.*, p. 27–28.

tremendous curiosity throughout the Commonwealth, and far beyond its borders." [73] In his speech that night Harry Flood Byrd dropped a bomb whose effects are still mushrooming throughout the state. "In my 20 years in the Senate," he began, "I have fought many lone battles. Rightly or wrongly, I have not always trod the popular road. I know the difficulties and heartaches of taking positions that are unpopular at the time." Then he launched an expected three-pronged attack against Truman for his record on civil rights, the Taft-Hartley Act, and the national debt. Referring to his recent primary victory over Francis Pickens Miller, Byrd continued: "I was nominated as a Virginia Democrat and during the campaign repeatedly stated that I was not a Truman Democrat." He called Trumanism "the dominant issue" of the Eisenhower-Stevenson campaign. To his knowledge Stevenson had not repudiated Trumanism; therefore, "I will not, and cannot, in good conscience, endorse the national Democratic platform or the Stevenson-Sparkman ticket. Endorsement means to recommend and this I cannot do." [74]

Republicans were elated, liberal Democrats enraged, organization spokesmen for Stevenson bewildered. [75] Editorials generally hailed Byrd's courage. "One of the best speeches [he] has ever made and one of the best of the many speeches that have been made in the 1952 presidential campaign," exclaimed the Lynchburg *News*. Byrd "riddled the Truman administration. He took it apart, exposed it to the gaze of all and threw its pieces in the garbage can." [76] The Roanoke *World News* only regretted that Byrd did not actually endorse Eisenhower. [77]

Far different, however, was the reaction of straight-ticket Democrat Francis Pickens Miller:

The implications of Senator Byrd's statement for the Democratic party in Virginia are so serious that it will be some time before the

[73] Richmond *Times-Dispatch*, Oct. 15, 1952.

[74] Richmond *Times-Dispatch*, Oct. 18, 1952.

[75] See Richmond *Times-Dispatch* and Richmond *News Leader*, Oct. 18, 1952, for various reactions to Byrd's address.

[76] Lynchburg *News*, Oct. 18, 1952.

[77] Roanoke *World News*, Oct. 18, 1952.

full consequences of his action can be determined. Senator Byrd has refused to endorse the Democratic platform and the Democratic ticket. It would appear that by refusing to support the ticket, he has broken his pledge of honor and has betrayed the party. Under the leadership of Governor Battle . . . we will carry Virginia for Stevenson and Sparkman in spite of Harry Byrd.[78]

Virginia voters were the last to have their say. They swept Eisenhower to victory in 1952, backed him in 1956 when Byrd kept absolute silence, and continued behind Richard Nixon four years later when the Senator again refused to endorse any presidential candidate (see Table 9). "I have found at times that silence is golden," said an aging Byrd in 1960 to the guests

Table 9   Presidential Voting in Virginia (1948–1960)

Year	Candidates *	Percentage of state vote
1948	Truman (D)	48.2
	Dewey (R)	41.3
	Thurmond (States' Rights)	10.4
1952	Stevenson (D)	43.5
	Eisenhower (R)	56.5
1956	Stevenson (D)	38.4
	Eisenhower (R)	55.4
	Andrews (States' Rights)	6.2
1960	Kennedy (D)	47.0
	Nixon (R)	52.4
	Coiner (Conservative)	.5

    * Several minor candidates have been omitted. Percentages are rounded off to the nearest tenth and thus do not always total exactly 100.

[78] Richmond *Times-Dispatch*, Oct. 18, 1952. Miller later charged that "William M. Tuck, ex-governor and member of the Virginia delegation, is reliably reported to have said to a friend while chatting on the floor of the [1952] convention hall that Senator Byrd had just made a deal with the Republicans that he would throw Virginia to Eisenhower in November provided the Republicans gave him no opposition." The existence of any such deal is highly questionable. See Miller's "The Struggle for Democracy in Virginia," p. 12 (MS dated Feb. 1, 1956; in Hutchinson Papers).

who thronged the annual August picnic in his apple orchards at Berryville.[79]

Byrd's golden silence must ultimately be viewed as a product of the peculiar one-party politics of the South. The climate of national and southern politics actually pushed Byrd to the point where silence seemed the only alternative. Critics of this policy often made one of two mistakes. Those who denounced Byrd for not joining the Republican party, "where he really belonged," ignored a century of southern history. Those who saw golden silence as an insidious betrayal of the Democratic party ignored the nature of Harry Byrd.

The Civil War ended only twenty-two years before Byrd was born. Young Byrd and his fellow Southerners saw the Republican party as the brutal victor in that war, the agent of a painful Reconstruction, and the champion of Negro rule in the South. The Democratic party became the haven of the white South, the chance to wrest power from a motley lot of carpetbagger and Negro Republicans. Byrd, a young man of distinguished Virginia ancestry and grand political aspirations, naturally became a Democrat. For him there was no other choice.

The present spectrum of party philosophies had not fully emerged when Byrd began his political career. The Republican party, as viewed by young Governor Byrd in the twenties, was very much the party of big business. Calvin Coolidge's famous remark that "he who builds a factory builds a temple" had little appeal to the farmers of Virginia. The Republican connection with Reconstruction and Wall Street was more than enough to keep the Virginia courthouse machine in the Democratic fold.

Senator Byrd had arrived in Washington in 1933 quite ready to support President Roosevelt's programs. He had been thrilled by the President's 1932 campaign promise to cut federal spending by 25 per cent, but when Roosevelt called for more spending to break the depression Byrd quickly became disillusioned. With each passing year Senator Byrd and the national Democrats moved farther apart. In 1948 the Senator could no longer simultaneously advance his party and his prin-

[79] *Time,* Aug. 17, 1962, p. 14.

ciples. A painful choice confronted him. All his boyhood impressions, his growing seniority, and his sentimental attachments bound him to the Democratic party. Yet Truman's spending and civil rights proposals angered and alarmed him. What could he do? To go Republican was unthinkable; to support Truman impossible. The result: golden silence.

Golden silence had many not so golden consequences, even for Senator Byrd. Professional politicians revere party regularity as holy writ, and Byrd's silence branded him a black sheep to many fellow Democrats. The Senator had always strayed from the fold on Senate votes; in 1948 the *Congressional Quarterly* termed him the least Democratic Democrat on the basis of crucial roll call votes that year.[80] But independence on issues was one thing; defection at the time of a national election was something else. Byrd's failure to support Truman in 1948 so incensed vice-presidential nominee Alben W. Barkley that he compared Byrd's unfaithfulness to that of the housewife who dispensed her favors to the man next door but withheld them from her husband.[81] The silence of 1960 prompted Senator Joseph S. Clark's (D., Pa.) attempt to remove Byrd from his chairmanship of the Senate Finance Committee.[82] To many Democrats outside the South, Byrd was the Benedict Arnold of Berryville. Willis Robertson, although just as conservative, at least nominally supported the Democratic ticket at election time and often experienced less friction in his contacts with fellow Democratic senators.

Most Virginians, however, were unconcerned with the ground rules of professional politics and admired their senior Senator for his principle-over-party stance. The exact number of votes which golden silence swung to Republican presidential candidates can never be determined, but most observers agree that Byrd's recalcitrance was instrumental in pushing Virginia into the Republican column in 1952, 1956, and 1960.[83]

[80] See Richmond *News Leader,* July 22, 1948.

[81] Washington *Post,* July 23, 1965.

[82] See Richmond *Times-Dispatch,* Dec. 11, 1960, for a running account of the Clark-Byrd feud.

[83] Wright (p. 110) claims that Byrd was all-powerful in Virginia in presidential elections. "There is little doubt in anyone's mind that if Harry Byrd on any

These election results indirectly supported golden silence, but Byrd's primary campaign with Francis Pickens Miller in 1952 is the most accurate yardstick of Virginia's approval of the Senator's policies.

Trumanism was clearly the great issue of this campaign. Miller was not content to attack Byrd's voting record; he declared early in the campaign that President Truman had "made the right decision on every one of the great issues." [84] The statement haunted him throughout the race and stamped him squarely as the Truman candidate. The Senator, of course, denounced Trumanism across every inch of the Old Dominion. Friends recall him stomping Virginia under the July sun, eyes twinkling in his ruddy face, his curly hair slightly mussed. He mounted the platform in his famous double-breasted white suit, then assumed his classic speaking pose—feet together, hands resting lightly on the rostrum. He spoke quickly, raising one hand repeatedly to drive home a point. "I've been asked what kind of a Democrat I am. Well I believe still in the Democratic platform of 1932—the best platform ever written. I'm a Virginia Democrat, a true Democrat, and if any further definition is needed, I am not a Truman Democrat." [85] Crowds applauded with their hands and with their ballots. Byrd, the Virginia Democrat, whipped Miller, the national Democrat, with 62.7 per cent of the vote.

---

one of these occasions [1952, 1956, or 1960] had issued even a one-sentence statement in favor of the Democratic nominee, the results would have been reversed."

[84] Richmond *Times-Dispatch*, July 17, 1952.
[85] Richmond *News Leader*, July 9, 1952.

Chapter 4

Troubles for the Organization
1949-1954

T HE 1950's were troublesome years for the Byrd organization. In retrospect Tuck's administration seemed almost a
placid pond. Sandwiched between golden silence and the
school desegregation controversy was an episode which many
Virginians have long since forgotten but which has played a
significant role in the organization's recent woes. This was the
Young Turk revolt—an attempt by young, predominantly
urban state legislators to challenge the organization's tax and
spending policies in the 1954 session of the General Assembly.

The Young Turk revolt represented far more than a fleeting
or spontaneous uprising of young delegates feeling their oats.
It was the first significant setback for the organization which
had held sway over Virginia's public life for years. The Young
Turks could deadlock the powerful Byrd machine only after
persistent complaints moved a significant bloc of legislators to
unite and oppose the force which seemed to control the course
of their own future political careers.

In one sense the Young Turks constituted a plea to the Byrd
organization to recognize change. The Byrd oligarchy, long in
possession of undisputed power, held to old formulas which
had been successful but which were becoming more obsolete
with each passing year. For the first generation of Byrd leaders
slogans such as pay-as-you-go worked magic, but now the old
clichés were wearing thin. Already in certain key urban and

suburban areas politicians echoing the traditional rhetoric were finding audiences unsympathetic.

The Turks did not seek to destroy the Byrd organization. They were neither willing nor able to accomplish that. The Byrd political empire had not been built in a day; neither would it fall in one. The Young Turks were, however, a menacing cloud on the horizon of Virginia's political skies.

The post-World War II decade witnessed an upheaval in local government. Virginia's urban and suburban centers, especially, confronted a host of new problems with which they were ill equipped to deal. It was essential that the state lend a helping hand to the localities at this time. If it allowed them to struggle alone, it did so only at its own eventual peril.

Inflation hit Virginia localities hard. Almost as soon as World War II ended, prices surged upward. A substantial increase occurred in the cost of almost everything local governments bought or borrowed, including personal services, materials, supplies, equipment, construction, and money. In 1957 Professor Rowland A. Egger estimated that "local government budgets are about 65 per cent higher than they were a decade ago, solely as a consequence of the decline in the purchasing power of the dollar. This is a hard fact, which the local governments did not create and which they cannot control." [1]

Localities required large additional revenues merely to stand still. And they could not stand still. Population increased, particularly in Virginia's urban areas, and local governments were confronted by demands for new streets, sewers, water mains, fire protection, police protection, school buildings, health facilities, and welfare claims. Professor Egger concluded, "We can add an open-ended 65 per cent to the cost of local government [1947–1957] which results from larger populations, larger areas, and larger and more expensive service programs for the inhabitants of the cities and towns." [2]

Increase in local revenues from 1947 to 1957 met "all of the increased costs attributable to inflation, but somewhat less than two-thirds of the increased cost due to the demands for the

[1] "Putting Our Financial House in Order," *Virginia Municipal Review,* XXXIV (Oct. 1957).
[2] *Ibid.*

expansion and improvement of local services." [3] This is where the trouble arose. Net county debt in Virginia, which had actually dropped from 1931 to 1947, rose in the next decade as localities struggled to meet increasing demands.[4] What contributed most to the increase was a vastly accelerated schoolbuilding program. Gross county debt rose from $20,190,187 in 1947 to $165,571,487 in 1956. Of this debt 62 per cent was owed by the six largest urban counties (Arlington, Fairfax, Henrico, Norfolk, Princess Anne, and Chesterfield).[5] There population increased most rapidly and demands for services were loudest.

It would be misleading to imply that the "squirearchy" of the Byrd organization ignored the plight of urban and suburban localities. It did not. Changing conditions required the Byrd organization to cooperate with local governments in education, health, welfare, and other fields of joint state and local endeavor. The organization responded in 1950 by creating a State Commission on Local Debt to aid the localities, upon request, in the flotation of long-term indebtedness. The Department of Taxation by 1946 was assisting localities in devising improved assessment methods.[6] Owing primarily to the Tuck tax measures of 1948 and the Battle school fund,[7] state school appropriations amounting to only $52,230,000 in 1946–48 increased to $138,702,000 in 1956–58, a sizable amount even after adjustment for inflation.[8] The question is not whether the organization responded to the localities' plight but whether it responded adequately. And by the 1954 session of the General Assembly the Young Turks were ready to answer with a resounding NO.

Signs that the Byrd organization was growing rusty had appeared long before the Young Turks entered the scene. The

---

[3] *Ibid.*

[4] J. G. Bennet, "County Debt in Virginia," *University of Virginia News Letter*, May 15, 1957.

[5] *Ibid.*

[6] See F. C. Forberg, "Assessment: Recent Developments in Virginia," *University of Virginia News Letter*, Dec. 15, 1960.

[7] See pp. 98–99.

[8] M. M. Sutherland, "State Spending: Trends in the General Fund Budget," *University of Virginia News Letter*, Jan. 1, 1959.

grievances which the Turks harbored against the organization
had been aired freely but unsuccessfully by prominent Virginians five years before in the Democratic primary of 1949. As
Tuck's administration drew to a close that year, the organization's popularity was at a low ebb. Tuck had been colorful and
aggressive, but his boldness had made enemies. His corporate
and individual income tax increases angered many businessmen and ordinary citizens. His "anti-Truman" bill infuriated
straight-ticket Democrats, particularly in the Fightin' Ninth
District of southwest Virginia, where two-party competition
flourished and party loyalty was a sacred duty. As the organization faced the 1949 primary, its normally smooth-sailing bark
faced choppy seas.

The race quickly developed into a three-cornered tussle between the organization's John Stewart Battle, its determined
foe, Francis Pickens Miller, and a middle-of-the-roader, Horace
Edwards. Battle dutifully carried the organization banner
throughout the fray, and Miller mounted a strong attack. He
described the organization as a "political clique of backward-
looking men" [9] whose "methods of conducting political warfare
have made it contemptible to decent citizens." [10] "We have
inadequate services in many departments of government,"
Miller charged, "because of the backward-looking, unimaginative, and undemocratic leadership of the Byrd machine." [11]
Byrd himself was described as the "absentee landlord" of Virginia politics, who ran things through "overseers." Combs was
the "chief overseer" or "operating boss." [12]

Miller repeated all the stock charges against the Byrd machine. Battle defended the organization with dignity and
aplomb. Yet it was the third candidate, Horace Edwards, who
added a new and interesting turn to the whole affair. Although
Edwards was to finish with only 15 per cent of the total vote,
the significance of his campaign was great.

Edwards was only forty-six on the eve of the race, but already
he had fashioned a most impressive set of organization credentials. While a young man in the House of Delegates from 1933
to 1938 he had been one of the few members from Richmond to

[9] Latimer, p. 33.   [10] Richmond *Times-Dispatch,* July 29, 1949.
[11] *Ibid.,* July 30, 1949.   [12] Latimer, p. 33.

side with the organization's point of view. One day in 1940 while vacationing at Virginia Beach, Edwards received a call from Combs informing him that he would soon be appointed chairman of the Democratic State Central Committee.[13] Delighted and at first somewhat incredulous that he should have received the appointment at such an early age, Edwards served diligently, and he was selected in 1944 for a second term.

All this time he worked to build his candidacy for the governorship. By 1949 he had assembled an impressive following. He was particularly strong in the Ninth District, where he had campaigned for Franklin D. Roosevelt and Democratic Congressman John Flannigan. His home city of Richmond also seemed to provide solid support, and he found scattered backing throughout the Fourth, Fifth, and Sixth Districts.[14] When he made the traditional pilgrimage to Senator Byrd, he hoped to be rewarded by the coveted nod. But Byrd played coy, intimated that it might be better to wait a few go 'rounds, and hinted at others ahead of him.[15] Edwards, after all, was still young and had, as one observer put it, that "glittering, scrubbed look a small boy maintains for as long as three minutes around dinnertime."[16] And in the Byrd organization seniority was the rule, and state Senator John Battle at fifty-eight was senior.

Edwards soon concluded there was little room at the top for a youthful, urban member of the organization's progressive wing, but he nevertheless refused to move over. "The bee was in my bonnet,"[17] he remarked, and quickly he determined to run his own race with or without Senator Byrd's approval. In the campaign he mounted he gave a sharp appraisal of the organization—not so much an embittered, emotional harangue as a reasoned portrayal of its faults, including an alternative to the fiscal policies of the Byrd Democrats.

Edwards' program contained much to interest urban areas.

[13] Interview with Horace Edwards, Jan. 6, 1967.

[14] This assessment of Edwards' initial strength is based on (1) the Edwards interview; (2) Latimer, p. 33; (3) study of the Richmond newspapers' account of the 1949 campaign; and (4) final election results.

[15] Edwards interview.　　　[16] Richmond *Times-Dispatch*, March 22, 1949.

[17] Edwards interview.

Although he had considerable rural backing and courted the farmer's vote, his program offered hard-pressed urban localities far more than they had previously received. From 1946 to 1948 Edwards had been mayor of Richmond and there had learned the difficulties of a steadily growing city—the struggle to avoid debt and the need to raise additional revenue to meet the expanding demand for more expensive public services. "The Byrd organization was then too indifferent to local governments and the major problems confronting urban areas," Edwards maintains.

I felt if I ran, I could do something for local governments, do something for schools, and establish a Department to counsel the localities on bonds, fiscal planning, schools, sanitation and the like. The pay-as-you-go policy was putting us years behind. We could have had roads quicker from bond issues and generated industrial development from the improved highways. Urban areas, moreover, were pumping considerable revenue from gasoline taxes into the pay-as-you-go fund and receiving little in return.[18]

"The issue in this gubernatorial campaign is crystal clear," Edwards said in one campaign speech after another. "That issue is: Our schools and our 500,000 school children, the future citizens of our State. The future of the schools rests on but one point—how to finance them. . . . We must have school buildings. Twice $64,000,000 will about meet emergency school building needs in the next four years. Surpluses in the State treasury present and future at best could finance only 20 per cent of these school building needs." How would Edwards finance them? By a 2 per cent tax on all retail sales.[19]

Edwards had arrived at a sales tax proposal only after much thought. Well aware that many localities were suffering under heavy debt, he termed unthinkable Battle's campaign proposal that the state should loan money to localities for school construction. This was no time to increase the bonded debt of the counties, cities, and towns with soft, inflationary dollars, he claimed.[20] Edwards believed Tuck's increase in income and

[18] *Ibid.*   [19] Richmond *Times-Dispatch*, June 15, 1949.
[20] *Ibid.*, April 12, 1949.

corporation taxes was unbearable, especially for urban areas. "I contend," he said,

that the present taxes, including the Federal tax and the increased State taxes which go into effect this year, are approaching the confiscatory stage so far as small business and industry are concerned. . . . To think of increasing revenues from present sources is out of the question. Indeed, a real adjustment of some of them is indicated to equalize the tax burden. A sales tax with its broad base seems to me to be the most equitable new tax. Not only would this spread the cost over so many that it would be burdensome to none, but also it would impose a tax upon the tourist business, which is at present our least-taxed big business.[21]

The sales tax proposal promised simultaneously to remedy the organization's neglect of public schools, to bail out localities with revenue from a lucrative new tax source, and to change the tax structure from its too exclusive reliance on individual and corporate incomes.

As the campaign progressed, top leaders of the organization became increasingly concerned lest Battle and Edwards split the normal organization vote and allow Miller to squeak in ahead of them with his solid backing from the militant antiorganization faction. Since Virginia had no primary runoff law then, Miller's victory appeared quite possible. While Byrd had clearly given Battle the nod (and as the campaign went on he kept nodding harder and harder), much of Edwards' support was proving remarkably tenacious. Edwards even commanded several key organization leaders in the heart of the Southside —for example, state Senator Charles Moses and an influential young delegate from Nansemond County, Mills E. Godwin.[22] The organization thus faced imminent defeat unless Edwards' support could somehow be taken from him.

A month before the campaign's close, Combs, Kellam, and several other Byrd lieutenants met in austere seclusion to try to salvage the situation by uniting the organization behind Battle. They devised the slogan "A vote for Edwards is a vote for

[21] *Ibid.*, Feb. 15, 1949.   [22] *Ibid.*, March 4, 1949; July 13, 1949.

Pickens Miller" and immediately put it into circulation.[23]
Combs traveled and telephoned to courthouses throughout the
state, and prayed, pleaded, pestered, and pressured the middle
and lower echelons of the Byrd organization to fall in line
behind Battle and save the state from a Miller takeover.[24] One
courthouse official in Franklin County wrote his assistant: "Mr.
Combs, Chairman of the Compensation Board, who sets your
salary and mine for our work as Commissioner and Deputy
Commissioner of the Revenue, is very much interested in
seeing John S. Battle elected for governor. Since Mr. Combs is
a good friend of ours I think it would be to our interest to get
every vote we can for Mr. Battle." [25]

While Combs worked behind the scenes, Byrd summoned
the faithful to Battle's side on July 9 in a major speech at
Harrisonburg. Byrd labeled Miller "the CIO-supported candidate," painted a sinister backdrop of labor bosses and doctri-
naire liberals outside the state trying to force Miller's nomination, and warned that it would be a "tragedy" if "those who
believe in sound government" divided their votes between
Battle and Edwards and permitted Miller to win with a minority of the primary vote. The only thing to do, Byrd emphasized,
was to get behind John Battle.[26]

Edwards was caught in a whipsaw between Battle and
Miller. Miller cut into whatever anti-Byrd support Edwards
enjoyed by the counter slogan that "A vote for Edwards is a
vote for Battle." During the week following the slogan ex-
changes between Battle and Miller, Edwards received hundreds of telegrams from persons withdrawing support in order
to avoid a Miller triumph.[27] The candidate who once had had
at least a chance to get the nomination now stood naked between two viciously warring factions. Aware that Combs was
taking away virtually all his support, Edwards lashed back. He
attacked Combs as chairman of the State Compensation Board,

[23] Latimer, p. 33; Edwards interview.   [24] Latimer interview, Jan. 4, 1966.
[25] C. B. Perdue to B. R. Dillon, July 19, 1949 (Robert Whitehead Papers,
Series 1, Box 13, Alderman Library, University of Virginia).
[26] Richmond *Times-Dispatch,* July 10, 1949; Latimer, p. 34.
[27] Latimer, p. 33; Edwards interview.

accusing him of having "perverted" the Board into "a political agency, pure and simple. . . . The first step in re-establishing the confidence of our people in this important agency . . . ," he claimed, "is to replace E. R. Combs, its chairman. This I propose to do." [28]

After that remark, Edwards sped quickly down the road to disaster. Virginia Republicans, at the behest of one of their most prominent figures, entered the primary in support of Battle,[29] and Byrd Democrats pushed in last-minute unison behind Byrd's anointed. The final vote showed Battle the winner, though he lacked the usual comfortable majority:

Battle	135,426	42.8 per cent
Miller	111,697	35.3 per cent
Edwards	47,435	15.0 per cent
Arnold	22,054	7.0 per cent [30]

Spokesmen for the organization claimed that Miller received no more than the usual percentage of the antiorganization vote and that the Edwards-Arnold [31] backing would have gone for Battle in a two-way race. The opposition wrote that "much has been accomplished by reason of the campaign. Had the Republicans stayed out of the primary, we would, of course, have nominated Colonel Miller for Governor. It is a disgusting spectacle when a political leader has to go into the Republican Party and secure the votes with which to keep his organization in power." [32]

Two ominous facts emerged from the 1949 campaign. The organization no longer triumphed with the old finesse; for the first time it had had to strain to win. And a young, urban figure had seriously questioned the organization's commitment to ex-

[28] Richmond *Times-Dispatch,* July 13, 1949.

[29] Major Henry A. Wise, old-guard Taft Republican leader and former Virginia member of the GOP National Committee, publicly urged Republicans to enter the Democratic primary and vote for John Battle (Latimer, p. 34).

[30] Figures rounded off to nearest tenth. This accounts for total of 100.1 per cent.

[31] Remmie Arnold was a conservative Petersburg businessman whose presence in the primary served further to fragment the "normal organization" vote.

[32] Hutchinson to J. B. Mapp, Aug. 5, 1949 (Hutchinson Papers, Box 17).

panded public services. Although Edwards had urged a tax rise
at a most inopportune time, he had spoken for a group of
moderate citizens who were becoming disillusioned with the
state's stinginess at a time of climbing local debts and needs.
Edwards virtually disappeared from the state's political scene
after the election. His complaints, however, were soon to be
voiced again.

John Stewart Battle was fifty-nine years old when he was
inaugurated governor of Virginia on Wednesday, January 18,
1950. A man of great dignity and homespun sincerity, he
looked and spoke the part of governor. The son of a Baptist
minister, Battle was born at New Bern, North Carolina. He
grew up in Petersburg, Virginia, took his law degree in 1913 at
the University of Virginia, and soon developed a prosperous
law practice in Charlottesville. After two terms in the Virginia
House of Delegates he was elected to the state Senate in 1933.
He became chairman of the Senate Finance Committee in the
middle 1940's and received the organization's blessing to run
for governor in 1949 when his appealing simplicity and reserve
were badly needed. Tall, gray-haired, and ruggedly handsome,
"Jawn" Battle succeeded in checking for a time the slowly
gathering storm.

Foremost on Governor Battle's agenda for the 1950 session of
the General Assembly was an appropriation to localities for the
construction of badly needed classrooms and schools. The
Tuck tax increases had poured an "embarrassment of riches"
into the state treasury and Battle had promised to use the
accumulating surplus to help meet school room shortages.
After debating whether localities should be required to put up
matching funds—which Battle opposed—the 1950 Assembly
appropriated $45,000,000 for school construction grants to the
localities with the understanding that the 1952 Assembly
would vote $30,000,000 more.[33]

The Battle school program was an innovation in Virginia
public finance. The Virginia General Assembly had never before voted outright grants for school construction, though it

[33] *Acts of Assembly, 1950,* p. 12; *Acts of Assembly, 1952,* p. 1262.

had long granted low interest loans to localities for the purpose.[34] Traditionally the cities and counties bore the cost of school construction while the state helped to provide administrative costs and teacher salaries. The virtual cessation of school construction during World War II and the school-age population explosion after the war had swamped localities with demands for new construction. Finally the Byrd organization stepped forward to lend a helping hand.

Other events in the 1950 Assembly were not in so progressive a vein. Harry Flood Byrd, Jr., had entered the state Senate in 1948, representing the same district that his father served from 1916 to 1924. The young senator was expected to share his father's views on taxation and spending and already he was disturbed over grumblings that the Tuck tax increases made Virginia a high-tax state. He also resented criticism that asserted the state government was technically violating Section 188 of the state constitution, which stipulated that "no other or greater amount of tax or revenues shall, at any time, be levied than may be required for the necessary expenses of government." He countered with a bill directing that if general fund revenues for a fiscal year exceeded budget estimates by X per cent, then individual and corporation income tax payers would receive a reduction of X per cent on their income tax bills.[35] Although the bill passed with little opposition (32–5 in the Senate, 72–24 in the House), some legislators concerned over the state's apparent lag in meeting capital outlay needs did not like it. The bill would automatically wipe out any potential general fund surpluses, which in Virginia had traditionally been used to pay for new buildings and equipment. Many saw the measure as a step in "Little Harry's" gubernatorial bid,[36] and indeed the bill was to play a controversial role in Virginia politics for the next several years.

During the Battle years a spirit of unwonted independence was infecting several of the younger members in the General Assembly. The *Times-Dispatch* observed in 1952 that "a group of younger Delegates—including Dodson and Rutherfoord of

[34] See *Acts of Assembly, 1950*, p. 16.

[35] *Ibid.*, pp. 965–68; Latimer, p. 39.   [36] Latimer, p. 40.

Roanoke, Boothe of Alexandria, Page of Norfolk, Cochran of
Staunton and perhaps a few others—are winning reputations as
non-conformists within the regular organization. In other
words, they appear to be less hesitant to 'buck' the organization
than is the case with many of the older men within the organization fold." [37]

A small incident involving these younger delegates had
ruffled Battle's "era of good feeling" toward the close of the
1950 General Assembly. It was an old-timer, however, who
initiated the difficulty. For years Robert Whitehead of Nelson
County had waged a one-man battle against the organization
in the House of Delegates. The Assembly's most able orator,
Whitehead "would clinch his fist and swing his right arm up
and down as if flaying the backs of the majority. His point
finished, he would rear back, his great oven mouth snapped
shut and turned down at the corners, a lank white cowlick
falling across his forehead, his blue-gray eyes glaring." [38] In the
closing days of the 1950 General Assembly, Whitehead had
persuaded the younger members of the House of Delegates to
amend the Battle administration's budget bill so as to add an
extra $1,000,000 for increases in teacher pay.[39] Administration
leaders opposed the amendment ostensibly on the grounds that
it would unbalance the budget (an unspeakable horror in
Harry Byrd's Virginia), but in fact because its adoption would
be a slap in the face of the organization's leadership and an
opening for a possible Whitehead gubernatorial campaign in
1953. The Byrd-controlled Senate defeated the Whitehead
amendment, but the House refused to adopt the Senate version. The deadlock which developed on the final day of the
session kept the Assembly convened until 4 A.M., long past its
normal expiration period of midnight. It was clear to all that
the struggle involved prestige and politics far more than
money. Finally several House members who normally followed
the organization but had deviated on the teacher pay increase
were summoned one by one for conferences upstairs in the
governor's office. "It is not known exactly what processes of

[37] March 2, 1952.   [38] Friddell, p. 69.   [39] Latimer, p. 37.

reasoning and persuasion were used," observed one experienced reporter. "It is a matter of record, however, that enough votes were changed to bring the House in line, and agree finally to reject the teacher pay amendment." [40]

The 1950 General Assembly thus witnessed a revolt in miniature, if indeed there was a revolt at all. The fight on the Whitehead amendment was yet another indication that the Byrd organization was allowing its obsession with a balanced budget to overshadow its commitment to public education and other vital state services. The early 1950's would have been the ideal time for the Byrd organization to shift gradually from an economy-minded to a public-school-minded attitude. It did not do so, and consequently it invited trouble in the years ahead.

For the most part, however, the Battle years, especially the first two (1950–51), were relatively quiet ones for Virginia politics. As the 1952 Assembly ended, the Washington *Post* declared that the organization was "enjoying a rare measure of public good will." It hit a low point in 1948–49; "then it started on an upward trend. It is partly, no doubt, as a result of Miller's blasts [in 1949] that the more hardboiled manifestations of machine operation have been little in evidence since that campaign." E. R. Combs, who had voluntarily stepped down from his Compensation Board post in 1950, now seemed "merely an affable old gentleman . . . diluting organization doctrine with the milk of human kindness." [41]

Thomas B. Stanley was the organization's choice for governor in 1953 to succeed Battle. Stanley had toiled long for the organization with the hope that one day it would be his turn to run for governor. For seventeen years he had served in the House of Delegates, with three terms as speaker (1942–46). He then moved to Congress to represent the Southside's Fifth District. Although he never had much popular appeal, Stanley was friendly and unpretentious, and through the years he developed a substantial following in the inner ranks of the organi-

[40] *Ibid.*, p. 38.   [41] March 23, 1952.

zation. A wealthy furniture manufacturer from southside Henry County who had married the daughter of another wealthy furniture manufacturer, both Stanley and his wife had been generous contributors to the organization's campaign war chest.

By 1949 Stanley's affability and donations had done much to legitimize his longstanding quest for the governorship. It appeared that he was finally in line for the nod. But the organization's fortunes were so shaky that year that he was passed over for Battle, who was felt to be the stronger candidate. Reluctantly Stanley withdrew from consideration and waited another four years. In 1953 he was given the go-ahead sign.

He rode to victory in a listless primary, winning over state Senator Charles R. Fenwick, an organization backer with somewhat less perfect credentials.[42] Robert Whitehead, who had considered the race, withdrew because of inadequate financial support and his own feeling that the state, in the light of the Eisenhower-Byrd victories in 1952, was trending "toward the most extreme conservatism." [43] Whitehead also acknowledged that the primary run-off law passed in 1952 had greatly increased the difficulties for an antiorganization candidate.[44]

Stanley was not to have the usual pushover Republican opponent in November. His foe was state Senator Ted Dalton, an attractive and tireless campaigner who gave the organization the scare of its life. The usual issues and ingredients of a Virginia election were present, and Dalton gave them all a thorough airing. Campaigning in "tan suit, white shoes, and a buoyant mood," [45] Dalton struck hard at the machine but without arousing animosities. He advocated an overhaul of Virginia

[42] Fenwick came from Arlington, Va., which was outside the organization's immediate sphere of influence; he had been defeated in a race for lieutenant governor in 1945, and he had not been speaker of the House of Delegates or a congressman as had Stanley. All these factors made him a relatively weak candidate.

[43] Latimer, p. 55.

[44] The organization passed the law to avoid a repetition of the 1949 Democratic primary in which, because there was no primary run-off law, Miller, the antiorganization candidate, nearly won.

[45] Richmond *Times-Dispatch*, Aug. 12, 1953.

election laws by repealing the poll tax, strengthening the absentee ballot law, and lowering the voting age to eighteen. He criticized the appointive powers of circuit judges and called for "popular election of members of school boards." He saw the judges as "cogs in the political wheel whereby appointments are made which show the touch of political expediency." [46] Virginia's industrial development was emphasized with a pledge to appoint an official "whose entire duties should be directed toward obtaining new and increasing industry in Virginia." [47] Dalton further urged a minimum annual salary of $2,500 for teachers, the establishment of a Virginia Institute of Psychiatry, and state appropriations of "at least $2.50 per patient day for care and treatment of cases in mental hospitals." [48]

The only bland aspect of the campaign was Stanley's performance. Called "colorless and disappointing" by most editors, it caused Dalton to charge that the "big chiefs" of the Democratic organization were trying to sell Virginians "a silent Indian" under "a smokescreen campaign." [49] The most Stanley would venture was, "If I were permitted but one plank in my program, I would have no difficulty in making the selection. It would be a continuation of the sound fiscal policies which have characterized our State government as far back as we can remember." [50] Stanley refused to enlarge on his program, and it was evident by late September that his whole campaign might capsize. Newsmen came to call him "Mr. No Comment," [51] and a Republican victory in Virginia became a distinct possibility.

The campaign closed amid three unexpected developments which diverted attention from Stanley's personal performance. The first shook the Democratic organization to its foundation. A federal grand jury indicted Sidney S. Kellam, the state Democratic campaign manager, on income tax evasion charges. Kellam professed "shock, surprise," charged he had been framed by Republicans in a "politically motivated" holdup, and resigned as Stanley's campaign manager, all the while defending

[46] Richmond *News Leader,* Aug. 13, 1953.
[47] Richmond *Times-Dispatch,* Aug. 23, 1953.   [48] *Ibid.,* July 24, 1953.
[49] *Ibid.,* Nov. 1, 1953.   [50] Richmond *News-Leader,* Sept. 4, 1953.
[51] Latimer, p. 59.

his innocence and pleading to the public not to let "this personal attack against me affect your appraisal of the fine, outstanding nominees of our party or your action when you go to the polls." [52] Later Kellam was exonerated and acquitted of the charges. Although the episode first appeared to damage the Stanley campaign, most observers think it shocked and aroused previously lethargic Democratic leaders to turn out the vote and smash the Republicans. [53]

The second crucial development came when Dalton proposed a $100,000,000 bond issue to improve Virginia highways. He was careful to stress that the issue would be revenue bonds, not general obligations of the state government, and would be paid off by pledging a portion of anticipated gas tax revenues. [54] Nonetheless, Byrd construed the proposal as a slap at his sacred pay-as-you-go, and entered the campaign with both fists flying. Dalton's plan, Byrd claimed, would bypass constitutional bars against state debt and would "junk our sound fiscal system based upon freedom from debt." Dalton replied that "while the Senator is talking so much about Virginia's being free from debt, let him do some explaining about the localities in Virginia which have carried a large part of the load for the State in governmental requirements and now owe a total debt of astronomical proportions." [55] But Dalton had committed a major political blunder. He had given the Old Master an entree into the campaign, and the fight now seemed more between Dalton and Byrd than Dalton and Stanley.

The third development may or may not have hurt the Republicans. On October 21 Francis Pickens Miller, the foremost leader of antiorganization Democrats in Virginia, suggested that his supporters might wish to enter the general election on behalf of the Republican nominee. While saying that he himself would vote the straight Democratic ticket, he commended Dalton's platform and repeatedly advised other Democrats that they were under no obligation to vote for Stanley who, said Miller, had "conducted a campaign without parallel in the memory of living men for its lack of voter appeal." Byrd pounced on Miller's speech, charging a "strange coalition be-

[52] Richmond *Times-Dispatch*, Oct. 16, 1953.   [53] Latimer, p. 60.
[54] Richmond *Times-Dispatch*, Oct. 20, 1953.   [55] *Ibid.*, Oct. 22, 1953.

tween Mr. Dalton and Mr. Miller." He added that Miller's "implacable hatred of me" had led him to try to destroy the Democratic party.[56]

"Thus," said one reporter, "the 1953 campaign roared to a finish, with Harry Byrd coaching, quarterbacking, carrying the ball—and Stanley—for the Democratic ticket." [57] A cartoon by Fred O. Seibel in the *Times-Dispatch* summed up the campaign. It showed Dalton atop the GOP elephant and working hard, while Stanley was sitting nonchalantly on a Democratic donkey being pulled across the line by a sweating, straining Byrd.[58] When the votes were tallied, Virginia went for Stanley, but by an uncomfortably close margin (225,878 to 182,887). Dalton's vote, not Stanley's victory, was the noteworthy item.

Stanley was approaching the governor's mansion on very wobbly legs. "It seems in order to urge him to do a lot of thinking before his inauguration in January, and to develop a more affirmative approach to the problems of the Commonwealth," declared the *Times-Dispatch*. "His uncertain grasp of the issues during the primary campaign and then during the contest just ended, caused Virginians to wonder how a man with so long and honorable a career in the General Assembly and in Congress could seem so baffled and distraught." [59] It was evident that the new governor lacked the leadership qualities of his predecessors, and difficult times for the organization could be foreseen.

When the 1954 General Assembly convened, ominous signs hung in the air. If ever a man needed E. R. Combs, that man was Tom Stanley. Yet Combs, on doctor's orders, was vacationing in Florida. "Without Ebbie Combs," said one editorial, "Mr. Stanley's problems of leadership—already difficult enough—will be just about doubled. His departure creates a whale of a hole in the administration's lineup, right at kick-off time." [60]

From the first it was apparent that the Governor had lost control. He committed the unforgivable by violating one of his few popular campaign pledges only minutes after he had been in office. To the dumbfoundment of many who had heard the

[56] Latimer, p. 61.   [57] *Ibid.*   [58] *Ibid.*, p. 62.
[59] Richmond *Times-Dispatch*, Nov. 4, 1953.
[60] Richmond *News Leader*, Jan. 13, 1954.

Governor promise "no increase in taxes," Stanley in his inaugural address proposed a one-cent hike in the gasoline tax. It was necessary, he contended, to improve Virginia's highways. Legislative leaders, unimpressed and annoyed that they had not been consulted beforehand, quickly consigned the gas tax rise to oblivion.[61]

Somewhat staggered by this defeat, the Governor was soon confronted by a full-scale revolt in the House of Delegates. Under the leadership of Delegates Armistead Boothe of Alexandria, Stuart Carter of Fincastle, George Cochran of Staunton, and Walter Page of Norfolk, a group of young, predominantly urban legislators, aptly called the Young Turks, moved almost completely away from the Governor's influence. Boothe, who led the revolt, was a former Rhodes Scholar and an articulate moderate. In the 1950 Assembly he had introduced bills calling for repeal of state segregation laws affecting all forms of public transportation and for the establishment of a Virginia Civil Rights Commission to study economic, educational, and other phases of race relations in order to recommend corrective measures.[62] Two years later he led a number of urban legislators who called for a special session to reapportion the state legislature.

The Young Turks represented a new political breed in Virginia. The foremost members of the group averaged only thirty-seven years of age; almost all had earned college and graduate law degrees (see Table 10). Many had served in World War II and had traveled far beyond the borders of Virginia. They had returned to the state aware that all governments did not run on the gospel according to Harry Byrd. In the postwar years the Young Turks entered politics. They were concerned over the growing demands on state and local government and eager to play some role in shaping state policy. Yet the Byrd organization, steeped in the tradition of balanced budgets and pay-as-you-go, demanded long apprenticeship. The Turks (most of whom represented districts which, historically, had been marginal territory for the organization) soon became impatient.

[61] Reichley, p. 15.   [62] Richmond *Times-Dispatch,* Jan. 8, 1950.

The Young Turks differed significantly from Moss Plunkett, Martin Hutchinson, Francis Pickens Miller, and the older antiorganization leaders. Neither blindly following nor blindly opposing organization policy, the Turks, in the words of one prominent Virginia editor, "reserved the right to do their own thinking on issues that seemed crucial to them." [63] They never adopted an all-or-nothing attitude toward the Byrd organization as Plunkett and Miller had done. Although certain of its policies greatly disturbed them, most Young Turks in 1954 considered themselves bona-fide members of the organization and part of its emergent, forward-looking wing. Delegate Stuart Carter put it this way: "The antiorganization forces would have Virginia throw out the present board of directors and elect a new board. I'd like to keep the present board but have it become more progressive." [64]

The old antiorganization leaders generally attempted to take the Byrd machine by storm and batter it down from without. Their tactics generally consisted of verbal barrages from nonelective positions with little institutional power. The young Turks challenged the organization not with verbal attacks but with a significant number of General Assembly votes. They fought power with power and, as a result, stymied the organization in a way that the more extreme critics of an earlier generation had never done.

The Turks were above all respectable; they offered many moderate Virginians the first real alternative to orthodox organization doctrine. Many Virginians regarded Plunkett and Miller as erratic,[65] and even those who had reservations about the Byrd organization still preferred it to the "dangerous" programs of the older antiorganization leaders. Plunkett's proposal to redistribute much of the tax burden "on the basis of ability to pay" [66] terrified business and the urban well-to-do. The Turks, however, offered a middle course between the radical reformers and the low-tax, low-service formula of the old Byrd organization.

The Young Turks emphasized important issues. They conceded, even admired, the organization's integrity and cen-

[63] *Ibid.*, March 15, 1954.   [64] Richmond *News Leader*, Feb. 19, 1954.
[65] See Key, p. 29.   [66] Richmond *Times-Dispatch*, July 12, 1945.

Table 10 Prominent Young Turks (1954)*

Name	District	Age (1/1/54)	Educational background	Profession	First elected to House for session of
Armistead L. Boothe †	Alexandria (city)	46	University of Virginia B.A.; Oxford University, B.A. (Rhodes Scholar)	Lawyer	1948
Stuart B. Carter	Botetourt, Craig (counties)	47	Western Reserve University; University of Virginia; Cumberland University LL.B.	Lawyer, farmer, businessman	1950
Joseph E. Blackburn †	Lynchburg (city)	33	Lynchburg College B.A. (Phi Beta Kappa); Washington & Lee University LL.B.	Lawyer	1954
George M. Cochran †	Augusta, Highland (counties) Staunton and Waynesboro (cities)	41	University of Virginia B.A., LL.B.	Lawyer	1948
Eveland C. Compton †	Albemarle, Greene (counties)	37	Virginia Polytechnic Institute B.S.	Farmer	1954

Name	Locality	Age	Education	Occupation	Year
Walter A. Page †	Norfolk (city)	36	Washington & Lee University; University of Virginia LL.B.	Lawyer	1948
John F. Rixey †	Norfolk (city)	27	University of Virginia B.A., LL.B.	Lawyer	1954
Julian H. Rutherfoord †	Roanoke (city)	41	Roanoke College	Insurance agent	1948
Toy D. Savage †	Norfolk (city)	32	University of Virginia B.A., LL.B.	Lawyer	1954
William B. Spong †	Portsmouth (city)	33	Hampden-Sydney College B.A.; University of Virginia LL.B.	Lawyer	1954
Charles W. Wampler	Rockingham (county) Harrisonburg (city)	38	Bridgewater College; Rutgers University	Farmer, feed manufacturer	1954
John C. Webb †	Fairfax (county) Falls Church (city)	38	Washington College of Law LL.B.	Lawyer	1954

Source: General Assembly Manual, 1954.

* These twelve delegates were selected as leaders in the Young Turk revolt on the basis of five critical roll call votes on the conference reports of H.B. 32 recorded in the *Journal of House Delegates, 1954*, pp. 980–1001; newspaper coverage of the Young Turk revolt, Jan. 1–March 19, 1954; and discussions with Jim Latimer and George Kelley, political reporters of the Richmond *Times-Dispatch* and Norfolk *Virginian-Pilot*, respectively.

† World War II veteran.

tered their attack where the organization was most vulnerable —on its record of public services. The Turks were very much aware of the inflationary pressures and expanded demands for public services which besieged Virginia's localities. They also knew that many hard-core organization representatives were not granting adequate state funds in aid.

The showdown came shortly before adjournment. Under the Byrd Tax Credit Act administration forces had directed that a general fund surplus of $7,000,000 be returned to the taxpayers. The Turks, however, felt the money should be appropriated for state needs, primarily to boost Virginia's sagging school system. On adjournment day the matter seemed deadlocked. Organization strength, concentrated in the Senate, insisted the money be returned. The Turks, under the leadership of Armistead Boothe in the House of Delegates, refused to go along. Both houses remained adamant through thirty-six hours and five conference reports; it appeared no solution was in sight.[67]

As the hours wore on [wrote the Richmond *News Leader*], the lines stiffened, the cleavage deepened. Principle became confused with politics, and politics with personalities, and rights with wrongs. On the Senate floor, old friends glared stonily at each other, and then looked away. In the House, remarks were exchanged that will not be forgotten. Over both chambers a pall settled, of stale smoke and raw temper, and fancied grievances. In time, many of the members forgot precisely what it was they were fighting about; it became an endurance contest, a team engagement; it became vaguely dishonorable to quit, or shift position, and men talked it up as halfbacks will talk to linesmen: "You okay?" "You're sticking?" And in time it became ludicrous, almost childlike. More was being lost than possibly could be gained, and little after 10 o'clock last night the drama ran its course.[68]

The House in an angry mood was prepared to adjourn when Senator Landon R. Wyatt, of Danville, a strong Byrd backer,

[67] *Journal of the House of Delegates of . . . Virginia, Session 1954* (Richmond: Division of Purchase and Printing, 1954), pp. 980–1001.
[68] Richmond *News Leader*, March 15, 1954.

moved to reconsider the fifth conference report, and his motion brought an end to the impasse.[69] Both sides accepted a compromise whereby $2,186,500 of the $7,000,000 was appropriated and most of the remainder was credited to the taxpayers.[70] The crisis was ostensibly at an end, but there were now definite signs of a new political order in Virginia.

"It is in the nature of political machines that they must periodically undergo a reorganization," says Key in commenting on the "immortality" of the Byrd organization in 1949. "Leaders grow old—and careless. Public demands change, and political hierarchies have difficulty in adjusting themselves to the new requirements for political survival. Able though the leaders of the Virginia machine are, it is unlikely that they can manage a frictionless succession to produce a high command canny enough to keep the organization in power in perpetuity." [71] Byrd, Combs, Tuck, Battle, Smith, and others who had ushered in the organization's long reign were aging. Events now made it clear that the time had come for the organization to rejuvenate itself with younger leaders and progressive policies. Virginius Dabney put the situation most succinctly:

Commentators appear to agree—and we have seen no Virginia paper which expresses a contrary view—that the Democratic "organization" came out of the session of 1954 definitely weakened. The manner in which the Young Turks in the House fought the machine to a standstill, and ended by forcing it to go in reverse, is recognized as a political portent of great magnitude.

This does not mean that the "organization" is on the rocks; it *does* mean that its leadership had better do some hard and heavy thinking. With its grip shaken badly by recent events, it should, among other things, adopt a more hospitable attitude toward its younger members.[72]

[69] See A. D. Howard, "Byrd Organization" (History Thesis, University of Richmond, May 1954), p. 67; *Journal of the Senate of Virginia, Session 1954* (Richmond: Division of Purchase and Printing, 1954), pp. 1155–56.

[70] *Journal of Senate, 1954,* pp. 1155–56; *Journal of House, 1954,* pp. 1000–1001.

[71] Page 34.   [72] Richmond *Times-Dispatch,* March 19, 1954.

Since the Byrd organization had never welcomed youth to its inner councils, many young men had "defected" to the Republicans or antiorganization Democrats. The Young Turks, in turn, paid dearly for their independence. Those who arrived in the Senate in 1956 were shunted to inferior committees, and their hopes of running as statewide organization candidates quickly dimmed. Several insiders now admit that the organization handled the Young Turks too harshly and closed the doors to youth everywhere.° Others continue to feel that the organization was right in demanding a long and proven obedience in return for its powerful backing. Virginius Dabney regrets that the organization and progressive leaders such as Armistead Boothe never formed a mutually beneficial alliance. Both forces might have met at the middle of the road.[73] Instead, animosity developed, and two Young Turks of 1954 became such seasoned politicians by 1966 that they challenged the machine for higher stakes.

It seemed in the spring of 1954 that the once luminous star of Virginia's Byrd organization was at last beginning to dim. Battle's tough primary fight in 1949, Stanley's narrow victory over Dalton in 1953, and the Young Turk revolt in the General Assembly of 1954 all indicated gradual slippage and decline. Although the organization had continued to give Virginia honest, principled, and gentlemanly conservatism, many tough questions went unattended. Was the state's prime purpose to balance budgets or to promote public schools? What value was the debt-free state with debt-ridden localities? What role, if any, could urbanites and youth play in the organization's inner councils? For the past five years, the organization's answers to these and other questions had satisfied a steadily decreasing segment of the Virginia electorate. In the spring of 1954, however, a new issue appeared on the horizon which was to retrieve the fortunes of the Byrd organization. The issue was school desegregation, and under the banner of "massive resistance" the Byrd machine quickly refueled its sputtering engines.

[73] Interview, Aug. 29, 1966.

Chapter 5

Massive Resistance
1954–1960

IF WE can organize the Southern States for massive resistance
to this order [of the Supreme Court in the school segregation cases] I think that in time the rest of the country will
realize that racial integration is not going to be accepted in the
South." [1] This fateful statement was issued from the Washington office of Senator Harry Flood Byrd on February 24, 1956.
Within moments "massive resistance" became the battle cry for
all Virginians who wanted to fight even token compliance with
the Supreme Court's decision to end racial segregation in
public education.

Massive resistance was truly Virginia's issue of the century.
The profound changes hinging on its outcome should not obscure the human crises which enveloped its major participants.
Caught between belief and circumstance, political leaders
faced anguished decisions. "I lived in hell," said J. Lindsay
Almond, Jr., governor of Virginia from 1958 to 1962 and in
many ways the tragic hero of the entire episode.[2] Few would
doubt his word.

Massive resistance held an especially significant place in the
long life of the Byrd organization. During this crisis the power

[1] Richmond *Times-Dispatch*, Feb. 25, 1956.
[2] Quoted in W. G. Harris, Jr., "J. Lindsay Almond, Jr. and the Politics of
School Desegregation in Virginia, 1954–1959" (unpublished honors paper, Yale
University, 1966), p. 22.

components of the organization stood most fully exposed, and the usual discreetness of its operations yielded to more blatant and naked display. Massive resistance was also the last triumphant gesture of the old order of Virginia politics—a twilight performance where the hard-core coalition of the old Byrd organization hoisted its last great hosannas. Yet in the end massive resistance gave Virginia a new political direction. Within a decade it brought to the old commonwealth new leaders and new outlooks.

Virginia did not respond uniformly to the Court ruling in *Brown* v. *Board of Education*. Extreme variance in local conditions and attitudes caused a wide spectrum of reaction to the desegregation decree. Which reaction would dictate the policy of the Byrd organization? That was the vital question.

A study of the distribution of Negroes throughout the Old Dominion in 1950 will help to illuminate the reasons for Virginia's differing responses to the school integration crisis. It will not provide the magic key with which to unlock all the complex political attitudes and activities in Virginia, but it will present a helpful and necessary perspective on massive resistance. With this approach, not one, but four, Virginias emerge.[3]

The *black belt* in 1950 consisted of thirty-one contiguous southside and tidewater counties where the percentage of Negroes in the population ranged from 40 to 81 (see Map II). South of the James, fanning out toward the Piedmont and along the North Carolina border lay the eighteen populous counties of the black belt. Brunswick typified these areas where social change in the face of the traditional racial caste system was most difficult.[4] These highly rural, courthouse-controlled counties of the black belt or Southside (the areas overlap to a considerable extent) also exerted a prodigious influence over state policy.[5]

[3] The present discussion follows, in many respects, Robbins L. Gates, *The Making of Massive Resistance: Virginia's Politics of Public School Desegregation, 1954–1956* (Chapel Hill, N.C.: University of North Carolina Press, 1962), pp. 1–12.

[4] *Ibid.*, p. 3.

[5] Compare Maps I and II for the overlapping boundaries of the black belt and the Southside.

Between the black belt and the comparatively Negroless counties in western Virginia lay the *middle ground* (see Map II). Here Negroes in the population varied between 10 and 40 per cent. Although the center of this area lay in the Piedmont, several detached counties to the east and Bath County in the west prevented it from being contiguous. Some manufacturing had taken hold here, and professional men, business executives, and skilled labor were able to find a home. Stanchly conservative, the middle-ground avoided the more extreme racial positions held in portions of the black belt. "White attitudes toward caste run the gamut," wrote Robbins Gates, "and extremes are generally tolerated, if not respected. Negroes residing in middle-ground counties still live in a caste structured society, but it is doubtful that many of them would care to trade places with their brethren in the black belt." [6] The middle ground represented Virginia's ideological and political mean, and the percentage of its Negro population (23) practically duplicated that of the state (22.2).

The third group of Virginia counties constituted the *white belt* (see Map II), where Negroes comprised less than 10 per cent of the population. The Shenandoah Valley stretching from Frederick to Rockbridge County and the mountain counties of southwest Virginia represented the bulk of the white belt, but the three suburban counties of Arlington, Fairfax, and Henrico also had relatively low percentages of Negro residents. The white belt was far less a political monolith than either the middle-ground or black-belt counties; the conservatism of the Shenandoah Valley and Henrico was balanced by more liberal voting habits in southwest Virginia, Fairfax, and Arlington. Most Virginians in the white belt west of the Blue Ridge appeared to at least one native son as "a different breed of Virginian—thrifty, relatively progressive, acknowledging the traditional Virginia mores, but lacking the deep emotional attachment that one finds in other sections of the state." [7]

Virginia's cities in 1950 will not fit the rather neat categories of the counties. The smaller ones generally reflected the atti-

[6] *Ibid.*, p. 7.   [7] Phillips, "Virginia," p. 49.

Note to Map II

Negro population percentages in Virginia counties follow:

Accomack 34.2	Chesterfield 20.9	Greensville 59.3	Montgomery 5.3	Roanoke 8.5
Albemarle 18.6	Clarke 17.2	Halifax 44.0	Nansemond 65.3	Rockbridge 8.6
Alleghany 8.3	Craig 0.5	Hanover 30.8	Nelson 27.0	Rockingham 1.9
Amelia 49.9	Culpeper 27.9	Henrico 9.9	New Kent 54.0	Russell 2.5
Amherst 27.9	Cumberland 55.7	Henry 24.2	Norfolk 16.3	Scott 1.1
Appomattox 24.7	Dickenson 1.4	Highland 2.9	Northampton 53.5	Shenandoah 1.8
Arlington 4.9	Dinwiddie 64.6	Isle of Wight 51.9	Northumberland 40.8	Smyth 1.6
Augusta 5.1	Elizabeth City 20.5	James City 46.5	Nottoway 43.9	Southampton 60.9
Bath 10.5	Essex 46.1	King and Queen 53.8	Orange 26.7	Spotsylvania 23.9
Bedford 19.0	Fairfax 10.0	King George 27.4	Page 3.7	Stafford 12.9
Bland 2.0	Fauquier 26.3	King William 46.1	Patrick 8.4	Surry 63.8
Botetourt 10.1	Floyd 4.3	Lancaster 41.2	Pittsylvania 30.9	Sussex 65.6
Brunswick 57.8	Fluvanna 35.1	Lee 1.1	Powhatan 43.6	Tazewell 6.1
Buchanan 0	Franklin 14.6	Loudoun 18.8	Prince Edward 44.6	Warwick 31.2
Buckingham 42.8	Frederick 2.2	Louisa 39.8	Prince George 30.3	Warren 8.0
Campbell 23.7	Giles 2.5	Lunenburg 43.9	Prince William 11.9	Washington 3.2
Caroline 51.4	Gloucester 31.3	Madison 23.1	Princess Anne 23.5	Westmoreland 45.5
Carroll 1.5	Goochland 50.0	Mathews 24.9	Pulaski 7.5	Wise 4.2
Charles City 81.0	Grayson 4.4	Mecklenburg 49.5	Rappahannock 17.7	Wythe 4.7
Charlotte 40.9	Greene 13.5	Middlesex 41.9	Richmond 34.4	York 26.2

Negro population percentages in Virginia's independent cities follow:

Alexandria 12.4	Falls Church 1.8	Newport News 43.2	South Norfolk 23.0
Bristol 7.1	Fredericksburg 6.3	Norfolk 29.7	Staunton 10.9
Buena Vista 4.2	Hampton 37.2	Petersburg 42.2	Suffolk 36.7
Charlottesville 18.2	Harrisonburg 6.3	Portsmouth 38.4	Waynesboro 8.2
Clifton Forge 18.1	Hopewell 14.8	Radford 7.0	Williamsburg 13.0
Colonial Heights 0.2	Lynchburg 22.0	Richmond 31.7	Winchester 8.3
Danville 30.2	Martinsville 29.3	Roanoke 15.9	

Map II. Negro Population Percentages in Virginia (1950)

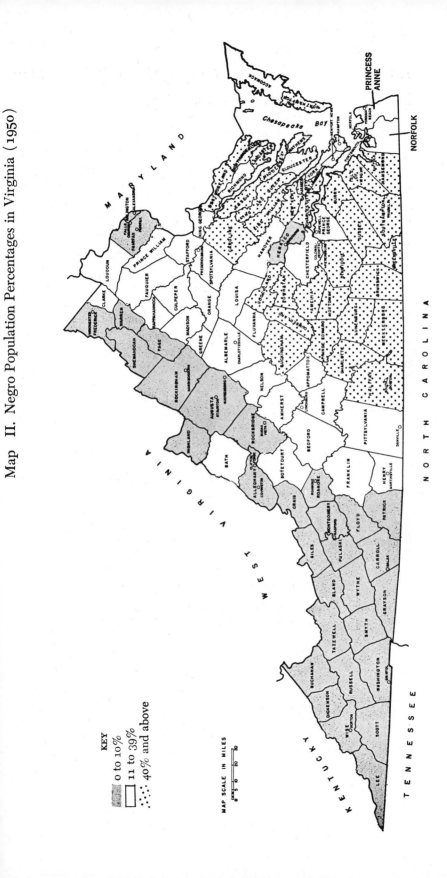

KEY

0 to 10%
11 to 39%
40% and above

MAP SCALE IN MILES

tudes of the surrounding counties. This was especially true in western, white Virginia in the numerous small mountain and valley towns. Two slightly larger cities of middle-ground Virginia, Lynchburg and Charlottesville, did not significantly deviate from the traits of the region as a whole, and a third, Danville, with a Negro population of 30 per cent, was closely akin to the black belt. Petersburg and Suffolk were the two most distinctively black-belt cities in the state. Virginia's five major metropolitan areas (Richmond, Norfolk-Portsmouth, Newport News–Hampton, the Washington suburbs, and Roanoke) were laws unto themselves. They did, however, share common urban characteristics which differentiated them from the rest of the state. Here, says Gates, Negroes can "form a relatively complete community of their own within the city, where they can support doctors, lawyers, merchants, and others of their own race. Here they are most articulate, best organized, and least cowed by the doctrine of white supremacy. What may be no more than his own church for the rural Negro becomes a compact economic and social community for his urban counterpart." [8]

Before the Supreme Court edict the integration of public schools in Virginia was not an overt political issue. Most Virginians accepted the provision in Section 140 of the state constitution that "white and colored children shall not be taught in the same school." The handful of whites in Virginia who conscientiously believed in integration despaired of ever bringing it to pass. After the Court decree, however, the question was not merely one of pro or anti integrationist views. The conscientious integrationist frequently found allies in those who favored compliance with the Supreme Court verdict as the law of the land and in those who accepted token integration in preference to closing public schools. Segregationists often found it easier to declaim on the rights of states and the wrongs of courts rather than to debate the strict pros and cons of white supremacy and school segregation. The primary effect of the Court's ruling in Virginia was to veil in new terminology what had previously been a matter of integration vs. segregation.

[8] Pages 11–12.

In black-belt and southside Virginia many whites were not at all eager to accept the nuances of the new situation. For them the issue was sharply focused; the lines were clearly drawn. Bill Tuck, now representing the Southside's Fifth Congressional District, presented these views:

There is no middle ground, no compromise. We're either for integration or against it and I'm against it. . . . If they [other Virginia areas] won't stand with us then I say make 'em. We cannot compromise. . . . We may have to have 5, 10 or 100 special sessions or even have the Assembly stay in constant session. . . . If you ever let them integrate anywhere the whole state will be integrated in a short time.[9]

Tuck's attitude was understandable. Southside Virginia with its high proportion of Negro residents was potentially most affected by the Court ruling. Where the Negro lived in largest numbers, he was seen to pose the greatest long-term threat. In Brunswick, where Negroes comprised almost 60 per cent of the population, they traditionally had a low economic and educational status and almost no political influence.[10] The specter of large-scale Negro voting power, economic mobilization, and social advance terrified many southside whites. The Negro, properly organized, might one day come to share in the control of county government. To the Southside the integration of public schools seemed a first step to limitless Negro gains.

Moreover, the black belt was in an excellent position to determine state policy. As Table 11 illustrates, organization candidates ran splendidly in the black belt and only slightly less well in the middle ground. The white belt and urban centers seldom provided large majorities. Stanley owed his governor's chair to the loyal black-belt courthouses. They gave him almost 75 per cent of the vote, whereas he barely scraped by in the cities and actually fell short of a majority in the white belt. Senator Byrd relied on the black belt for some of his most impressive margins. No one could better explain the influence of these southside and black-belt voters on the Byrd organization than Al-

[9] Richmond *Times-Dispatch*, July 28, 1956; Gates, p. 133.
[10] See Chapter 1.

mond, governor of Virginia at the height of massive resistance. Part of an agrarian, small-town society, these voters possessed in Almond's view, a "consolidation of mores and outlook. . . . The vote is not only large but solidified in support of the Organization, and as a result the Southside has exercised a power disproportionate to its part of the over-all population of the state." "There would have been no hard, unyielding core of

Table 11   Byrd Organization in Black-Belt, Middle-Ground, and White-Belt Counties and Independent Cities

| | | | | Percentage of vote polled by organization candidates | | | |
Year	Office	Candidates *	State	Black belt	Middle ground	White belt	Cities
1946 P	Senator	*Byrd* Hutchinson	63.4	74.7	68.6	64.8	55.1
1949 P	Attorney general	*Almond* Plunkett	67.2	72.5	69.9	65.3	63.6
1952 P	Senator	*Byrd* Miller	62.7	71.6	64.2	58.4	61.3
1953	Governor	*Stanley* Dalton	54.7	73.9	62.8	48.2	53.0

Source: Adapted from Gates, *Making of Massive Resistance*, p. 24.
* Byrd organization candidates are italicized.
P A primary.

massive resistance in Virginia," he continued, "if there were no Southside. Virginia as a whole was opposed to racial mixing in the public schools, but outside of the Southside the state evinced more of a willingness to face reality." [11]

The political efforts of southside segregationists were carefully and tightly organized. In October 1954 sheriffs, clerks, legislators, and many courthouse professionals throughout the black belt supported the formation of an innocuously named

[11] Norfolk *Virginian-Pilot*, June 8, 1964.

group—the Defenders of State Sovereignty and Individual Liberties.[12] The Defenders, as the group soon came to be called, was the official voice of the defiant segregationists in Virginia. The officers, as announced at the time of formation, were all Southsiders, and the thirteen Defender chapters were concentrated in Petersburg and twelve southside counties.[13] From this base the Defenders expanded across the state. On its first anniversary it had twenty-eight active chapters with approximately five thousand members. It retained its own counsel, employed a full-time executive director, maintained an active state headquarters at Richmond, and published a monthly newsletter entitled *The Defenders' News and Views*.[14] Estimates of Defender membership in August 1956 placed it at twelve thousand, and the sixty local chapters extended from Norfolk to Martinsville and Danville to Arlington.[15] If the Defenders boasted particularly aggressive chapters in such moderate areas as Arlington, Norfolk, and Charlottesville, it never found elsewhere in Virginia the broad-based support it enjoyed in the Southside.

The Defenders must not be confused with the White Citizens' Council, the Ku Klux Klan, or other societies which have traditionally agitated the South. Most southside Virginians were gentlemen with a high sense of dignity and integrity. They disdained cross burnings, riots, and fanatical waving of the Confederate flag.[16] Robert B. Crawford, a Farmville laundryowner and president of the Defenders, abhorred cheap violence and emotionalism almost as much as he did school integration. Moreover he was not eager to isolate the Defenders in an extreme position remote from access to political power. American conservatives must work together, he believed, to oppose racial integration and "other efforts to destroy the Constitution." [17] Membership in the Defenders was not

---

[12] See Richmond *Times-Dispatch*, Oct. 27, 1954; Gates, pp. 36–38.

[13] Richmond *Times-Dispatch*, Oct. 27, 1954.

[14] *Southern School News*, Sept. 1955; Gates, p. 48.   [15] Gates, p. 160.

[16] Both Muse (*Massive Resistance*, p. 10) and Gates (p. 161) suggest this view of the Defenders.

[17] Quoted in Gates, p. 161.

obtained through any secret or primitive initiation ceremony. The application read (almost soberly) as follows:

I am a white, law abiding citizen of the United States of America, and a resident of the City/County of _____, Virginia. I am not a member of any organization detrimental to the peace or welfare of the U.S.A., nor do I ever intend belonging to any such organization.

I believe the segregation of the races is a right of the state government; in the sovereignty of the several states and in the freedom of the individual from government controls.[18]

The Defenders seemed quite respectable. The members, conservative, nonviolent, with substantial official support, were in a position to influence the top leaders of the Byrd organization. It was the Defenders operating from its predominantly southside base which pushed organization policy from token compliance to massive resistance. Virginia's reaction to the Supreme Court's decision was at first relatively moderate. Yet organization policy became very much like a canoe which, first drifting downstream in mild waters, soon followed more turbulent currents and eventually plunged over the waterfall.

Governor Thomas B. Stanley was obliged to deal with the first stages of the school integration crisis. Already shaken by his strenuous race with Dalton and legislative battles with the Young Turks, Stanley now faced a crisis of even greater proportions. An affable and likable man little suited to high political drama, Stanley received the Court integration ruling in his customarily mild manner. "I am confident," he stated on May 18, 1954, that

the people of Virginia will receive the opinion of the Supreme Court calmly and take time to carefully and dispassionately consider the situation before coming to conclusions on steps which should be taken. . . . I contemplate no precipitate action, but I shall call together as quickly as practicable representatives of both state and local governments to consider the matter and work toward a plan which will be acceptable to our citizens and in keeping

[18] *Ibid.*

with the edict of the court. Views of leaders of both races will be invited in the course of these studies.[19]

But Stanley was not to be allowed to pursue this line of thinking. Almond, attorney general at the time, believes Byrd reacted unsympathetically to Stanley's mild pronouncement. "I heard, I don't know," he said, "that the top blew off of the U.S. Capitol." [20] Pressure came from other quarters also. On June 20, 1954, twenty southside legislators met in the Petersburg firehouse under the chairmanship of state Senator Garland Gray to express officially their "unalterable opposition to the principle of integration of the races in the schools." By June 25 Stanley realized how "wrong" his previous moderation had been. "I shall use every legal means at my command," he now declared, "to continue segregated schools in Virginia." [21]

Any notion of voluntary compliance with the Court had by now been discarded. The school integration crisis entered its second phase when legal methods for compromise or circumvention were sought. On August 23 Stanley appointed, not a biracial commission as had earlier been hinted, but a thirty-two member, all-white, legislative commission to study the problems created by the Court decision and to formulate a course of action. Although each congressional district had at least two commission members, the southside's Fourth District was represented by six, the First by five, the Fifth and Eighth by four each, and the Seventh by three.[22] The rural, black-belt, Byrd-backing counties dominated the commission. To no one's surprise, the new commission selected as its chairman state Senator Garland Gray, who had led the recent anti-integration meeting at the Petersburg firehouse.

While the Gray Commission pondered a solution, sentiment on the integration issue began to harden. On the far right was the Defenders of State Sovereignty and Individual Liberties. At the left was the NAACP. The efforts of this organization were necessarily limited to testing in federal courts the validity

[19] Richmond *Times-Dispatch*, May 18, 1954.
[20] Norfolk *Virginian-Pilot*, June 8, 1964.
[21] Richmond *Times-Dispatch*, June 21, 26, 1954.   [22] *Ibid.*, Aug. 29, 1954.

of Virginia's massive resistance laws. Few members of the state legislature were openly sympathetic to the Negro cause, and there was little chance of electing any more in the heated political climate of the late 1950's. Governor Stanley, moreover, had carefully excluded Negroes from the decision-making process within the state. The NAACP had to concentrate its efforts in a less dramatic but more congenial arena, and it achieved gradual but noticeable judicial success.

Vaguely identified in the public mind with the NAACP was an organization formed on February 22, 1955. The biracial Virginia Council on Human Relations announced its purpose to prepare Virginia for peaceful desegregation. It would achieve this not through political activity but by "workshops, program planning, personal consultation, speakers, books, printed materials and other such educational methods." [23] The most significant thing about this group was its impotence. Its leadership included several clergymen, college professors (but no presidents or deans), social workers, clubwomen, and a representative of the state leadership of the AFL. [24] Conspicuously absent were members of the business and professional communities and other segments of the private white power structure. Few whites wished to risk the subtle social and political ostracism which came with being an integrationist, and many moderate businessmen felt that their influence would be most effective if they worked at the integration problem "from within." At any rate, the lack of any powerful integrationist sentiment in 1955 in Virginia which might have countered the Defenders was an ominous sign.

The Gray Commission, meanwhile, after one rather turbulent public hearing and more than a year's deliberation, finally submitted its report on November 11, 1955. The Gray Plan, as it came to be called, seems moderate in retrospect, for it tacitly admitted the possibility of token integration and urged only that no child be required to attend an integrated school. [25] It contemplated local control of the degree of integration within

---

[23] *Ibid.*, Feb. 23, 1955.   [24] Gates, p. 53.
[25] The Gray Plan was reprinted in the *Race Relations Law Reporter*, I (Feb. 1956), 241 ff.

a particular school district. The plan made two basic recommendations. The first was a pupil assignment plan, whereby local school boards assigned students on the basis of individual health and aptitude, availability of transportation, and "the welfare of the particular child as well as the welfare and best interests of all other pupils attending a particular school." This last criterion allowed local school boards to sidestep the intent of the Court ruling.

If federal courts overruled segregationist placement procedures of a local school board, an escape hatch was still available. A system of tuition grants from public funds would be established to aid any pupil who chose to attend a private and presumably segregated school in preference to a newly integrated public one. To facilitate this, the Gray Commission urged amendment of the compulsory attendance law to provide that no child be required to attend an integrated school.

One major legal obstacle prevented the immediate enactment of the tuition grant proposal. Section 141 of the Virginia constitution provided that "no appropriation of public funds shall be made to any school or institution of learning not owned or exclusively controlled by the State or some political subdivision thereof." As tuition grants were to be given to students attending *private* schools, immediate amendment of Section 141 was necessary. A special session of the General Assembly, convened on November 30, 1955, provided for a popular referendum in which the voters would determine whether or not a limited constitutional convention should be called for the purpose of amending Section 141 to permit the proposed tuition grants.[26]

The ensuing referendum battle was "one of the most spirited campaigns in the state's history."[27] The campaign statements revealed for the first time the full spectrum of forces and views on integration in Virginia. As might be expected, the Defenders supported the tuition grant proposal as the least that should be done to prevent enforced integration. The NAACP and the Virginia Council of Human Relations were equally determined

[26] Muse, *Massive Resistance*, p. 16.   [27] *Southern School News*, Jan. 1956.

to defeat it. It was, however, the middle-road attitudes which carried the greatest long-range significance, and they merit particular attention.

On December 19 several leading opponents of the tuition grant proposal formed an organization known as the Virginia Society for the Preservation of Public Education. Its chief support lay in the urbanized Tenth District, where Armistead Boothe, leader of the Young Turk revolt of 1954, functioned as acting chairman. Boothe gave the group its campaign theme when he stated that the grants "will not work, are unconstitutional, we will have nothing when we get them, and the price we have to pay for an unconstitutional false hope in undercutting the public schools is too high." [28] These public school savers attracted little official support outside the Tenth District, but they pioneered an approach to the integration question which in the next two years became widespread. Boothe and his cohorts were among the first to oppose Virginia's growing defiance on nonracial grounds. Instead of blasting the tuition grant proposal in terms of race, they posed as champions of public schools. Such a posture would never win over adamant segregationists but would increasingly attract moderates, whose support would have to be enlisted if massive resistance were to end. [29]

Predictably the Byrd organization threw its influence behind tuition grants. Yet beneath seeming unanimity there was discord. There was much to indicate that all members of the ruling circle were not committed to endless defiance. Two thorny questions began to emerge. Would the organization continue to support local option on desegregation even if it meant integration in several of the state's more moderate localities? Would it press defiance of the Court to the point of closing public schools? Senator Byrd in his press release of December 17 had urged adoption of tuition grants, but he carefully refrained from commenting on the other main feature of the Gray Plan—local option. Colgate Darden, governor of Virginia from 1942 to 1946, urged fellow leaders of the Byrd

[28] Richmond *Times-Dispatch,* Dec. 20, 1955.   [29] Gates, p. 76.

organization to pledge their support of free public schools.[30] Even within the camp of tuition grant proponents it was clear that a more moderate element was emerging. Few doubted that Senator Byrd, Governor Stanley, and Congressmen Tuck, Abbitt, and Smith would support a stanchly segregationist stance. But such respected figures as ex-Governors Battle and Darden hinted their preference for preserving public schools, even if token integration eventually came to pass.

At the time of the referendum, however, any split in the organization was carefully hidden. Almost to a man the organization rallied behind the Gray slogan that "no child be required to attend an integrated school." The result was an overwhelming endorsement of tuition grants by a vote of 304,154 to 146,164. The largest majorities, of course, came from black-belt and middle-ground counties. In the white belt and the cities the tuition grants gained considerably less support. The percentages of the voters favoring legalization of the grants were as follows: black belt, 84.3; middle ground, 80.1; white belt, 56.4; and cities, 60.3.[31] The success of the referendum determined the organization's high priests to lead Virginia into an even more defiant stance.

The decision to make resistance truly massive was unexpectedly aided in the early months of 1956 by a dynamic young editor of the Richmond *News Leader,* James Jackson Kilpatrick, Jr. Although a native of Oklahoma, Kilpatrick had learned Virginian modes of thought, and he seldom failed to cast his editorial appeals in an irresistibly Virginian way. He was easily one of the most gifted phrasemakers of the national press. Kilpatrick, moreover, attacked all forms of liberalism with crusading zeal. "I was on horse and the pen was a lance," he remarked of his involvement in the massive resistance crisis.[32]

No more ideal spokesman for the view of the organization could be found. In a stream of books and editorials Kilpatrick articulated the case of the southern segregationist. "I have,"

[30] Richmond *Times-Dispatch,* Dec. 18, 21, 1955.   [31] Gates, p. 89.
[32] J. J. Kilpatrick, *The Southern Case for School Segregation* (New York: Crowell-Collier, 1962), p. 8.

wrote Byrd, "a great respect for Jack, who has, in a very brilliant fashion, aroused the country to the evils of the Supreme Court's decision."[33] Kilpatrick made massive resistance "respectable"; if the political compulsions for massive resistance lay in southside Virginia, its intellectual justification lay behind Kilpatrick's pen.

Because of its destructive effect upon the stability of law and the permanence of long-established institutions [Kilpatrick was later to write in *The Southern Case for School Segregation*], the school decision, in my own view, surpassed *Scott* v. *Sanford* in the area of jurisprudence gone mad. In one stroke, the Warren Court violated those precepts of judicial restraint and constitutional interpretation which it most frequently has insisted on in the past; it transformed itself into a superlegislature—more, it usurped the functions of constitutional amendment that lie with not fewer than three-fourths of the States. Abandoning law, the court wedded sociology; discarding eighty years of unbroken precedent, members of the court substituted their own notions of psychology and moral fitness for the plain and palpable meaning of the Fourteenth Amendment in terms of racially separate public schools.[34]

Besides being bad law, *Brown* v. *Board of Education* seemed to Kilpatrick an indefensible infringement on states' rights:

Unless . . . the rightful powers of the States [are] guarded from continued encroachment, the whole organism of American government will be subtly transformed, without the expressed consent of the people governed, from the federalism that has provided its greatest strength to an immoderate centralism that will prove its greatest weakness. In maintaining its case, the South is no longer fighting the question of separate schools or even a question of race relations at all; it is contending, rather, for the preservation of an American plan of value to all the States and all the people. What is lost to the Southern States, in terms of political powers, is lost to all States; and the imposition of court-ordered prohibitions in one field

[33] Byrd to J. L. Almond, Nov. 14, 1958 (Almond, Executive Papers, Box 35).

[34] Kilpatrick, *The Southern Case for School Segregation*, p. 105 (copyright Crowell-Collier Press, 1962).

makes the next imposition that much easier. By the court's decree of 1954, the South's largest, most expensive, most important, most cherished public institutions—our public schools—were thrown into potential jeopardy and chaos. Whose most cherished institutions will be next? [35]

There was another, more emotional basis for Virginia's opposition. The Old Dominion was a proud state; she intensely disliked being told that her way of life was "not good enough" by nine justices of the Supreme Court. Yankees, moreover, seemed inherently incapable of understanding the South. Virginia to Kilpatrick was "tobacco and peanuts; the gem that is Williamsburg, the plantation country, the somnolent Northern Neck, Mr. Jefferson's University, the hunt country, the changelessly changing capital city where I write." [36] How then could anyone outside the South ever really understand?

In late 1955 Kilpatrick was busily searching for a way to oppose the Court decision. Finally he disinterred the doctrine of Interposition, by which the state asserted its sovereignty to resist and even nullify the effects of what it considered an unconstitutional and intolerable federal ruling. For over two months the editorial page of the Richmond *News Leader* was devoted to Interposition.[37] Kilpatrick lavished his verbal resources on the doctrine and carefully traced its history during the early years of the American Republic and under the old southern patriarch, John C. Calhoun. So great was his influence and so intense was Virginia's opposition to the Court decision that the 1956 session of the General Assembly overwhelmingly adopted an Interposition resolution "to resist this illegal encroachment upon our sovereign powers, and to urge upon our sister States, whose authority over their own most cherished powers may next be imperilled, their prompt and deliberate efforts to check this and further encroachment by the Supreme Court, through judicial legislation, upon the reserved powers of the States." [38]

[35] Kilpatrick, *The Southern Case for School Segregation,* p. 106 (copyright Crowell-Collier Press, 1962).

[36] *Ibid.,* pp. 19–20.   [37] Nov. 21, 1955, to Feb. 2, 1956.

[38] *Journal of Senate, 1956,* p. 146.

More serious matters than Interposition were taking shape in the winter of 1956. Speaker Moore, Byrd's close friend and confidant, introduced in the General Assembly a resolution calling for a continuation of segregated schools throughout Virginia in 1956–57. Virginius Dabney in the *Times-Dispatch* led a chorus of dissent to the resolution from editors across the state. Reminding readers of the Gray Commission's pledge that any city, county, or town which wished to integrate could do so, Dabney called the Moore resolution a "repudiation of assurances" on local option given by many members of the organization in the recent referendum on tuition grants.[39] Although consideration of the Moore resolution was "indefinitely postponed" by the Senate Rules Committee,[40] the course the organization's high command was set to pursue was clear.

Massive resistance was on the move. Heartened by the tuition grant referendum and Interposition, the organization's leaders gathered on July 2, 1956, for a secret conclave with Senator Byrd in Washington.[41] With Governor Stanley, state Senator Gray, and Representatives Tuck and Abbitt all known to be present, the decision was made to go all the way. A series of meetings in Stanley's Richmond offices completed the midsummer madness. Southside Congressman Watkins Abbitt was a frequent caller on the Governor and he often presided over the drafting of the massive resistance laws.[42] These were ready by mid-August when Governor Stanley summoned the General Assembly together for what was to be known as a "very special session."[43]

"In the historic capital of the Southern Confederacy," wrote Muse, "100 miles south of Washington and the Supreme Court, crowds filled the galleries of the House of Delegates on the morning of August 27, and Confederate flags fluttered."[44] Noticeable that morning were copies of a propaganda sheet known as the *Virginian.* A Confederate soldier stood at the masthead, and various Negrophobic photographs depicting

[39] Feb. 13, 1956.   [40] *Ibid.*, March 10, 1956.
[41] Muse, *Massive Resistance*, p. 28.
[42] Norfolk *Virginian-Pilot*, June 8, 1964.
[43] Muse, *Massive Resistance*, p. 28.   [44] *Ibid.*, p. 29.

"integration as it really is" spread across its pages. "Let fathers and mothers travel to the capital," the *Virginian* urged, "and see the fate of our children decided. . . . Let Virginians from every crossroad and byway journey to Richmond on this day of days." [45]

The Virginia legislature is not generally a body bereft of reason. On August 27, 1956, however, extremism was in the air. The massive resistance legislation proposed to the session by Governor Stanley and the ensuing political crises were unique products of heated and trying times. Massive resistance caught the Old Dominion out of character. Political compulsions, constitutional considerations, and simple race prejudice can all be invoked to explain these events, but many, familiar with the gentlemanly tone of the Byrd organization, regarded the hardening of massive resistance with a certain measure of disbelief.

By the end of the 1956 special session Virginia resembled a modern Nineveh with its numerous rings of labyrinthine walls. The outer wall was a three-man state Pupil Placement Board to which local school districts were to refer all Negro applications to white schools. Although not explicitly stated in the bill, the Pupil Placement Board in practice was to do its utmost to preserve segregated schools. If Negroes disputed the Placement Board's decision in federal courts, as they undoubtedly would, the district school would be ordered to admit them or face contempt-of-court charges. In that event the second stage of defense would come into play. The governor was required to close all schools under court order to integrate and to remove them from the public school system. He was then to engage in an attempt to reopen them on a segregated basis by persuading Negroes to withdraw their applications. If, by some chance, a local school was willing or ordered to open on an integrated basis, state funds were to be cut off from the schools in that district. With state funds withheld, a locality would face two alternatives: it could try to operate integrated schools, using only local funds, or it could close its schools and, under other bills in the Stanley program, provide tuition grants from state

[45] Quoted, *ibid.*

and local funds for private (segregated) schools if adequate private school facilities were available.[46]

The massive resistance legislation did not pass the General Assembly unopposed. Moderates in the legislature hoped to insert a local option provision in the fund cutoff measure by which localities so desiring could avoid the more extreme consequences of Virginia's massive resistance laws.[47] The original Gray Plan had included a local option provision, but this suggestion had been trampled in the tuition grant and Interposition stampede. Now moderates attempting to resurrect local discretion on integration clashed with the hard core of the Byrd organization. Senator Mills E. Godwin, organization stalwart from the southside city of Suffolk, led the massive resistance drive. Claiming that "integration is the key which opens the door to the inevitable destruction of our free public schools," he further asserted that "integration, however slight, anywhere in Virginia would be a cancer eating at the very life blood of our public school system." A state policy for Virginia such as Governor Stanley had outlined, Godwin continued, "is needed as a deterrent to those localities in Virginia which have, or may indicate, a willingness to integrate. . . . The [Supreme Court] decision is either right or wrong. If we think it is right, we should accept it without circumvention or evasion. If it is wrong, we should never accept it at all. Men of conscience and principle do not compromise with either right or wrong." [48]

Local option forces were beaten 59 to 39 in the House but only 21 to 17 in the Senate. The voting patterns were predictable. Southside and black-belt legislators voted 20 to 1 against local option in the House and 11 to 1 against it in the Senate. The seven Republicans in the legislature were unanimously for local option, and delegations from Richmond, Norfolk, Roanoke, and the immediately adjacent Washington suburbs supported it 25 to 5.[49] But hard-core organization elements finally

---

[46] See *Acts of Assembly, Extra Session 1956;* Gates, pp. 167–90; and Muse, *Massive Resistance,* pp. 28–34.

[47] Gates, p. 183.   [48] Richmond *Times-Dispatch,* Sept. 5, 1956.

[49] See Gates, p. 186, for a detailed analysis of the voting patterns on the local option provision.

pushed through their entire resistance program. Across the state, school closings and fund cutoffs would be mandatory to prevent threatened integration. Abandoning the cherished conservative principle that local problems can best be handled by local governments, the Byrd organization clamped on every corner of a varied Virginia the racial axioms and attitudes of the Southside and the black belt.

When the legislature adjourned, Thomas B. Stanley had weathered his last crisis. The end of his long term was coming into view, and he must have felt considerable relief that future Young Turk revolts and Supreme Court decisions would find him not in Richmond but in his country home at Stanleytown. In the governor's mansion for the next four years would be a very different man—one whose temperament seemed light years away from Stanley's low-keyed amiability.

J. Lindsay Almond, Jr., ostensibly fitted the organization mold. The son of a poor, retired Southern Railway engineer, he spent his boyhood on the red-clay family farm in Orange County.[50] Young Virginians often romped for hours over old Confederate battle fields, and Almond did the farm chores and watched the turkey flocks just four miles from the Wilderness Thicket where the legendary Stonewall Jackson was mortally wounded by one of his own men.[51] And the boy who was later to become the Demosthenes of the Old Dominion, practiced speech making. "I would declaim to the trees," he said. "I made the best speeches I've ever made. But my only applause was the zephyr rustling the leaves."[52]

Orange had long been an organization county, and the young Almond spent much of his time at the knees of courthouse veterans. Never in his future political career did he forget that the courthouse was the power nerve of Virginia politics. As a young lawyer in Roanoke, he found time to work for Harry Byrd's 1925 gubernatorial campaign. Byrd demonstrated his gratitude in 1932 by helping Almond perform a

[50] *Time,* Sept. 22, 1958, p. 16.
[51] *Ibid.;* Norfolk *Virginian-Pilot,* June 7, 1964.
[52] Norfolk *Virginian-Pilot,* June 7, 1964.

minor miracle by defeating for re-election, in the Democratic caucus of the General Assembly, the incumbent judge of the Roanoke hustings court (the urban counterpart of the circuit court). "My opponent was not friendly to Byrd," Almond recalled. "I am sure Byrd knew that. . . . Had Byrd hinted to the legislative leaders that I was not acceptable, I would not have been elected. He told me later that he had been helpful." [53]

In 1945 Almond won the Sixth District congressional seat with the blessings of the Byrd organization. He underlined his conservative voting record in Washington with elaborate denunciations of communism and the CIO. Once he warned Congress of "subversives on the Federal pay roll" and urged it to resist communism's "concentrated, insidious, blatant, contumacious and deadly deliberate design" against the government of the United States. "Shall we bolster . . . the ramparts of Greece and Turkey," he asked, "and negligently refuse to take cognizance of the lethal curse of a viper nestled in our own bosom?" [54]

When Battle faced an unusually strong challenge in the 1949 gubernatorial primary, Almond's popularity and rhetorical talents were most helpful to the ticket. At the behest of the organization's hierarchy Almond traded his $15,000 congressional salary for the $9,860 job as attorney general.[55] He filled the last portion of the deceased Harvey B. Apperson's term, campaigned effectively for Battle, and seemed to maneuver himself into position for the 1953 gubernatorial election.

Yet a view of Almond as the organization's fair-haired boy has only a superficial validity. He was taking the traditional steps to the governor's mansion, and he persistently, though good-naturedly, strove to work his way into the organization's hierarchy. "I hate so damn bad to see your term expire," he once ribbed Tuck while asking him to a football game at the University of Virginia, "that I want to bask as much as possible in the shadow of your fine company as well as your official greatness." [56] Almond's relations with the organization's high

---

[53] *Ibid.*   [54] *Congressional Record,* July 15, 1947, pp. 8957–58.
[55] *Time,* Sept. 22, 1958, p. 16.
[56] Almond to Tuck, Oct. 21, 1949 (Tuck, Executive Papers, Box 25).

command were, however, on uneasy ground. A "stout, white-haired orator of the old school," Almond "little resembled the suave, disciplined politicians in gray flannel suits generally associated with the Byrd machine. He never felt completely at home with the machine leaders, nor they with him, although he scrupulously followed the organization line and sought to integrate himself in that powerful group. His greatest political asset was his ability to impress crowds of ordinary people—a talent of which Byrd and his associates were instinctively suspicious." [57]

By organization standards Lindsay Almond was, moreover, a bit too erratic. There was little doubt of his basic conservatism, but occasionally he wandered. In Congress he broke with Byrd by supporting the Marshall Plan and the Truman doctrine of aid to Greece and Turkey, though this in itself was not too serious.[58] But when Byrd refused to support Harry Truman in 1948, Almond campaigned actively for the national ticket. "The only sane and constructive course to follow," he said in a remarkable speech that year in Norfolk, "is to remain in the house of our fathers—even though the roof leaks and there may be bats in the belfry, rats in the pantry, a cockroach waltz in the kitchen, and skunks in the parlor. . . . We cannot take our inheritance and depart into a far country. Where shall we go and to what shall we return?" [59]

The episode in Almond's career which could not be overlooked was his letter of endorsement for Martin A. Hutchinson, who had been nominated by President Truman for the Federal Trade Commission. Hutchinson had been the antiorganization opponent of Senator Byrd in the 1946 Democratic primary, and Byrd was so incensed at his nomination that he succeeded in blocking Senate confirmation. "Before I wrote the letter," said Almond, "I talked with Mr. Combs and gathered the impression that Senator Byrd wouldn't have anything to do with the appointment, one way or another. I gave an honest appraisal of the man's character and ability, without any thought of offending Senator Byrd or anyone else." [60]

[57] Muse, *Massive Resistance*, p. 40.
[58] Norfolk *Virginian-Pilot*, June 7, 1964.   [59] Quoted, *ibid.*   [60] *Ibid.*

When Almond sought Byrd's nod in 1953, he was not encouraged. It was evident that Stanley had the inside road. "The general tone of the conversation was not encouraging," Almond said of his interview with Byrd.

Very friendly and no feeling in it, but I knew enough about the situation to know that had I run I wouldn't have had his support. . . . I saw that I had reached the end of the political road unless I went out on my own. I made up my mind that if I was to be shelved, the people would have to do the shelving. I began cautiously laying the foundation that would be my approach to the governorship in 1957. I accepted nearly every opportunity to speak on public issues, and, at considerable sacrifice, I kept myself before the people.[61]

"What a pleasure it would be to go to some place and not have to make a damn speech," Almond once complained.[62] For the next four years, however, Almond's rhetorical talents were much in demand. As attorney general he was the "little David" defending the laws of the commonwealth from the "Goliath of the federal judiciary." [63] He attacked integration, federal bureaucracy, and all the other leftist demons. Publicly Almond appeared the political go-getter, the spellbinding orator, and one of the most massive of all resisters.

That, however, was Almond the politician. Almond the lawyer strongly suspected that massive resistance had a limited legal future. He was too realistic to think otherwise. In 1950 Almond had indicated that state law and recent federal rulings required that a qualified Negro applicant, Gregory Swanson, be admitted to the University of Virginia for graduate study—a ruling which must have rankled in Senator Byrd. "Don't you kid yourself," said the NAACP special counsel, Thurgood Marshall. "He is a good lawyer." [64] Precisely because he was a good lawyer, Almond quickly perceived the vulnerability of the Stanley program of resistance. He told Stanley that the fund cutoff law would never survive a test in either state or federal

[61] *Ibid.*, June 8, 1964.
[62] Almond to Tuck, Nov. 9, 1948 (Tuck, Executive Papers, Box 25).
[63] Norfolk *Virginian-Pilot*, June 8, 1964.   [64] *Time*, Sept. 22, 1958, p. 15.

courts: "I said to the governor, 'I'll draft anything you want but I'm telling you it's no good.' " [65] Stanley asked someone else to draft the bill.

Almond's public utterances occasionally hinted that massive resistance was legally doomed. "What can you do in the face of overwhelming power?" he once asked. Massive resistance meant resistance "by all lawful and honorable means. . . . This is a government of laws, not men." And when the showdown came, Virginia would have little choice but to submit. "This state can't secede from the Union," said Lindsay Almond. "Virginia has no desire for it." [66]

Politician Almond could not afford the luxury of the legal view. Legal cautions were buried beneath stump oratory. The organization had narrowly survived a formidable challenge in the gubernatorial primary of 1949, and Republicans had almost defeated Stanley in 1953. Almond wished to avoid another close call. Massive resistance was widely regarded at the time as giving the organization "a new lease on life," a chance to revitalize its sagging supremacy. [67] By playing on segregationist emotions, Almond might restore organization majorities to their former strength. In the approaching gubernatorial election of 1957, therefore, he followed the segregationist line unreservedly.

First Almond had to outmaneuver state Senator Garland Gray for the Democratic nomination. Gray had repudiated the moderate suggestions of the plan which bore his name and now was clearly the first choice of Senator Byrd and the organization's highest councils. Almond, however, anticipated Gray by announcing his candidacy on November 17, 1955, almost a year before the election. [68] At once endorsements from the organization's middle and lower echelons began to pour in. Gray made a hurried estimate of his own strength, reluctantly assumed Almond to be unbeatable, and by December 6 withdrew his name from consideration to avoid "a division among the propo-

[65] Norfolk *Virginian-Pilot*, June 8, 1964.

[66] *Time*, Sept. 22, 1958, pp. 17–18.

[67] Muse, "Durability," *Reporter*, Oct. 3, 1957, pp. 28–29.

[68] Norfolk *Virginian-Pilot*, June 8, 1964.

nents of segregated schools." [69] Senator Byrd's endorsement followed five days later.

After a primary with only nominal opposition, Almond faced Ted Dalton, the Republican who had almost defeated Stanley just four years before. "We will oppose," read Almond's platform, "with every facility at our command, and with every ounce of our energy, the attempt being made to mix the white and Negro races in our classrooms. Let there be no misunderstanding, no weasel words, on this point: We dedicate our every capacity to preserve segregation in the schools." [70] Dalton, on the other hand, launched a systematic attack on massive resistance. He called the state Pupil Placement Board "the most flagrant example of centralized power that has been witnessed in Virginia and America since the adoption of the Tenth Amendment to the Constitution" and saw the fund cutoff measure as "a road that can only end in massive integration or the closing of the public schools of Virginia." [71] Because he advocated a locally administered pupil assignment plan and token compliance with the Court's decision, Dalton was quickly branded an integrationist. Eisenhower's decision in the fall of 1957 to send troops to enforce school integration in Little Rock, Arkansas, cost him thousands of votes. "Little Rock knocked me down to nothing," said Dalton in explaining his meager 36.5 per cent of the vote. "It wasn't a little rock, it was a big rock." [72] Almond, confident in his recent mandate, looked to four years of continued defiance.

Less than nine months after Almond's inauguration lightning struck. Virginians had listened to talk of last-ditch defiance and school closings to avoid integration, but many believed that massive resistance belonged only to the somewhat hysterical world of political campaigning. On Friday, September 12, 1958, Warren County High School was closed under Virginia's massive resistance laws. Under Court order to integrate, the Warren County school superintendent and Board of Education received the following notice from Governor Almond:

[69] Muse, *Massive Resistance*, pp. 41–42.
[70] *Southern School News*, Oct. 1957.   [71] *Ibid.*, July, 1957.
[72] *Ibid.*, Dec., 1957.

Pursuant to the provisions of Chapter 9.1 of the Code of Virginia, the Warren County High School is closed and is removed from the public school system, effective September 15, 1958, and all authority, power and control over such school, its principal, teachers, other employees and all pupils now enrolled or ordered to be enrolled, will thereupon be vested in the Commonwealth of Virginia, to be exercised by the Governor.[73]

Within days little mountain-locked Warren County had company in crisis. On September 19 Lane High and Venable Elementary schools in Charlottesville were closed and taken over by the Governor. School closures next hit Norfolk, the center of Virginia's largest metropolitan area, where almost 10,000 students suddenly found themselves without classrooms.[74]

Virginians were stunned. Generally unprepared for the closings, parents, pupils, politicians, and public school personnel sought some system of education to replace the public schools. In the smaller localities their efforts met with some success. Warren managed to accommodate 780 of approximately 1,000 displaced high school students in thirty makeshift classrooms in the county seat of Front Royal. Methodist, Baptist, and Episcopal Sunday school buildings, a museum of the United Daughters of the Confederacy, and a youth center were all rapidly transformed into classrooms. Teachers shifted from the public school to the private schools. Funds for the private school experiment in Warren were donated by a local union and segregationist well-wishers throughout the South who considered the Warren school a martyr to their cause. The private school in Warren, therefore, generally had "an atmosphere of normal routine and of permanency." [75]

Charlottesville was also able, in large part, to cope with the problem: 862 of its 1,080 displaced high school students attended a private school sponsored jointly by the segregationist Charlottesville Educational Foundation and the pro-public-school Parents' Committee for Emergency Schooling. Most of the pupils from Venable Elementary School attended either

[73] *Ibid.*, Oct., 1958.   [74] *Ibid.*   [75] Muse, *Massive Resistance*, p. 114.

the private Robert E. Lee School or classes operated in private homes by members of the PCES. Only 175 children were unaccounted for and presumably not in school.

In Norfolk it was different. Almost 3,000 of the approximately 10,000 pupils affected by the public school closings were not receiving any real education as late as December 1958. Four thousand had been accommodated in very loosely organized tutoring classes, another thousand transferred to schools in the contiguous city of South Norfolk, and over 1,600 transferred to public and private schools in other areas. Here it was most evident that educational improvisations had failed to take the place of public schools. Lack of adequate facilities, disruption of established routines, and the questionable legality of state tuition grants combined to make substitutes for public schooling a rather hazardous experiment.[76] And as public schools remained closed throughout the fall in Norfolk, Warren, and Charlottesville, and further closings threatened elsewhere across the state, the pressures on Almond began to mount.

The defiant segregationists never relaxed their efforts. Time after time Defenders from the Southside called on Almond to urge him to new heights of defiance. "They had all kinds of schemes, all revolving around the theory of Interposition," Almond recalls. "I'd say, 'Our Navy is depleted and the Army is gone, and we just don't have the power to rebel against the federal government.' "[77]

If Almond ever thought of easing resistance, the stern figure of Harry Byrd loomed in the background. Byrd knew that southside Virginia formed the heart of his political organization and southside Congressmen Tuck and Abbitt were never far from the Senator's ear. Then, too, Byrd was a conservative who concurred in Kilpatrick's views of the rights of states and wrongs of courts. Yet there was something else which profoundly influenced the Senator's actions. Almost a century before, the North, after much bitter combat, had succeeded in effecting a fundamental change in the life of the Southland. At

[76] *Ibid.*, pp. 111–13.   [77] Norfolk *Virginian-Pilot*, June 9, 1964.

that time Virginia had provided the Lees, Jacksons, and other military giants who nobly acquitted themselves in a great but losing cause. Now in the twilight of Byrd's career the Northerner was once again knocking at the door and intruding upon Byrd's beloved Virginia. The South again needed leadership, and Harry Flood Byrd was there to provide it. Virginia would set the pattern of defiance for the entire South in its effort to maintain its own way of life. "We face," said the Senator in September 1958, "the gravest crisis since the War Between the States." The forces of integration are "working on the theory that if Virginia can be brought to her knees, they can march through the rest of the South singing HALLELUJAH." [78] Since early in 1956 Byrd had been engrossed in a movement to unite the representatives of southern states in defiance of the Court's ruling. The Southern Manifesto, issued on March 12, 1956, and signed by 101 southern members of Congress represented, said Byrd, "a part of the plan of massive resistance we've been working on and I hope and believe it will be an effective action." More than one informed observer believes that Virginia's massive resistance encouraged the deep South to defy the courts even after Virginia had submitted. [79]

The organization's high command made it clear to Almond in a series of letters and visits that he was not to forsake the resistance. "I am receiving very large correspondence from my friends over the State . . . ," Byrd wrote Almond, "and every letter is positive and emphatic for continuation of our resistance." [80] Byrd also wrote to Attorney General Harrison commending him on a resistance speech: "On Page 20, you mention the revulsion that will occur when the people of America realize what enforced integration means, and you say the overwhelming majority of the people, knowing the issues, agree with the fight that we wage. . . . I do hope measures will be taken along the lines of your statements in Richmond to continue our resistance." [81] Tuck was even more adamant. "I have

[78] *Time*, Sept. 22, 1958, p. 15.   [79] Muse, *Massive Resistance*, pp. 27, 172.
[80] Byrd to Almond, Oct. 16, 1958. This and later quotations from letters in this chapter are taken from Almond, Executive Papers, Box 35.
[81] Byrd to A. S. Harrison, Oct. 16, 1958.

every confidence," he wrote Almond, "that you will handle the matter in such a way as to keep the schools on a segregated basis, if operated at all. I fear your turning the schools back to the localities, and hope you will not do so. There are many foundations, such as the Ford and Rockefeller Foundations, and other organizations in the country that would embrace the opportunity to finance the localities in order to break down our segregation policy." [82] When further school closings threatened, Tuck assured Almond of his "support in every honorable and just step you take to prevent our schools from being integrated and to resist this federal tyranny, and I am not in favor of taking any half-way measures." [83]

Almond tried to arrange a meeting with Byrd. "I hope we can get together for a talk on this terrible crisis," he wrote the Senator in early November. When his first efforts were unavailing, he again wrote Byrd hoping "in the near future you and I can sit down for a long talk relative to our problems." [84] When, after numerous requests, he finally did talk to Byrd, Almond found him intractable. "He expressed concern," said the Governor, "as to what his Southern colleagues in the Senate would think if Virginia gave up." [85]

Pressure on Almond came from quarters other than the Defenders, southside Virginia, and Senator Byrd. As the months dragged on and the schools remained closed, many citizens grew uneasy. Several communities had organized groups of "public school savers," who petitioned the Governor to reopen the closed schools and return the children to classes. Closing schools to prevent integration was considerably less glamorous in December than in September, and few Virginia localities now envied the once dramatic circumstances in Norfolk, Charlottesville, and Warren. Almond was "very much interested in the expression of popular sentiment," as he knew that the "sentiment would reflect itself in the legislature." [86] As yet the rumblings of scattered public school savers and PTA's were not

[82] Tuck to Almond, Sept. 8, 1958.   [83] Same, Jan. 14, 1959.
[84] Letters of Nov. 3 and Dec. 22, 1958.
[85] Norfolk *Virginian-Pilot*, June 9, 1964.
[86] *Ibid.*

enough to convince him that public sentiment demanded the slackening of resistance.

More powerful forces soon came into play, however. The Virginia press, with its long tradition of conservatism and organization sympathy, nonetheless realized the futility of unending defiance. In October and November 1958 even segregationist editors indicated their disapproval of radical resistance. By December 1958 the press had issued a concerted call for retreat:

Richmond *Times-Dispatch:* We respectfully suggest to Gov. J. Lindsay Almond the appointment of a committee from the Virginia General Assembly, charged with the duty of outlining a positive school program for the commonwealth.

Lynchburg *News:* Political leaders in the commonwealth . . . know that they are licked. . . . There is nothing left to do but devise the best possible methods of slowing down the integration process.

Charlottesville *Daily Progress:* It is dangerous nonsense to suppose that 100 per cent segregation in education can be preserved.

Norfolk *Ledger Dispatch:* A month ago this newspaper, which had been an advocate of massive resistance from the beginning, suggested that the program was approaching a dead end and that the time had arrived . . . for a new approach.[87]

To this chorus of moderation and modification was added a cautious but significant statement from Kilpatrick. In an address to the Richmond Rotary Club on November 11 Kilpatrick explained: "I believe the time has come for new weapons and new tactics. I believe the laws we now have on the books have outlived their usefulness, and I believe that new laws must be devised—speedily devised—if educational opportunities are to be preserved and social calamity is to be avoided." He further recognized the possibility that there might be integration in some public schools in Virginia under new legislation, and he presented tentative plans which included local referendums on the question of school closings.[88]

[87] Quoted from *Southern School News,* Dec. 1958.   [88] *Ibid.*

By November 20 a controversy arose over the relative positions of the state and national flags at the state Capitol. The
Governor touched off comment with his statement that state-
owned buildings would not be permitted to fly the United
States flag over the Virginia flag. Moreover, when only one staff
was available, the Virginia flag, not the Stars and Stripes would
stream. The week of angry debate which ensued provoked a
certain comic relief from columnist Charles McDowell in the
Richmond *Times-Dispatch:*

> O! Say, can you see by the dawn's early light,
> Is it up, is it down, since the twilight's last gleaming?
> Is the flag of the state at a similar height?
> Are both of them there, so co-equally streaming?
> After video's glare, the bombast in air,
> Is it clear that the flags are now dually there?
> O! Say that our far-wrangled banners at last,
> Are secure, and this Capitol tempest is passed.[89]

Throughout the crisis Almond's fire and brimstone oratory
had clashed with his devotion to legal processes and his recognition of the inevitable. Almond, in addition, abhorred violence
in Virginia and respected more than most the rights of the
Negro. Under pressure to do so on a number of occasions, he
never lent himself to "any move of intimidation or reprisal with
respect to Virginia's Negro citizens." When the Norfolk city
council sought to close the city's Negro high schools in a spite-
ful tit-for-tat, the Governor replied sharply that this "would be
a vicious and retaliatory blow against the Negro race." It hurt
him to have the public link his name with the demagoguery
and vindictiveness of Orval Faubus in the Little Rock crisis.
Almond had few intimate friends, stood always aloof, and
throughout tried to bear his cross alone.[90]

Two people tried to help him resolve these pressures. His
tall, rather austere wife, Josephine, had kindled his ambitions
in the early years and now stood ready to offer advice. "If I had
just listened to Josephine," Almond later mused, "I wouldn't

---

[89] Quoted in Muse, *Massive Resistance*, p. 101.   [90] *Ibid.*, pp. 81–84.

Senators A. Willis Robertson and Byrd at Chamber of Commerce Dinner, 1950

Governor John S. Battle, Senator Byrd, and Former Governor William M. Tuck at Byrd's Annual Apple-Orchard Picnic, 1951

J. Lindsay Almond, Jr., at a Campaign Rally, 1953

have made the errors I did." [91] The other helpful person was Attorney General Albertis S. Harrison, well able to keep a cool head under fire. In mid-September Almond and Harrison had initiated a suit to test the validity of the school-closing and fund cutoff laws in the Virginia Supreme Court of Appeals.

As the court neared its decision, Almond was obliged to contend with a potent antiresistance force. Business had supported Almond in 1957 when he promised to aid the state's industrial development. As massive resistance unfolded, however, businessmen were becoming more and more concerned. Nothing would shatter Virginia's stability and retard her economic growth so much as a closed public school system. Dr. Lorin A. Thompson, director of the University of Virginia's Bureau of Population and Economic Research, emphasized this in *Some Economic Aspects of Virginia's Current Educational Crisis.* Pointing out that the school situation had already caused many skilled workers to leave Virginia and deterred new industries from coming, Thompson predicted that "the damaging effects of the present dislocation will be more apparent one, two or five years hence." [92] Business leaders were alarmed and overcame their previous reluctance to get involved in the massive resistance issue.

In December 1958 twenty-nine businessmen, industrialists, and bankers, representing the economic power structure of Virginia, met with Governor Almond for an important dinner conference in the stately Rotunda Club in Richmond. The businessmen told the Governor that massive resistance was hurting the state's reputation and undermining its development. Almond gave no hint that he would change his course, but he left the meeting with the realization that business had added its influence to the growing antiresistance sentiment in Virginia.[93]

Massive resistance was teetering, and the courts gave it a final push. The Virginia Supreme Court of Appeals declared on

[91] Norfolk *Virginian-Pilot*, June 8, 1964.
[92] Quoted in *Southern School News,* Jan. 1959, and in Muse, *Massive Resistance*, pp. 108–9.
[93] Muse, *Massive Resistance*, p. 110.

January 19, 1959, that both the school-closing and the fund
cutoff measures were contrary to Section 129 of the Virginia
constitution, which required the state to "maintain an efficient
system of public free schools throughout the State." "That
means," wrote Chief Justice John W. Eggleston in the majority
opinion of *Harrison* v. *Day* "that the state must support such
public free schools in the state as are necessary to an efficient
system, including those in which the pupils of both races are
compelled to be enrolled and taught together, however unfortunate that situation may be." [94]

On the same day a three-judge federal district court in Norfolk declared in *James* v. *Almond* that Virginia's school-closing
statutes were "in violation of the Fourteenth Amendment to
the Constitution of the United States" and therefore void. So
long as the state maintained a public school system, the court
said, "the closing of a public school or grade therein . . .
violates the right of a citizen to equal protection of the laws." [95]

Almond determined to make one last try. In a television
broadcast the day after the court rulings he raised segregationist hopes with a just-begun-to-fight cry:

To those in high place or elsewhere who advocate integration for
your children and send their own to private or public segregated
schools; to those who defend or close their eyes to the livid stench
of sadism, sex immorality and juvenile pregnancy infesting the
mixed schools of the District of Columbia and elsewhere; to those
who would overthrow the customs, morals and traditions of a way
of life which has endured in honor and decency for centuries and
embrace a new moral code prepared by nine men in Washington
whose moral concepts they know nothing about; . . . to all of these
and their confederates, comrades and allies, let me make it abun-
dantly clear for the record now and hereafter, as governor of this
state, I will not yield to that which I know to be wrong and will
destroy every semblance of education for thousands of the children
of Virginia. [96]

"I don't know why I made that damn speech," Almond said
later. "I saw the whole thing crumbling. I was tired and dis-

[94] Quoted in *Southern School News,* Feb. 1959.   [95] *Ibid.*
[96] Richmond *Times-Dispatch,* Jan. 21, 1959.

traught. I agonized and gave vent to my feelings, which never should have been done. My underlying thought and motivation was to show the people that we had done everything we could do." [97] Senator Byrd found satisfaction in it, however. "The notable speech of Governor Almond last night will further stiffen the resistance," he said.[98] Tuck sent a congratulatory telegram to Almond, saying the speech "should give our people great encouragement." [99] "Congratulations," wired Abbitt, "on the splendid presentation of our situation. It was the finest speech I have ever heard you make." [100] But it was the last time that Abbitt, Tuck, or Byrd ever found satisfaction in Lindsay Almond.

One week later, a sobered governor came to address the General Assembly in what many observers have termed his "finest hour." "Whatever may be said of his course up to that point," wrote Muse, "however much he may himself have contributed to the malevolent hysteria which prevailed, when the hard-pressed Governor called the legislature and the state back to sanity, he displayed a combination of courage, eloquence and skill which was admirable. He did what a leader in Arkansas, with whom his name had been unjustly coupled, has never dared to do. He set an example which to some extent many another Southern leader in time must follow." [101]

Alone in front of the General Assembly, with Speaker Moore, the younger Byrd, Godwin, Gray, and all the powers of the organization listening somewhat incredulously, Lindsay Almond calmly explained his plans to end the resistance. He appointed a commission headed by Senator Mosby Perrow to study the school problem further, called for repeal of the compulsory school attendance law, urged the enactment of a tuition grant plan independent of public school appropriations, and recommended a law against bombing threats.[102] He advanced no new plans to forestall court-ordered integration in the coming semester, and on February 2, 1959, twenty-one

[97] Norfolk *Virginian-Pilot*, June 9, 1964.
[98] Muse, *Massive Resistance*, p. 129.   [99] Tuck to Almond, Jan. 21, 1959.
[100] Abbitt to Almond, Jan. 21, 1959.
[101] Muse, *Massive Resistance*, pp. 131–32.
[102] Almond, *Address to General Assembly*, Jan. 28, 1959.

Negro children were taken into formerly white schools of Norfolk and Arlington without incident.[103]

Massive resisters, though deprived of the Governor's influence, closed ranks for a final assault. Their attempts to revive resistance in the January special session were defeated 22 to 17 in the Senate.[104] When the Perrow Commission completed its work and the General Assembly reconvened on March 31, the resisters attended in full force. Over five thousand angry Virginians, mostly from the Southside, assembled in front of the Capitol and applauded when Edward J. Silverman, a voluble orator from a small southside town, called on the legislature to "regain the leadership" which had been "so shamefully surrendered in recent weeks."[105] Angry with the Governor for failing to appear, these hard-core resisters tried mightily to urge the legislature to renewed defiance.

Within the General Assembly the battle raged. The thrust of the Perrow recommendations was a shift from the statewide massive resistance policy to local option in dealing with the school problem. The bill providing for local assignment of pupils was the bone of furious contention, just as the local option question had dominated Stanley's special session over two long years before. Against the new bill in the Senate fight were organization leaders: Byrd, Jr., Button, Godwin, Gray, Moses, McCue, Wyatt, and their allies. In the meantime the Governor had marshaled together, under the local option banner, a makeshift alliance. Senators Perrow, Fitzpatrick, Fenwick, Willey, and Stuart, all with organization backgrounds, stuck with the Governor. With them were the handful of Republicans (Dalton, Landreth, and Wolfe) and a number of former Young Turks, moderates, and antiorganization liberals (Boothe, Breeden, Haddock, and others). When the House-approved assignment bill came to the Senate, normal procedure would have been to refer the measure to the Senate Education Committee. There, however, the Byrd organization majority would have consigned the measure to an early grave. To by-

[103] Richmond *Times-Dispatch*, Feb. 3, 1959.
[104] *Journal of Senate, Extra Session 1959*, p. 74.
[105] Muse, *Massive Resistance*, p. 161.

pass the committee, the Governor's forces proposed that the Senate resolve itself into a committee of the whole. The motion carried by the razor-thin margin of 20 to 19 only when moderate Senator Stuart B. Carter of Botetourt County, who was recuperating from a stomach ulcer operation, was hurriedly summoned to Richmond and carried into the Senate on a stretcher. His vote broke what otherwise would have been a 19–19 deadlock.[106]

The rift between Almond and the hard-core Byrd organization was now complete. Later that year in his annual apple orchard picnic Byrd said, "I stand now as I stood when I first urged massive resistance." [107] But Governor Almond had ended massive resistance in Virginia forever, and the Senator knew it. "Almond speaks with feeling of his break with Byrd," wrote Norfolk columnist Luther J. Carter in 1964. "If he had never been part of the Byrd Organization inner circle, and if his philosophy and that of the Senator's never were quite congenial, at least Almond had earned by his political talents high associate status. One may believe that this was as important to Almond emotionally as it was politically." "I naturally dreaded," said Almond, "to break with the people with whom I had long been associated and for whom I had the highest respect. A torturing dread that you recoil from." [108]

Almond battled the organization with varying success for the remainder of his term. He pushed through the General Assembly a dramatic increase in the budget which the economy-minded organization strenuously opposed. But Byrd, Jr., and Speaker Moore succeeded in killing Almond's proposal for a state sales tax. "If these gentlemen [Byrd, Jr., and Moore] want to play it rough, that suits me, for the remainder of this administration and for the days to come after the close of this administration," Almond said in a televised appearance.[109]

J. Lindsay Almond, Jr., was a pivotal figure in the history of

---

[106] See *Southern School News*, May, 1959, and Muse, *Massive Resistance,* pp. 160–64, for detailed accounts of this session.

[107] Muse, *Massive Resistance,* p. 166.

[108] Norfolk *Virginian-Pilot,* June 9, 1964.

[109] Muse, *Massive Resistance,* p. 167.

the Byrd organization. His decision to abandon massive resistance marked the first major policy matter on which Senator Byrd, southside Virginia, and courthouse conservatism did not have their way. The Almond alliance was at best a motley and makeshift operation; in the legislature moderate organization men, Republicans, former Young Turks, and liberals combined in shaky ranks for thin majorities. Outside the legislature, business leaders, moderate voices in the press, many churchmen, PTA groups, and citizens more interested in public schools than segregation gave the Governor their support. Though far from ideal, Almond's course of action proved considerably more palatable to Negroes, labor, and dedicated integrationists than that of Senator Byrd. The Almond alliance did not remain completely intact after the Governor's term, and even during that term its day-to-day existence was precarious. Almond never posed a serious threat to Senator Byrd's control of the organization. What he did do was to head a functioning alliance in which traditional powers no longer played a major part and, by so doing, pioneered policies and coalitions which Albertis Harrison held and Mills Godwin extended in the gubernatorial races of 1961 and 1965. He emerged from his anguished political and personal decisions as the forerunner of a more modern and moderate Democratic party in Virginia.

In time, massive resistance came to seem more and more a political nightmare. Its architects gained little stature. The massive resisters failed for the most part to resurrect the nobler sentiments of the Civil War. No succeeding generations would nurture the cult of their lost cause. Instead a newer Virginia saw massive resistance as the end of an era—an era which ended in aberration.

For many Virginians, massive resistance did seem an aberration. How had the Old Dominion, whose race relations had been termed "perhaps the most harmonious in the South," [110] come to close its public schools? Some have argued that massive resistance served a good purpose in that it provided time

[110] Key, p. 32.

to cool emotions and to demonstrate the inadequacies of various resistance schemes, time in which the inevitability of some integration could come to be accepted without violence.[111]

For such an argument, however, the evidence is thin. Virginia's massive resistance developed slowly; emotional currents did not stampede the statewide leadership into defiance. Over two years elapsed between the initial Supreme Court decision in May 1954 and the adoption of massive resistance legislation in September 1956. Governor Stanley's first reaction to the Court decision was a mild one, and the original Gray Plan (1955) seemed moderate in its provision for local option. Yet all initial gestures of moderation were deliberately repudiated in favor of piecemeal adoption of more extreme measures—Interposition, resistance legislation in the summer of 1956, and the subsequent school closings in the fall of 1958. Massive resistance appears more a calculated maneuver than an emotional imperative. There were intense segregationist pressures on the organization throughout the period, but they were localized and might have been more realistically confronted had the organization accepted from the first a policy of token compliance with the Court decision, a stand similar to that of North Carolina. Instead, the rhetoric of resistance, far from helping southside and rural Virginia adjust to new conditions, raised false hopes for an eternity of segregation.

Muse suggests that "Virginia's political leaders, instead of being hog-tied in constructive impulses by the prejudice of their constituents, were actually more extreme in their opposition to school desegregation than the people of the state as a whole." [112] This is true, although the "people of the state as a whole" were opposed in varying degrees to integrated public schools, judging from the 1956 tuition grant referendum and the 1957 Almond-Dalton race. In Byrd's Virginia, however, "the people of the state as a whole" did not always make the crucial decisions. In massive resistance the organization refused to allow the principle of localism to operate, and in effect

---

[111] This is now the organization's standard justification for massive resistance. See Latimer, p. 66.

[112] *Massive Resistance,* p. 163.

imposed on "the people of the state as a whole" the attitudes of the state's most extreme part.

That massive resistance developed as it did was not surprising in the light of Virginia politics in 1955. The courthouse cliques in the Southside and other rural counties of Virginia constituted the state's most reliable political force. State leaders were courthouse bred; the state legislature was apportioned to favor rural areas; state spending (what there was of it) never failed to give rural roads and schools at least a fair share. In 1955 southside and rural conservatives dominated the state leadership, the state legislature, and state policy. For years they dictated Virginia's course. And they did not suddenly surrender their customary control just when the issue that mattered most to them was at stake.

Byrd influenced the development of massive resistance as much as did the structure of his state machine. More than any other individual, Byrd pushed Virginia into defiance. Byrd helped to "correct" Stanley's first mild reaction to the Court decision, and Byrd was the first to hint, during the tuition grant referendum, that the local option feature of the Gray Plan would be dropped. Byrd coined the phrase "massive resistance" in February 1956, and he presided over the midsummer conference (1956) in Washington when the decision was taken to go all the way. He encouraged Lindsay Almond to block integration, and Almond forsook massive resistance only over the adamant objections of Harry Byrd.

Byrd's motives, however, were different from those of many of his fellow resisters. Race prejudice was not a primary factor with Byrd as it was with Tuck and with Abbitt, who had suggested that where white schools were closed by threatened integration localities should consider closing Negro schools also.[113] Byrd had never been known as anti-Negro; indeed, while governor he had passed a stiff antilynching law to protect Negro citizens from mob violence. His massive resistance stand was undoubtedly motivated to some extent by the dependence of his organization on the rural white vote, yet even

[113] *Southern School News,* Dec. 1958.

this consideration was not paramount. In 1956 Byrd helped to organize the Southern Manifesto; massive resistance for him meant the "coalition between the 11 Southern States" which would "strengthen the position of the individual state." [114] Byrd's pride in Virginia demanded that the Old Dominion not be the first southern state to capitulate. "Let Virginia surrender to this illegal demand" stated Byrd in 1956, "and you'll find the ranks of the other southern states broken. . . . If Virginia surrenders, if Virginia's line is broken, the rest of the South will go down, too." [115] The traditional power structure of the Byrd machine and Byrd's own Old South ethic made Virginia ripe for massive resistance.

The organization might not have courted segregationist favor had it enjoyed its customary control of the Virginia political situation in 1955. From 1949 to 1954, the five years preceding the Court decision, it was evident that the Byrd organization was fighting to hang on. John Battle narrowly won his 1949 primary fight, Ted Dalton almost defeated Tom Stanley, and the Young Turks had become impatient with their exclusion from the decision process and with the low levels of service which the organization provided. The Byrd organization was in trouble at home, and the Supreme Court decision offered a neat diversion to a "foreign, federal bogeyman." Attention was momentarily turned away from basic conflicts on fiscal matters and focused on the integration question. The strategy seemed successful. Byrd remarked jubilantly to Almond of "the intensity of the feeling and the great support you have in your work to prevent integration." [116] "For the first time I am getting some active support from the labor people," Byrd wrote several days before his re-election to the Senate in 1958. "Billy Prieur called me and said the CIO leaders in Norfolk have made a public statement for me. This I never expected." [117] Tuck reminded Almond that "the people are one hundred per cent behind you in your determination to keep our schools from being integrated . . . and the harder and the tougher the going is the

---

[114] Quoted in Muse, *Massive Resistance*, p. 27. [115] Latimer, p. 79.
[116] Byrd to Almond, Oct. 10, 1958. [117] Same, Oct. 31, 1958.

more the folks will unite behind you." [118] The high command gloried in the return of political prosperity with the integration issue. "This will keep us in power another 25 years," a top organization man is supposed to have said at the height of the resistance.[119]

The view that massive resistance was Virginia's spontaneous, segregationist response to the Court's ruling is both partial and misleading. Race prejudice was an important overt factor in the situation, but it was often manipulated by more potent backstage forces. Massive resistance stands as a logical, though not an inevitable, product of the declining days of Harry Byrd's Virginia.

[118] Tuck to Almond, Sept. 9, 1958.
[119] Latimer, p. 73. This is perhaps the most famous "anonymous" quote in Virginia politics.

Part II
The Changing Commonwealth

Chapter 6

Urban Growth

Like his avowed spiritual ancestor, Thomas Jefferson, Harry Byrd cherished his own dream of an agrarian utopia. "The prosperity of Virginia depends primarily upon agriculture," the young governor had said in his inaugural address of 1926.[1] Four years later, in his farewell speech, he emphasized that Virginia's "rural population has been the bulwark of the State in the past, and agriculture should be advanced in every practical and reasonable way."[2] Years afterward Virginia's governors took the same view. "Our farms constitute the bedrock of the State's progress," said Tuck in 1945. "It is important for Virginia to remain an agricultural State."[3]

By 1960 agrarian Virginia had begun to disappear. For years the commonwealth had held urbanization and industrialization at bay, but by 1960 the urban areas, which for the first forty years of the twentieth century had grown slowly, claimed 55 per cent of Virginia's population (see Table 12). The state's rural farm population was then only one-tenth of Virginia's total.

The urban boom in Virginia was part of a similar trend throughout the South. From 1940 to 1950 the South's rate of urban growth was almost twice that of the nation's, and Flor-

[1] *Inaugural Address, Feb. 1, 1926.*
[2] *Address to General Assembly, Jan. 8, 1930.*
[3] Richmond *Times-Dispatch,* July 19, 1945.

ida and Texas were the only southern states outpacing the Old
Dominion in the swiftness of urban and metropolitan expansion.[4] In 1940 the urban percentage of the South's population
was 20 per cent below the national average; by 1960 it was only
10 per cent lower.[5] In 1960 seven of the former Confederate
states had a majority of urban residents. Only in Mississippi

Table 12   Virginia's Rate of Urban Growth
(1900–1960)

Year	Population	Per cent Urban	Rural
1900	1,854,184	18.3	81.7
1910	2,061,612	23.1	76.9
1920	2,309,187	29.2	70.8
1930	2,421,851	32.4	67.6
1940	2,677,773	35.3	64.7
1950	3,318,680	47.0 *	53.0
1960	3,954,429	55.6 *	44.4

Source: U.S. Bureau of the Census, *Population, 1960*, I, A,
U.S. Summary.
* Urban and rural population percentages for 1950 and 1960
follow the definition of urban places adopted by the 1950
census. The adoption of this broader definition exaggerated
the jump in Virginia's urban population from 1940 to 1950.
Under the old definition Virginia's population would have
been 41.4 per cent urban in 1950 and 48.7 per cent urban in
1960.

did the cities contain noticeably less than 40 per cent of the
total population.[6] The population of standard metropolitan
areas in the South increased from 1950 to 1960 at a rate thirteen times as great as the population living outside such areas.[7]
With this growth came technicians, businessmen, managers,

[4] See J. M. Maclachlan and J. S. Floyd, Jr., *This Changing South* (Gainesville: University of Florida Press, 1956), for a thorough statistical study of the
changing complexion of the South from 1940 to 1950.
[5] U.S. Bureau of Census, *Population, 1960*, I, A, *United States Summary*, p.
29.
[6] *Ibid.*, pp. 33–35.   [7] *Ibid.*, p. xxxvi.

factories, assembly plants, educational opportunities, and higher incomes. The old agrarian South receded before the onslaught. Rural farm population dropped sharply in all eleven states of the old Confederacy as sharecroppers and agricultural workers left the farms for employment in cities both North and South. The exodus cut the Negro-white population ratio in the South to 1 in 5, and in 1960 less than 50 per cent of all American Negroes lived in southern states.[8]

The urban revolution initiated political upheaval as well. "The old line 'wool hat' politician who perennially shouted his mighty defenses of the rural way of life to a responsive constituency now finds himself speaking more and more in a vacuum," wrote Thomas D. Clark in *The Emerging South*.[9] The breed of the southern spellbinder was not yet extinct, but it no longer predominated. In 1960 the rural stumper competed for attention with more modern, managerial-minded southern governors such as Terry Sanford of North Carolina, Ernest F. Hollings of South Carolina, and Carl E. Sanders of Georgia. Southern segregationists no longer found it quite so safe to rouse the voters with undisguised appeals to race. Candidates who courted backlash on the campaign trail, once in office, wooed industry with equal zest.[10]

The Southern Governor's Conference of 1959 demonstrated an awareness of new industrial currents by reversing the ancient southern position of opposition to the tariff. Urging Congress and the President "to consider at all times the protection of the national security and the domestic economy in decisions affecting the amount and extent of foreign imports," [11] the governors united with the North in resisting foreign competition to domestic industry. More important than the tariff was a recognition that cross burnings, lynchings, school bombings, and school closings would not attract new industry. An expression

[8] D. W. Grantham, "The South and the Reconstruction of American Politics," *Journal of American History*, LIV (Sept. 1966), 233.

[9] New York: Oxford University Press, 1961, p. 273.

[10] Alabama's Governor George Wallace, for instance, launched a determined effort to bring new industry to Alabama.

[11] Quoted in Clark, p. 273.

of the new attitudes of moderation was the election of Lindsay
Almond president of the 1959 Southern Governor's Conference.

The political transformation of the South lagged behind its
demographic development. Rural black belts, long the citadels
of political power in the South, did not easily surrender their
ancestral hegemony. Diehard segregationists prepared to fight
tenaciously as their traditional grip on state politics was threatened. Many areas in the deep South seemed all but impreg-
nable to moderating influences. "Urban upstarts," on the other
hand, were unwilling to submit to rural reaction. In the urban
South, Negroes were freer to participate politically,[12] workers
could more easily join unions, party loyalties were not so rigid,
and regional consciousness was not so strong. Pressures for
municipal reform, expanded public services, and legislative
reapportionment reflected the growing urban influence.[13] Although the agrarian South resisted, the urban revolution forced
on the region political attitudes and structures of increasing
maturity. Nowhere was this more evident than in the Old
Dominion.

Historically Virginia's development had been slow. Each
decade from 1790 to 1930 showed Virginia's rate of population
growth considerably below that for the nation. From 1880 to
1930 the Old Dominion lost one-third of its natural increase in
population because Virginians migrated to other states in
search of better employment opportunities.[14] Negroes accounted for much of the exodus during this fifty-year span, and
their proportion of the state's population dropped from 42 to 27
per cent.[15] During the twenties the outmigration reached an
all-time high. More than 100,000 whites and 100,000 nonwhites

---

[12] Key, p. 673.   [13] See Grantham, p. 234.

[14] Holm, "Changing Va. Economy," p. 1.

[15] Key notes that from 1900 to 1940 the number of Virginia counties over 50
per cent Negro dropped from 36 to 18. "The shrinkage of the black belt," he
continues, "is probably of greater importance than the simple decline in Negro
population percentages for entire states." That massive resistance was on the
whole nonviolent and that it was ultimately abandoned probably owed much to
the drop in Virginia's Negro population during the first half of the century and
the resultant modification of white attitudes (p. 672).

left the state, and Virginia ranked as the eighth slowest-growing state in the nation.[16]

The thirties proved to be the pivotal period in Virginia's fortunes. The depression halted migration in the first half of the decade, and the expansion of federal activities later gave a much needed boost to the Virginia economy. Continued expansion of government activity helped to account for Virginia's remarkable 23.9 per cent population increase in the 1940's—a figure nine percentage points above that for the nation.

The pattern of growth within the state provides the greatest political interest. During both the 1940's and 1950's Virginia's five largest metropolitan areas grew rapidly.[17] In the fifties they increased by almost 550,000 persons, an average rate of 40 per cent—double that for the state as a whole. These metropolitan areas, comprising only 32 per cent of the state's population in 1940, contained 48 per cent of all Virginians by 1960. The most dramatic increase occurred in Virginia's Washington suburbs, where expansion of federal employment raised the population from 134,068 to 539,618 in twenty years (see Table 13).

Virginia's moderate-sized cities and smaller metropolitan areas averaged a 13 per cent growth in population during the decade of the fifties—somewhat below the 19.5 per cent rate for the state as a whole. These areas nevertheless continued to constitute approximately one-fifth of the state's population.[18]

Rural Virginia (that part of the state which lay outside the five large and twelve smaller metropolitan areas) gained less than 2 per cent in population during the fifties, and many counties experienced sharp population declines. The mechanization of farming and coal mining in southwest Virginia sent many rural residents to the cities in search of new jobs. Many of the Byrd organization's traditional strongholds suffered population setbacks. The central southside Virginia counties such as Brunswick, Mecklenburg, Prince Edward, Lunenburg, Charlotte, and Halifax lost from 4 to 12 per cent of their

---

[16] Holm, "Changing Economy," p. 1.

[17] See E. E. Holm, "Virginia Grows Metropolitan," *Virginia Economic Review*, XIV (Jan. 1961), 2.

[18] *Ibid.*, p. 6.

population during the decade. Many counties along Virginia's coastal plain beyond the impact of Richmond and Hampton Roads experienced moderate losses. Highly rural counties in Virginia's Piedmont (Orange, Madison, Nelson, Louisa) failed to show substantial growth.[19] Demographic gains accrued—unhappily for Byrd—primarily in those counties on the outer fringes of metropolitan and suburban areas.

Table 13   Virginia's Rate of Metropolitan Growth (1940–1960)

Metropolitan area	Population			Change	
	1940	1950	1960	1940–50	1950–60
				%	%
Virginia portion of Washington, D.C., area	134,068	303,328	539,618	126.2	77.9
Richmond	266,185	328,050	408,494	23.2	24.5
Norfolk-Portsmouth	258,927	446,200	578,507	72.3	29.7
Newport News–Hampton	93,353	154,977	224,503	66.0	44.9
Roanoke	112,184	133,407	158,803	18.9	19.0
Total	864,717	1,365,962	1,909,925	58.0	39.8
State total	2,677,773	3,318,680	3,966,949	23.9	19.5
Metropolitan areas as per cent of state total	32.3	41.2	48.1		

Source: Adapted from Holm, "Va. Grows Metropolitan," p. 2.

As Virginia became a more urban state, its economy became more varied. By 1960 the once farm-centered Virginia was more diversified than its southern and western neighbors— North Carolina, Tennessee, Kentucky, and West Virginia.[20] Agriculture, which at the turn of the century, accounted for almost one-half of Virginia's employment, by 1960 claimed less than one-tenth. Manufacturing was the largest employer, accounting in 1960 for 20 per cent of the state's labor force. Virginia possessed an unusually varied number of industries.

[19] U.S. Bureau of the Census, *Population, 1960,* I, 48, *Virginia,* pp. 27–29.
[20] See Holm, "Changing Va. Economy," p. 8.

Textiles, chemicals, and food products—the three largest manufacturing categories—accounted for only 37 per cent of the total manufacturing work force. Almost every area of the state felt the impact of new plants. Manufacturing development in Virginia from 1950 to 1960 concentrated in the Shenandoah Valley and the area from Roanoke to Galax even more than in the traditional manufacturing centers of Richmond and Hampton Roads.[21] In no other ten-year period of Virginia's history had so many large national corporations come to the state, and economists forecast even greater growth in manufacturing during the next decade.[22]

Federal employment supplemented manufacturing as a second vital component in the Virginia economy. For its size Virginia participated in more federal government activity than any other state in the nation. The 133,000 military personnel stationed in Virginia in 1960 constituted one-thirteenth of the national total and the 131,000 federal civilian workers living in the state one-eighteenth. Government workers accounted for almost one-fifth of Virginia's employed labor force by 1960.[23]

Agriculture, tourism, rail transportation, mining, port activities, fisheries, retail and wholesale trade, utilities, business and professional services rounded out the Virginia economy, which by 1960 ranked as one of the nation's healthiest.[24] An important question, however, remained. How would this new Virginia react to the established political organization of Senator Byrd?

Although Virginia governors beginning with Byrd had encouraged the influx of new industry to Virginia and middle-class business and professional men found much to admire in the state's government, the organization's policy was often unappealing to the urban electorate, and metropolitan Virginia became increasingly rebellious. Virginia's urban growth lent uncertainty to the predictable operations of the courthouse commonwealth, and most organization leaders did not welcome the change. Byrd's greatest failure was his consistent

[21] J. L. Knapp, "New Plants in Virginia," *Virginia Economic Review*, XV (Sept. 1963), 2–3.
[22] Holm, "Changing Va. Economy," p. 5.   [23] *Ibid.*, pp. 5, 8.
[24] See *ibid.*, pp. 1–11.

refusal to modify the decaying doctrines of a rural past to ease Virginia's urban growing pains.

Nowhere was this refusal more evident than in the field of education. Urban growth had only intensified the South's chronic educational crises:

The current rise of industry and the intoxicating promises of the atomic age have caught the South disastrously short in educational preparation [stated Thomas Clark]. Before 1940 southerners found it easier to reconcile their lower educational achievements by saying they were good enough for a floundering rural society and to serve the professions. Too few southern educators prior to 1945 had thought constructively in terms of intense urbanization. . . . If the South is ultimately to realize its promise, the new leadership will have to be soundly educated. Instead of a pink-cheeked colonel wearing a string tie, ruffled shirt, frock coat, and broad-brimmed planter's hat, the new southern human symbol will most likely be a less flamboyantly clad doctor of philosophy, who is a specialist in physics or business management. He will know more about atomic energy and corporate management than his aged prototype knew about slaves, staple crops, and cotton factors. If this new spokesman for the South is to be a trained scientist, the new southerner of necessity must be superior to his father in basic educational preparation in order to find profitable employment.[25]

The urban revolution found Virginia educationally underprepared. Virginia economist Edwin E. Holm called attention to this in the summer of 1963:

The changing economy is having more impact on our educational needs than at any time in our history. The material presented will show (1) the very rapid occupational upgrading taking place and (2) the growing need for persons to be able to adapt to changing jobs within a lifetime. In Virginia these trends are moving more swiftly than in the nation because the State's economy matured more slowly until recent times and is now growing and changing more rapidly than nationally.

Because of these changes, a strong basic education is required

[25] Clark, p. 275.

more than ever before along with the need for more specialized training and flexibility for continuing education and training during adulthood. . . . What Virginia does about education and training will be the single most important factor determining the rate of growth and the type of growth obtained in manufacturing.[26]

As late as 1963 teacher salaries in Virginia were thirty-sixth in the nation, nearly $1,000 below the national level.[27] Expenditures per pupil in average daily attendance in 1963 placed Virginia above many other southern states but fortieth in the nation and almost $100 below the national average.[28] The Old Dominion had a lower percentage of its eligible population in high schools, colleges, and graduate schools than almost any other state in the Union including its sister states of the South (see Appendix VII). No sales tax had yet been enacted to produce needed revenue for public schools. The organization's hierarchy opposed instead of helped the Young Turks and Almond in their efforts to provide increased revenues for education. When the machine did aid education, as in the Battle grants for school construction, it did so only after campaign pressure from opposition forces. Local municipal and suburban governments were inundated with demands from parents to accommodate the rapidly expanding school-age population, the development of the urban economy pleaded for educational improvement, and the effort to attract more industry demanded a mature school system, but the Byrd organization did not respond.

Massive resistance was adopted just when the pressures of population growth and the urban economy most demanded a stable, smoothly functioning public school system. The lack of a progressive and imaginative school policy had already alienated many urban citizens, and massive resistance and the closing

[26] "The Importance of Education in the Economic Development of Virginia," *Virginia Economic Review*, XIV (July 1963), 1, 6.

[27] *Book of the States, 1964–65*, p. 206.

[28] *Ibid.*, p. 212. Virginia would have ranked far lower had not certain localities taxed themselves heavily for better public schools. The amount of public school revenue coming from state sources was practically the lowest in the nation (Washington *Post*, July 21, 1965).

of public schools damaged even more severely the organization's strength in urban communities. School closings crippled the large city of Norfolk, and had federal District Judge Albert V. Bryan not postponed integration orders in Arlington County until February of 1959, a school shut-down there would have further embittered relations between the Byrd organization and another of the state's major metropolitan areas. Virginia's massive resistance was finally ended by the powerful urban press and the business community. They were unwilling to see Virginia's children without education, and they would not permit a threat to continued industrial development.

If massive resistance disturbed or angered many urban whites, it completely estranged the Negro from the organization. During the years 1940–60 Negroes were rapidly becoming powerful influences in urban Virginia. Since 1930 the movement of Negroes to southern cities had been as important a factor in the changing complexion of the region as the better publicized phenomenon of Negro migration to the urban North.

This influx of Negroes to the city was particularly noticeable in Virginia in the 1950's. Nonwhite population rose 26 per cent in that decade in Virginia's urban corridor (in 1960 a strip of twenty counties and fourteen cities stretching from Virginia's Washington suburbs to Richmond and Hampton Roads), while Negro population in the rest of the state actually declined. Net migration of nonwhites to the corridor amounted to 10,142; the rest of Virginia, predominantly rural, lost 71,546 Negro citizens through emigration.[29] Highly rural southside Virginia suffered the sharpest Negro losses.

Negroes in Virginia's urban communities were far more powerful than their rural counterparts. The two strongest Negro political organizations in Virginia were based in Richmond and Hampton Roads. Negro newspapers operated in Norfolk, Richmond, and Roanoke,[30] and they stimulated effective political

[29] L. A. Thompson, "Virginia Population Changes: Age and Color 1960 and 1970," *University of Virginia News Letter*, June 15, 1961.
[30] Gates, p. 12.

action. In 1960 Negroes in Virginia's counties still outnumbered those in the cities, but over 56,000 of the latter had registered to vote while fewer than 44,000 county Negroes were exercising the franchise.[31] Improved communications, more sophisticated leadership, higher levels of income and education, and less repressive white attitudes all enabled the Negro to play a larger role in municipal politics than he ever had in county government. After massive resistance Virginia politicians had perforce to respect the influence of the urban Negro, and the Byrd organization was not on good terms with this sector of the electorate. A decade after enactment of the resistance legislation the Richmond Negro press called two prominent colleagues of Byrd "ultra conservatives who have fanatically opposed progress of the colored man throughout their political lives. Their ugly records show they have consistently fought against legislation aimed at elevating us to first-class citizenship. . . . The oppressive Byrd machine must be demolished. With our new voting strength . . . we can do a lot to help wreck it." [32]

Youth supplied much of the momentum for Virginia's remarkable urban growth. Rapid increases and declines in an area's population seldom occur without modification of the age composition. In Virginia's case the relation of urban growth to change in age was easy to predict. Professor Lorin A. Thompson has given reasons for urban youthfulness in Virginia:

Areas of rapid population increase are dependent upon *inward migration* in addition to natural increase. Such migrations are selective with respect to age, since rapidly expanding areas are those with opportunities for employment. Such opportunities attract young adults in substantial numbers. As these young people settle in the new communities, new families are established and more children are born. These changes, in turn, enlarge the need and demand for schools, public utilities, residential construction, and the like. The areas of slow growth, stationary, or declining population are those in which the opportunities for employment have not

---

[31] Official voter registration records, 1960.
[32] Richmond *Afro-American,* July 9, 1966.

expanded sufficiently to absorb the young people coming into the labor force as they complete their education. The result is outward migration.[33]

Statistics offer confirmation. Rural areas in southside and southwest Virginia suffered most from the disproportionate exodus of the young. In the southside's Brunswick County, for instance, 1,687 persons from twenty to twenty-four years of age in the 1950 population became by 1960 a mere 988 adults in their early thirties. Dickenson County in southwest Virginia experienced similar attrition. Only 1,150 remained in 1960 of the 1,834 youngsters in their early twenties in 1950. Conversely, urban and suburban areas registered large population increases of young adults. Suburban Henrico County, for example, counted only 4,333 citizens in their early twenties in 1950. A decade later there were 10,390 persons in their early thirties. Rates of increase and decrease in the young adult bracket were much more dramatic than population changes for counties and cities as a whole.[34]

Urban youth, though it could not be called antiorganization, had reason to be disenchanted with state policy in the 1950's. The rapid influx of young families to cities and suburbs created unfilled demands for schools and public services. The Young Turks represented in part an attempt by young, urban legislators to penetrate the organization's high command without undergoing the traditional apprenticeship. The organization for the most part rejected the Turks and elected to continue under an aging rural leadership and the parsimony of pay-as-you-go. Pressures also came from urban youth to modify the state's bottle-only liquor laws to allow local option on liquor by the drink. This move was designed to bring revenue to the state, promote the tourist trade, and bring better eating and entertainment opportunities to Virginia's cities. Rural legislators killed the proposal in committee.[35] The young urbanites felt no blind allegiance to the Democratic party because of its

[33] "Va. Population Changes," p. 2.
[34] U.S. Bureau of the Census, *Population, 1960*, I, 48, *Virginia*, pp. 78, 81, 85.
[35] See Richmond *Times-Dispatch*, Feb. 12–13, 1960.

Civil War role. Byrd and his contemporaries had joined the Democratic party for reasons increasingly irrelevant to new generations of Virginians. The party loyalties of younger Virginians were largely based on the present alignment of the national parties—an alignment quite different from that of Byrd's Reconstruction childhood. The Republican party of 1960 lured young conservatives; the Democratic party appealed to their more liberal contemporaries.[36] The concept of a Byrd Democrat began to appear a confusing anachronism.

[36] Nowhere is this more evident than in Virginia's colleges. At the University of Virginia, for instance, it is the accepted practice for a conservative interested in politics to join the Young Republican Club.

Chapter 7

Metropolitan Dilemmas

A. *Virginia's Washington Suburbs*

T HE Byrd organization was always weakest in the counties adjacent to the District of Columbia. By 1950 these suburbs were beyond Byrd's influence, and for the next fifteen years the ties that bound were few and far between.

For three and one-half decades, from 1930 to 1965, Virginia's Washington suburbs were the most rapidly growing section of the state. During the 1950's, for example, the four main localities which comprised the area—Fairfax and Arlington counties and the cities of Alexandria and Falls Church—grew by more than 236,000 in population, averaging a 78 per cent increase, four times the rate of the state as a whole.[1] The growth of these suburbs stemmed from the phenomenal federal expansion that began in the mid-thirties with the New Deal, continued through World War II, and accelerated again with the war in Korea. By 1950 governmental activities, both civilian and military, accounted for approximately 40 per cent of the area's employment. Although federal employment leveled off after the Korean War, population in the Virginia suburbs of Washington continued to boom. The greatest job expansion now came in service industries (wholesale and retail trade, business and personal services, finance, and construction), indicating that the area was deficient in these activities after the boom of basic governmental employment in the thirties and forties.[2]

[1] Holm, "Va. Grows Metropolitan," p. 2.   [2] *Ibid.*, p. 3.

The Virginia suburbs of Washington enjoyed the most comfortable and sophisticated standard of living in the state. In 1960 median family income for the Tenth Congressional District (which the Washington suburbs comprised) was $8,392 —over $2,000 above any other district in the state.[3] Rural farm population had practically disappeared by 1950, and the percentage of persons employed in white-collar occupations in 1960 was twenty points higher than the next most prosperous section of Virginia. Unemployment was negligible.[4]

These flourishing suburbs of northern Virginia quickly assumed a progressive attitude toward public services. The adult population boasted the most extensive educational background in Virginia, and over 90 per cent of the 14- to 17-year-olds of the area were enrolled in school, compared to a statewide percentage of 81.[5] Teacher salaries in Arlington and Falls Church in 1960 exceeded $6,000, and those in Alexandria and Fairfax were well over $5,000.[6] The state capital of Richmond was the only other place in Virginia where salaries actually reached the $5,000 mark.

The northern Virginia suburbs met the challenge of better public services on their own. Arlington was one of the two counties in Virginia which refused to let the state government take care of its system of secondary highways. It kept the administration of its road financing in its own hands, "fearing," said one observer, "that some funds could be taken away from what it considers as its rightful share in the distribution of available funds for highways" if it participated in state road programs.[7] The superior school system in northern Virginia owed nothing to any generosity of the Byrd organization.

[3] *Congressional District Data Book (88th Congress)*, p. 513.

[4] *Ibid.*, p. 514. The Tenth District had 68.3 per cent of its working force employed in white-collar occupations, the 3rd, 48.4 per cent, with the state average 40.4 per cent.

[5] U.S. Bureau of the Census, *Population, 1960*, I, 48, *Virginia*, pp. 141–43.

[6] Virginia Commission on Public Education, *Virginia Schools in the Space Age—A Continued Evaluation of the Curriculum, Teacher Training, and Related Matters* (Richmond: Department of Purchases and Supply, 1961), pp. 67–70.

[7] Gottmann, p. 481.

While striving to respond to the strain which population growth placed on public education, many Virginians in this area had lost patience with the parsimonious platitudes of the Byrds.

Virginia's Washington suburbs were generally in no mood to tolerate massive resistance. Negroes comprised a mere 6 per cent of the area's population by 1960, and few citizens saw the sense in closing schools to avoid token integration. Although Arlington, the first locality in northern Virginia to face imminent integration, had a vocal segregationist minority, the clear majority of its citizens backed the Arlington Committee to Preserve Public Schools and worked to spread the movement through the state.[8] Arlington and Norfolk, moreover, were the first Virginia localities to integrate public schools, and each did so without violence.

Although these Washingtonian-Virginians differed with the Byrd organization on questions of public services and massive resistance, these issues were not the primary source of conflict. Differences between the organization and northern Virginia ran much deeper. A tacit feeling persisted on both sides that the Washington suburbs lying within Virginia's borders were not really part of the Old Dominion or its culture and traditions. Arlington, and to a slightly lesser extent Fairfax, Falls Church, and Alexandria, belonged functionally and economically to the nation's capital far more than to Virginia. The National Airport, the famous National Cemetery, many military establishments, and the whole complicated hub of highways by which Washington communicates with the area south of the Potomac are in Arlington. Several square miles of its territory are directly managed by federal authorities. The residents of Arlington and Fairfax patronize the stores of downtown Washington.[9] Federal employment stimulated the area's rapid growth and has been primarily responsible for its high standard of living. Powerful economic and geographical factors separate the Tenth District from the rest of the state.

No more than one-third of the residents of the northern

[8] Muse, *Massive Resistance*, p. 88.   [9] See Gottmann, p. 480.

Virginia suburbs in 1960 were natives of the state. Only one-quarter of Arlington's total 1960 population was born in Virginia, and but 35 per cent of Fairfax County was "native-son." This contrasted sharply with the state as a whole, where 70 per cent of the population was native Virginian.[10] Harry Byrd appealed to much of the Old Dominion as the quintessence of the Virginia gentleman with blue-blood ancestry, impeccable integrity, refined manners, and an almost mystic identification with Virginia's past. Virginia, wrote one reporter, was a government "of the gentry, by the gentry, and for the gentry," [11] while another noted the Byrd organization had "faithfully and honestly represented the needs, the aspirations, and the prejudices of that small aristocracy of farmers and businessmen who, as the 'best people' have controlled the destinies of Virginia since Colonial times." [12] The "Old Virginia" appeal diminished sharply in the Washington suburbs, however. Northern Virginians lacked no admiration for gentlemen, but they were not awed by Byrd's aristocratic descent. People in Arlington and Fairfax who had no ancestral ties in Virginia, who came to the state as adults, and who held jobs outside Virginia in downtown Washington, were naturally more immune to the "mystique of the Virginia gentleman" and the uniquely "Virginian" aura which surrounded Harry Byrd.

In the same way many "old" Virginians disdained the newcomers who inhabited the northern Virginia suburbs.[13] Marshall Fishwick, a student of the commonwealth's mind and culture, caught this attitude when he constructed a typical conversation with that most Virginian of all Virginians—the Virginia Lady:

"Next you'll lambast the Byrd machine" [the Lady remarks to her guest]. "There isn't a state in the Union as basically satisfied

[10] U.S. Bureau of the Census, *Population, 1960,* I, 48, *Virginia,* pp. 141–43.
[11] Richard Cope, "The Frustration of Harry Byrd," *Reporter,* Nov. 21, 1950, p. 23.
[12] Phillips, "New Rumblings," June 19, 1949, p. 10.
[13] At times, the disdain was not discreet. Delegate Frank Moncure of Stafford County once branded the Washingtonian Virginians "a bunch of crackpots and pinks" (Washington *Post,* June 14, 1957).

with the way it's being run as Virginia. Don't all the country people like Mr. Byrd?"

"Yes, but the cities don't. Up around Arlington—"

"That's not Virginia. Virginia starts at Fredericksburg. We ought to lop off those northern counties and give them to the Yankee bureaucrats who live there. People in the real cities, like Richmond and Danville and Petersburg—the ones that amounted to something in General Lee's day—are very content with Mr. Byrd. And so am I." [14]

The Byrd organization was not much more interested in the growth of "those northern counties" than the Virginia Lady. In 1952 Virginia created a new congressional district—the Tenth —to accommodate the rapidly expanding population of the Washington suburbs. Yet the organization's hierarchy was never hospitable to the idea that this new arrival ought to have any real say in state policy. Its apportionment of the state legislature seriously slighted the Tenth District. This fastest-growing part of the commonwealth by 1956 had at least four fewer representatives in the General Assembly than any of Virginia's nine other congressional districts.[15] Delegates from the Washington suburbs were generally the most anti-Byrd in the legislature. The only Tenth District representatives who had any strong attachment to the Byrd organization were Delegate James Thomson of Alexandria, brother-in-law of Harry Byrd, Jr., and state Senator Charles Fenwick of Arlington, who came to the Senate in 1948 and remained as a respected member of the organization's more progressive wing. Most other Tenth District legislators—Armistead Boothe, Kathryn Stone, Omer Hirst, John Webb, and John Donovan—often fought the organization as a hopeless but high-spirited minority.[16]

Another factor made traditional political practices in the Old Dominion seem absurd to many Washingtonian-Virginians. Many of the migrants to the area carried with them the politi-

[14] Marshall W. Fishwick, *Virginia: A New Look at the Old Dominion* (New York: Harper and Brothers, 1959), p. 259.

[15] See Appendix V.

[16] See Gates for an account of the minority role which Tenth District delegates often played in the massive resistance era.

cal party identification of their former states. This party identification generally approximated the views and platforms of the
national parties far more closely than it did party alignments in
Virginia. These out-of-staters transplanted to the Washington
suburbs a reasonably competitive, nationally oriented two-
party system alien to the conservative Democrats of the Byrd
organization. For many northern Virginians, the one-party politics of a southern state and Senator Byrd's golden silences
seemed so much nonsense. In the Washington suburbs liberals
voted heavily in Democratic primaries for any opponent of the
Byrd organization, while many conservatives waited until November to lend their ballots to a strong Republican challenge.[17]
As early as the Democratic primary of 1949 the organization's
John Battle was roundly defeated in the Washington suburbs
by Francis Pickens Miller, and Byrd, a landslide statewide
winner in the 1952 Democratic primary, carried only 52 per
cent of the Tenth District vote. In every major statewide race
from 1953 through the summer of 1966 the Byrd organization
fell considerably short of a majority in Virginia's Washington
suburbs. The Tenth District was the only section in Virginia to
grant Republican Ted Dalton a majority in his race against
Almond in 1957. The organization's standing reached its lowest
ebb when Albertis Harrison barely managed to collect one-
third of the Tenth District vote in the Democratic primary of
1961.

The Virginia Democrats of the Byrd organization grew even
more disturbed as the cancer of Washington's suburban growth
spilled beyond Arlington, Fairfax, Alexandria, and Falls
Church into the next tier of counties. These four counties of the
northern Piedmont (Clarke, Fauquier, Loudoun, and Prince
William) traditionally gave the Byrd organization some of its
most luxurious majorities. During the fifties, however, suburban expansion doubled Prince William's population and caused

[17] The party breakdown in the Washington suburbs has been described as
follows: 30 per cent Democratic (¾ newcomers, ¼ old Virginians), 20 per cent
Republican (¾ newcomers, ⅓ old Virginians), and 50 per cent independents.
The independents "vote 'em as they see 'em and their votes cannot be
'delivered'" (Washington *Post*, June 14, 1957).

Table 14   Byrd Organization in Northern Piedmont
(Prince William, Loudoun, Fauquier, Clarke Counties)

Year	Office	Organization candidate	Vote in northern Piedmont
			%
1945 P	Governor	Tuck	85.7
1946 P	Senator	Byrd	83.3
1952 P	Senator	Byrd	80.6
1953	Governor	Stanley	74.6
1957	Governor	Almond	72.4
1961 P	Governor	Harrison	63.5
1966 P	Senator	Byrd, Jr.	59.4

P A primary.

significant rates of growth in Loudoun, Fauquier, and Clarke. By 1965 the northern Piedmont had become the most rapidly growing region of the state, increasing its population by 30 per cent since 1960.[18] This growth slowly undermined the organization's strength. The factors which neutralized Senator Byrd in the immediate Washington suburbs began to operate in the northern Piedmont, though with greatly diminished intensity. Table 14 records the gradual erosion of organization strength in the area.

B. Richmond

One-hundred miles and forever separated Richmond, Virginia, from the Washington suburbs. For the Byrd organization the capital of the old Confederacy beamed a warm light, softening somewhat the disappointments of the Tenth District. Yet as the years progressed, problems arose which strained, though never snapped, the bonds between the Richmond community and Senator Byrd.

[18] Bureau of Population and Economic Research, University of Virginia, *Estimates of the Population of the Counties and Cities of Virginia as of July 1, 1965* (Charlottesville, 1966), p. 6.

Congressman Howard W. Smith, 1965

Governor Mills E. Godwin, Jr., 1966

Richmond in 1950 appeared a bustling manufacturing center, with chemicals, paper, food, and metal products in its output. It was the "cigarette capital of the world," where all major brands, save Camels, were produced.[19] It has been claimed by Chamber of Commerce enthusiasts that the cigarettes made in Richmond each year, if placed end to end, would reach to the moon and back 11 times, or encircle the earth 200 times.[20] Richmond was the financial hub of Virginia as well as its main trade and shopping center. Its attractive downtown section lured shoppers from Charlottesville, Lynchburg, Norfolk, Danville, and even Washington.[21] Population in Richmond and the surrounding suburban counties of Henrico and Chesterfield pushed forward at healthy increases of 25 per cent during both the forties and fifties, and by 1960 the metropolitan area included the cities of Hopewell and Petersburg and was rapidly penetrating the counties of Hanover, Charles City, Prince George, Dinwiddie, and Powhatan.[22] Although not so prosperous as the Washington suburbs, income and educational studies showed Richmond and its outlying counties the second most comfortably situated section of the state, enjoying to the full most conveniences of modern, urban life.[23]

But Richmond's heart was in the past. Behind its industry and trade lay a "land of gracious living" where the old manners and the old leisure still remained. Symbols of its golden age graced the streets, as in stately leaf-laced Monument Avenue where equestrian statues of Confederate greats still stalked the land. In central Richmond stood the state Capitol, designed by Thomas Jefferson, the White House of the Confederacy, and the homes of John Marshall and Edgar Allan Poe. Fashionable clubs, small, pillared houses, and antebellum grace existed beside a restless suburban and industrial sprawl.

Harry Byrd appealed strongly to Richmond's love of the past. One day his statue may mingle with those of Lee and

[19] Gottmann, p. 487.

[20] See J. J. Kilpatrick (ed.), "Public Office in Richmond, Virginia, 1900–1964" (MS at offices, Richmond *News Leader*), p. 129.

[21] Gottmann, p. 487.   [22] See Holm, "Va. Grows Metropolitan," pp. 2–4.

[23] See U.S. Bureau of the Census, *Population, 1960*, I, 48, *Virginia*, pp. 141–45; *Congressional District Data Book* (*88th Congress*), pp. 511–20.

Washington; his name will always evoke the respect which Richmonders hold for integrity, sincerity, and gentlemanly deportment. The white community in the Richmond area was one of the most conservative in the state and admired the Senator as a national champion of the conservative cause. Yet the Byrd organization clashed with Richmond's more progressive phase and seriously endangered its standing.

Richmond's efforts at municipal reform gave the most substantial evidence of the city's progressive impulse. Ostensibly divorced from the larger arena of state politics, these efforts nonetheless had indirect impact there. In the late thirties Richmond suffered from an antiquated, bicameral council-mayor form of government. A twenty-man Common Council and twelve-member Board of Aldermen argued needed ordinances for seemingly interminable lengths of time.[24] Each of the two bodies was burdened with powerful committees which prevented important bills from ever reaching the floor. Appropriations in excess of $100 required the approval of two-thirds of the aldermen. The entire process was fettered by the worst features of logrolling and ward politics. If, by some miracle, a controversial measure ever cleared the Council, it still faced the veto of the mayor, who was elected every two years by the city at large.

Richmond, even more than Virginia, deserved Key's designation of "political museum piece." As late as 1937 many streets in the heart of the city were still paved with rough, old-fashioned cobblestone. The Council had been considering since 1918 what improvements should be made in the city's collapsing jails, yet no steps had been taken. It required tremendous public pressure in the mid-thirties to push through the Council an ordinance for a public library, though there had long been widespread demand for one.[25] Soon all agreed that the situation was intolerable.

[24] The ensuing description of the bicameral council-mayor government is taken from *Why the Richmond Chamber of Commerce Favors the City Manager Plan for Richmond* (Richmond, 1947) and Richmond *Times-Dispatch*, Jan. 24, 1937.

[25] Richmond *Times-Dispatch*, Jan. 24, 1937.

Efforts to change Richmond's form of government came to a head in the formation of the Richmond Citizens' Association (RCA) in the summer of 1946.[26] The organization consisted at that time of approximately two thousand members, a majority of them middle- to upper-middle-class people who lived in Richmond's large and prosperous West End. In the next two years RCA won a series of political victories which brought change to Richmond's old form of government and gave the city new and more progressive governmental machinery. A new charter provided a unicameral City Council of nine non-partisan members, all of whom faced election every two years from the entire city. The nine councilmen selected from their number a mayor, whose functions were chiefly ceremonial. While the Council framed broad policy directives, a professional city manager, appointed by the Council and responsible to it, directed the administration of the government and appointed heads of the city's various departments.

Advocates of the new charter hoped it would give Richmond streamlined and responsive government, and for a while these hopes were apparently realized. In the five years following the adoption of the new charter, the staid old capital awakened to its responsibilities in a new age. Expenditures for public improvements from 1948 to 1953 came to $25,000,000—a sum greater than the city had appropriated for public projects during the past eighteen years. The Council authorized the construction of miles of improved streets, and buses replaced Richmond's outmoded streetcars. A modern $1,000,000 airport terminal and a $2,000,000 water purification plant were constructed. The Ninth Street Bridge was repaired at a cost of nearly $85,000, and the seating capacity of the City Stadium was doubled. School construction progressed rapidly. Natural gas was installed for cooking and heating in Richmond homes at an initial saving of nearly 25 per cent to customers of the city-owned gas utilities.[27] The Richmond Citizens' Association presided over the spirit of reform and selected able candidates for municipal elections.

The reformist momentum subsided after 1953, however, and

[26] See *ibid.*, Nov. 6, 1946.   [27] Richmond *Times-Dispatch*, June 20, 1953.

the once-spirited association became complacent, confused, and even the target of corruption charges. By 1962 petty feuding in the Council had replaced devotion to municipal progress. In 1963–64, however, reform efforts were renewed by an organization named Richmond Forward. The new group exemplified the principles and ideals of the original Richmond Citizens' Association. The New York *Times* praised Richmond Forward as a "managerial uprising," a movement whose "candidates were bankers, manufacturing executives, and stock brokers—representatives of Richmond's 'downtown crowd' of business leaders." [28] At its first general meeting on November 26, 1963, Richmond Forward resolved "to do something about Richmond's lack of progress through positive action at City Hall" and stated its intention "to elect a Council of excellently qualified people who are determined to run the affairs of Richmond on a businesslike basis." [29] The Richmond Forward slate featured prominent businessmen, such as James C. Wheat, Jr., senior partner in the J. C. Wheat & Co. securities firm, but a definition of the group as business-controlled would be far too narrow. Richmond Forward candidates also included "Sonny" Cephas, a Negro real estate dealer, and Eleanor Sheppard, former RCA regular who helped stimulate the women's efforts which played a vital role in the RF movement.

As the summer of 1964 approached, Richmond Forward, encouraged by business and civic leaders but with powerful appeals to Negroes, housewives, and citizen reformers, closed ranks against the incumbent Council. Critical of the "personal bickering, petty politics, and negative thinking" of the present Council, Richmond Forward pledged to relieve traffic congestion by financing the construction of a system of expressways, to take all necessary steps to improve Richmond's public school system, to develop a technical-vocational school program, to build a modern sports coliseum, and to improve public housing, parks, and industrial development.[30] In a hard-fought election, Richmond Forward gained six of the nine council seats. A

[28] June 11, 1964.
[29] Kilpatrick (ed.), "Public Office in Richmond, Virginia, 1900–1964," p. 83.
[30] Richmond *Times-Dispatch*, April 15, 1964.

record 30,900 persons voted in what Newman Hamblet, department store executive and early initiator of RF, termed "Richmond's greatest community victory." [31]

Richmond's municipal reform movements reflected in even the most conservative urban area a progressivism which far outstripped state government under the Byrd organization. The emphasis on public improvements at the municipal level eventually pushed candidates for statewide office into more positive programs. The gap between standstill state government and dynamic municipalities became ever more embarrassing until, by 1965, even the Byrd organization was ready to take a progressive stand.

Municipal politics and the Richmond reform movement had their most profound consequences outside the city's white, conservative establishment. The Richmond press and the business and professional community, the two most powerful elements in the reform movement, had too much in common with the Byrd organization to forsake it permanently. They stayed within the organization to exercise a restraining influence, as in massive resistance, or to urge a more progressive policy in the area of public services. Voting in Richmond's Precinct 32 reflected the typical attitude. The precinct lay in the middle of Richmond's prosperous West End and included the fashionable Windsor Farms area. A bastion of genteel but strict conservatism, Precinct 32 granted the organization's Albertis S. Harrison 90 per cent support in the hotly contested 1961 gubernatorial primary. Here Barry Goldwater defeated Lyndon Johnson 1066 to 173 in the 1964 presidential election.[32] Yet this conservative, Byrd-oriented precinct also initiated and overwhelmingly supported progressive, public-service-minded municipal reform slates and served as the home and enthusiastic backer of FitzGerald Bemiss, the moderate state senator who frequently gained Negro support in elections and who opposed

[31] Richmond *News Leader,* June 10, 1964.

[32] See J. J. Kilpatrick (ed.), "The Precinct Book: Voting in Richmond and Henrico County Precincts" (MS at offices of Richmond *News Leader*), for details on voting patterns of Precinct 32 and others in Richmond and Henrico County.

extreme organization policies in the legislature. This precinct typified the city's split progressive-conservative personality, and its residents represented the attitudes of the Byrd organization's more moderate wing.

The Richmond Negro took a very different view. During the fifties the city's Negro population increased from 32 to 42 per cent, and since then it has climbed so rapidly that, barring annexation of surrounding territory, it will top 50 per cent before 1970.[33] In 1958, at the apex of massive resistance, a group labeled Crusade for Voters determined to organize and increase the Richmond Negro's participation at all levels of politics. The Crusade, as the organization was familiarly called, was to enjoy a greater longevity than massive resistance. It plagued the old Byrd organization incessantly and served as a reminder that the organization which had managed to blunt or neutralize the Negro and other potentially hostile segments of the Virginia electorate before massive resistance faced powerful and deep-seated resentment afterward.

The Crusade has been described as a "firm, responsible and sophisticated Negro leadership which speaks softly and carries a big stick of political . . . power by commanding support of the Negro community." [34] It has been guided by its chairman, Dr. William S. Thornton, the head of its Research Committee, Dr. Franklin Gayles, a small, articulate hierarchy of Negro business and professional men, and faculty members of Virginia Union University. Closely linked to the NAACP, the Crusade advocated due-process advancement for the Negro race. After interviewing candidates and scrutinizing their political backgrounds, Thornton, Gayles, and their six comrades on the Executive Committee urged the support of those candidates they thought most helpful to the Negro cause. Public announcement of the Crusade's endorsement was traditionally withheld until the Sunday before election, when Negro ministers informed their congregations of the Crusade's decision.[35] The Crusade also stamped its choices on thousands of sample

[33] Kilpatrick (ed.), "Public Office in Richmond," p. 130.
[34] Washington *Post,* July 29, 1962.
[35] Richmond *Times-Dispatch,* July 17, 1965.

ballots which scores of poll workers distributed each election day at every Negro precinct.[36] Between elections the Crusade stimulated political interest through voter registration drives, political education meetings at Slaughter's Hotel, and the pronouncements of the weekly Richmond Negro newspaper, the *Afro-American.*

Table 15   Negro Voting Registration in Richmond, Norfolk, and the State (1957–1964)

	Negro registrations		
Date	Virginia	Richmond	Norfolk
1957	89,146	12,486	10,221
1958 *	91,757	12,346	9,888
1959	94,255	15,364	10,873
1960	100,424	15,641	11,486
1961	105,471	16,396	11,886
1962	110,953	17,355	11,945
1963	108,313	17,335	10,085
1964 (April) †	117,031	18,161	10,071
1964 (Oct.)	173,832 ‡	29,927	15,801

Source: State Board of Elections, official voter registration lists.
* Formation of Crusade for Voters.
† Repeal of poll tax for federal elections, January 1964.
‡ Includes those registered for federal elections only.

After its inception in 1958 Crusade for Voters enjoyed an astounding success. Its candidates encountered varying fates at the polls, but the group clearly established itself as the dominant political influence in the increasingly powerful Richmond Negro community. The steep increase in Negro voter registration was only a partial criterion of the success of the Crusade's efforts. Table 15 shows a gradual upturn in Negro voters until 1964, when repeal of the poll tax for federal elections and the terror of Barry Goldwater's candidacy caused an even sharper increase in Negro registration. Norfolk, the city with the second largest concentration of Negro voters in the state, remained considerably behind Richmond during this period.

[36] Richmond *Afro-American,* July 8, 1961.

The Negro in Richmond left his imprint on municipal politics long before the Byrd organization deigned to notice him. In the city his vote counted, but in statewide elections the Negro still played a negligible role. The Negro vote in Richmond rose steadily, until by 1966 it constituted approximately 42 per cent of the total vote cast in the city's Council elections. But more important, Negroes sought and occasionally won seats on the Richmond City Council. As early as 1948 Oliver W. Hill won election to the Council, and in 1964 a second Negro, B. A. Cephas, won a Council seat by finishing second in a field of twenty-one. Three Negroes won Council seats by comfortable margins in the 1966 elections. But while elective offices were opened to Negroes on the municipal level, the doors to the state legislature and the inner councils of the Byrd organization remained shut.

Cooperation and communication between white and Negro were far easier in an urban environment such as Richmond than on the state level. Hill was twice endorsed by the Richmond Citizens' Association, and Richmond Forward took care to include a Negro (Cephas) on its slate in 1964. It endorsed two Negroes, Cephas and Winfred Mundle, in 1966. These endorsements represented an appeal to expanding Negro influence, and the Negro community was not unresponsive. The Crusade for Voters in 1964 endorsed five Richmond Forward candidates and all of them won.[37] Negroes and the business and professional leadership of Richmond Forward have disagreed quite sharply on several issues since the 1964 elections,[38] but the white and Negro leaders of the city did form loose alliances in municipal politics before similar coalitions were feasible at the state level.[39] It is impossible to estimate how much effect the cooperation, or at least respect, between the Negro and white leaders in Richmond had in paving the way for the

[37] Richmond *Times-Dispatch*, June 8, 1964.

[38] Sharpest disagreement centered on the length of councilmanic terms, annexation problems, and the proposed route of a new expressway (Richmond *Times-Dispatch*, June–Nov. 1966).

[39] Negroes had occasionally supported the Byrd organization before the massive resistance era, but the Negro never obtained the respect in state affairs which he did in municipal politics.

remarkable coalition Mills Godwin constructed in his 1965 gubernatorial campaign. Certainly the Byrd organization's traditional disdain for appealing to Negro support was lessened in 1965 by the fact that its local arm in West End Richmond had tried to incorporate the Negro into the Richmond Forward movement a year earlier.

The Crusade's influence in the Negro political community did not go unquestioned or unchallenged. A rival Negro political group, Voter's Voice, accused the Crusade in the 1964 municipal election of "working hand-in-glove with Richmond Forward" to defeat all opposition.[40] The Crusade responded to this and to the challenges of political splinter groups by emphasizing the need for Negro political solidarity. "We say there is an effort to split our vote because in the past, we have been too successful and Negroes are fast becoming a political influence in the city of Richmond," the Crusade claimed. "In the long run our solid vote is more important to us than any candidate. If we make a mistake in selecting a candidate, we can vote him out of office in the next election, but if we allow misinformed persons or slick politicians to split our solidarity we will turn the clock back fifty years for the Negroes in Richmond." [41] The Negro press echoed this refrain. "The [1966 Council] election," wrote the Richmond *Afro-American,* "also provided a victory for the Crusade for Voters which, thank God, remained the solidifying force in our community, despite sinister efforts from inside and out to splinter our vote and destroy the Crusade which had five of its seven candidates to emerge as winners." [42]

Obviously the Crusade wished to smother any rival Negro political organization, but solidarity was far more than a mere political maneuver. The Negro was replacing even southside Virginia as the most monolithic voting bloc in Virginia politics. Precinct 64, for example, a bellwether of Richmond's Negro political strength, heavily supported Crusade-endorsed candidates. In the critical 1961 gubernatorial primary A. E. S. Stephens, who ran an antiorganization campaign, defeated Harri-

[40] Richmond *Times-Dispatch,* June 12, 1964.
[41] *Ibid.,* June 8, 1964.   [42] June 25, 1966.

son in this precinct 438 to 53, and Lyndon Johnson polled 1,770 votes to Barry Goldwater's 6 in 1964.[43] Negro voting strength was more fragmented in the multicandidate races for City Council and the state legislature than in head-on battles between two candidates for statewide office. In the latter, Negroes generally followed the Crusade endorsement with 90 per cent support. In a multicandidate field many Negroes still leaned to the Crusade's endorsements, but others voted only for Negro candidates (ignoring any white, Crusade-backed ones), followed Negro splinter group endorsements, or marked a familiar name which had not received Crusade support (see Appendix VIII).

By 1967 the Crusade had not endorsed a Byrd candidate in a statewide Democratic primary, but it was turning more and more to Democrats in the November elections. It continued to endorse Republicans when the Democrat appeared particularly unwelcome (i.e., Harry F. Byrd, Jr.), but since the Goldwater candidacy, the Crusade moved farther toward the Democratic camp. It endorsed five Democrats and only one Republican (a Negro) for the state legislative race in 1965.[44] This leaning may be quite temporary, however, for the Crusade's endorsements are historically independent of party affiliation.

The rapid expansion of a tightly organized Negro vote unquestionably constituted the greatest single hazard to the Byrd organization in the Richmond area. While opponents of the organization solidified their strength, the prosperous, stanchly conservative suburbs of Richmond in Henrico and Chesterfield counties increasingly split their vote between conservatives of various political parties. The Republican party carried votes which before went to Byrd Democrats, and the arrival of the Conservative party in 1965 further fragmented conservative strength. The Republican gains resulted partly from the party's more conservative national image, the increasingly liberal hue of the national Democratic party, and the efforts of young, attractive Republican candidates for state office who appealed

[43] Kilpatrick (ed.), "Precinct Book," p. 74.
[44] Richmond *News Leader*, Nov. 1, 1965.

to the many young couples who settled in Henrico and Chesterfield in the fifties. The combined population of these two counties increased by approximately 90 per cent during that decade, and the heaviest gains were among young adults.[45] In 1962 a little known Republican, Dr. Louis H. Williams, defeated veteran Democratic Congressman J. Vaughan Gary in Chesterfield County and nearly carried Henrico. A twenty-six-year-old Goldwater Republican, Richard D. Obenshain, carried Chesterfield and Henrico counties in 1964 against David E. Satterfield, a conservative Democrat, and Edward E. Haddock, a liberal independent. In the gubernatorial race of 1965 Republican Linwood Holton beat Mills E. Godwin, the Democratic nominee, in both Henrico and Chesterfield but he ran behind the Conservative party candidate in the latter county. Henrico and Chesterfield were united in a conservative point of view, but dangerously splintered in party preference.

The old Byrd organization had cause for concern. Yet the Confederate capital was too conservative ever to let the Byrd organization completely down so long as the organization represented the most reliable conservative force in Virginia politics. And until the mid-sixties there was little doubt that it did.

C. Hampton Roads

Hampton Roads was Virginia's largest and liveliest metropolitan complex, accounting in 1960 for 20 per cent of the state's population. The estuary of the James River divided it into the two smaller areas of Newport News–Hampton and Norfolk–Portsmouth, and more than 70 per cent of the population lived in the latter.[46]

"Norfolk's makeup," wrote Guy Friddell, "is a blend of N's—Navy, NATO, natives, and new-comers, especially North Caro-

[45] U.S. Bureau of the Census, *Population, 1960,* I, 48, *Virginia,* pp. 28, 80, 85.
[46] Holm, "Va. Grows Metropolitan," p. 4.

linians—but it operates largely on nerve." A city with its share
of aristocrats and more than its share of parvenues, Norfolk
was simultaneously part of Virginia, North Carolina, Washington, and the world. "It is a city of shopping centers," continues
Friddell,

one merging into another, sometimes so vast that when thoroughfares intersect the motorist knows the eerie sensation of knowing no
street boundaries, simply cruising an unlimited asphalt bay, in
which he could just as easily be going any one of four ways. Some
find the scene sterile, but riding through the jumping, jittery neon
night by bold, flamboyant signs of weird off-color colors of red,
green, and orange is like driving through a three-dimensional Stuart
Davis painting.[47]

Norfolk got its motion from the ocean. Its metropolitan area
in 1960 listed over 35 per cent of its population as having
moved into their homes after 1958. Only the Washington suburbs had grown more quickly than Hampton Roads. Norfolk-
Portsmouth registered a 72 per cent population increase from
1940 to 1950 and a 30 per cent increase the following decade,
while Newport News–Hampton recorded 66 and 45 per cent
gains for the same two periods.[48] The slower growth during the
1950's reflected the declining employment opportunities of
those years. Over 40 per cent of Norfolk-Portsmouth's labor
force obtained its livelihood either as military or civilian employees at the area's military installations. Here was the nation's largest naval concentration, scattered throughout the
area but with two large blocks at the Naval Shipyard at Portsmouth and the Naval Base and Air Station at Norfolk.[49] After
World War II and the Korean War, naval activity slowed
somewhat, and population growth consequently diminished.
Hampton Roads was also a great commercial port, and it was a
large exporter of coal. Its growth was further hurt in the mid-
fifties because of the slackening world demand for this com-

[47] Pages 44, 45.
[48] U.S. Bureau of the Census, *Population, 1960*, I, 48, *Virginia*, p. 139.
[49] Holm, "Va. Grows Metropolitan," pp. 2, 4, 5.

modity.[50] The area's economy climbed slowly in the late fifties, however, and port activities, manufacturing, tourism, and the redevelopment of downtown Norfolk with a strong invitation to new industry forecast a healthy economy even when employment in the naval installations declined. "If the Navy left," observers used to say, "Norfolk would sink." [51] By 1960 such a calamity appeared to be less and less a possibility.

Although Hampton Roads was not a wealthy area,[52] it was, by Virginia standards, both cosmopolitan and avant-garde. Hampton Roads and Norfolk showed a verve and willingness to experiment which was quite "un-Virginian." "A handful, or even a loner," said Friddell, "will launch an idea, while others watch, smiling, the quixotic quest, and if it succeeds, as it generally does, smile at themselves for having smiled at its chances." [53] Before 1920 Norfolk abandoned a ward system for a city-manager form of government, but immediately after World War II Norfolk found itself a "sailor town," and "hot bed" city with its streets falling into disrepair and corruption and prostitution running rampant. Angered by the American Hygiene Association's designation of Norfolk as one of the most demoralized centers in the world, the city's blue bloods and community leaders carried a reform crusade into the 1946 Council race and won. During the next four years the reformers brought in a new city manager and improved the town's housing, streets, waterworks, and zoning codes.[54] In 1949 the Council appropriated $25,000 to study the slums, and Norfolk was ready to become the first city to execute a loan and grant under the Housing Act of 1949. Soon Norfolk became a model of urban renewal. The momentum of the cleanup of the postwar years was maintained, and Norfolk in 1964 became the first Virginia locality to enact its own sales tax, touching off a chain of similar taxes across the state.[55]

[50] Gottmann, p. 498.   [51] Friddell, p. 43.
[52] Median family incomes, for instance, in 1960 ranked noticeably below Richmond and the Washington suburbs.
[53] Page 44.
[54] Interview with George Kelley, chief political reporter of the Norfolk *Virginian-Pilot*, Jan. 16, 1967.
[55] Friddell, p. 44.

From the 1920's to the 1960's William L. Prieur was the clerk
of the Norfolk court and the organization's kingpin in the city.
Prieur was one of the original Byrd followers; he took over in
the early 1920's from the old-time, iron-fisted boss of Norfolk,
James V. Trehy. Billy Prieur quickly became a member of
Byrd's kitchen cabinet; at one time he was second only to
Combs in influence. "You either worshiped or loathed him,"
said one observer. "There was little middle ground." [56]

For over forty years Prieur augmented his power in the
Norfolk courthouse by doing small favors for constituents, getting people jobs, using to the full his influence on state patronage, and closely supervising the appointive powers of Norfolk's
corporation court judge. When segregationist Fred Duckworth
became mayor of Norfolk in 1950, Prieur introduced him to
Byrd and the three quickly became congenial. Yet Prieur, for
all his efforts, could scarcely control Norfolk, not to mention all
Hampton Roads, and the area slowly slipped away from Byrd's
influence.

Traditionally Prieur and the Norfolk wing of the organization were better able to deliver the vote to Byrd than to lesser
organization candidates. It was to Prieur's credit that the organization was for so long able to muster a respectable showing
in an area which easily might have proved disastrous. If the
organization broke even in Hampton Roads, it could coast to
victory with large margins in central and southside Virginia.
Byrd himself defeated Hutchinson in the 1946 primary and
Miller in the 1952 primary with approximately 55 per cent of
the Norfolk vote. Battle, Stanley, and Harrison were able to
emerge from their toughest elections with about 47 per cent of
the Norfolk ballots. Elsewhere in Hampton Roads the picture
varied. Portsmouth was traditionally stanch antiorganization
territory in Democratic primaries but religiously Democratic in
the general elections. Newport News gave antiorganization
Democrats slim majorities, but Hampton was unpredictable.
The only reliable organization territory in Hampton Roads was
Princess Anne County and the city of Virginia Beach. The

[56] Kelley interview.

political genius of Sidney Kellam maintained them as an organization stronghold.

Hampton Roads trended more and more against the organization after 1950. For a long time the area had all the common urban complaints against the Byrd organization and many special ones besides. If Hampton Roads was not as hostile to the Byrds as the Washington suburbs, it was only because some of its dissatisfactions were less acute. Although it was underrepresented in the General Assembly, it was not so badly underrepresented as were the Washington suburbs.[57] In former Governor Colgate W. Darden (1942–46), Billy Prieur, and Sidney Kellam, Hampton Roads had respected public figures in statewide office and in the organization's upper echelons. But Hampton Road nonetheless grew discontented with the organization, which thereby lost many thousands of votes.

Pay-as-you-go brought little but grief to the residents of this area. The sprawling Hampton Roads complex desperately needed additional bridges, tunnels, and highways faster than pay-as-you-go policies could finance them. And the state constitution virtually prohibited the issuance of state-backed bonds for highway construction.[58] To ameliorate traffic problems in Hampton Roads required a roundabout method of highway financing which cost the residents of the area dearly. Special commissions were authorized by the state to issue revenue bonds for highway, bridge, and tunnel construction. These revenue bonds were paid off by revenue from tolls and did not obligate the commonwealth of Virginia or any of its political subdivisions in any way.[59] Without the benefit of the state's gilt-edged credit rating behind them, the special commissions were forced to issue bonds at unnecessarily high interest rates, and Hampton Roads residents were forced to submit to excessive tolls to pay off the bonds.[60] By 1960 there was no "free" approach to the city of Norfolk except through North Carolina,

[57] See Chapter 2.   [58] See Constitution of Virginia, Sec. 184-a.
[59] See S. J. Makielski, Jr. "State Authorities: Virginia's Governmental Paradox," *University of Virginia News Letter*, July 15, 1965.
[60] The Norfolk *Ledger-Dispatch*, Feb. 17, 1966, gives a crisp account of the difficulties of this type of financing.

and tolls "had become a real factor in the cost of living." [61] As the residents of Hampton Roads had only to gaze a few miles south over the North Carolina border to witness state-backed, toll-free, bond-financed highways, they naturally were incensed at the lack of a similar policy in Virginia.

The most elemental needs of the Hampton Roads area had to be financed in this circuitous manner. The Elizabeth River Tunnel Commission was empowered to issue bonds and collect and fix tolls to construct a tunnel between the cities of Portsmouth and Norfolk.[62] The Chesapeake Bay Bridge and Tunnel Commission operated a toll facility connecting the Virginia mainland with the tip of the Eastern Shore, Accomack and Northampton counties. Most distressing to Hampton Roads citizens, however, were the "package deals" of the Virginia General Assembly. In one such instance the State Highway Commission in the early fifties issued toll revenue bonds totaling $95,000,000 to construct both the Hampton Roads Bridge-Tunnel system connecting the peninsula and Norfolk and a bridge over the Rappahannock River between the more remote locations of Greys Point and White Stone.[63] The residents of Hampton Roads paid the bulk of the tolls required to retire bonds involved in the construction not only of their own bridge but also of a bridge in a less urban and less traveled area. Many Norfolk residents believed that the Rappahannock River Bridge was constructed not to meet traffic volume but to please Senator Robert O. Norris, an elderly power in the Byrd organization whose constituency the bridge was to serve.[64]

Public school policy caused as much trouble for the Byrd organization in Hampton Roads as did highway finance. Of all Virginia localities Norfolk was hardest hit by massive resistance. Its white public school system was closed completely. Massive resistance had begun in Norfolk almost as a joke. People did not believe, in the early fall of 1958, that the schools

[61] Kelley interview.

[62] See Makielski and Virginia State Chamber of Commerce, pp. 63–64, for a description of the highway needs financed by the special commission approach.

[63] Virginia State Chamber of Commerce, p. 64.   [64] Kelley interview.

really would close. Yet they did close, and Muse has recorded the consequences:

Less than 4,500 of the nearly 10,000 displaced pupils in that city [Norfolk] were being accommodated in local private school classes. Approximately 948 pupils had been transferred to the public schools of the contiguous city of South Norfolk; 1,621 had been officially transferred to public or private schools outside the area, and a few others had transferred without requesting transcripts of their records. Between 2,500 and 3,000 Norfolk children were receiving no education or tutoring of any kind.[65]

Norfolk residents have a touching way of reflecting on the crisis which the organization's massive resistance policy inflicted on them. They remember the pupils affected by the public school closings as "The Lost Class of 1959."

No area desired liquor-by-the-drink more than Hampton Roads. The state's bottle-only liquor laws especially hurt a port city such as Norfolk and seriously hampered its night club and restaurant business. The resort town of Virginia Beach also suffered heavily.[66] In many sessions of the General Assembly bills were introduced to provide localities the option of selling whiskey by the drink, but the bills were always pigeonholed. Hampton Roads heartily endorsed the local option measure; the Byrd organization and its rural chieftains did not. The result was an additional source of friction between the organization and Hampton Roads.

Byrd's golden silences in the presidential elections also hurt the organization in Hampton Roads. The area contained progressive and stubbornly Democratic sentiment. Portsmouth, for instance, has handsomely supported the Democratic presidential candidate since 1928. A few lieutenants of the Byrd organization in the Hampton Roads area, e.g., Sidney Kellam, were also ardent Democrats on the national level. Since the whole area's economy was tied to the federal government through the vast employment generated by the U.S. naval

[65] Muse, *Massive Resistance,* p. 111.
[66] See F. R. Blackford, "Sidney Severn Kellam," *Virginia Record,* LXXXVII (March 1965), 8.

installations in Hampton Roads, it was wise to have the national Democratic administration sympathetic with the locality. Byrd's golden silences did little to help, and they did not endear him to the residents of Hampton Roads.

The Negro vote became an increasingly influential factor in the Tidewater's political life. Moses Riddick, a Negro member of the Nansemond County Board of Supervisors, spent the late 1950's and early 1960's organizing chapters of the Virginia Independent Voters League throughout Hampton Roads. This Negro political group claimed to influence some 200,000 Negro voters across the state, but it had its strongest impact in the Tidewater area. There by October 1964 almost 47,000 Negro voters were registered in Norfolk, Portsmouth, Newport News, Hampton, Chesapeake, Virginia Beach, Suffolk, and Nansemond County.[67] The number of registered Negro voters in Hampton Roads practically doubled between 1957 and 1964, though the largest gain came in 1964 as a result of the repeal of the poll tax in federal elections. "Negro registrations in Tidewater now run between 50,000 and 60,000," claimed one informed observer in 1966, "and their effect on political life is simple to explain. Any time the white vote splits and Negroes vote as a block, the Negroes decide who wins the election."[68]

By the mid-sixties a group of liberal Democrats led by Norfolk state Senator Henry Howell began to campaign on a platform of letting Norfolk—and also the state—"out of the Byrd cage."

D. *The Urban Corridor*

"The American megalopolis," the standard textbook is fond of saying, "stretches from Boston to Washington." And so our school children have been led to believe. But the textbooks may one day (in their *n*th revisions) come to change this

---

[67] Official voter registration records, 1957–64.   [68] Kelley interview.

definition to include Virginia. By 1960 the southern tail of megalopolis cut through the Old Dominion in a band of twenty counties and fourteen cities which political scientists have termed the *urban corridor*.[69] The corridor is a meandering strip of the state. It starts at the Washington suburbs, heads south through Fredericksburg and Richmond, and then swerves east to the Tidewater and Hampton Roads (see Map III). Most of Virginia's population growth from 1940 to 1960 took place within this urban corridor, and it was here that Virginia changed from a predominantly rural to an urban state.

The Byrd organization found but little support in the corridor. The policies which had proved such honey on the farm turned to vinegar in the urban household. The frugality of the Byrd organization was obliged to confront the urban demand for "quadrupled" state services. Massive resistance proved a ubiquitous liability. The growing Negro vote, the ethos of municipal reform, the disenchantment of the influx of young urbanites with the "old" Byrd machine, the organization's apportionments and almost exclusively rural hierarchy, growing Republican sentiment in the Richmond and Washington suburbs, resentment at pay-as-you-go, urban support for liquor-by-the-drink, the golden silence of Virginia Democrats—all these were factors which undermined the organization's standing in the urban corridor area.

Residents there inflicted political misery on the Byrd organization at election time, especially in the crucial Democratic primaries, where clear-cut philosophical differences were most apparent. At the very least, Byrd candidates in the Democratic primaries from 1945 to 1966 gained 8 per cent more of the vote outside the corridor than within it, and as the years advanced, the organization's political fortunes within the corridor turned steadily downward (see Table 16).

Even more dismaying than these declining percentages was the growing domination of the corridor over the state's political life. Virginia's electorate was no longer small, white, and predominantly rural. Clear statewide majorities no longer came

[69] See L. A. Thompson, "Recent Population Changes in Virginia," *University of Virginia News Letter*, Feb. 15, 1961, p. 4.

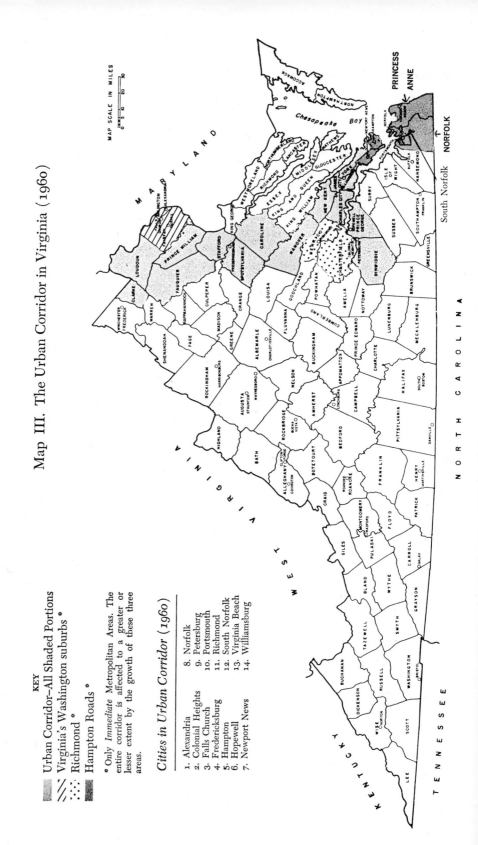

Map III. The Urban Corridor in Virginia (1960)

KEY

Urban Corridor–All Shaded Portions

Virginia's Washington suburbs °

Richmond °

Hampton Roads °

° Only *Immediate* Metropolitan Areas. The entire corridor is affected to a greater or lesser extent by the growth of these three areas.

Cities in Urban Corridor (1960)

1. Alexandria
2. Colonial Heights
3. Falls Church
4. Fredericksburg
5. Hampton
6. Hopewell
7. Newport News
8. Norfolk
9. Petersburg
10. Portsmouth
11. Richmond
12. South Norfolk
13. Virginia Beach
14. Williamsburg

from the small towns, farms, and courthouse counties which had religiously supported the organization from the late 1920's to the 1960's. In 1945 Virginia's urban corridor cast only 43 per cent of the statewide Democratic primary vote. In 1966 it cast almost 60 per cent of the total primary vote (see Table 17). This percentage will apparently increase appreciably in the years ahead.

Table 16   Primary Vote for the Byrd Organization in and out of the Urban Corridor (1945–1966)

Year	Office	Organization candidate	Urban corridor vote	State vote outside corridor
			%	%
1945	Governor	Tuck	62.0	76.2
1946	Senator	Byrd	54.1	70.4
1949	Governor	Battle *	36.7	47.6
1952	Senator	Byrd	58.2	66.4
1961	Governor	Harrison	52.7	61.1
1966	Senator	Byrd Jr.	45.2	59
1966	Senator	Robertson	43.8	59

* Battle's percentages are lower than those of organization men in other elections because he had three opponents, Edwards, Miller, and Arnold.

It was the single greatest irony of Virginia politics that the high command of the old Byrd organization proved political magi in a static rural environment and floundered so hopelessly in a dynamic urban one. That the organization's mighty coped so inflexibly with megalopolis in Virginia cost them dearly. Younger members such as Mills Godwin saw the old boat sinking and wisely hit the lifeboats. Others went down with the ship or grabbed a fragment of the wreckage to keep afloat in their own small domains. But like those on the "invincible Titanic," many in the Byrd organization never saw the iceberg. On one of his climbs up the Blue Ridge, Senator Byrd gazed over the valley below and the hills and mountains afar. "I love those mountains," he said. "I like to look out over the ridges

Table 17   Percentage of Vote Cast by Urban Corridor in Major Democratic Primaries and General Elections (1945–1966)

Year	Office	Vote by Urban Corridor
	Democratic Primary	
		%
1945	Governor	42.8
1946	Senator	42.5
1949	Governor	44.0
1952	Senator	45.2
1961	Governor	52.9
1966	Senator	59.2
	General Elections	
1953	Governor	40.1
1957	Governor	44.0
1965	Governor	49.4

and valleys and watch the changing shadows." [70] In the Virginia of his latter years, something more than the shadows was changing.

[70] Washington *Post,* July 22, 1965.

Chapter 8

The Republican Party

For years the Republican party's struggle in the South was a David and Goliath contest in which the Democratic giant was seldom so much as bruised. Southern Republicans before 1950 wavered, said Key, "between an esoteric cult on the order of a lodge and a conspiracy for plunder in accord with the accepted customs of our politics." [1] The prime goal of these intriguers was to keep the party as weak as possible in the South so that each of the faithful might one day, when the national party won, cut a big slice of the federal pie. Winning local elections might disastrously broaden the party's base, and the story persists of the old-line Virginia Republican who cooled the enthusiasm of a young upstart who wished to build up the party by reminding him that Virginia already had more deserving Republicans than jobs. [2] The patronage mongers encountered a fatal dry spell, however, during the long years of the Roosevelt administration, and the leadership of the party in the South from 1932 to 1948 passed to more respectable businessmen who resented Roosevelt's policies, regarded the local party as an expensive hobby at best, entertained no foolish notions about winning local elections, [3] and were often, in

---

[1] Page 277.   [2] *Ibid.*, p. 292.
[3] Alexander Heard, *A Two-Party South?* (Chapel Hill, N.C.: University of North Carolina Press, 1952), p. 110.

Key's words, "overwhelmed by the futility of it all." [4] Although southern Republicans did enjoy an occasional success, their party's plight in the first half of the twentieth century could be seen only in various shades of hopelessness.

Observers of southern political life asked whether a strong two-party system was a necessary or even a desirable feature of the region's politics. Defenders of the one-party faith (among whom were numbered many prominent southern Democrats) praised the benefits of seniority under the one-party system, extolled the "good government" the Democratic South had enjoyed, and pointed to the Democratic primary as a substitute for the competitive two-party system in the rest of the country. Opposing points of view were fully aired, they claimed, in the rough and tumble of the major party primary.

This constituted little more than a gloss of the problem of the fundamental differences between one-party and two-party political systems. Key has suggested significant differences between the two-party system and one-party factionalism. [5] In the most extreme cases the lack of two-party competition contributed to confused multifactionalism in the primary contests of many southern states. In some southern Democratic primaries as many as eight different candidates entered the lists. In such a free-for-all primary an irrelevant localism and "friends 'n neighbors" vote was accentuated in the election of officials, whereas in a two-party election the geographical distribution of party strength was usually more stable. Without competitive party labels and traditional party policy guideposts, voters had real trouble learning what a candidate espoused. The factions in the Democratic primary were often transitory groupings, trumped up for a particular candidacy, and destined to fade away shortly after the election. The continuity of name, leadership, and following that accompanied an organized political party was often absent.

"Individualistic or disorganized politics," explained Key,

---

[4] Page 293.

[5] Key (pp. 298–311) and Heard (pp. 10–13) form the basis for the following discussion of the general differences between one and two-party systems.

"places a high premium on demagogic qualities of personality that attract voter-attention," whereas "party machinery, in the advancement of leaders, is apt to reject those with rough edges and angular qualities out of preference for more conformist personalities." [6] In the free-for-all of unrestrained factionalism candidates resorted to stunts, spectaculars, mudslinging, and other attention-getting tactics to win. In the one-party factionalism of the South the spellbinder often had the edge.

Once in office the governor of a multifactioned one-party state often had little or no party program to bind him, no need to think of the future welfare of the party, and no guarantee that his legislature was committed to any of his ideas. He gained office not through well-oiled party machinery but through his own personal appeals. No debt of gratitude did he owe the party and never would he need to rely on Democratic unity to fend off challenges of a strong Republican opposition. He was his own man, and the state's course rested on his individual talent and whim.

Of all the southern states, Virginia had most successfully avoided the unhappy consequences of a virtual one-party system. The primary battles between the organization and the core of Plunketts, Hutchinsons, and Millers who persistently challenged the machine resembled, at least vaguely, two-party politics. Both the organization and the opposition appeared year after year and election after election with the same leaders, platforms, and followings. There was localism in the elections, of course, but it was not predominant. There were many examples of home-town boys who ran very poor races in their home towns.[7] Strength between the organization and the oppo-

---

[6] Key, pp. 304–5.

[7] Martin Hutchinson and Francis Pickens Miller, two chief antiorganization leaders, lost their home towns of Richmond and Charlottesville to Byrd in the Democratic senatorial primaries of 1946 and 1952. The most important evidence of the limited influence of localism in Virginia elections, however, is the poor showing of antiorganization candidates in counties immediately surrounding their home county. For example, A. E. S. Stephens, the anti-Byrd candidate in the 1961 Democratic primary, won his home county, Isle of Wight, but lost each of the three contiguous counties of Nansemond, Southampton, and Surry. This would be quite a rarity in the multifactioned southern states.

sition was also geographically distributed, much in the manner of a two-party system.

Virginia did not experience the showmanship and demagoguery that Key suggested a loose one-party factionalism bred. The Old Dominion did not nurture a Huey Long or Gene Talmadge. Governors Darden, Tuck, Battle, Stanley, Almond, Harrison, and Godwin, if of varying degrees of competence, were all gentlemen. Tuck and Almond were certainly colorful, but they were quite different from the demagogues of the deeper South. Most Virginia governors entered office with sympathetic legislatures, distinct platforms, and a commitment to the continuing welfare of the Byrd organization and its principles. Far from being chaotic or discontinuous, Virginia politics for many years was dreary in its continuity.

Why, then, did the commonwealth need a two-party system if its own Democratic party system so closely approximated two-party competition? To begin with, competition between the organization and its opposition was often more apparent than real. Although the antis were never at a loss for words, they frequently were at a loss for money, manpower, and other campaign hardware. They never maintained anything like a continuing and dependable second-party apparatus. To oppose the organization, Miller, Plunkett, and Hutchinson had to put together fleeting coalitions of the disgruntled. If Virginia never suffered from the chaos of one-party factionalism, it did suffer from the lack of a competitor equal to the Byrd organization. There was no powerful political force to urge the organization to a more progressive stand in public services or to force it to bid actively for the support of Negro, labor, and other minority votes.

The growth of the Virginia Republican party gradually encouraged the organization to do all of these previously unthinkable things. It was not the only factor which made the organization step lively, but unquestionably it introduced a ferment into Virginia politics which had not previously existed. Many of the same forces which encouraged the growth of the anti-Byrd elements in the Democratic party also contributed to the development of a stronger and more active Republican party.

Virginia Republicans had never been as weak as their comrades in most of the other southern states. Historically the
Virginia Republican party was the third strongest in the eleven
former Confederate states, ranking behind those of Tennessee
and North Carolina, but significantly ahead of the Florida,
Texas, Arkansas, and Alabama parties and far ahead of the
Georgia, Louisiana, South Carolina, and Mississippi parties,
which were virtually extinct.[8] Table 18 indicates that Republi-

Table 18   Percentage of Total Vote Received
by Republican Candidates for Governor in
Virginia (1945–1965)

Year	Candidate	Percentage of vote *
1945	Landreth	31.0
1949	Johnson	27.4
1953	Dalton	44.3
1957	Dalton	36.4
1961	Pearson	36.1
1965	Holton	37.7

* Republicans generally received a slightly higher percentage
of the major party vote than of the total vote due to the presence of
minor candidates. In the 1965 election, however, the presence
of the Conservative party caused Holton to receive over 44 per
cent of the major party vote and only 37.7 per cent of the total
vote.

can candidates for governor in Virginia generally were able to
collect approximately one-third of the total vote.

An analysis of the geographical distribution of the strength
of Virginia Republicans is the most helpful tool for understanding the nature of the present party. Map IV reveals the varying
degrees of Republican strength in Virginia on the basis of races
for the presidency, the United States Senate, the governorship,
the United States House of Representatives, and the Virginia
General Assembly over the last twenty years (1947–66). Republican ratings in Virginia's localities varied from 0 to 56,

[8] Heard (pp. 54–73) evaluates the strength of the Republican party in each
of the eleven former Confederate states.

Note to Map IV

This index to Republican strength in Virginia from 1947 to 1966 is computed as follows:

A majority vote for a Republican candidate for President, governor, or U.S. senator .... 2 points
A majority vote for a Republican candidate for U.S. representative .... 1 point
Representation by a Republican senator in a Virginia General Assembly session .... 1 point
Representation by a Republican delegate in a Virginia General Assembly session .... 1 point

Counties and their points follow:

Accomack 4	Chesterfield 11	Greensville 4	Middlesex 8	Roanoke 39
Albemarle 11	Clarke 5	Halifax 2	Montgomery 44	Rockbridge 12
Alleghany 11	Craig 7	Hanover 9	Nansemond 0	Rockingham 19
Amelia 8	Culpeper 6	Henrico 13	Nelson 1	Russell 4
Amherst 1	Cumberland 8	Henry 1	New Kent 9	Scott 42
Appomattox 2	Dickenson 0	Highland 20	Northampton 6	Shenandoah 37
Arlington 22	Dinwiddie 0	Isle of Wight 0	Northumberland 13	Smyth 36
Augusta 18	Essex 9	James City 9	Nottoway 4	Southampton 0
Bath 8	Fairfax 26	King George 7	Orange 8	Spotsylvania 2
Bedford 11	Fauquier 7	King and Queen 4	Page 17	Stafford 9
Bland 16	Floyd 56	King William 9	Patrick 0	Surry 0
Botetourt 23	Fluvanna 6	Lancaster 9	Pittsylvania 2	Sussex 2
Brunswick 2	Franklin 12	Lee 18	Powhatan 8	Tazewell 10
Buchanan 6	Frederick 7	Loudoun 8	Prince Edward 8	Warren 4
Buckingham 4	Giles 7	Louisa 5	Prince George 4	Washington 17
Campbell 9	Gloucester 6	Lunenburg 2	Prince William 3	Westmoreland 9
Caroline 3	Goochland 3	Madison 12	Pulaski 16	Wise 0
Carroll 52	Grayson 44	Mathews 11	Rappahannock 2	Wythe 20
Charles City 10	Greene 21	Mecklenburg 2	Richmond 11	York 7
Charlotte 2				

Independent cities and their points follow:

Alexandria 11	Hampton 9	Newport News 5	Radford 40	Suffolk 4
Bristol 10	Harrisonburg 15	Norfolk 6	Richmond 9	Waynesboro 16
Charlottesville 6	Hopewell 6	Petersburg 4	Roanoke 24	Williamsburg 13
Danville 8	Lynchburg 18	Portsmouth 0	Staunton 16	Winchester 10
Fredericksburg 6	Martinsville 7			

The index has not been computed for any counties or independent cities not in continuous existence throughout this twenty-year period

Map IV. Republican Strength in Virginia (1947–1966)

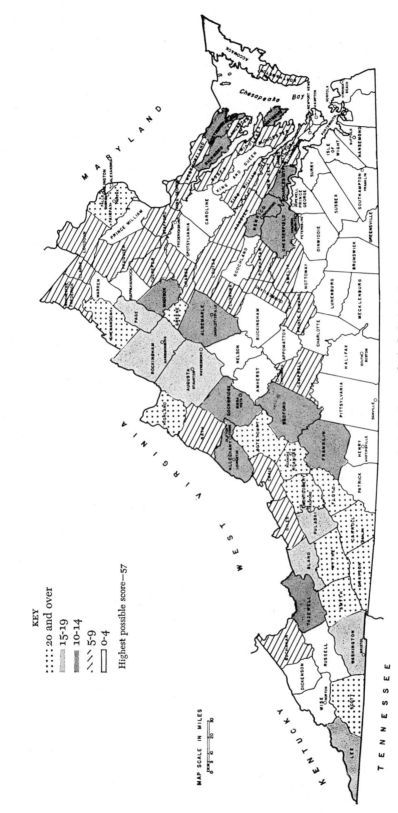

KEY

∴∴∴ 20 and over
15-19
10-14
5-9
0-4

Highest possible score—57

MAP SCALE IN MILES
0 6 20 30

with 57 being the highest possible Republican score. Localities with Republican ratings from 20 to 56 indicate a Republican party of significant strength; in those with ratings of 10 to 20 the party was an occasional threat. A loyal Republican was little more than a curiosity in most counties and cities with ratings of less than 10.

The map demonstrates that Republicans fared better in the western part of Virginia than in the central and coastal portions. The chain of counties running from Botetourt through Carroll and Grayson and over to Lee County in the far southwest tip of Virginia formed the main area of Republican strength. Pockets of Republican support also appeared throughout the Shenandoah Valley and in the Washington and Richmond suburbs. The party's fortunes were barren, however, in that long stretch of southside Virginia from Nansemond to Patrick County and only slightly less dismal in the tract of central piedmont Virginia from Loudoun to Culpeper to Fluvanna and Buckingham. The Tidewater and coastal areas offered Republicans little but hope.

Republican fortunes in Virginia rose with the hills.

A modest line of low hills along the western fringe of Loudoun County in its northernmost section of Virginia, the Blue Ridge boldly rises higher and expands in width as one follows it southwards [reported Jean Gottmann]. In the southernmost section, near the North Carolina line, it can boast the highest summits of Virginia, and it encompasses entire counties within its range, such as Floyd, Carroll, and Grayson, while in the north its main crest . . . serves rather as a boundary between counties. The main change occurs in the vicinity of the Roanoke Gap, to the south of which the Blue Ridge is a much more complicated chain of mountains than to its north.[9]

The Blue Ridge was backed by endless ribbons of mountains and valleys in western and southwestern Virginia which sharply differentiated this section of the state from its eastern two-thirds. The sprawling Southside halted abruptly before the mountains of Carroll and Floyd Counties, and Virginia became

[9] Gottmann, p. 191.

almost a different land. Here among the endless mountain chains of the Southwest lived the "highland Republicans."

Highland or mountain Republicans long constituted the citadels of that party's strength in the South. The principal concentrations of these Republicans lay in southwestern Virginia, western North Carolina, and eastern Tennessee.[10] Republicans in these areas elected their candidates for county offices and the state legislature frequently and for Congress occasionally. They regularly returned majorities for Republicans in state-wide contests. Although they seldom threatened the Democrat's control over state government, they were lively enough to keep the major party honest. Outside North Carolina, Tennessee, and Virginia, however, the mountain Republicans were much less powerful. They controlled several counties in northern Georgia and Alabama and the Ozarks region in Arkansas, but they were seldom taken seriously by the dominant Democrats.[11] In the upper South, however, they provided a basis for the possible rebirth of the two-party system.

The mountaineers were Republicans not by choice but by inheritance. Their origin traced directly to the Civil War. In the debate over slavery the highlanders of small landholdings and few slaves found themselves at loggerheads with the plantation counties of the lowlands, where slave labor could be profitably worked. Table 19 shows the slave and white populations in various areas in antebellum Virginia and illustrates how few slaves resided in the mountainous country west of the Blue Ridge.

The strength of Democratic loyalties in Virginia in 1960 was closely related to an area's slaveholdings of a century before. In the Southside, where the slave population actually outnumbered whites in the antebellum years, Democratic fortunes were at their zenith in 1960 (see Map IV). In the other tidewater and piedmont counties east of the Blue Ridge where slaves were slightly less numerous, Democratic loyalties by 1960 were a bit less stubborn. West of the Blue Ridge where slaves were scant, the Republicans were relatively strong.

[10] Key, p. 281.   [11] *Ibid.*, pp. 281–82.

The reason for the correlation is clear. "When the slavery issue evolved to the question of secession, the stoutest opposition in the South came from the hill folk who had least to lose from a national party adverse to slavery," wrote Heard. "They wanted to mind their own business and stay in the Union." [12]

Table 19   Population (Slave and White) of Virginia * in 1860

Region	Counties	Square miles	Slave population	White population
Southside	22		173,109	128,303
All other tidewater & piedmont counties	46		250,990	322,703
East of the Blue Ridge	68	26,778	424,099	451,006
West of the Blue Ridge	80	37,992	66,766	596,293
Virginia as a whole	148	64,770	490,865	1,047,299

Source: Reprinted by permission from *Cavalier Commonwealth: History and Government of Virginia*, by William E. Hemphill, Marvin W. Schlegel, and Sadie E. Engelberg. Copyright © 1963, 1957 by McGraw-Hill Inc. See p. 231.
* West Virginia was still a part of Virginia at this time.

During the war and its aftermath the Republican party became the champion of the Unionists. This pleased many of the mountaineers. "The highland yeomanry did not want to fight a rich man's war," observed Key. "The Democratic party was, or at least became, the planters' party and the war party. The Democratic party forced the hills into The War and for this it has never been forgiven." [13]

The lowlands have likewise never forgiven the Republicans. The party of Lincoln razed and obliterated antebellum grace and prosperity, and the lowland South has never forgotten. In Virginia the money value of half a million slaves, amounting to approximately half a billion dollars at pre-Civil War prices, was a total loss since the federal government freed the slaves without compensating the owners. A report of the Virginia House of Delegates in 1877 itemized a total of $300,000,000 in property losses other than those in slaveholdings during the preceding sixteen years.[14] Poverty hung over much of the Old

[12] Page 41.   [13] Page 283.   [14] Hemphill *et al.*, p. 342.

Dominion during Reconstruction, and the Republican party took the blame.

The scars of the Civil War still determined the party structure of Virginia in 1950. After a thorough study of party loyalty in the South, Heard in 1952 concluded that "all over the world hereditary influences affect party affiliation, but the intensity of hereditary Democratic and Republican strength in the South should sober those tempted to believe party realignments can occur overnight. Only the deepest upheavals jar voters loose from their habitual moorings."[15] By 1950, however, the upheavals had not occurred.

We have already observed how the former slaveholding citadel of southside Virginia cast a dominant influence on the Democratic party in the state. The mountain counties likewise exerted a powerful influence on the nature of the present Virginia Republican party. From 1902 to 1922 the southwestern counties elected a Republican Congressman while the rest of the state remained overwhelmingly Democratic. Largely because of its history and geographical base, the Republican party in Virginia pursued a uniquely progressive course.

The Republican party has often been called the "liberal" party in Virginia. Prominent Republican leaders objected to this definition, however. They preferred to characterize their party as more "progressive" or less "segregationist-minded" than the Virginia Democrats.° The latter description had substantial validity. The Republicans claimed political strength in mountain areas where Negroes were simply not a major problem. Ted Dalton and Floyd Landreth, the two most distinguished Republicans in the 1950's, hailed from the highlands, and they advocated programs far more moderate than the Byrd organization ever espoused. Dalton, in his 1953 gubernatorial platform, called for repeal of the poll tax and he drafted specific plans for the expansion of public health and education services in Virginia.[16] He urged bond financing of Virginia's roads at a time when Byrd Democrats were religiously clinging

---

[15] Page 45.

[16] See Chapter 4 for an account of Dalton's 1953 gubernatorial campaign against Stanley.

to pay-as-you-go. Dalton's platform in the 1953 race against Stanley was so progressive that Francis Pickens Miller, the chief antiorganization Democrat in Virginia, termed it a "genuine Democratic document" and invited his followers to back the personable Republican.[17]

The inherited loyalties of black-belt, southside Virginians to the Democratic party and southwest mountaineers to the Republican party played a significant part in the stands of their gubernatorial nominees in the 1957 general election. Almond was forced to court southside Virginians and advocate massive resistance. The Republican, Dalton, on the other hand, who came from Radford and a mountain constituency, advocated token integration as a solution to the Supreme Court decision—at the time a dangerously "liberal" stance. Dalton carried only a cluster of mountain counties and the Washington suburbs.[18] The Republicans, however, by taking such stands, always left the door open to the Negro vote, and the Negroes did give the Republicans substantial support in the 1957 and 1961 gubernatorial races and in some lesser local contests.

While Virginia's political parties still related to the Civil War, the national parties were undergoing profound transformations. The party of Lincoln became the party of Hoover, and in the years immediately following World War II the Republicans were clearly the country's foremost conservatives. The New Deal years and Truman's civil rights program reversed the old Democratic notions of white supremacy, and the national Democratic party began more and more to woo urban voting blocs outside the South. That the Virginia political parties did not keep pace with these national shifts but generally stood pat along Civil War lines is testimony to the imprint which that great conflict left on the state. It was inevitable, however, that the national parties would alter traditional party alignment in Virginia and cause friction, confusion, and the painful abandonment of habitual preferences.

Conservative Virginia appeared, on the surface, an ideal

[17] Latimer, p. 61.
[18] See Chapter 5 for an account of the 1957 gubernatorial race.

target for the Republican party. The conservative stance of the national party, especially in Congress, provided incentive for local Republicans to fashion a strong party apparatus in the state. If the Republicans could enlarge their traditional mountain base by courting conservative voters throughout the state, competitive two-party politics might emerge at last.

Two-party politics was so slow in coming to Virginia, however, that observers no longer wondered "when" but "whether." The Byrd organization's tight grasp on the conservative voters left a conservative Republican party very little growing room. Key observed "that in the mountain counties of southwestern Virginia the Republicans are fighters, but that in most of the remainder of the state they are a faction of the Byrd organization."[19] The lines between Byrd Democrats and Republicans were indeed fuzzy, for Senator Byrd had so faithfully represented the Republican point of view in Congress that local Republicans often found it sacrilege to criticize him.

This was most noticeable in the 1949 Democratic primary. When John Battle faced an unprecedented challenge from liberal Democrat Francis Pickens Miller, the Republicans alertly jumped to the rescue. Major Henry A. Wise, an old guard Taft Republican leader and former Virginia member of the GOP National Committee, publicly urged Republicans to enter the Democratic primary and vote for John Battle in order to repel the "alien influences" trying to take over the state.[20] The Battle camp let it be known Republicans would be welcomed. On primary day more than 316,000 Virginians voted in the Democratic primary while fewer than 9,000 voted in the Republican primary.[21] It was the first Republican state primary ever held in Virginia, and the Republicans have not seen fit to hold one since. Later Miller estimated that some 50,000 Republicans had voted in the primary—considerably more than Battle's margin of victory.[22] Ted Dalton made the same point:

[19] Page 285.
[20] See the Richmond *Times-Dispatch*, Aug. 5, 1949, for editorial comment.
[21] The Republican primary had no opposed race for governor; two little known candidates were battling for nomination as lieutenant governor.
[22] Latimer, p. 34.

Strange as it may seem, the Republican Party in Virginia, although dead on its feet, last year was the deciding factor in the election of John S. Battle as Governor. . . . [Republicans] deserted our own first gubernatorial primary and flocked to the Democratic primary to support Battle. . . . The Byrd organization may deny that it owes its political neck in the state government to the Republicans . . . but the county and precinct workers know otherwise.[23]

Again in 1952, on the floor of the Virginia Senate, Dalton stated:

We of the minority party have cooperated and helped you. . . . When you were *in extremis* in the gubernatorial primary of 1949, thousands and thousands of us rallied and saved your necks by electing the fine gentleman who now sits upstairs in the Governor's chair. . . . We're not asking for a payoff. All we want is a fair and square deal. . . . If you keep turning us down, our people will say we've got to look elsewhere for friends.[24]

The peculiar situation of the Virginia Republican party was even more evident in the elections for Congress and the United States Senate. Three Republican congressmen rode to victory in Virginia on the Eisenhower landslide of 1952, and all three faced tough re-election challenges in 1954. Although William Wampler in the Ninth District was narrowly defeated, the other two Republicans, Richard Poff in the Sixth and Joel Broyhill in the Tenth, ran better without Ike than they had with him. In the latter districts the Democratic nominees were not firm organization men. Many Byrd Democrats disapproved of their party's nominees and discreetly supported the Republicans, who moderated party affiliation and ran as conservatives, tossing occasional bouquets in Byrd's direction. A reporter visiting Poff's campaign headquarters in Roanoke did not find the word "Republican" visible on any sign, placard, or pamphlet, save on some leaflets sent in from national GOP headquarters.[25]

Senators Byrd and Robertson did not face a Republican challenge from 1950 to 1964. Even after the Republican resurgence of 1952–53, the party was unable to draft a candidate

[23] Washington *Post*, Sept. 3, 1950.
[24] Richmond *Times-Dispatch*, Feb. 13, 1952.   [25] Latimer, p. 67.

with a ghost of a chance of upsetting Virginia's conservative junior senator, A. Willis Robertson. The Republican dilemma was expressed by one reporter in the following "Help Wanted" sign:

Republican notice—Urgent! Need candidate for United States Senate. Prefer man able to juggle issues deftly with flair for catching votes from both parties, both sexes. Experience unnecessary. Working capital of at least $100,000 advisable but will consider less. Make us an offer. Apply Republican State Convention. Roanoke July 17.[26]

The two GOP congressmen, Poff and Broyhill, were opposed to seeing one of their own party challenge the two Democratic giants in the Senate. Stuart D. Baker, an Arlington businessman who was thinking of running against Robertson in 1960, publicly accused Poff and Broyhill of blocking attempts to nominate an opponent to the junior senator from Republican ranks.[27] That the GOP congressmen were opposed was not surprising. They were not eager to have Republican campaign funds diverted from the congressional to the senatorial level and they did not wish to irritate Robertson, a tough campaigner, with a Republican opponent for fear the Senator would carry the state on a Democratic unity appeal and swamp whatever local Republican chances existed.

It was surprising that Virginia Republicans had the temerity to nominate an opponent to Byrd in 1964. "For the first time since 1946, Virginia Republicans nominated a candidate to run against Senator Byrd," the *Times-Dispatch* reported. "It took considerable prodding, pulling and tugging to line up a majority [at the Republican convention] behind May." [28] The Richmond *News Leader* had earlier noted that "an informal poll of GOP leaders who arrived early at the Hotel Jefferson meeting place indicated that a ⅔ majority [of the Central Committee, which was necessary to nominate a candidate] might be extremely hard to come by. Almost to a man they were reluctant to challenge Byrd, unchallenged by Republicans since 1946." [29]

[26] Richmond *Times-Dispatch*, June 4, 1954.   [27] *Ibid.*, June 20, 1960.
[28] *Ibid.*, June 28, 1964.   [29] Richmond *News Leader*, June 27, 1964.

But the Republicans dutifully nominated a candidate and braced themselves for protest from the GOP rank and file across the state. Representative Joel Broyhill recorded his strenuous objections, and the chairman of the Mathews County Republican Committee resigned in protest to the Republican challenge to Senator Byrd. Calling himself a personal friend of the GOP nominee, he nevertheless viewed the entire proceeding as a "grave and regrettable mistake on the part of the Republican Party. . . . I am a conservative and feel that Senator Byrd has consistently and courageously endeavored to protect the conservative principle in the federal government, therefore, I cannot vote against him." [30]

The sympathy between Democratic Senator Byrd and the Republican party extended to the upper levels of American politics. In a speech attacking the Byrd machine, Miller charged that in 1949 the "machine solicited and obtained very substantial financial assistance from Republican sources in Pennsylvania. These Republican sources," Miller added, "were affiliated, as might have been expected, with the worst wing of the Republican party—the Taft wing." [31] Byrd and Taft naturally had many common views and interests, but the Virginia senator did not confine his amenities to any one section of the Republican party. Eisenhower appreciated Byrd's golden silence, which helped him carry Virginia in 1952 and 1956, and it was persistently rumored that the President was thinking of appointing Senator Byrd as Secretary of the Treasury. Byrd, in turn, had kinder words for the Eisenhower administration than for any Democratic President. Republican senators went out of their way to help Senator Byrd. Senator Thruston Morton of Kentucky, former national GOP chairman said in a news conference in Richmond: "I will try in my gentle way to dissuade anyone who wants to run against Senator Byrd in the event he runs in 1964." [32]

The general feeling that the Democratic Byrd organization was at times a wing of the national Republican party and that the Virginia Republican party was at times a wing of the Byrd

[30] Richmond *Times-Dispatch,* July 1, 1964.   [31] Latimer, p. 105.
[32] Richmond *Times-Dispatch,* Jan. 24, 1963.

organization made it difficult for the Virginia Republican party to make any headway. Nevertheless, there remained the fact that party alignments in Virginia were diametrically opposed to the national party alignments. These different alignments influenced the entire Virginia political system and pushed Senator Byrd into a very ticklish situation.

Byrd tried to resolve the dilemma by applying to political parties one of the South's most reliable political tools—the venerated slogan of states' rights. The idea was to insulate the state parties from their national counterparts in every conceivable manner. This led to four distinct (though inevitably overlapping) political categories—two national parties and two state parties. The national party was, in Byrd's view, little more than a confederation of autonomous state parties, each of which reserved the right to veto decisions of the party's national conventions and to withhold support from presidential candidates.[33] The concept of a national party affiliation was invoked only when seniority and committee chairmanships were at stake.

In his desire to sever the state and the national parties, Harry Byrd had the structure of Virginia politics behind him. Byrd was above all a master political structuralist. Because of the poll tax laws, legislative apportionment and committee assignments, the circuit judge system, the State Compensation Board, the makeup of county government, the role of E. R. Combs, the appointive powers surrounding the governor, and many other shrewd devices, Virginia was tailored for Harry Byrd and his machine.[34] Only social forces of vast proportions could ever succeed in destroying this carefully fashioned struc-

[33] This belief of Byrd's angered the antiorganization Democrats more than any other. Miller wrote that "the basic issue is whether there is or is not a National Democratic Party, and if there is such a party what should be the relation to it of Democrats in the several states. This is a momentous issue. If Byrd's concept of the Democratic Party were to be accepted, the plight of this country would, in the course of time, resemble the plight of France. We would become cursed with 'splinter' parties—the only real difference being that whereas France's 'splinter' parties represent different ideologies or interests, ours would represent different States" ("The Struggle for Democracy in Virginia," pp. 17–18).

[34] See Chapter 2 for an analysis of the structure of the Byrd machine.

ture. As further testimony to his brilliance, Byrd's states' rights concept of political parties was ingeniously reinforced by Virginia's election laws.

Elections in Virginia were carefully scheduled so as not to attract an unduly large number of voters, who might upset the expected results. A large number of simultaneous elections would only open the way for unnecessary political excitement and coattail voting, an unsettling spectacle for the gentlemen of the Byrd organization. Virginia chose its governor in the odd year after the presidential elections.[35] State senators were elected in the other odd year.[36] The Virginia election cycle rotated as follows:

Year	Offices Elected
1952	President and Congress
1953	Governor and Virginia House of Delegates
1954	Congress
1955	Virginia State Senate and Virginia House of Delegates

Every state official was elected in a different year from federal officials. State and national issues were separated to the greatest possible extent, and every precaution was taken to eliminate the carryover of enthusiasm from a party's national candidates to its state nominees. If Virginians in a presidential contest followed the Republican nominee, a year always elapsed before the election of governor, thus giving any general ardor for the Republican party sufficient chance to cool. The Virginia Republican party was robbed of any opportunity to benefit significantly in gubernatorial elections from the popularity of the more conservative Republican presidential nominees. Virginians were reminded by this system that Democratic governors could be very different from Democratic presidents. It was unfortunate that Byrd was unable to separate the elec-

[35] See Code of Virginia (1966), Title 24, Sec. 148. All references to the Code are quoted from *Virginia Election Laws, in Effect as of July 1, 1966* (Richmond: Department of Purchases and Supply, 1966).

[36] *Ibid.*, Sec. 13.

tion of President from that of the congress. Had it been possible, the Virginia senator might well have attempted it.

Byrd's states' rights concept of political parties was also confirmed by prevalent interpretations of Virginia's party loyalty oath. One political reporter summed them up in this way:

Another peculiarity of Virginia presidential election laws and customs was born of political expediency after the 1928 presidential elections, in which thousands of Virginia Democrats were scared by the Pope and Demon Rum into giving Virginia's electoral votes to the GOP ticket for the first time since Reconstruction days. After the 1928 election, in which Byrd and the organization chiefs worked hard for the Al Smith ticket, Virginia turned to the 1929 elections of Governor. The Democratic organization had to cope with the problem of luring the Democrats back into the fold and putting down the threat of a possibly resurgent prohibitionist faction.

This was the background: The State Democratic Party Plan, then and now, provides rules of party regularity and eligibility for participation in Democratic primaries. Any candidate in a primary and members of party committees must sign a loyalty pledge which says, in effect, that the signer supported all Democratic nominees in the last preceding general election and promises to support all Democratic nominees in the next general election. People who vote in Democratic primaries are presumed to subscribe to the same pledge; if challenged, they may be required to sign it. . . .

It was necessary in preparing for the 1929 Democratic primaries to open the door, legally and officially, for all organization Democrats who bolted to Hoover to return to the Democratic primary. Attorney General John R. Saunders found enough leeway in the phrasings of law and party plan to conclude: presidential electors are not nominees of the Virginia Democratic party within the meaning of the law or the party plan.

Therefore, Virginians who voted for Hoover were not by that voting action barred from running or voting in the 1929 Virginia Democratic primary. It is still a matter of some wonder and controversy how Saunders could reach such a solemn conclusion, in view of the language of the party plan which then and now says the Virginia State Democratic convention "shall *nominate* so many Presidential electors as the state of Virginia is entitled to . . ." The explanation may lie in the sovereign state party theory that national party nominees are *not* necessarily state party nominees.

The Saunders opinion has been re-affirmed by three Attorneys General since 1929. Because the state legislature has done nothing to overrule it, and because the state Democratic Convention has done nothing to overrule it, the passage of years has given it the force of law. Thus, in Virginia, a voter can vote for a Communist or a Fascist or a Hottentot for President—if such extremes were available on the ballot—and still remain a Democrat in good standing so long as he went along with the Democratic nominees for State and Local Office.[37]

There was yet another practice in Virginia politics which helped to undermine the concept of national party loyalty. Voters in Virginia did not register their party affiliation. There was nothing on the registration books to designate a voter Republican, Democrat, or whatever.[38] The law gave aid to the "now-you're-a-Republican, now-you're-a-Democrat" operation. Voters could support different party candidates on the national and state levels without the nagging feeling that their registration suggested they do otherwise.

Most important, however, was the impact of Byrd's states' rights theory of political parties on the growth of the Virginia Republican party. On this question there was little agreement. One view contended that Byrd put the state in a frame of mind which made it impossible for the Republican party to develop. The lack of a sense of strict party loyalty in Virginia crippled attempts of a minority party to recruit a loyal following in the state. Had Byrd insisted on party loyalty at all levels of government, one official argued, he might have driven "thousands" of conservatives headlong into the Republican fold,° particularly in the urban corridor where inherited party loyalties did not

[37] Latimer, pp. 30–31.
[38] See Code of Virginia (1966), 24–52 to 24–119.2 for a description of Virginia's registration laws.

control voting behavior to the same extent as in rural Virginia. In Richmond, for instance, Byrd's repudiation of the Stevenson-Sparkman ticket in 1952 gave an official blessing to a powerful new force in Virginia politics, the Virginia Democrats for Eisenhower. Their organizers and leaders were well-to-do, non-officeholding business and industrial leaders who were stanch supporters of Harry Byrd. Among them were Robert V. Hatcher, president of Atlantic Life, who became state chairman of the Democrats for Eisenhower, and Thomas C. Boushall, chairman of the Board of Directors of the Bank of Virginia, who became treasurer of the Eisenhower Democrats.[39] With abundant manpower and funds they exploited the opposition of conservative Virginians to the liberal economic and civil rights planks of the Democratic platform. These men, however, were all Democrats on the state level. When Ted Dalton appealed for their support just one year later in the gubernatorial race of 1953, Mills F. Neal, a leader of the Democrats for Eisenhower, issued a sharp rejoinder. Democrats for Eisenhower had differed only with the national Democratic party, Neal pointed out. "These Democrats had no criticism of the Democratic Party within the state." [40]

Thus many natural recruits of the Republican party remained Byrd Democrats because, as some would have it, Senator Byrd never backed a national Democratic ticket and even encouraged Virginia businessmen and conservatives to chart an independent course in presidential elections. Had Byrd urged Virginia into line behind the national ticket, it might have been disastrous for the Democratic party in the state.

Yet another school of thought contended that Byrd's golden silences and states' rights views, far from stunting the Republican party, were the greatest factors in that party's recent growth. "Every time a Democrat crosses a party line," ventured the state Republican chairman, I. Lee Potter, in 1961, "it becomes easier for him to do it in a subsequent election. We want them to know we have good candidates for state offices as well as national office. . . . Let them know the Republicans are

[39] Latimer, p. 51.   [40] Richmond *News Leader,* June 23, 1953.

getting ready for the state elections this year and the congressional elections next year." [41] This view alarmed many local Democrats, especially in the Sixth, Ninth, and Tenth Districts where two-party competition seemed a growing reality. They feared that defections from the Democratic party at the national level were finally seeping down to local contests. Republican Congressmen were relatively safe in the Sixth and Tenth Districts after 1952. Republican state legislators were running stronger races in the Shenandoah Valley, and even the supposedly Democratic First and Third Districts witnessed strong Republican congressional challenges in 1956 and 1962, respectively. [42] Senator Byrd's golden silences seemed to some to open the dikes for a flood of Republican victories in Virginia.

Almond was one who worried that Byrd's lax view of loyalty to the national party was weakening the Democratic party within the state. "I find both in the Roanoke and Lynchburg area," wrote Almond to Byrd of the 1958 congressional elections, "that Poff's friends are emphasizing with telling effect statements that Poff [6th District Republican congressman] is acceptable to you and that Poff has always cooperated with and followed your leadership in the Congress, and that a vote for Poff would in no wise embarrass Senator Byrd." [43]

It was almost inevitable that the Republican party in Virginia would benefit from the conservative stance of the national party. Byrd's problem was how to minimize this gain. Structurally—in Virginia's election and registration system—the Senator's aims were brilliantly implemented as he interposed every conceivable barrier between the state and the national Republican party. Whether golden silence forestalled or accelerated the growth of the Virginia Republican party must remain a question. The two cogent but irreconcilable viewpoints can never be conclusively resolved.

[41] Richmond *Times-Dispatch,* Feb. 26, 1961.

[42] In 1956 Democratic incumbent Edward J. Robeson barely nudged out Republican Horace E. Henderson 31,839 to 30,799. In 1962 veteran Democrat J. Vaughan Gary edged little known Republican Louis H. Williams 28,914 to 28,566.

[43] Almond to Byrd, Oct. 16, 1958.

Those seeking to measure the strength of the Virginia Republican party were too often tempted to look at the number of Republican congressmen or the percentage of the vote won by Republican candidates for the governorship or the Senate. A more reliable index is the number of seats controlled by the party in the state legislature. State legislatures were most influential in southern states. These bodies posed one of the greatest obstacles to Republican resurgence. In Virginia the

Table 20 Republican Representation in the Virginia General Assembly (1948–1964)

Year	Republican delegates (100 Seats)	Republican senators (40 Seats)
1948	8	2
1950	7	2
1952	6	3
1954	5	3
1956	6	3
1958	6	3
1960	4	2
1962	5	2
1964	11	3

Source: *General Assembly Manual, 1948 to 1964.*

legislature was the organization's testing ground where young conservatives gained experience before making their first state-wide race. Legislators often proved valuable local campaign leaders for the state leaders of the organization. Even more important, Democrats in the legislature ensured that election procedures would benefit the Democratic party.

For many years Republican strength in the Virginia General Assembly was pitifully low. Table 20 demonstrates only the slightest variance in Republican fortunes from year to year.

Virginia hospitality was not extended to the few Republicans in the state legislature; no Byrd Democrat would place a Virginia Republican on a committee of real significance. Republicans in the state Senate were virtually barred for years from the Finance Committee, which considered most fiscal measures, and the Privileges and Elections Committee, which handled election laws, apportionment, and many other delicate procedures.[44] The Democrats were not above an occasional gerrymander when the opportunity arose. The Fifth Congressional District for many years jutted out from western southside Virginia to include Wythe County. Wythe used to be in the Ninth District, and the Ninth used to be Republican. Forty years ago the Democratic state legislature removed Wythe to the Democratic Fifth District in order to make the Ninth safer for the Democrats.[45] As recently as 1964 Democrats found a convenient solution to reapportionment problems by placing two incumbent Republican senators in the same district.[46]

Republican candidates for governor found Democratic control of the state legislature a serious problem in most campaigns. Voters were uneasy that contention between a Republican governor and a Democratic legislature might weaken the state for the four-year term. Dalton, in his 1953 campaign, remarked that "I cannot believe that any member or candidate for the General Assembly would be little enough to block constructive legislation because it came during the administration of a Republican Governor. . . . I know, for instance, that no legislator in Virginia would be so partisan as to deny the proper appropriations for the mentally ill, the children in epileptic colonies, or persons suffering from tuberculosis."[47] Touching as it was, Dalton's appeal could not obscure the realities of partisan politics. Republicans suffered in races for the state legislature because they could not win favors from a Democratic governor; Republicans suffered in gubernatorial races because they could not obtain the cooperation of a Democratic legislature.

What plagued Republicans most, however, were the powers

[44] See *General Assembly Manual, 1946 to 1966,* for Republican committee assignments.

[45] Latimer, pp. 14–15.

[46] See *General Assembly Manual, 1964 and 1966,* for shifts in legislative districts.

[47] Richmond *News Leader,* Aug. 12, 1953.

of the circuit judge.[48] Elected by the General Assembly, these judges were invariably Democrats who controlled patronage in even the most Republican county. The judge acted as a powerful Democratic persuader for any citizen with an eye to appointive office. This patronage network often gave Democrats the decisive edge in areas of brisk two-party competition. In the Southwest, where party rivalry abounded, charges of scandal followed almost every election. Republicans claimed that Democrats, through the judge's control of the Welfare Board, used threats of welfare withdrawal to intimidate impoverished and illiterate voters.[49] Far greater controversy centered on another of the circuit judge's appointments, the Electoral Board. Of the three members on each board, two had to be of the party whose candidate won the most recent gubernatorial election (i.e., Democrat).[50] The Electoral Board appointed all election judges, precinct registrars, and clerks, thus assuring Democrats in doubtful counties of sympathetic election officials. With Democrats interpreting the voters' lists, counting the ballots, and tallying the totals, Republicans, if they were not the victims of fraud, at least suspected trickery in every close election.

The Republicans were most critical of the handling of absentee ballots. Absentee ballot scandals arose in southwest Virginia regularly. Democratic election judges and precinct registrars determined the validity of all "mail ballots," and officials were tempted to overlook irregularities in absentee voting in any close election. Yet abuses occasionally became too flagrant to ignore. In 1954, three Democrats, including two election officials in Banner precinct of Russell County, were convicted in a federal district court of conspiring to violate Virginia's absentee voters law in the 1952 general elections. The three, it was found, had taken the absentee balloting procedure almost entirely into their own hands. Of the 62 supposed absentee voters interviewed by the FBI, 53 had not applied for the ballots as required by law, others could neither read nor write and had received "help" in marking their ballots, and 19 did

---

[48] See Chapter 2. [49] Richmond *Times-Dispatch,* Nov. 15, 1959.
[50] Code of Virginia (1966), 24–29.

not even know that votes had been cast in their names. The attorney for the defendants issued a quaint plea: "Whatever these men did was done not with criminal intent . . . but for the love of the party. . . . They perhaps took shortcuts in things that could have been done legally. All the votes cast would have been cast that way anyway." [51]

The Ninth District continued the undisputed champion of absentee voting by casting 4,780 such ballots in the 1954 congressional election—nearly twice as many as the rest of state.[52] Republicans laid their slim defeat that year to "black satchel" politics and hundreds of illegal mail ballots.[53] In the 1959 state Senate contest in Lee and Scott counties, Republicans again alleged many of those who voted by absentee ballot "were illiterates . . . bought by money and whiskey . . . pressured into voting with threats of being arrested or having their welfare cut off." The Richmond *Times-Dispatch* remarked that in Lee County "a total of 2,895 mail ballots were voted out of 10,500 ballots of all kinds. This is well in excess of 25 per cent. Does anybody really believe that nearly 2,900 citizens of Lee were unable to get to the polls on election day and had to vote by mail?" [54]

Republican attempts to repeal absentee balloting invariably failed. State Senator M. M. Long, a Democrat from Wise County, responded to one such measure in 1948 by proposing his own bill to remove some of the safeguards erected around the absentee ballot by the 1946 General Assembly. The veteran Democrat explained that officials found the law cumbersome to administer and wished greater freedom in handling the ballots. The Senator's views were understandable. Wise County was the most notorious in the state for election irregularities.[55] "Just try to do something about these practices in the General Assembly and listen to the howl from most of the Southwest Virginia contingent," one indignant editor later remarked. "Any effort to make violations of the block poll tax payment law a felony is certain to be greeted by all kinds of fervent

---

[51] Richmond *Times-Dispatch*, Nov. 30, 1954.   [52] Latimer, p. 105.
[53] Richmond *Times-Dispatch*, April 6, 1956.
[54] *Ibid.*, Nov. 15, 1959.   [55] Heard, p. 92.

wails and bogus arguments. Ditto for any effective suggestion for stopping the notorious mail ballot frauds which have been a stench in the nostrils of the state for generations." [56]

The editor touched on a second grievance of Republican candidates. Although illegal block poll tax payments were regularly made by both parties, the Republicans were the more infrequent offenders because the county treasurers who handled such payments were generally Democrats. The perennial Republican call for poll tax repeal was not wholly altruistic. Dalton contended that the poll tax militated against Republicans because Democrats were treasurers in 90 per cent of Virginia's towns and counties and therefore in a better position to see to it that organization supporters were qualified to vote. [57]

Even where Republicans were treasurers, they were unable to outdo their opponents. Maneuverings in Lee County from 1955 to 1956 showed the Democrats at their shrewdest. There Republicans had emerged apparent victors in hotly fought contests for four county offices. The Democrats charged, however, that the former Republican treasurer, C. C. Combs, had refused to accept a $7,500 check from the Democrats to cover poll tax payments for approximately 4,000 voters, even though he had earlier accepted a similar $2,800 payment from Republican sources. The attorney for the Democrats claimed they had been "tricked" into an agreement whereby the Democratic Electoral Board would give the GOP access to certain voter records and the Republican treasurer would accept block payments of poll taxes. When the GOP refused to accept the Democrats' payments, the Democrats charged in court that the GOP had already paid poll taxes in block, illegally. [58] Any election contest involving county office had to be tried by a tribunal of three circuit judges, who were always Democrats and from whom there was no appeal. [59] The Democratic court upheld the Democratic charges that the GOP illegally had paid poll taxes

[56] Richmond *Times-Dispatch,* July 6, 1956.
[57] Richmond *News Leader,* March 25, 1953.
[58] Richmond *Times-Dispatch,* May 31, 1956.
[59] Code of Virginia (1966), 24–431; 24–439.

for hundreds of voters for the November 1955 elections. It further nullified the election of Republicans as county sheriff, treasurer, commissioner of revenue, and commonwealth's attorney.[60] Later the judge of the Lee County circuit used his powers of appointment to fill the vacancies in the four offices with three of the Democrats who had been candidates in the recently contested elections.[61]

Ted Dalton commented on this in his speech to the Republican state convention at Roanoke on July 21, 1956. He claimed that three of the Democrats appointed in Lee County

admittedly had participated in the very act for which the Republicans were removed. It is a poor rule [he continued] that won't work both ways. . . . The Democratic organization has waxed strong and almost invincible through the use of the poll tax in restricting the electorate in Virginia and perpetuating themselves in office. I have yet to hear of one single instance where a Democrat has been removed from office because he participated in, or was the beneficiary of, the payment of poll taxes of others than himself and family. . . . To my certain knowledge most of the Democratic leaders of this state, including members of Congress, state officials, and county office holders by the hundreds, have year in and year out been paying the poll taxes of their supporters and party stalwarts.[62]

Block poll tax payments, though prohibited by law, nonetheless constituted a major campaign expenditure. A Democratic leader of much experience has estimated that $75,000 was spent by the two parties for poll tax payments in the Ninth District's hotly contested 1954 congressional election.[63] For poll taxes as for other campaign expenditures, Democrats had access to the funds. The costs of statewide campaigns in Virginia were often low because the state's dominant political apparatus depended on courthouse organization, not publicity, to win elections. In the factional politics of Florida or Arkansas large sums were required just to become known,[64] but in Virginia

[60] Richmond *Times-Dispatch*, July 6, 1956.   [61] Latimer, p. 106.
[62] Roanoke *Times*, July 22, 1956.   [63] Latimer, p. 105.
[64] Key (pp. 463–85) discusses in some detail campaign financing in the South.

Byrd's nod was worth far more than a $100,000 campaign contribution. Expenses in Virginia general elections were also low because few conceded the Republican candidate a chance to win. Businessmen, who in Virginia as elsewhere in the South, were by far the biggest campaign contributors, had a notorious fondness for winners (assuming, of course, that the winners will not rock the businessman's boat). As a result, Republicans often were obliged to run on a shoestring (see Table 21).

Table 21   Reported Campaign Expenditures in Recent Gubernatorial Elections

Year	Office	Candidates	Reported expenditures *
1953	Governor	Stanley (Dem.)	$ 73,138.00
		Dalton (Rep.)	39,895.00
1957	Governor	Almond (Dem.)	78,526.00
		Dalton (Rep.)	42,801.00
1961	Governor	Harrison (Dem.)	29,163.00
		Pearson (Rep.)	15,682.00
1965	Governor	Godwin (Dem.)	218,067.00
		Holton (Rep.)	79,164.00

Source: State Board of Elections, expense accounts filed by candidates within thirty days after the election in accordance with Section 24–442 of the Virginia Code.

* These expense accounts are at best a general guide to the relative levels of party expenditures. The reports account only for what the candidate, his campaign manager, and state headquarters spent in his behalf. They do not account for expenditures of local groups in the hinterland or the considerable sums spent by local headquarters in a large city such as Richmond or Norfolk. The biggest items of expense in Ninth District politics, illegal bloc payment of poll taxes and "whiskey money," could never be included. The law requires that the candidate report expenditures "to the best of his knowledge and belief," and truthful compliance with this provision may represent only from ½ to ⅔ of the total. Sources of campaign contributions are never reported.

In the light of all these obstacles it is remarkable that Virginia Republicans ever won anything. Yet the minority party, ignoring the odds, at times offered the Byrd organization a game opposition. One big reason was Ted Dalton. Byrd said he had never seen anybody like Ted Dalton. The two party chiefs often hunted together before the 1953 campaign, and Dalton, spying a man working in a field miles across the valley on a distant mountainside, would go striding over to talk with him and shake his hand.[65]

Theodore Roosevelt Dalton hailed from the traditional mountain strongholds of the Republican party. He was born in Carroll County in southwest Virginia on July 3, 1901, and became commonwealth's attorney of Radford from 1929 to 1937. In 1944 when a vacancy occurred in the old twenty-first senatorial district of Montgomery, Franklin, and Roanoke counties and the city of Radford, Dalton ran, won, and withstood two subsequent Democratic challenges. The tall, jovial state senator was, by 1952, ready to give the Republican party its first show of life since 1928–29.

Old-guard Taft Republicans controlled much of the Virginia Republican party before 1952. When Curtis M. Dozier of Richmond retired as national committeeman that year, Dalton won the intraparty maneuverings to succeed him.[66] He publicly pursued a fence-sitting policy in the Taft-Eisenhower struggle until his own election; then he swung the Virginia delegation behind Eisenhower at the 1952 convention. That fall Eisenhower carried Virginia by over 80,000 votes and three Republicans got into Congress on his coattails. One of the new congressmen, Richard Poff, was Dalton's young law partner for whom he had engineered the Republican nomination. With a banner year behind them, Virginia Republicans prepared to assault the governorship.

He gave us "the closest call we ever had," said Senator Byrd of Dalton's race against Stanley in 1953. "Until he made that speech, he was as good as elected." [67] That speech was Dalton's proposal for a road bond issue of $100,000,000, to be secured by gas tax receipts. Bonds were bonds to Byrd, and he came "flying into the campaign, wattles flaming, spurs flashing, and turned it, just barely." [68] The Republicans, who in a normal gubernatorial race might win one-third of the vote, ended with 45 per cent.

[65] Friddell, p. 71.   [66] Latimer, p. 58.   [67] Friddell, p. 70.   [68] *Ibid.*

Those two years, 1952–53, long stood as a high-water mark of Republican resurgence. After them the party half-hibernated. Eisenhower's appeal, in Virginia as elsewhere, proved to be largely personal and nonpartisan. It was not easily translatable to gains on the local level. In the 1954 elections Republicans were unable to oppose Senator Robertson and actually lost their Ninth District seat. In 1956, despite a resounding Eisenhower victory in Virginia, local Republicans proved unable to gain, though they did come within 1,100 votes of beating Edward J. Robeson, the bland incumbent in the First Congressional District. The next year when Dalton opposed Almond in the massive resistance race, Dalton was branded an integrationist and lost by landslide margins. "What's happened to Virginia Republicans' once bright hope of building strong two-party state competition on the presidential victories won by Mr. Eisenhower in the Old Dominion?" a reporter asked at the party's low ebb in 1958. "This year Virginia Republicans have nominated only three congressional candidates including the two GOP incumbents. They have let the Ninth District, historically a GOP strong point, go by default. They chose not to nominate a Senate candidate against Senator Byrd. Enthusiasm and money, two important ingredients for political success, are lacking. Does this . . . mean that the GOP is slipping into new and deeper political depression in Virginia?" [69]

No little fortitude was required to keep alive the party's morale. Republican leaders became experts at radiating optimism. "We have had a temporary setback," said Dalton after his 1957 gubernatorial loss, "but we are not discouraged and we'll keep fighting to build two-party competition." [70] Dalton himself kept fighting, often to the considerable irritation of Democratic leaders. "I have tried," Almond wrote to Byrd in 1958, "to avoid running discussions with Dalton, but he was so brazen with some of his statements that I felt I must reply. He has never realized that the votes were counted in the gubernatorial election of 1957 and certified as final by the General Assembly, of which he is a member." [71]

[69] Richmond *Times-Dispatch*, July 20, 1958.   [70] *Ibid.*, Nov. 11, 1957.
[71] Almond to Byrd, Dec. 22, 1958.

Frequently intraparty bickering followed Republican slumps at the polls. Dalton charged in 1955 that the GOP would never get anywhere "with only a half-baked organization" and he swore that two-thirds of the district, county, and city chairmen were not "doing a thing." [72] Even sharper were the remarks of Page County Republican Chairman I. R. Dovel to State Chairman Potter in the wake of the weak Republican challenge in the gubernatorial race of 1961. "If you cannot provide any better leadership than you have," Dovel exclaimed, "a good start would be for you to resign so that you can be replaced by someone who desires to try to build something worthwhile. . . . [Republicans] cannot build an organization in Virginia by depending upon the Byrd crowd to carry our state every four years for the Republican national ticket." [73]

It was evident that as late as 1960 Virginia Republicans, like most opposition elements within the Democratic party, found themselves unable to move against Byrd. "Virginia has had clean government which satisfied the hopes and aspirations of the people who were doing the voting," admitted one Republican leader. "It's tough to fight success." °

The Republican future, however, looked far brighter in 1960 than its past. Throughout the lean years Republicans found solace in the thought that Byrd, Robertson, Tuck, and Smith would one day retire, that Virginia Democrats would lose their high command and vast congressional seniority, that liberals would then capture the Democratic party, and that conservative Virginians would finally see the light and become Republicans.

A more realistic view depended not on the retirement of the senior Byrd leaders or on a *deus ex machina* Republican President. It demanded the slow toil of precinct build-up while the currents of urban growth, population explosion, and Negro voting power undermined the old Byrd consensus. Byrd's courthouse machine was undergoing increasing stress. Virginia was becoming too diverse, too fluid, and too closely tied to national currents for a one-party monopoly to endure.

[72] Richmond *News Leader,* April 4, 1955.
[73] Richmond *Times-Dispatch,* Nov. 26, 1961.

The Republican party had developed along a progressive and nonsegregationist course which proved a liability in the massive resistance period but an asset in the more modern and metropolitan Virginia of the 1960's. The chief project for Virginia Republicans was to add to their traditional mountain base sufficient strength to challenge Democrats on an equal basis. The suburbs of the state's big metropolitan centers provided an ideal target for Republican hopes.

Republicans had long demonstrated more strength in the suburbs than in the large tracts of rural Virginia east of the Blue Ridge. Map IV shows varying degrees of Republican strength in the suburban counties of Roanoke, Arlington, Fairfax, Chesterfield, and Henrico, and it indicates that in each of these heavy voting areas the Republican cause was far from hopeless. Median family income in these counties ranged in 1960 from $450 to $3,700 above the state median ($4,964). Educational background was likewise significantly higher than that of the state as a whole.[74] Many white-collar, suburban areas had proved congenial for the national Republican party,[75] and each of these suburban counties had reasons for being an actual or potential Republican area in Virginia. Roanoke and Botetourt counties shared the mountain heritage of the Republican party. They had few Negroes, little or no traditional attachment to the Democratic party, and had long been friendly to Republican candidates. Roanoke County supported Republican presidential nominees from 1948 to 1964; it regularly gave large majorities to Republican Congressman Richard Poff and frequently to Republican gubernatorial and state legislative candidates.

Arlington and Fairfax counties in the Washington suburbs were occasionally sources of Republican strength. The area's income and educational levels, the highest in the state, indicated at least some Republican affinities. Its residents, over

[74] U.S. Bureau of the Census, *Population, 1960,* I, 48, *Virginia,* pp. 141–45.

[75] It would be misleading to oversimplify the positions of the major national parties by depicting the Republicans as the party of the white-collar suburbs and the Democrats as the party of the blue-collar "city core." The author wishes merely to note that the national Republican party does have substantial, upper-middle-class, suburban appeal.

two-thirds of whom were born outside Virginia, brought to the commonwealth the national party affiliations of their native states—in many cases Republican. This progressive section often voted Republican in protest to the Byrd organization, especially in Virginia's gubernatorial elections. Republican presidential candidates (with the notable exception of Goldwater) carried the area easily, and a Republican congressman, Joel Broyhill, consistently overcame tough Democratic challenges.

The Richmond suburbs were less Republican than those of Roanoke and Washington. The two large suburban counties of Henrico and Chesterfield nonetheless showed signs of moving toward the GOP. Among the most conservative counties in the state, they gave Goldwater two-to-one majorities in 1964 and backed Republican candidates for Congress in 1962 and 1964. Republican Linwood Holton defeated the Democratic nominee for governor in both counties in 1965. There were also little noticed Republican gains on the local level. In 1963 the largest subdivision of Henrico rejected a Byrd Democrat and sent a Republican to the Board of Supervisors.[76] Chesterfield elected a Republican to the state legislature in 1966. Most responsible for these recent Republican gains were the party's conservative national image and the entrance of Negroes, labor, and assorted liberals into the state Democratic party.

The Republican party also found itself able to court both the Negro vote and that of the rural conservatives, though it is unlikely it will ever achieve much simultaneous success among these two groups. Republicans generally had taken a less segregationist stand on racial issues than the Democrats; Dalton spoke against massive resistance, and poll tax repeal was for a long time the foremost plank in the party's platform. "We can't turn our back on 20 per cent of the vote," explained one prominent Republican. "We must continue to seek Negro support." ° Another swore that Virginia Republicans "will never appeal to redneck thinking." °

Yet the party could eventually get the "redneck" vote, if only

[76] See Richmond *News Leader*, Feb. 2, 1967, for an article on L. Ray Shadwell, Jr., and his political career.

because the rednecks would have no place else to go. The time would come when the major parties in Virginia could no longer afford to take an openly segregationist stand, and rural segregationists would eventually have to join the more conservative of the two major parties. Republicans, benefiting from a conservative national image, felt they could attract conservative Democrats who would forsake party before philosophy.

The Republicans regarded youth as their most valuable long-range asset. Their leaders explained the party's attraction for the young as follows:

Our party is above all a party of young people. The Byrd organization has been growing stale and its appeal is primarily to the past. Young conservatives interested in the present alignment of our national parties are flocking to the Republicans. The Byrds, moreover, have always dealt harshly with youth. Witness the Young Turks who got their heads pinched off for disagreeing with the high command. Young people are downright opposed to monopoly of government by a single party and are joining the Republicans whom they know will experiment with new ideas. Our recent gains in the suburbs result from the influx of so many young families there.

This is not partisan self-delusion. Republicans courted the young voter by running youthful candidates in contrast to the older men of the Byrd organization. In 1952, when the party elected three congressmen in the Eisenhower landslide, Joel Broyhill, at thirty-three, was the oldest of the three. Richard Poff was twenty-nine and William Wampler a mere twenty-six. The 1965 Republican gubernatorial candidate, Linwood Holton, was but thirty-nine.

The party, as well as the candidates, was young. The Republican precinct organization in the Third District found approximately nine-tenths of its workers under forty years old. Most of the Third District leadership was under forty-five.° Teen-age Republican clubs abounded in the area's high schools, and Young Republican clubs were gaining members in the state's colleges.

Hope is often the most valuable capital of a minority party.

Suburban voters, Negroes, rural conservatives, youth—all these the Republican party could hope to attract, though not simultaneously. Among these groups signs of Republican strength still remained conjectural, nebulous, or embryonic. Yet the signs were there and increasingly they became more tangible. The Republican party by the mid-1960's was still not ready to compete on an equal footing with state Democrats. But neither was it the mountain-locked party of its yesteryear nor an amiable group of Taftite conservatives bound in the beaks of the mighty Byrds.

Part III
New Face to the Old Dominion

Chapter 9

The Harrison Administration

THE veterans of the Byrd organization emerged from the 1950's battle-scarred but still alive. There had been fiscal, racial, and election problems and divisions within the organization's once so harmonious ranks. Underneath the political turmoil ran the currents of urban growth, a youthful electorate, Republican resurgence, and Negro voting power—the full consequences of which had yet to be measured.

Harry Byrd had fought desperately to keep his organization together. When Battle had been seriously challenged in the 1949 primary, Byrd and Combs toiled to rally the faithful to Battle's side. When Republican Ted Dalton threatened Stanley in the 1953 gubernatorial race, Byrd entered the campaign and dragged Stanley to victory. When the Senator sought to retire in 1958,[1] former Governors Battle and Tuck immediately lined up for his Senate seat and the organization stood on the brink of a historic bloodletting. Byrd, to preserve harmony, ran again.[2]

The old warhorse found himself embroiled in the bitterest fights of his lifetime. In the 1950's even silences were contro-

---

[1] "Six years ago," Byrd wrote Almond in announcing his retirement, "I promised my wife I would not be a candidate for re-election. Since then as you know she suffered a stroke and is confined to her bed. She is making a great fight and I feel I should be with her at our home" (letter of Feb. 11, 1958). But Byrd eventually yielded to intense pressures from friends, admirers, and political associates around the state that he run for re-election.

[2] Latimer, p. 87.

versial, and Byrd's "golden" ones in presidential years stirred protest from Democrats throughout Virginia. At the end of the decade Byrd fought the toughest battle of all when he and Almond clashed over massive resistance.

Byrd had used his powers in the fifties to preserve the *status quo,* not to change it. A rigid posture in the midst of a changing electorate invited grave trouble, and to this immortal law even the Byrd organization was no exception. In 1960 Harry Byrd, after thirty-five years at the helm, was still the Olympian figure of Virginia politics. But the incomparable and irreplaceable Combs had died three years before, and even the Senator looked weary from his long, long struggle.

Albertis S. Harrison had the organization's support for governor in 1961. As Battle had been chosen twelve years earlier to salve the ill feelings of the Tuck years, so Harrison was the man to cool the state after the Almond administration and massive resistance. Harrison appealed to conservatives, moderates, old guards, and Young Turks. His composed and middle-road course as attorney general during the massive resistance crisis had alienated only the most diehard segregationists. Stately and silver-haired, Harrison was a country gentleman in the grand old tradition of Harry Byrd's Virginia. Commonwealth's attorney of the Southside's Brunswick County from 1932 to 1948, he then came to the state Senate, where he remained for ten years until his race for attorney general in 1958. In the 1961 primary he was joined by state Senators Mills Godwin and Robert Button, two archconservatives, to comprise the organization's ticket.

A. E. S. Stephens, then lieutenant governor, headed the opposing ticket. A Byrd man for most of his thirty-year political career, he began to deviate in the middle fifties when the desire to run for governor took hold. Although he was from the Southside's Fourth District, Stephens had alienated the stanch segregationists there by openly siding with the Almond-Perrow forces in forsaking massive resistance. His relations with Moore, Tuck, Gray, and other powers in the machine's high command had been cool for some years.[3]

[3] *Ibid.,* p. 98.

Stephen's announcement for governor had aroused such scant enthusiasm by late February that he almost decided to withdraw. He changed his mind, however, when Armistead Boothe, state senator from Alexandria and a leader of the Young Turk revolt, agreed to run for lieutenant governor on a ticket with him.[4] T. Munford Boyd, a law professor at the University of Virginia, joined the team as candidate for attorney general, and the traditional pro- and anti-Byrd primary factions emerged once again.

Stephens certainly fancied himself a typical antiorganization leader, for he charged that the Byrd machine's inner circle was bossing Virginia politics, arbitrarily destroying ambition, and crushing incentive among younger Democrats who failed to conform to the machine mold. His charges sounded somewhat odd, because he had sided with the organization most of his long political life. Harrison responded by recalling some of Stephens' 1959 statements which commended both Byrd and the organization in glowing terms.[5] Harrison won the primary comfortably, 199,519 to 152,639. He gained majorities from almost every county in the state outside southwest Virginia and the Washington suburbs.

The closer and, indeed, more significant race was between Godwin and Boothe for lieutenant governor. Here was a clearcut contest between a southside massive resister and an urban progressive, each with unique but devoutly loyal followings. Boothe called Godwin "a penny-pinching school closer," while Godwin retorted that Boothe was soft on integration and had tried to sink Virginia's right-to-work law.[6] From the sharp confrontation Godwin emerged the victor, 187,660 to 157,176, but the results clearly indicated that massive resistance, abandoned in actuality over two years before, was now waning even as a political battle cry. Godwin carried Virginia's cities by the slight margin of 1,000 votes and his victory rested in large part on runaway margins in the Southside.

The Harrison-Godwin campaign was the last statewide race which the classic Byrd coalition was able to win in style. Harri-

---

[4] *Ibid.*, p. 99.   [5] *Ibid.*, p. 100.   [6] *Ibid.*

son triumphed behind courthouse and corporation, with sprin-
kled support from conservative Republicans and moderate
Democrats. The reliable machine which had placed Byrd, Pollard, Peery, Darden, Tuck, Battle, Stanley, and Almond in the
governor's chair delivered once again for its latest son. Taking
57 per cent of the statewide vote, Harrison collected 71 per
cent from the Southside. The urban corridor, which by now
cast over half the total primary vote, gave the organization less
than 53 per cent. The traditional election lineup in Virginia
was evident: Negroes, labor, liberals, many urbanites, and
straight-ticket Democrats opposed the Byrd candidate, but the
Byrd candidate still won. In the next four years, however,
coalitions, policies, and electoral results would be radically
transformed.

The Harrison years were an Indian summer for the organization. Virginia politics moved from the turbulent fifties into a
brief period of harmony and calm in which the old order still
reigned. Inauguration day had always been a happy occasion
for Senator Byrd, and Harrison's was no exception. The festive
gathering gave the Senator a rare opportunity to reminisce
with old friends and admiring followers from every section of
Virginia.[7] Inauguration also meant one more campaign survived
and one more administration launched with the Senator's
blessing. Byrd's good humor was marred only by the thought
that outgoing Governor Almond had dared defy him on massive
resistance just a few short years before. "I was seated within
two feet of him," Almond said. "I spoke—I have always spoken
—and he grumbled something, I don't know what. He was very,
very cool." [8]

Although it never reconciled Byrd and Almond, the Harrison
administration healed most animosities of the massive resistance era. Race no longer dominated all debate, the Washington
Post reported. "Perhaps the best that can be said of Governor
Albertis S. Harrison, Jr., who is widely regarded as an ineffec-
tual leader, is that his administration encouraged a calm transi-

---

[7] Muse, *Massive Resistance*, p. 44.
[8] Norfolk *Virginian-Pilot*, June 9, 1964.

tion to a time when the issues of state government could be freely debated again." [9]

State services, on the eve of the Harrison administration, were in the same dreary condition as before. Due partly to local apathy and partly to the policies of the Byrd organization, Virginia's commitment to public services had sunk to new depths. The National Education Association found that Virginia's 1961 per pupil expenditures for schools in relation to per capita income placed the Old Dominion last among the forty-eight states covered in the survey.[10] The 1961 per capita expenditure of the state for welfare programs amounted to $2.66 — again low enough to give the commonwealth undisputed claim to last place.[11] The highways told a brighter story: Virginia ranked thirty-sixth among the forty-eight states in per capita highway expenditures from 1958 to 1962 and thirty-seventh in per vehicle highway expenditures for the same years.[12]

The low level of public services was not surprising in the light of the tax structure. In 1962 Virginia had the lowest gross tax burden in the nation: state and local taxes amounted only to 7.2 per cent of per capita income.[13] Virginia continued to collect revenue from individual and corporation income taxes

[9] Washington *Post*, July 20, 1965.

[10] See National Education Association, *Rankings of the States, 1963*. It should be noted that this statement does not mean that the absolute level of teacher salaries or per pupil expenditures were lower in Virginia than in any of the other states. It means that Virginia's school effort, as measured by state school expenditures as a percentage of state wealth, ranked forty-eighth among the forty-eight states in the survey.

[11] See *Book of the States, 1962–1963*, p. 218; R. E. Dawson and J. A. Robinson, "The Politics of Welfare," in *Politics in the American States*, ed. Herbert Jacob and K. N. Vines (Boston: Little, Brown and Co., 1965), Table 6, pp. 392–93. There are numerous other measures for state welfare programs which might have been used. The one employed by Dawson and Robinson, however, takes into account only state expenditures and incorporates *both* the number of persons on welfare rolls and average payments per recipient. Many other indexes of state welfare provide a very partial or misleading picture of welfare programs.

[12] See R. S. Friedman, "State Politics and Highways," in Jacob and Vines (eds.), Table 3, p. 433.

[13] Clara Penniman, "The Politics of Taxation," in Jacob and Vines (eds.), Table 3, pp. 308–9.

and it ranked ninth among the states in the percentage of its total revenue derived from these sources. No general sales tax had been adopted. By 1962 thirty-seven states had put such taxes into effect and relied on the proceeds for one-quarter to one-half of their total revenue.[14] Virginia, however, refused to budge.

Thus Virginia politics was much the same at the start of Harrison's administration as it had been during the Tuck years immediately following World War II. The level of public services, the tax structure, the election coalitions, even the low percentage of voter turnouts told much the same tale in 1962 as they had in 1945.[15] That they did so was somewhat incredible. Francis Pickens Miller, Ted Dalton, Robert Whitehead, and the Young Turks had all demanded from the Byrd organization a more progressive stand on public services in the early fifties. Horace Edwards in 1949 and Governor Almond as late as 1960 pleaded for the adoption of a sales tax to meet state needs, but both were stymied by unusual political circumstances. Urban growth, Negro organization, the political emergence of a new generation all forewarned the Byrd organization that its courthouse conservatism faced a rocky future. Repeated cries came to abandon the poll tax. Yet as Harrison took office, the basic problems still existed, though massive resistance had diverted attention from them for a while.

Nor was Harrison to lead Virginia through major reforms. He broke little new ground during his term of office, though he did put Virginia in a frame of mind for future progress. The General Assembly enjoyed its most harmonious period since Battle's governorship. "You couldn't start a fight down there with a hand grenade," grumbled veteran state Senator Ed McCue.[16]

Harrison spent much of his time promoting the state's indus-

[14] U.S. Bureau of the Census, *State Tax Collections in 1962* (Washington, 1962), Tables 1, 3–5.

[15] In the 1960 presidential election only 33.4 per cent of Virginia's voting age population went to the polls as compared with a national average of 63.8 per cent. Virginia thus ranked forty-sixth in turnout for this election. See Lester W. Milbraith, "Political Participation in the States," in Jacob and Vines (eds.), Table 3, pp. 38–39.

[16] Norfolk *Virginian-Pilot*, Nov. 16, 1966.

trial development. Here lay his path of quiet improvement and progress without controversy. In his opening address to the General Assembly the new governor emphasized the "demand that Virginia have an active and vigorous industrial development program." He proposed the "transfer of the functions of industrial development and planning, advertising, and public relations from the present Department of Conservation and Economic Development to [the office of] the Governor" to enable the chief executive to be "more closely identified and familiar with all activities designed to promote industrial development." [17]

For the next four years Harrison spoke often of Virginia's attraction for industry; he met with large companies considering locating in the state; he poured funds and advice into the newly elevated Division of Industrial Development.[18] "There is no doubt that he gave industrial development a more prestigious position in over-all state operations than any previous Virginia Governor," one top official declared.° In this respect Harrison moved to meet the demands of the times. Publicly suggesting that other states had been both "more aggressive" and "more successful" [19] than Virginia in attracting industry, he began to talk less of Virginia's glorious past and more of its present needs.

Virginia in the early 1960's experienced a period of sustained economic and population growth. The trends of development noted during the 1940's and 1950's continued for the most part from 1960 to 1965. The major difference was that the state's political arm was at last beginning to augment its economic progress instead of ignoring or actively working against it. The commonwealth recorded a 12 per cent population growth rate from 1960 to 1965, over 40 per cent above that for the nation.

---

[17] *Address to General Assembly*, Jan. 15, 1962.

[18] Box 5 of Harrison's Executive Papers in the Virginia State Library reveals the extent of Harrison's effort to attract industry to Virginia. The letters written to industrial prospects, the brochures published to advertise the state's attraction to new business, and the personal attention which the Governor paid to this field surpassed that of any previous administration and clearly marked this as the area of Harrison's greatest concern.

[19] *Address to General Assembly*, Jan. 15, 1962.

Of this increase, one-third was due to inmigration from other states.[20] Every subdivision of the urban corridor boasted a higher percentage increase in population than any region outside the corridor. Virginia's metropolitan areas expanded at an average rate of 16 per cent as compared with an average rate of 7.5 per cent for the rest of the state. By 1965 these metropolitan areas contained 53.4 per cent of the state's total population.[21]

Growth within the metropolitan areas focused on the suburban counties. Many cities, such as Richmond, Roanoke, Lynchburg, Norfolk, and Portsmouth, showed little population growth and, in some cases, an actual decline. But the suburbs were booming; Henrico County noted a 20 per cent increase for the five years, Chesterfield 29 per cent, Campbell 18 per cent and Roanoke 20 per cent. Even more important was the spill of metropolitan areas into counties which before had been uninvolved in urban expansion. The four counties comprising the northern Piedmont, Clarke, Fauquier, Loudoun, and Prince William, grew more rapidly than any other section of the state. They recorded a 30 per cent population increase as a result of the overflow from the Washington metropolitan area. The growth of the Richmond-Petersburg-Hopewell complex spread into the traditionally rural counties of Hanover, Prince George, and Dinwiddie. In the early sixties rural Virginia was losing not merely its percentage of the state's population but of its land area as well.[22]

Rural areas fared variously during the early sixties. The Cumberland area in far southwest Virginia and the Eastern Shore at the opposite end of the state were the only regions to decline in population. Counties in central southside and southwest Virginia showed negligible gains. The Shenandoah Valley and the northwest Piedmont, however, gained second only to the urban corridor.

Virginia had pockets of unemployment, especially in far southwest Virginia. There the six counties in the coal region averaged unemployment rates of 8 to 10 per cent. Yet the state

[20] Bureau of Population and Economic Research, p. 1.　　　[21] *Ibid.*, p. 7.
[22] See *ibid.*, pp. 6–12.

as a whole surged ahead: unemployment was well below the national average. Approximately 328 new plants located in the state from 1960 to 1965, and personal per capita income averaged an annual 3.75 per cent increase after adjustments for inflation.[23] The growing prosperity contributed to the impression that the Byrd organization was entering an era of long-awaited "good times."

Byrd himself had never seemed in better spirits. Celebrating his seventy-fourth birthday on June 10, 1961, America's walking-est senator led a troup of breathless hikers up Old Rag Mountain, where he dedicated Byrd's Nest No. 1—a shelter he had donated to the hiking and camping public. "I've been climbing this mountain since I was 16 years old," he said. "Let's see—that's about 60 years, isn't it?"[24]

The bareheaded, ruddy-faced man in the old khaki pants and collarless, faded blue shirt was most comfortable on the Blue Ridge Mountain peaks of Shenandoah National Park. In the early 1960's Byrd may have reached the summit of his Senate career as well. The eighteen years following World War II were a period of great congressional influence when senior conservatives in House and Senate successfully stalled executive programs from the Fair Deal through the New Frontier. In one sense Byrd was more responsible for this course of events than Senators Richard Russell, Robert Taft, and Congressman Charles Halleck, since his Virginia colleagues and lieutenants controlled critical committees in both branches of the legislature. When Kennedy arrived in the White House, he found the torch passed to a new generation everywhere but in Congress. "It is an irony," remarked *Time* in 1962, "that, as he nears the end of his political life . . . Harry Byrd has arrived at a crest of effective power and influence. He has, in fact, become a symbol of the Capitol Hill rebellion against the young activist who lives at 1600 Pennsylvania Avenue."[25]

[23] See Division of Industrial Development and Planning, *Manufacturing Plants in Virginia Established since 1950* (Richmond, 1966), p. 1, and its *The Virginia Economy in 1965* (Richmond, 1965), pp. 4–5.

[24] Richmond *Times-Dispatch*, June 12, 1961.

[25] *Time*, Aug. 17, 1962, pp. 11–12.

The President gamely tried to outmaneuver Byrd as the 87th Congress drew to a close. His Medicare measure was buried beneath a packet of bills scheduled for hearings before the Finance Committee, which Byrd had chaired since 1955. If Kennedy was desperate to pass the measure, his haste was not contagious. Byrd moved at a turtle's pace, scheduling lengthy hearings on tax revision before Medicare. With the session rapidly drawing to an end, Kennedy decreed that Medicare be tacked onto a minor bill and brought to a Senate vote without being considered by Byrd's committee. But in the folkways of the gentlemanly Senate, it was risky to bypass a senior member such as Byrd. By a floor vote of 52 to 48 Medicare "died a premature death and the Administration suffered a sobering defeat." [26]

Kennedy's tax revision and tax cut proposals met much the same fate. By the end of the 87th Congress, Byrd and his colleagues had so hamstrung the young President that many observers pointed to a failure in leadership at the White House level. "In such an atmosphere," continued *Time,*

leadership must inevitably be taken over by the few legislators who really know what they stand for. Byrd knows what he stands for. So does everyone else. Byrd believes a dollar should be worth a dollar. This is still a popular notion in the U.S. And so, in one of the most crucial of all areas, Byrd has become a kind of unwavering banner around which the wanderers and wonderers of Capitol Hill can rally.[27]

On his seventy-sixth birthday, in the summer of 1963, the Senator was again hiking—this time to Mary's Rock to dedicate Byrd's Nest No. 3. A group of reporters tagged along and fired questions:

—What about 1964? Would Byrd run again next year?
—In due time the Senator would make the decision.
—What of President Kennedy's new civil rights legislation?
—Byrd saw it bringing on a southern filibuster and jeopardizing the President's tax reduction bill.

[26] *Ibid.,* p. 12.   [27] *Ibid.*

—On state matters. Had the time come to reconsider pay-as-you-go as a method of highway finance, to try something new?

—"I'd like to know what it would be. Pay-as-you-go has worked admirably." [28]

—What of the future of Virginia politics?

At this point, the Senator preferred to talk more about present and past wonders of nature in Shenandoah National Park. "It does me good just to see all these people out here," he said gazing at the hundreds of campers, young and old, cooking, eating, playing games, and enjoying the outdoor life. "Look at those children. You know it's good for them." At the dedication ceremony 250 people, including some who made the trip up in trucks, applauded as Byrd touched on his favorite theme. "Everybody ought to get out in the open," he said, "and not stay in the city and get smothered by gases. Let's get out in the open. That would be the salvation of our nation." There was applause, too, as Byrd, champion of outdoor life and rural virtues, said he expected to be mountain climbing "for a great many more years." [29]

Beneath apparent harmony, however, opposing forces gathered. Anti-Byrds still hoped to eliminate the poll tax, break golden silence, accelerate public services, and reapportion the legislature. Negroes, labor, youth, urbanites, and Republicans all demanded a greater say in the commonwealth's politics and policies. And within the next three years, their demands would all be partially granted.

In 1964, the third year of the Harrison administration, several sacrosanct practices and traditions of the old order of Virginia politics fell by the wayside. In 1964 far more than in any previous year national trends and federal decisions touched a reluctant Virginia. To some it seemed the commonwealth was at last entering the mainstream of national life; others contended that Virginia had always fared much better in the eddies.

[28] Richmond *Times-Dispatch,* June 10, 1963.   [29] *Ibid.*

The Warren Court had never been a favorite institution of conservative Virginians. In 1954 the Court's school desegregation decision had ushered in the stormiest period of twentieth-century Virginia politics. Now, ten years later, the Court again struck at the "Virginia way of life," and once again Virginia had to comply with its decision. This time, however, compliance came with far less anguish than in massive resistance.

On June 15, 1964, the Supreme Court handed down the *Reynolds* v. *Simms* decision ruling emphatically that the Fourteenth Amendment's equal protection clause required that the seats in both houses of a bicameral state legislature be apportioned on a population basis. "Legislators represent people, not trees or acres," wrote Chief Justice Earl Warren in the majority opinion. "Legislators are elected by voters, not farms or cities or economic interests. . . . To the extent that a citizen's right to vote is debased, he is that much less a citizen. . . . Diluting of the weight of votes because of place of residence impairs basic constitutional rights under the 14th Amendment just as much as invidious discriminations based on race or economic status." [30]

Virginia had done better than most states in its legislative apportionments. By 1960 there was not a single legislative body in a single state in which there was not at least a 2 to 1 population disparity between the most and least heavily populated districts. For example, disparity was 242 to 1 in the Connecticut House, 223 to 1 in the Nevada Senate, 141 to 1 in the Rhode Island House, and 99 to 1 in the Georgia Senate. [31] In the 1964 Virginia Senate the ideal constituency was 100,000 and districts ranged from 62,000 to 163,000. In the House delegates represented constituencies ranging from 22,000 to 95,000, with the ideal approximately 40,000. [32] The Court, however, found the disparities too large and ordered redistricting before the 1965 elections.

The 1962 General Assembly, as required by the state constitution, had reapportioned itself, but the reapportionment had

[30] *Reynolds* v. *Simms*, 377 U.S. 533.
[31] *Congress and the Nation*, p. 1525.
[32] Richmond *News Leader*, June 15, 1964.

only been a token one. One Senate seat was transferred from southwest Virginia to Fairfax County and another from Richmond to Henrico County, the latter making no real difference in urban-rural representation. Southwest Virginia also lost three delegates to Fairfax County and the cities of Alexandria and Virginia Beach. "Not enough," urban forces argued in the 1962 General Assembly, and northern Virginia lawmakers, later joined by Norfolk representatives, brought suit seeking more representation for urban voters.[33] The Supreme Court backed their pleas, and the Virginia legislature in the fall of 1964 found itself facing a very delicate task.

As it turned out, however, the 1964 reapportionment session was not so tempestuous as many had predicted. The Byrd organization left all its old stalwarts intact, threw two incumbent Republican senators into the same district, and carved up a couple of junior Democrats in underpopulated, rural areas. The Washington suburbs in northern Virginia acquired one additional senator and five more delegates, while Hampton Roads increased its Senate representation from 6 to 8 and House strength from 16 to 19. In all, eleven seats in the 140-man legislature were transferred from rural to urban areas,[34] not enough to transform the legislature but enough to tip the balance of power on close votes. "This area [Washington suburbs] is going to become more a part of the state," commented Armistead Boothe on the eve of the prospective switch. "That's what we're aiming our energies at. These new members of the legislature from urban areas aren't going to try to take over the state. No one's out to ruin the tobacco farmer. Along with responsibility comes wisdom. I really don't see radical departures into new fields of legislation." [35]

Delegate M. Caldwell Butler, Republican leader of the House from Roanoke, was less restrained. "Every close urban-rural conflict which in the past has resulted in a rural victory will now be an urban victory," he predicted. "I do think the urban strength reflected in the reapportionment plans could bring us almost into the 20th century." [36]

[33] *Ibid.*   [34] Richmond *Times-Dispatch,* Dec. 2, 1964.
[35] Richmond *News Leader,* Nov. 28, 1964.   [36] *Ibid.*

More important than the immediate transfer of the eleven seats was the assurance that future gains in Virginia's urban population would be met with proportionate gains in representation in the state legislature. Virginia might well have been spared the worst consequences of massive resistance in 1956 if the legislature had been apportioned on a population basis and urban forces had acquired the few extra votes needed to attach a local option provision to the massive resistance legislation. The Byrd fiscal policy and attitude on public services might also have been somewhat more flexible and progressive had urban areas had more representation in previous legislatures. Virginia's legislative future began to look quite different from Virginia's legislative past. The 1966 General Assembly, the first to convene on a reapportioned basis, demonstrated new verve and it set goals for itself which were before unthinkable.

Along with new state goals Virginia's Democratic party was slowly but surely perceiving a sense of responsibility to the national party—a responsibility overreaching even deep-seated differences on national issues. The Virginia Democratic party in 1964 openly acknowledged for the first time in many years more than a merely nominal affiliation with its national counterpart. The national Democratic party and its Virginia branch had been so seldom of the same frame of mind that many wondered aloud what was still holding them together.[37] From 1912 to 1960 Virginia delegations had only twice given first ballot support to the Democratic party's ultimate nominee, and those occasions were merely the perfunctory, second-term nominations of Wilson in 1916 and Roosevelt in 1936. Since Roosevelt's death relations had further deteriorated. Tuck, early in 1948, had introduced in the General Assembly his anti-Truman bill, and Byrd's golden silences had helped to hand Virginia's electoral votes in 1952, 1956, and 1960 to the Republican presidential nominee. The 1960 election was a case in point. Virginia Democrats went to the national convention instructed to support Lyndon B. Johnson. Byrd and Moore, though members of the Virginia delegation, felt no compulsion

[37] See Chapters 3 and 8 for a discussion of the Byrd organization's relationships with the national Democratic party.

to attend the convention. Instead they went to Switzerland for a bit of mountain climbing. The Senator heard from afar of Kennedy's nomination, however, and shortly after his return told a chuckling audience at his annual apple orchard picnic that in politics "silence is golden." While Byrd maintained his silence throughout the presidential election, Democrats for Nixon-Lodge movements appeared across the state and waged vigorous, well-financed campaigns. Nixon carried Virginia 404,521 to 362,327 despite the efforts of William C. Battle, the son of former Governor John S. Battle, to swing the Old Dominion to Kennedy.[38]

The successive Republican presidential victories in Virginia angered an increasingly large segment of straight-ticket Democrats, who thought Byrd's golden silences an outright betrayal of the national party. Concern mounted even among many conservative Virginia Democrats, who contended that voter defections at the top were contagious and were gradually seeping down to the local level. By the summer of 1964 sentiment began to build in various quarters for at least a cautious step by Virginia Democrats in the direction of the national party.

Those familiar with the tactics of the Byrd organization at state convention time were none too sure that such a step would be taken. Even the mildest state convention would be certain to pass a flood of resolutions endorsing states' rights and attacking civil ones. Moderate and straight-ticket Democrats concentrated on trying to wring from the convention an endorsement of President Johnson, the certain 1964 Democratic standard bearer.

It was rumored several days before the convention that there would be no effort by the hard-core organization leaders to prevent such a move. Governor Harrison and others had, in fact, planned to submit a mild endorsement of President Johnson for convention approval. Yet when Byrd checked into the Hotel John Marshall on the eve of the convention and learned of Harrison's intentions, he exploded. If a resolution endorsing President Johnson were presented to the convention, Byrd

[38] Latimer, pp. 96–97.

said, he would go to the floor and denounce it.[39] Later that night in a tenth-floor suite of the hotel Byrd held an hour-long summit conference with his son, Governor Harrison, and other leading Democratic officials.[40] No one could calm him. Even Judge Smith is reported to have emerged from the hotel room shaking his head and saying, "You just can't reason with him." [41] But Byrd prevailed, and the word of "no endorsement" was duly handed down the grapevine.

When the convention delegates assembled next day in Richmond's Mosque, the Democratic party faced an unprecedented struggle. Few could remember such a sultry afternoon, and delegates sweltering in the Mosque cursed the absence of air conditioning. Earlier that afternoon the organization-dominated Resolutions Committee had passed a statement admitting that Johnson "apparently . . . will be nominated" and appealing to him "in his campaign for election, to support and defend the Jeffersonian principles of separation of powers . . . among the executive, legislative, and judicial branches of the government." This timid stand was challenged on the convention floor by those who would forever rid "Democrat" of its Virginia and Jeffersonian prefixes. "Tidewater Don't Need Goldwater" read a Second District banner, and the Ninth District of southwest Virginia fairly bristled with "LBJ" signs. Folk singer Jackie Stephens had earlier entertained the convention with an ominously stirring rendition of "Will the Circle Be Unbroken?" [42] and received a much warmer reception than would any of the vaunted circle that afternoon. As soon as Governor Harrison read to the convention the noncommittal report of the Resolutions Committee, pro-Johnson forces began yelling, booing, and wildly waving their "Johnson for President" signs. Delegate Edgar Bacon of Lee County immediately seized the floor and offered a substitute:

Be it resolved that this convention endorses the election of Lyndon B. Johnson as President of the United States in the 1964 November

[39] Washington *Post,* July 23, 1965.
[40] Richmond *News Leader,* July 18, 1964.
[41] Washington *Post,* July 23, 1965.
[42] Richmond *Times-Dispatch,* July 19, 1965.

election and further endorses the nominees of the Democratic Party and urges all members of the party to join hands to work and vote for a Democratic victory for the entire ticket.[43]

The Bacon amendment sparked a cutting debate as the hoarse voices of the speakers strained to override the static of private pressurings and feverish pleadings taking place within doubtful delegations. "How could anyone oppose a resolution urging Democrats to support Democratic candidates?" Bacon asked. Easily, thought state Senator Charley Moses, Byrd wheelhorse from southside Appomattox County: "The loyalty pledge never intended us to support Democrats who espouse foreign ideologies. Johnson broke the pledge when he took my rights. For God's sake," pleaded the veteran state senator, "vote it down." Next, above the din, the voice of Representative Pat Jennings of the Fightin' Ninth: "Nothing has happened to cause us to turn our backs on Lyndon B. Johnson," Jennings argued. "Let's be Democrats from the courthouse to the White House." Former state Senator and Young Turk Stuart Carter then summoned Democratic unity in ousting the Sixth District's Republican congressman, Richard Poff. "How much longer," he ended, "are we going to rely on Jefferson and Jackson?"[44]

Delegates tensed as the roll call neared and the district chieftains grabbed floor microphones to report the vote. The process was marked by erratic and confusing changes in several districts, but the general picture was shockingly clear. As expected, the Ninth District, the Washington suburbs, and the Tidewater's Second District (Norfolk-Portsmouth) went unanimously for the Johnson endorsement.[45] Also as expected the southside Fourth District and the Third (Richmond area), under the leadership of Byrd backer J. Clifford Miller, Jr., both turned in unanimous unit-rule votes for no endorsement. Byrd's own district, the Seventh, predictably voted 109½ to 8½ against the Bacon amendment. What astounded most observers, however, was how poorly the organization fared in the four

---

[43] *Ibid.*   [44] Richmond *Times-Dispatch,* July 18, 1964.
[45] Vote taken from *ibid.,* July 20, 1964.

doubtful areas. The Fifth District in western southside Virginia, home bailiwick of Bill Tuck, had not imposed a unit rule on its convention vote. It saw many delegates in the western third of the district bolt the line, and finally went for no endorsement by the surprisingly slim margin of 57 to 42. Lack of a unit rule in Howard Smith's fiefdom, the Eighth, also cost the organization 20 votes. Most devastatingly, however, the Sixth District went 113 to 19 for Johnson, and Sidney Kellam, the party-first potentate of Virginia Beach, obtained a 70 to 25 vote for the Bacon amendment in the First District. Total— 633½ for endorsing Johnson, 596½ for no endorsement. Pandemonium ensued as Pat Jennings, delirious with joy, yelled, "We won boys, we won! It's been a long dry spell, but we won!" [46]

Byrd never appeared on the convention floor. His lieutenants had clearly been outmaneuvered, and the Senator's states' rights concept of political parties suffered irreparable damage. It was the first time in anyone's memory that the Byrd organization had suffered such a significant reversal at a state convention. "Does this upheaval signify a historic turning point in Virginia politics," asked the *Times-Dispatch*, "or is it just another momentary lapse like those which the Byrd organization has occasionally suffered in the General Assembly, only to come back stronger than ever? Does it indicate a presidential wind is blowing that will take Virginia back into the Democratic column for the first time since 1948? Is it, perhaps, a step that might contribute to the possible re-arrangement of party lines in Southern States—a possibility discerned faintly by some analyses of what happened earlier last week at the Republican National Convention in San Francisco?" [47]

The Virginia Democratic convention of 1964 was the first unmistakable signal that the state party was gradually but inevitably being nudged in the direction of its national counterpart. Some Virginia Democrats still contested this appraisal of their party's course and others contended that any leftward movement was proceeding with glacial slowness, but a modified realignment of party philosophies in Virginia was increas-

[46] *Ibid.*, July 19, 1964.   [47] *Ibid.*, July 20, 1964.

ingly perceptible. The Virginia Republican party had not significantly altered its position, but Virginia Democrats since the summer of 1964 moved, albeit haltingly, closer to the national Democratic fold. Few observers expected them to march in the Great Society parade, but equally few expected them to remain an almost exclusively conservative political party. The stanch presidential Republican—Harry Byrd Democrat appeared to be a slowly dwindling breed.

The presidential election of 1964 furthered the trend, at least among Virginia's top-ranking Democratic officials. The appointment of Sidney Kellam, Virginia's Democratic national committeeman, as campaign manager for the Johnson-Humphrey team, epitomized the movement toward a single Democratic standard. Kellam had long been a devoted Byrd lieutenant, had managed the campaigns of former Governors Battle and Stanley, but had also stressed party loyalty at both the state and national levels. "I have a feeling," remarked Kellam in early September of 1964, "that the people of Virginia, having received excellent government from the Democratic Party at the national as well as the state level over a great number of years, do not wish to see it pushed aside and supplanted by the Republican Party. If we are to prevent this, it will be necessary for all Democrats to unite and devote their time and attention to electing the Democratic nominees, whoever and wherever they are." [48]

Early in September, Kellam was the only politician of statewide stature who predicted Johnson would carry Virginia. Governor Harrison thought Goldwater ahead,[49] and indeed few would bet that conservative Virginia, which had supported Republican presidential candidates in 1952, 1956, and 1960, would now switch to Johnson. Yet by October so many novel and bewildering currents had beset the commonwealth that prognosticators studying the state's political skies resorted to the weatherman's classic forecast of "sunny weather ahead, marked by considerable cloudiness and more than a slim chance of rain." The state had indeed turned topsy-turvy, and

[48] Richmond *News Leader*, Sept. 3, 1964.
[49] Richmond *Times-Dispatch*, Sept. 4, 1964.

citizen movements exhibited a cross-fertilization of all party breeds. There were Virginia Democrats for Goldwater-Byrd, Virginia Republicans for Byrd, and two major candidates running for the same congressional seat both claiming to be the only true Democrat. Byrd, of course, was the only certain factor in all these political equations. Standing for a sixth full term in the United States Senate, he found both national tickets madly trying to clutch his coattails. "Barry and Harry" went the message on one gold-and-black bumper sticker, while another read, "Vote for Johnson-Byrd November Third." [50] It was rumored that Goldwater excluded Virginia on his southern speaking tour because he did not wish to be in the embarrassing position of standing on the same platform with Byrd's Republican opponent.[51]

Byrd's position on the presidential campaign was subject to the most intimate scrutiny. Officially he was silent. But this failed to satisfy reporters. "[Byrd's] presidential year silences have ranged from cool to hostile," one remarked, "but his silence this time seemed warm and friendly." [52] After all, Sidney Kellam, one of Byrd's foremost lieutenants, was managing the Johnson campaign, and many thought this provided a clue to the Senator's own attitude. Yet Byrd, Jr., Moore, Gray, Tuck, and others close to the Senator remained silent on the presidential race.[53] Virginians religiously sorted these myriad clues for some key to the Senator's "true" feelings. Byrd chose to remain majestically and enigmatically silent.

Two important Virginians spoke out for the national Democratic ticket in an emphatic manner. They were the state's highest elective officials, Governor Harrison and Lieutenant Governor Godwin. Both were southside Virginians; both had impeccable conservative backgrounds, and both had enjoyed the organization's approval in their every election. Godwin had his eye on the 1965 gubernatorial race and he realized his stance in the 1964 presidential campaign would have a critical bearing on his prospects. Yet both officials clearly associated them-

---

[50] Richmond *Times-Dispatch*, Oct. 4, 1964.   [51] *Ibid.*, Sept. 9, 1964.
[52] *Ibid.*, Nov. 8, 1964.   [53] See Richmond *News Leader*, Oct. 19, 24, 1964.

selves with the Johnson campaign by boarding the controversial Lady Bird Special as it whistlestopped through Virginia.

The Lady Bird Special was destined to excite symbolic commotion in Virginia politics long before it first whistled in the Virginia air. The red, white, and blue train was to carry Luci, Lynda, and Lady Bird Johnson through eight southern states, where Mrs. Johnson would issue gentle reminders of her husband's southern background. Long before the trip Virginia papers carried daily articles on the elaborate preparations for the journey and the women's pages buzzed with features on Lady Bird's projected wardrobe.[54] Not all the fuss centered on the clothes, however. There were some Virginians, especially in the Southside, who viewed the First Lady's journey as a full-scale invasion of the commonwealth's sacred soil. Those entrenching to resist this influence were horrified to learn that Lieutenant Governor and Mrs. Godwin expected to escort Mrs. Johnson on the Virginia leg of her trip. Their dismay knew no bounds when Harrison boarded the Lady Bird Special in Richmond, not merely as a southern gentleman meeting the First Lady of the United States, but as the governor of Virginia making a pro-Johnson campaign speech.[55] Harrison, who at the July state convention had acquiesced to Byrd's plan of no endorsement, by early October was making more than the customary gestures for the national Democratic ticket.

Lyndon Johnson carried Virginia with 53.5 per cent of the vote, and the state entered the Democratic column for the first time since the Truman victory in 1948. The reasons for Johnson's victory were numerous. The Harrison-Godwin endorsements and Kellam's unflagging efforts were undoubtedly important. Godwin emerged from the election with his gubernatorial hopes much increased, and Kellam in the aftermath of the Johnson sweep seemed a brilliant and supreme political strategist. Senator Byrd won 64 per cent of the total Senate vote against six opponents, but his defeated GOP adversary, Richard May, charged that Virginia's Democratic machinery

[54] See Richmond *Times-Dispatch*, Oct. 5, 1964; Richmond *News Leader*, Oct. 2, 1964.

[55] Richmond *Times-Dispatch*, Oct. 8, 1964.

had slipped from the hands of Harry Byrd. "I feel like it's no longer the Byrd machine now," May said. "It's the Kellam Machine." [56] John Carter, raucous right-winger from Danville, echoed the charge. "We have seen in this campaign," lamented Carter, "Sidney Kellam, disciple of political expediency par excellence, wrest the political leadership in Virginia from our very conscientious Senator Byrd without even a struggle. . . . [Kellam] bludgeoned half of the General Assembly into supporting Johnson for fear of political reprisals." [57] Although these comments were overstatements and Sidney Kellam was not to inherit the Byrd machine, it was clear in 1964 that the aging Senator was slowly relaxing the reins.

Johnson's victory in Virginia cannot be attributed only to the efforts and endorsements of leading Democratic officials. Many Virginians worried over Goldwater's casual approach to the bomb; others feared he would sabotage the Social Security system; and the farmers were disturbed by his views on price supports. All the issues which contributed to Goldwater's national defeat helped submerge him in Virginia.

The 1964 presidential election was the first election of modern Virginia politics. It marked a great watershed and set many of the trends which resulted in the political turnabouts and upheavals of the next two years.

In 1964, for the first time in over sixty years, Virginians could register and vote without paying a poll tax six months before election day. The twenty-fourth Amendment to the United States Constitution, ratified on January 23, 1964, banned the state poll tax as a prerequisite for voting in federal elections. [58] With poll tax barriers down, the number of registered voters in

[56] Blackford, "Kellam," p. 53.

[57] Richmond *Times-Dispatch,* Oct. 24, 1964.

[58] The pending repeal of the poll tax in federal elections stirred the General Assembly in a special session in the fall of 1963 to enact legislation requiring persons to furnish proof of continuing residence in the state if they desired to vote in federal elections. Such proof was to be furnished six months before each federal election by filing a certificate of residence with the county or city treasurer (*Acts of Assembly, Extra Session, 1963,* pp. 4–9). However, a federal district court on May 29, 1964, declared the legislation unconstitutional. See *University of Virginia News Letter,* Sept. 15, 1964, p. 1.

Virginia increased by 224,305 from April to October 1964. Over 150,000 of these new voters were registered for federal elections only and were not qualified to vote in state elections where the poll tax was still required.[59] Nonetheless, the rise in registrations during 1964 dwarfed the combined increases in registered voters of the last seven years.[60] Voting in the 1964 general election in Virginia passed the one million mark for the first time, an increase of 270,000 since the last presidential election in 1960. Forty-one per cent of Virginia's adult population voted in the 1964 presidential election—an impressive gain of eight percentage points above 1960. Virginia's level of voter participation, which was thirty percentage points below national turnouts in presidential elections from 1948 to 1960, moved to within twenty points of the national average in 1964 (see Table 22). Although turnouts in Virginia still compared poorly with national participation, the 1964 voting increases were significant. Poll tax removal and the resultant expansion of the Virginia electorate were soon to pose novel problems for political leaders accustomed to running in a state whose rate of voter turnout was among the lowest in the country and whose selective electorate was among the nation's most predictable.[61]

In 1964, for the first time in the 20th century, Negro voting power emerged as a powerful statewide political force. In 1964 Negro votes provided Johnson with his margin of victory in Virginia. Of the 175,000 to 200,000 Negroes registered to vote in November 1964, 125,000 to 150,000 are estimated to have voted, and at least 95 per cent of the Negro vote went to

[59] Official registration figures, April–October 1964. [60] See *ibid.*, 1957–64.

[61] Professor Ralph Eisenberg in a detailed analysis of the 1964 presidential vote in Virginia concluded that poll tax removal was the primary, though not the only, cause of the increased turnout: "This large and widespread increase in voting at a pace almost four times as great as the growth in the State's adult population and contrary to the direction of national participation suggests the impact of the removal of the poll tax upon the size and complexion of the Virginia electorate. . . . The widespread and uncorrelated nature of proportionate increases in voting throughout the State indicates that population growth was not the primary factor contributing to the record turnout. Rather, the increases seem attributable to the removal of poll tax payment as a voting prerequisite" ("The 1964 Presidential Election in Virginia: A Political Omen?" *University of Virginia News Letter*, April 15, 1965, p. 30).

Table 22 The 1964 Presidential Election in Virginia: Signs of an Expanded Electorate

Year	Total population 21 years and over	Total votes cast	Increase from preceding election	Increase from preceding election	Adult population voting in Virginia	Eligible adult population voting Nationally
				%	%	%
1948	2,015,000	419,256	23,872	6.0	20.8	51.5
1952	2,083,000	619,689	200,433	47.8	29.8	62.0
1956	2,198,000	697,978	78,289	12.6	31.8	60.1
1960	2,313,000	771,449	73,471	10.5	33.3	63.8
1964	2,532,000	1,042,267	270,818	35.1	41.2	61.1

Source: Ralph Eisenberg, "Virginia Votes for President: Patterns and Prospects," *University of Virginia News Letter*, Sept. 15, 1964; Ralph Eisenberg, "The 1964 Presidential Election in Virginia: A Political Omen?" *ibid.*, April 15, 1965.

Johnson.[62] An estimated 55,000 additional Negroes registered during 1964 [63] as a result of poll tax repeal, aversion to Goldwater, and the increasing sophistication of Negro political registration drives. "Lyndon B. Johnson 1770—Barry M. Goldwater 6," read the returns from Richmond's Negro Precinct 64. Other samplings from around the state told the same story (see Table 23).

Table 23 Returns from Selected Negro Precincts in Richmond and Hampton Roads in the 1964 Presidential Election

City	Precinct	Democratic	Percentage	Republican	Percentage
Richmond	62	2,138	99.3	14	0.7
Norfolk	4	2,022	99.0	21	1.0
Virginia Beach	Seatack	614	99.7	2	0.3
Portsmouth	Stuart, 3rd	2,290	99.5	11	0.5
Hampton	Pembroke	1,238	99.4	8	0.6
Newport News	Jefferson Park	1,325	100.0	0	0.0

Source: Eisenberg, "1964 Presidential Election," p. 32.

Virginia's southside Fourth District went Republican in 1964 for the first time in recent history. This tobacco growing, governor-producing area had long maintained unshakeable Democratic loyalties. The Fourth gave Truman a large margin in 1948. It backed Stevenson in 1952 and 1956 while the state went overwhelmingly for Eisenhower. And it voted for Kennedy in 1960. Johnson's support of the 1964 Civil Rights Act, however, was too much for southside segregationists. Backlash overrode traditional allegiances to the Democratic party and such counties as Appomattox, Brunswick, Buckingham, Lunenberg, Mecklenberg, Prince George, and Sussex went Republican for the first time in the century. The District as a whole backed Goldwater 45,700 to 42,800.

[62] Estimates of the number of Negro voters vary widely: the Richmond *Times-Dispatch*, Nov. 8, 1964, estimated 100,000 Negroes voted. Professor Eisenberg claimed "at least 160,000" ("1964 Presidential Election," p. 31).

[63] Official registration figures, April–October, 1964.

The urban majorities for Johnson smothered the votes of rural segregationists however, and the Tenth District (Virginia's Washington suburbs) cast over 35,000 more votes than the second heaviest-voting district to give Johnson a 105,200 to 63,700 victory. Just four years earlier the Tenth had voted for Nixon. The Norfolk-Portsmouth complex, the 2nd District, went for Johnson 57,700 to 35,900. Returns from these two highly urbanized areas reflected far more than a Negro voting bloc. They announced the day when the more moderate urban areas of the commonwealth were flexing their voting muscles.

Expanding electorate, Negro voting power, large returns from urban areas, and the growing estrangement of the Southside were easily read into the 1964 presidential election in Virginia. And there were many, many readers. But perhaps the most conscientious of all those who poured over the election returns was the Lieutenant Governor of Virginia, Mills E. Godwin.

Chapter 10

The Godwin Coalition
1965

MILLS E. GODWIN, JR., was above all a realist; he recognized that in politics winning elections was essential. He dealt deftly with every tool of his trade and learned that to keep a ship afloat, some of the cargo might have to be tossed overboard. A politician must retreat as well as attack, and Godwin had both skills in his repertoire. Working with power was more effective than revolt against it; party regularity had to be maintained even in the lean years, and votes not words were political currency. Godwin knew all this and acted upon it. He was a master practitioner of the political art.

Godwin was not a politician in the colloquial sense of the word. He was no backslapper or gladhander, nor did he beam a 1,000-watt smile. To flattery he was virtually immune; he saw behind it and let one know he did.

Although he was a realist and although he could compromise, Godwin was no opportunist. He was flexible in the long run, never bendable in the short. When he took a stand, he took it firmly and brought his booming voice to his aid. He was austere, more a born leader than a boon companion. He evoked confidence, not warmth. Because he could lead and because he could also change his course of leadership, Godwin has survived and flourished in the bewildering twists and turns of recent Virginia politics.

A native of Chuckatuck, Virginia, Godwin was educated in

southside Nansemond County, where he became class president
at his local high school. In college at William and Mary he
played basketball and developed into a crack debater. After
gaining his law degree at the University of Virginia, he worked
for three years with the FBI before he returned home to enter
the political fray. In 1947 the thirty-three-year-old lawyer, already a member of the Ruritan Club, the Masons, and the
Knights of Pythias, announced his candidacy for the Virginia
House of Delegates by opposing Willis E. Cohoon, representative from Nansemond-Suffolk since 1940.[1] Godwin won and he
moved to greater prominence when he was elected to the state
Senate in 1952 to fill the vacancy created by "Gi" Stephens' ele-
vation to lieutenant governor.

In the legislature Godwin sided with the Byrd organization
on almost every matter of consequence. His first real opportunity came during the massive resistance crisis when the hard-
core organization was shorthanded in the state Senate and
desperately needed Godwin's vote and rhetorical talent to
carry the fight for segregation to extreme conclusions. In his
support for massive resistance Godwin went far beyond the
call of duty and endeared himself to Byrd, Moore, Tuck, Abbitt, and the rest of the organization old guard. "We should not
enact, or amend, any statute which would recognize the validity of the Supreme Court's decision of May 17, 1954 relating to
our public schools," he exhorted an audience in August 1956.[2]
As floor leader for the Stanley massive resistance program in
the 1956 special session of the General Assembly, Godwin
denounced integration as leading to the inevitable destruction
of free public schools.[3]

When Ted Dalton proposed token compliance as a solution,
Godwin leaped to the attack. "The blunt truth," he replied, "is
that we cannot preserve segregation by permitting integration
either wholly or in part." [4] And in July 1958, just two months
before the school closings in three Virginia localities, Godwin

[1] Richmond *Times-Dispatch,* June 3, 1947.
[2] Richmond *News Leader,* Aug. 9, 1956.
[3] See p. 132 for quotations from his anti-integration speeches at this time.
[4] *Ibid.,* March 26, 1957.

pleaded eloquently for the "preservation" of Virginia's public school system: "The Governor of our state and our state leaders will exhaust every effort and avail themselves of every method legally open to them to keep our schools racially separate. . . . We are convinced our system of public free schools in Virginia cannot survive on an integrated basis." [5]

Godwin's view of the race problem stemmed in part from the fact that he represented that part of Virginia where Negroes were most numerous. His Senate district of Nansemond, Southampton, Isle of Wight counties, and the city of Suffolk claimed in 1950 respective Negro population percentages of 65, 61, 52, and 37. Here the racial situation was potentially volatile, and Godwin's theory of race relations never lost sight of this. Rather than leading to peaceful adjustment, racial mixing, he believed, ignited social violence, which could be avoided by accepting the segregated *status quo*. The closer the races were pushed, the more inflammable, he felt, became the situation. Integration in public schools merely represented the first step to integration in other spheres of life, and each new breach in the time-honored caste system of segregation would be accompanied by new possibilities for violence or at best an uneasy truce. The northern liberal saw integration as a moral absolute. He demanded speedy implementation, with an abatement of violence coming soon after the races adjusted to a new pattern of life less radical in practice than in prediction. The southern conservative viewed integration as a threat to a way of life upon which he had staked his feeling both of identity and superiority. Integration in public schools was the first mile on a long, tortuous, strife-stricken road at the end of which lay miscegenation and loss of racial distinction. At the very least, Godwin and others have argued, massive resistance delayed the unpleasant but inevitable. It allowed the Southside its catharsis. Virginia, having fought the good fight, could surrender with dignity and in peace. [6]

During the massive resistance years, however, Godwin's statements served more to agitate than to pacify, more to

[5] *Ibid.*, July 1, 1958.   [6] Latimer, p. 66.

prolong a forlorn hope than to open the way for gradual acceptance. Whether Godwin and others like him could have
survived politically by urging a more moderate course than
massive resistance was an important consideration. It was not
until well after the school closings in 1958 that Godwin's statements moderated their absolutist tone. In February 1959 he
wanted to eliminate integration if possible and "contain" the
problem at any cost. Mixing of the races in large areas of the
state, he said, would be the death knell of public schools.[7]

In the fall of 1959 and throughout 1960 Godwin mixed notes
of belligerent conservatism with hopeful suggestions of moderation. In October 1959 he urged all Virginia Democrats to
reconcile their differences and work for the "great good of the
state." It was, he said, "no time to sulk about dead issues." Yet
one week later Godwin called upon the American people to
"stir themselves to check the unbridled power of certain labor
organizations" whose "philosophy of getting something for
nothing is not compatible with private initiative and the free
enterprise system." [8]

Throughout this period Godwin and Governor Almond remained resolute political enemies. Almond claimed that Godwin told him in the April 1959 special session of the General
Assembly that local option on public school integration was the
only sensible course open to Virginia and that he would support it. "The next thing I knew, Godwin was denouncing it,"
Almond said.[9] Fortunately Godwin's vote was not needed. The
Senate approved the local option plan, 20 to 19.

The political feud continued at the 1960 General Assembly.
Almond proposed a 3 per cent general sales tax to finance a
large increase in the state budget and to provide fiscal help for
hard-pressed localities. Godwin aligned with Gray, Moore, and
Byrd, Jr., to smother Almond's program in committee, and the
Governor charged that committee appointments had been
"stacked and packed" with opponents of his measures.[10] The
defeat of his sales tax program stirred the Governor to claim
further that Byrd, Jr., Godwin, and Moore had "ruthlessly

[7] Richmond *Times-Dispatch*, Feb. 7, 1959.   [8] *Ibid.*, Oct. 18, 25, 1959.
[9] Norfolk *Virginian-Pilot*, June 9, 1964.   [10] Latimer, p. 94.

trampled upon the rights of the people without giving any consideration at all to the needs of the state." "It's apparent that the Governor dislikes for anyone to disagree with him," Godwin answered.[11]

Godwin's dedication to segregation, fiscal stinginess, anti-unionism, and the other tenets of Byrd politics aroused speculation that he and Byrd, Jr., might run together on the organization's ticket in the 1961 gubernatorial race.[12] Even at that time, however, the combination was judged a bit extreme, and Godwin ran with the organization's blessings for lieutenant governor on a slate with the more moderate Harrison. His 1961 primary pronouncements on industrial development, education, and urban growth were obscured by attempts to link his opponent, Armistead Boothe, to Robert Kennedy, the Supreme Court, and the NAACP.[13] His attacks on organized labor also drew notice. "I do not accept a new day or a new face for this commonwealth which will be molded and fashioned by the labor union bosses of Virginia or by any who do their bidding," he asserted in the wake of his opponent's endorsement by the AFL-CIO.[14] Godwin won an uncomfortably close victory, 188,000 to 157,000. Harrison, who had the more moderate background, got significantly better margins than his massive resister running mates.

Godwin did not ignore the election returns or the changing times. The Harrison administration provided an ideal climate for Godwin to moderate in, and he did just that. There were no issues on which the Lieutenant Governor had to take a stand, and Godwin spent his time on the banquet and barbecue circuit. For a while he spoke on innocuous topics, pledging his support to a healthy balance in the Virginia economy, the development of industry, and a return to proper moral and spiritual values. "His favorite theme," wrote one reporter, "is the virtue of Virginia." [15]

The apple pie and motherhood rhetoric had a powerful logic behind it, however. These speeches eased Godwin out of the

[11] Richmond *News Leader*, March 15, 1960.
[12] Richmond *Times-Dispatch*, April 21, 1960.   [13] *Ibid.*, June 12, 1961.
[14] *Ibid.*, April 26, 1961.   [15] Richmond *News Leader*, Jan. 30, 1964.

racial controversy and allowed him to meet hundreds of important Virginians on a more congenial basis than was possible
during the massive resistance era. After this cooling-off period
Godwin's speeches gradually became more substantive and
progressive. "My philosophy is in tune with Byrd-type conservatism," Godwin acknowledged in January 1964, "but I don't
think the status quo can or ought to be maintained." [16] Education was quickly becoming the major Godwin concern—not
segregated education, but improved, better-financed education.

The Lieutenant Governor took his most crucial stands later
in 1964. Amid the furor of the Democratic nominating convention and the subsequent presidential election, Godwin early let
it be known he was a straight-ticket Democrat who intended to
support the Democratic presidential slate and that he had, in
fact, "always voted for the Democratic nominee." [17] He rode
the Lady Bird Special through Virginia, all the time urging
votes for the Democratic ticket.

In December 1964, after the Johnson victory in Virginia,
Godwin was set to take another step forward. Hinting that the
demands of the state might require a general retail sales tax,
Godwin proposed that "the time may well be at hand when we
must examine and re-evaluate all of our existing sources of
revenue." [18] The speech helped to convince any remaining
doubters that Godwin's attitudes had changed significantly.

By late 1964 a Godwin-for-Governor movement was reaching band-wagon proportions. It drew support from many in the
organization's old guard who remembered Godwin's pro-Byrd
background and from many moderates and liberals who welcomed his recent change. Moderate Democrats were brought
to Godwin's side by the fear of a Byrd, Jr., candidacy.° Byrd,
Jr., and Godwin had taken almost identical stands before and
during massive resistance, but their views were quite different
in 1965. Moderates, convinced of Godwin's evolution, were
under no circumstances ready to assume the same of Little
Harry. He, like his father, had maintained strict silence and

[16] *Ibid.*   [17] Richmond *News Leader,* July 21, 1964.
[18] *Ibid.,* Dec. 10, 1964.

nonsupport for the national Democratic ticket in 1964. Edward
L. Breeden, Jr., influential, progressive state Senator from Norfolk, had endorsed Godwin in April 1964, and Kellam early
began to mention the Lieutenant Governor as the "likeliest
popular choice for Governor in 1965." [19] Godwin's gubernatorial support was immense at the time of his formal announcement in January 1965. One columnist wrote:

Well, when the endorsements of Lieutenant-Governor Godwin start
rolling in—and there will be a Niagara of them between now and
Friday—we will find that his support is somewhat breathtaking. He
will have most of the old line Byrd organization people from the
courthouses to the Capitol, a good many of the better-known
moderate types including the so-called Young Turks, and a vast
array of the straight-ticket Democrats including some who are
regarded as anti-organization. . . . I cannot think of many times in
the past hundred years or so when one man had so many labels and
symbols going for him.[20]

The *Times-Dispatch* observed that

when Richard S. Reynolds, the aluminum manufacturer who has
always been a relatively liberal down-the-line Democrat in national
and state elections, and State Senator Garland Gray who has been
anything but, team up to provide the financial sinews for Mills
Godwin's gubernatorial bid, we may assume that the day of well
nigh supernatural goings-on in the political realm is at hand. We
have here an almost unique phenomenon in the state's modern
political history.[21]

This "unique phenomenon" was so imposing that trial bal-
loons for other candidates popped almost before they got off
the ground. Even Byrd, Jr., decided to bide his time for a more
auspicious occasion, and Godwin, together with Delegate Fred
Pollard of Richmond and incumbent Attorney General Button,
entered the Democratic primary unopposed.

In the November election Godwin's major opponent was
Linwood Holton, the forty-one-year-old Roanoke Republican

[19] Richmond *Times-Dispatch*, June 20, 1964.　　[20] *Ibid.*, Jan. 10, 1965.
[21] Jan. 12, 1965.

long a leader in that party's affairs. A graduate of Washington
and Lee and the Harvard Law School, Holton campaigned
relentlessly. He met the people "eyeball to eyeball," darting
into barber shops, drug stores, merchant shops, and front
porches in search of votes and opinions. "If personal contact
with the voters was the only key to a successful candidacy,
Holton would be a runaway favorite," declared one reporter
two days before the election.[22] Holton, moreover, was a Ted
Dalton Republican, a progressive GOP leader from the southwestern hills. He flouted conservative extremists by calling for
"repeal of the Virginia poll tax" and an end to other voting
restrictions.[23] And he attacked the Byrd organization for its
record in public services. "Aren't you sick and tired of hearing
Virginia placed 46th, 48th, etc. in some area as critical as
public schools?" Holton asked, all the while campaigning
under the slogan "Make Virginia First Again." [24] He charged
Byrd Democrats with meeting state needs on a "crisis to crisis"
basis [25] and compared the machine's response to public needs
to an "old Model-T Ford" patched up with bailing wire as the
occasion demanded it.[26] Holton's big issue, however, was the
large surplus accumulated by the Harrison administration
which had not yet been appropriated for state services. "The
government of Virginia," he persistently claimed, "is hoarding
a financial surplus that will soar to 100 million dollars next year
while neglecting schools, roads, and other public needs. This
may be an achievement if miserly bookkeeping balances and
paper profits are our goals. But it is a devastating indictment of
mismanagement and nonplanning if better schools, colleges,
universities, roads, and other public facilities are our goals." [27]

While Holton criticized the Byrd organization for its laggard
role in public services, another group viewed with dismay the
quickening pace in Virginia politics. The Virginia Conservative
party was founded July 10, 1965, on the premise that Democrats, Republicans, and the Byrd organization were all swerv-

---

[22] *Ibid.*, Oct. 31, 1965.   [23] *Ibid.*, May 30, 1965.
[24] Richmond *News Leader*, July 1, 1965.
[25] Richmond *Times-Dispatch*, Aug. 3, 1965.   [26] *Ibid.*, July 5, 1965.
[27] *Ibid.*, June 24, 1965.

ing too far to the left. The party hoped to free Virginia from economic dependence on the federal government, stick to pay-as-you-go, eliminate "federal control" of the school system, and above all "to investigate and expose subversive influences." [28] The Conservative candidate for governor, William J. Story, Jr., a proud member of the John Birch Society, warned that Democrats and Republicans were "slowly moving down the road to socialistic, Communistic, Marxist control" of life in Virginia. Things had gone so far, Story suggested, that Virginians were going to wake up some Saturday morning and see a "big Asiatic, African, or even Caucasian policeman standing on the corner ordering everybody to stay inside that day." [29]

The Conservative party opened its political rallies with evangelistic fervor. A band blared "Dixie," and small children swarmed about the meeting place bearing placards and marching to the strains of "Stout-hearted Men." One youngster was generally clad in an Uncle Sam suit to symbolize the Conservative's dedication to patriotism. "Do you stand with liberty or do you stand with communism?" Story asked.[30] But Story seemed subdued beside John Carter, the Conservative candidate for attorney general. No public figure was immune from Carter's tongue lashings. President Johnson was an American Hitler who resorted to "chicanery, trickery, blackmail and bribery . . . who looks benign and quotes the Bible on the boob-tube." The Virginia Republican party was "the illegitimate offspring of the union of Marxism and the national Republican party." [31] Carter deplored the fact that the country had not "the intestinal fortitude to run Castro out of Cuba." Then shifting to a note of domestic humanitarianism, he opened new vistas of employment, pledging to put unwed mothers to work "if nothing more than swabbing down the streets." [32]

What most disturbed the Conservatives was the recent path of Mills Godwin. The national parties had long been rife with Communist influence, but that the Byrd organization should be so tainted—the Conservatives were aghast. Godwin was pub-

---

[28] *Ibid.*, July 11, 1965.   [29] Richmond *News Leader,* Oct. 1, 1965.
[30] *Ibid.*   [31] *Ibid.*, September 29, 1965.   [32] *Ibid.*, Oct. 1, 1965.

licly lumped with Martin Luther King, Thurgood Marshall, Arthur Goldberg, and Abe Fortas in an unholy alliance dedicated to the destruction of the American way of life. What galled the Conservatives most was Godwin's endorsement of Lyndon Johnson in the 1964 presidential election and his ride on the Lady Bird Special. Story thundered that Godwin was mistaken in the belief that he could "ride the Lady Bird Special into the Governor's Mansion." [33] Carter was more vehement: "Godwin was once a stalwart constitutionalist. But when the Lady Bird Special came charging into Richmond, who should climb aboard with dear old Albertis but Mills Godwin." "Where," Carter wanted to know, "were Mills Godwin and Albertis Harrison when George Wallace came to Richmond?" At this point the *News Leader* reported a standing ovation. [34]

The Conservatives campaigned most intensively and most successfully in southside Virginia. The emergence of this party symbolized an important change in Virginia's politics. Gone was the day when the Southside dictated state policy. Massive resistance had been forsaken, the Virginia Democratic party had endorsed Lyndon Johnson in 1964, and both major gubernatorial candidates courted moderate and liberal voting strength at the risk of losing southside conservatives. Thus the one-time bastion of Byrd organization strength had been slighted, and many southside Virginians looked elsewhere for a home. The Virginia Conservative party offered an outlet for frustrations. If it could not change recent trends, it could at least roundly denounce them.

Godwin seemed destined to infuriate the Conservatives further. Unruffled by their polemics or the criticism from his Republican opponent, Godwin campaigned as one who looked and acted as if he were prepared to sit in the seat of power. "Sweaty afternoons in crowded shopping centers and busy scurryings down the streets to thrust a welcome hand at a potential supporter are not really part of his makeup," wrote one reporter. "The Democratic nominee is in his milieu standing tall and smiling graciously as he meets quiet groups of the

[33] Richmond *Times-Dispatch*, Sept. 17, 1965.   [34] Aug. 20, 1965.

faithful flanked by local party stalwarts. . . . [Godwin] receives more than he greets and he does it with poise and grace." [35]

Godwin looked to Virginia's future, not its past. "Virginia stands in 1965 on the threshold of an undreamed-of future," he said in a keynote speech on September 8. "Our people are ready for new and bolder steps to keep pace with the times. I am determined that if you elect me your Governor, I will do all in my power to see that we are prepared" to keep up with and meet "the whirlwind of change." [36] Of Story, the Conservative candidate, he remarked: "Sometimes I think he sees a Communist behind every tree. He wants to turn the clock back I don't know how far. . . . He has not uttered one word about education or highways in his campaign, but talks more about alleged communists than the problems confronting the state." [37] Holton, Godwin implied, was an "inexperienced, irresponsible politician" with the absurd formula of "sky high promises" without new taxes.[38] When questioned about his previous support of massive resistance, Godwin replied firmly that the issue had been "long since settled. The program adopted in the General Assembly of Virginia bought valuable time during which people were able to adjust for conditions that were inevitably to come. As a result there has been a peaceful transition in Virginia." [39]

Most of all, Mills Godwin spoke of Virginia's need for improved public services. He pledged increased teacher's salaries, more capital outlays for college expansion, practical fringe benefits for teachers, and state participation in new areas such as summer schools, kindergartens, technical schools, and special education for the handicapped. He spoke of the need for long-range statewide planning and a planning division within the governor's office to analyze Virginia's needs and resources. He promised to redouble efforts to attract industry and tourists to Virginia. He urged constructive planning to make an orderly

[35] Richmond *Times-Dispatch*, Oct. 31, 1965.   [36] *Ibid.*, Sept. 8, 1965.
[37] Richmond *News Leader*, Oct. 5, 1965.
[38] Richmond *Times-Dispatch*, Sept. 30, 1965.
[39] Richmond *News Leader*, Oct. 27, 1965.

process out of urbanization with programs to solve water pollution, air pollution, and other attendant problems. He sought to update mental health facilities and enrich the cultural opportunities of the state.[40] Most important, he admitted that "if conditions indicate that we must seek new sources of revenue for this stepped-up program, then I will recommend new sources of revenue in accordance with the best thinking of our tax experts." [41]

Godwin's political support and his program attracted attention. Linwood Holton attacked the "incredible logic under which he [Godwin] was able on September 14, 1965 to send Armistead Boothe to Arlington to proclaim him a liberal in the finest tradition of the Great Society while he was also able on October 6, 1965 to send Bill Tuck to Danville to attest he was a true conservative in the tradition of Harry Byrd." [42] Godwin had fashioned a remarkable consensus within the Democratic party, but observers in Virginia rubbed their eyes more than once when organized labor gave Godwin its wholehearted endorsement.

The Byrd organization and organized labor had historically lived in enmity. Tuck had attacked labor throughout his term. Byrd had denounced the union bosses in every campaign. And Godwin, as recently as 1961, had counted antiunion pronouncements one of his most effective campaign aids. In 1964, however, organized labor began to re-evaluate its long-held position as the "crucified minority." In August of that year union leaders determined both to improve their public image and make themselves a political force in the state by supplying votes and funds in ample quantity to friendly candidates. The AFL-CIO convention promised increased public relations efforts and voted to levy an assessment of $1.50 per member per year for the next five years. Labor would have an annual $90,000 political war chest to implement its aims. Chief among these was to raise union enrollment from 65,000—the member-

---

[40] Godwin-Pollard-Button campaign platform, 1965 gubernatorial race (Richmond *Times-Dispatch*, Nov. 1, 1965).

[41] Richmond *News Leader*, Sept. 8, 1965.

[42] Richmond *Times-Dispatch*, Oct. 13, 1965.

ship of the Virginia AFL-CIO in 1964—to 275,000 by 1969.[43]
Legislative goals of a minimum wage in Virginia of $1.25 an
hour, the outlawing of professional strikebreaking activity, and
modification of the state right-to-work law were also endorsed.[44]

Godwin's candidacy gave the unions a unique opportunity.
He had moderated sufficiently to make an AFL-CIO endorsement feasible, and labor at last could back what appeared to be
a winning candidate. In 1965, moreover, the unions were particularly friendly with most Democrats, and the AFL-CIO
could also improve its image by supporting a respected political figure like Mills E. Godwin. For the first time in years the
organization candidate received the union endorsement in a
significant statewide election. The AFL-CIO statement admitted that in the past organized labor "disagreed with the dominant Democratic organization and its nominees. Recent state
Democratic administrations have not been anti-labor; neither
have they been pro-labor." But labor viewed the current race
as a "contest between radical extremism, anti-federal government and progressive moderation in moving the Commonwealth forward. . . . Mills E. Godwin, Democratic nominee for
governor stayed with his party and supported the Democratic
ticket in the last [presidential] election."[45]

Godwin's endorsement by the AFL-CIO rubbed salt in the
wounds of southside conservatives, most of whom regarded
unions as a dangerous force needing at all times to be closely
checked and guarded. But the labor endorsement encouraged
Negroes to move to Godwin's support, for the liberal forces on
the Virginia political scene had seldom been able to afford a
divided stance. The former advocate of massive resistance soon
received the endorsement of Richmond's Crusade for Voters
and Tidewater Virginia's Independent Voters League, the
two most influential Negro political groups in the state. Republicans who felt that Holton's progressive stands and calls for
poll tax repeal had entitled him to a share of the Negro vote
protested. Winfred Mundle, a prominent Negro Republican,

[43] *Ibid.*, Aug. 20–23, 1964.   [44] Norfolk *Virginian-Pilot*, Aug. 21, 1964.
[45] Roanoke *Times*, Oct. 13, 1965.

predicted that "no thoughtful Negroes will follow the suggestion . . . that we support candidates who, if they had their way
would have closed every public school in Virginia rather than
admit one Negro child to a white school." [46] Other Negroes
throughout the state dissented from the VIVL endorsement.
But the Republican party was so repugnant to the Negro in the
year after the Goldwater candidacy and Godwin had so re-
formed his political posture that most of the Negro vote lined
up behind him. Like labor, the Negro longed to be with a
winner, and Godwin's candidacy had every earmark of success.

By this time Virginia was so transformed that even informed
observers were befuddled. There were new looks to old faces
and new coalitions in which once "out" elements sought "in"
and once "in" elements sought "out." Campaign rhetoric and
programs had done a complete about-face, and Virginia was at
least temporarily developing a three-party system.

Columnist Charles McDowell, Virginia's political humorist,
was on hand, however, to make some sense of the situation.
Assume for the moment that a man familiar with the traditional pattern of Virginia politics retired in 1963 for a long nap
assuring himself that nothing would change for the next several
years. Upon awakening in 1965, he senses that politics in the
state have been turned upside down. He instinctively asks for
McDowell, who reassuringly has survived the political turmoil
and is ready to answer the distressed fellow's questions:

Q—I assume that this fellow Godwin, the Democratic nominee
for Governor, is the same old product of the Byrd organization—
isn't that right?

A—No, he is a new one. His program is progressive and he is a
modern realist, he says.

Q—It's all very well for him to say that, but what do the anti-
Byrd Democrats say? Are they all sitting on their hands, or are some
of them quietly advocating a vote for the Republicans?

A—They are working for Godwin. They say they are wild about
him.

[46] Richmond *News Leader*, Oct. 26, 1965.

Q—Well, that must mean this fellow Holton, the Republican, is somewhere to the right of Goldwater—am I correct?

A—No. His program is progressive and he is a modern realist, he says. He is one of the most attractive, hard-working candidates the Republicans ever had.

Q—In that case, let me get back to the Byrd candidate—he is for tight-fisted economy, isn't he?

A—No, he doesn't talk much about that. He talks about spending money to meet the needs of the state, and he seems to think new taxes will be needed.

Q—Well, he makes a point of being a big segregationist, doesn't he, like Byrd candidates have in recent times.

A—No. As a matter of fact, some of the most important Negro leaders in the state have endorsed Godwin, and he is expected to get a majority of the Negro vote.

Q—But wasn't he an advocate of massive resistance, or whatever you called it, in the past?

A—Yes, but that was in the past. Virginia is emerging from its past, as they say. Godwin has emerged very fast, like a rocket.

Q—The next thing you will be telling me is that Godwin is not running against organized labor, which has been one of the Byrd organization's most reliable tactics. You aren't going to tell me that are you?

A—Yes. Organized labor in Virginia has endorsed Godwin. Organized labor is part of what is called the Godwin Consensus.

Q—I identify that word with President Johnson. Godwin is running against President Johnson, isn't he?

A—No. He has his reservations, but he did support Johnson, and the Johnson leaders in the state are part of his consensus.

Q—Well, Senator Byrd didn't come out for Mr. Johnson in the campaign and hasn't given him much support since. Is Senator Byrd supporting this remarkable Godwin?

A—Oh, yes of course. Godwin is the Byrd organization candidate. You understood that much when we started. I have the feeling that you are losing ground.

Q—Wait a minute now, Buster, are you trying to tell me that Senator Byrd and the anti-Byrds and the straight-ticket Democrats and the Negro leaders and the labor leaders and the courthouse crowd and the old power structure (as we experts sometimes say) are all supporting Godwin?

A—Yes, and Bill Tuck and Army Boothe and, well, all the fellows.

Q—Are you putting me on?

A—Not unless I've been had, too.

Q—Well, don't disillusion me completely. Surely I'm right in saying that the basic power, the greatest pool of undeviating loyalty to the Byrd organization, still lies in rural Southside Virginia. . . .

A—No, not in this election. The Southside is giving the Byrd organization and Godwin a great deal of trouble. A lot of people down there are said to be bolting the organization to vote Conservative.

Q—Did you say somebody is bolting the organization to vote Conservative? Are you playing some sort of Halloween prank with me?

A—I am only trying to tell you, sir, that the Byrd organization candidate is not acceptable to some people who call themselves Conservatives, with a capital "C," and they have a candidate named Story who seems to regard both Godwin and Holton as liberals. Anyway the organization and Godwin are having trouble with conservatives in the Southside.

Q—You have now pushed me too far, and I must tell you that I don't believe anything you have told me about Virginia politics. Do you really have the vaguest idea what you are talking about?

A—That is a good question. I don't know whether this election has done it but I must confess that sometimes I don't think I understand Virginia politics.

Q—Let me ask you one last question anyway: Who is this fellow Kellam I keep hearing about in Virginia politics?

A—I don't handle metaphysical questions.[47]

On November 3, 1965, Mills E. Godwin, Jr., became the governor-elect of the Commonwealth of Virginia. He won by comfortable though not landslide margins, but he was the first

[47] Richmond *Times-Dispatch*, Oct. 31, 1965.

governor to go into office with a plurality, not a majority. The breakdown of the vote was as follows:

Mills E. Godwin Jr. (Democrat)	269,526	47.9%
Linwood Holton (Republican)	212,207	37.7%
William J. Story (Conservative)	75,307	13.4%
George Lincoln Rockwell (Nazi)	5,730	1.0%

Each party had something about which to gloat. The Republicans had mounted their liveliest challenge since Ted Dalton's candidacy in 1953. In sheer numbers Holton polled more votes than any Virginia Republican had ever attracted before. He bested the Democrats in 31 counties and cities and he carried both the Sixth and Tenth Districts convincingly. The Republicans also increased their representation in the Virginia House of Delegates from 11 to 12 and they picked up a fourth seat in the Virginia Senate.[48]

As Map V demonstrates, the GOP held its traditional mountain strongholds, Carroll, Floyd, Grayson, and others, and ran a creditable race in the Southwest, where two-party competition had always been strong. More interesting, however, was the Republican showing in the Shenandoah Valley. Loyalty to the Democratic party was less rigid in the Valley than it was east of the Blue Ridge,[49] but few expected the counties of Rockingham, Shenandoah, and Augusta to give Holton such substantial margins.

East of the Blue Ridge Mountains the Republican party ran strongest in suburban areas. In the Washington suburbs of Arlington and Fairfax counties, a contested area, Holton benefited from memories of Godwin's massive resistance. In the Richmond suburbs of Henrico and Chesterfield counties, many conservatives switched to Holton in the wake of Godwin's endorsement by Negro and labor groups. In Roanoke County, Holton profited from a heavy home-town vote and traditional

[48] Technically the Republicans had only 11 members of the House of Delegates, as Rufus V. McCoy missed the filing deadline in Russell and Dickenson counties and had to run as an independent with Republican support. In the Senate, Republican J. Kenneth Robinson won that party's fourth seat in a special election on December 14, 1965. See *General Assembly Manual, 1966*, for Republican representation in the 1966 legislature.   [49] See Map IV.

Map V. Vote by Parties in the 1965 Gubernatorial Election

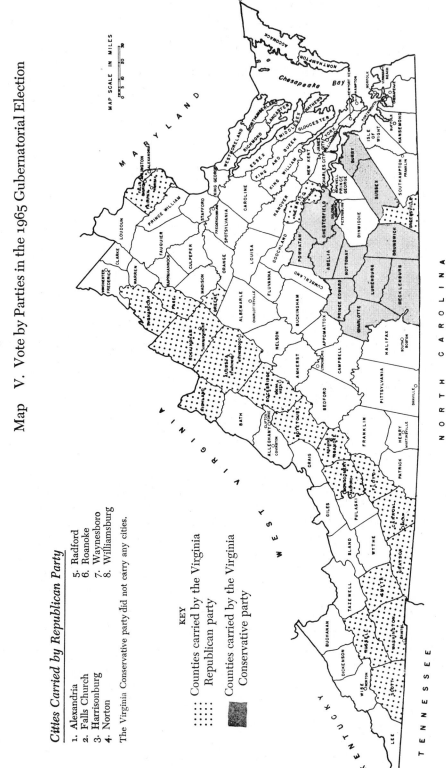

Cities Carried by Republican Party

1. Alexandria   5. Radford
2. Falls Church   6. Roanoke
3. Harrisonburg   7. Waynesboro
4. Norton   8. Williamsburg

The Virginia Conservative party did not carry any cities.

KEY

⋮⋮⋮⋮⋮ Counties carried by the Virginia
        Republican party

▨ Counties carried by the Virginia
    Conservative party

Republican loyalties. In the five heaviest-voting suburban counties in the state, Holton outpolled the Democratic nominee, 54,000 to 44,000.

The Republican party could also take consolation in knowing that Democrats no longer regarded it lightly. Godwin campaigned in a calm, confident manner, but the Democratic party took no chances. Four years before, Harrison had listed $27,663 in campaign expenditures against Republican Clyde Pearson. In 1965 the Democratic ticket spent $215,567, almost eight times as much. Over $150,000 of that amount was used in newspaper, radio, billboard, and television advertising, clearly indicating that Mills Godwin and his colleagues were not going to rely solely on the steady, unpublicized operations of the courthouse machine to push them to victory. Holton's performance appeared even more creditable considering that his reported campaign expenditures were $79,165, about one-third of the Democrats'.[50]

Holton's major contribution to the Republican party could not be measured by financial reports or voting returns. His candidacy returned the Virginia Republican party to a moderate course after the Goldwater disaster in 1964. Goldwater's candidacy had attracted diehard segregationists in the Southside to the Republican party for the first time in years, and Holton might have followed this appeal with right-wing rhetoric of his own. The Republican candidate not only refused to do this, but instead worked hard for Negro support. He endorsed poll tax repeal, promised the appointment of a Negro to the State Board of Education, placed Negroes high in his campaign organization, and bore down hard on Godwin's prior identification with massive resistance.[51] If Holton was unsuccessful in his appeal for Negro votes, he at least steered the party away from the momentary temptation to adopt a far right-wing position.

The Virginia Conservative party also had every right to be pleased with the election returns. Story had been given 6 or 7

[50] "Official Reports of Campaign Expenditures," filed by Harrison, Godwin, and Holton at State Board of Elections in Richmond.

[51] Richmond *News Leader*, Nov. 3, 1965.

per cent of the ballots in most advance speculation. He ended
by polling over 13 per cent of the total vote. As expected, his
candidacy was most successful in central southside Virginia,
and all the eleven counties he carried were clustered in or near
this area (see Map V). Although they failed to carry them, the
Conservatives cut deeply into the normal organization vote in
southside counties such as Pittsylvania, Halifax, Campbell, and
Southampton, in suburban counties such as Henrico and
Hanover, and in central Virginia near Louisa, Fluvanna, and
Goochland. The protest of segregationists against Godwin's
moderation had been even sharper than expected, and the Conservative party raised a "here to stay" banner after the 1965
election.[52]

The Democratic party was also satisfied; it won respectably
and for the first time on a program of unlimited future. The
all-out economy and massive resistance platforms of past administrations had lost their usefulness, and a few of the more
astute members of the Byrd organization knew that sooner or
later a switch would have had to come. Godwin made it—dramatically and just in time. He managed to retain a large chunk
of the old-line Byrd organization, which was primarily responsible for his winning effort in two-thirds of Virginia's counties.
But more moderate and liberal urbanites also gave Godwin's
candidacy a big boost. In Hampton Roads, for instance, Godwin's endorsement of President Johnson and his progressive
program made him an attractive candidate, and he emerged
from the relatively liberal and traditionally Democratic Hampton Roads area with his biggest majorities. Liberal, straight-
ticket Democrats also pushed Godwin to a narrow victory in
the Ninth District of southwest Virginia and, though he lost the
Tenth District in the Washington suburbs, he would have been
badly defeated there had he not shifted to a progressive stand.

The Negro vote indisputably provided Godwin's margin of
victory. Of the 60,000 Negro votes cast in the election Godwin
is estimated to have received 50,000.[53] Richmond's ten largest

[52] Richmond *Times-Dispatch*, Nov. 4, 1965.

[53] Estimate formed from Richmond *News Leader*, Nov. 3, 1965, and conver-
sations with political reporters of Richmond *Times-Dispatch*, Richmond *News
Leader*, and Norfolk *Virginian-Pilot*.

Negro precincts, which in 1961 had given the Republican gubernatorial candidate a margin of 2,800 votes, gave Godwin a
3,000 vote margin. Precincts in other Negro areas followed suit.

The election analyses and post mortems, predictably varied.
Tuck grunted that Godwin had seriously erred in seeking the
Negro vote, which had not delivered, which "almost goos-
egged" Godwin among southside whites, and ended by making
him Virginia's first minority governor.[54] Holton, Godwin's defeated opponent, did not see it that way. "Of the votes cast for
Godwin and myself we got 45%. . . . If 30,000 votes had
switched or half the Negro vote, we could have won." [55] Outgoing Governor Harrison claimed that liberals who thought
they had captured Godwin were "going to be in for a rude
awakening." Godwin, Harrison explained, was not the John
Lindsay type nor was he "a New Deal, Fair Deal, Great Society
type." [56]

Kilpatrick, editor of the Richmond *News Leader,* outlined
the task of the new governor:

Were ever such bedfellows united in one boarding house? Here
were Byrd Democrats, anti-Byrd Democrats, Goldwater Republicans, Negroes, whites, pro-labor and anti-labor, somehow tented
together in an uneasy coalition based upon affection for Senator
Byrd, Democratic habit, pure pragmatism, respect for Mr. Godwin,
and a good deal of what's-in-it-for-me.

Mr. Godwin's fearfully difficult and delicate task, as Governor,
will be to keep this shaky political structure from becoming alto-
gether unglued. He has said publicly that he made no committ-
ments of any sort either to the Negro bloc or to the AFL-CIO; he
also has made evident his own distaste for most of the programs of
LBJ's great society. Yet the combination of factors that produced
his plurality must propel him, almost inevitably, into gestures and
actions calculated to please some of his supporters without actually
offending anyone else.

Thus Mr. Godwin must be sufficiently conservative to hold the
"Byrd Democrats" of the 32nd Precinct, and sufficiently liberal to
retain the crucial support of the "anti-Byrd Democrats" of the 46th.

[54] Conversation with Tuck, June 27, 1966.
[55] Richmond *News Leader,* Nov. 18, 1965.   [56] *Ibid.,* Nov. 3, 1965.

He cannot afford to lose the support of the State's business elements; he cannot afford to lose the Labor spokesmen either.

· · · · ·

It may be that Mr. Godwin is just the man to bring off the balancing act. He will go into office with a friendly Assembly and a bulging treasury. The state no longer is racked by the racial tensions of a decade ago. He himself wants earnestly to be a good Governor and to move the State forward. Most of the pressing issues before the Commonwealth, chief among them the question of a Statewide sales tax, can be resolved with a little give-and-take and few wounded feelings. As we commented in our editorial of endorsement two weeks ago, Mr. Godwin is a professional at politics. In this uncertain time, we may be grateful for an attractive pro at the wheel.[57]

[57] *Ibid.*

Chapter 11

The Sales Tax Legislature
January – March 1966

I NAUGURATION DAY, Saturday, January 15, 1966. Cold, raw,
and overcast. Virginians huddled together on the Capitol
lawn to brave the icy wind. Most felt repaid for their exposure
to the cold when the inaugural address of Governor Godwin
signaled that Virginia's government might at last be shaking off
its winter mantle:

For a dozen years, we have wrestled with a question that tore at
the foundations of a society more than three hundred years old.
Now the major decisions have been made. If they do not please us
all, they are realities with which we all must live, and within which
we must continue to preserve the system of government which
produced them.

. . . . . .

The feeling grows that we are only beginning to realize the
potential that is ours, that the incoming tide already rolling across
Virginia and the South has not nearly reached its flood.

. . . . . .

If there is a watchword for our time, it is to move, to strike out
boldly, to reach for the heights.

. . . . . .

Virginia is of the South. She always will be, and she will guard
and cherish the high principle, the warmth, the humanity, that have
marked our region.

But the South is also of the nation.

.   .   .   .   .

The Commonwealth we love will always be Virginia, but Virginia too is of the nation, and it is by the nation's standards that we are now called upon to judge her. . . .

.   .   .   .   .

We can take no rest until all our public schools—not just some—will compare with any in the nation; until all our colleges and universities—not just some—can hold up their heads in any company; until all our sons and daughters—not just some—have the same chance to train their minds and their skills to the utmost.

.   .   .   .   .

It is my duty as Governor to offer a positive plan of action. This I will do Monday, first in the field of education, then in highways and in other areas of opportunity and of need, for we must move Virginia forward everywhere.

.   .   .   .   .

We make a mistake, as their leaders, if we get too far ahead of our people. But we make a greater mistake if we fall too far behind them.

I have made a compact with myself that my own errors will be in the former category. I would be accused of having too much faith in the people of Virginia, rather than too little.

If I could choose a text for our State it would be from the twelfth chapter of St. Luke.

"For unto whomsoever much is given, of him shall be much required. . . ."

As we look across a Virginia bountiful beyond belief, those words recall for us her traditions. They speak to us of her destiny. They command us to our clear duty.

Our answer will be judged by our works. May those works be touched with greatness.[1]

The new governor had sounded the challenge, but the path which lay ahead was a treacherous one. Godwin had to steer his program through the Virginia General Assembly and the

---

[1] *Inaugural Address*, Jan. 15, 1966.

thicket of local interests therein. For this program to survive intact would be nothing less than a minor miracle.

The 1966 General Assembly was the first to meet on a reapportioned basis. As a result of Court-ordered reapportionment urban areas gained 11 members in the 140-member legislature, primarily at the expense of rural southwest Virginia. The gains came in the two most progressive metropolitan areas in the state: Virginia's Washington suburbs picked up 1 more senator and 5 new delegates, and Hampton Roads increased its Senate strength from 6 to 8 and House representation from 16 to 19.[2]

There was no danger of an urban takeover, however. Freshman Delegate Thomas Moss from Norfolk pinpointed the metropolitan dilemma: "Although I see an opportunity for greater urban representation at the General Assembly we are still faced with the problem of committee membership." Observing that the speaker controlled all committee assignments in the House, Moss predicted that "unless some of the new urban representatives are placed on these [crucial] committees, we will still have difficulty in passing any bills affecting and beneficial to the urban areas."[3]

Committee membership now became crucial. In the House, Speaker Moore was not likely to let things slip out of conservative control by assigning new liberals to important committees. Moreover, the rural stalwarts of the Byrd organization still chaired almost every significant committee. Chairman of House Appropriations was John H. Daniel of Charlotte County. Garnett S. Moore of Pulaski and Sam E. Pope of Southampton presided over the Courts of Justice and Education Committees respectively. The Privileges and Elections Committee, the most politically sensitive in the House, had as its chairman John Warren Cooke, majority leader of the House and Byrd loyalist from Mathews County.[4]

In the Senate the rural citadels of the old Byrd organization still held the reins. Of the 40-member Senate, 18 represented

[2] See *General Assembly Manual, 1964* and *1966.*

[3] Richmond *News Leader,* Dec. 27, 1965.

[4] See *General Assembly Manual, 1966,* pp. 54–58, 148–156, for list of committee chairmen and members.

predominantly rural constituencies, 18 predominantly urban or
suburban constituencies, and 4 came from districts of mixed
complexion. While the voting strength of the full Senate thus
split fairly evenly, committee membership was a different matter. In the Senate Privileges and Elections Committee, for
example, rural forces outnumbered their urban counterparts 7
to 3, with 3 members representing mixed districts. Of the 13
members on this critical committee, 10 were closely affiliated
with the Byrd organization. Byrd conservatives chaired not
only the Senate Privileges and Election Committee but the
Finance, Courts of Justice, General Laws, Welfare, Public Institutions, and Education Committees as well. Senator Garland
Gray headed the Democratic caucus, which appointed the
important Senate Steering Committee, a group comprised of
one representative from each congressional district which recommended all committee assignments.[5] Gray, though not as
potent as speaker Moore in the House, had far more institutional power than any other single senator.

The legislative power structure in 1966 was still topheavy
with Byrd conservatives. New forces, however, forced the Byrd
conservatives to be more receptive to new ideas than they
might have wished. Certain key figures in the Byrd organization faced major challenges in congressional and senatorial
races later that year, and the organization could not afford to
antagonize anyone by autocratic tactics in the General Assembly. The result was that the organization's old guard relaxed
"its rigid policy of reserving the choicest committees as a preserve for the politically faithful." A moderate-to-liberal Democrat from the Tenth District and a liberal from Norfolk fared
"spectacularly well in the Senate committee assignments compared with the olden days when ramrod controls were more in
order." [6]

It was, moreover, merely a matter of time before increased

[5] Richmond *News Leader*, Dec. 27, 1965.
[6] Richmond *Times-Dispatch*, Jan. 17, 1966. The moderate-liberal from the
Tenth District was Senator Robert C. Fitzgerald, who was appointed to the
Senate Finance Committee. The Norfolk liberal was Senator Henry Howell,
appointed to the Welfare and General Laws Committees.

urban strength in the legislature would work its way into the
committee power structure as well. Age was rapidly overtaking
the veterans of the legislative battles of the 1940's and 1950's.
Of the legislators who had backed Tuck in his labor wars,
battled the Young Turks, pushed for massive resistance, and
now dominated crucial committee chairmanships, Moore was
68 years of age, Gray 64, M. M. Long 80, Lloyd Bird 71, John
Daniel 69, E. O. McCue, Jr., 64, Dr. J. D. Hagood 76, and
Landon Wyatt 75.[7] They remained to make certain that Virginia did not change too quickly, that the new forces sweeping
the state did not immediately tear down the structure of economy and Byrd conservatism built so carefully and maintained
so religiously for forty years. Yet the old guard now faced a
new governor, of Byrd background but a born-again moderate.
Godwin had no desire to destroy all relics of Harry Byrd's
Virginia, but under his leadership in the 1966 General Assembly a new day unmistakably dawned.

The Governor's major objective for the 1966 session was the
enactment of a general statewide sales tax. Additional funds
were needed for public schools, highways, mental hospitals,
and other vital state services. Still another factor prodded the
state to move quickly on the sales tax proposal. Municipalities,
fiscally starved for many years, had in 1964 decided to levy
sales taxes of their own. When Godwin took office, fifteen
municipalities across the state had imposed local sales taxes,
while Virginia's counties lacked the authority to enact similar
levies. The possibility loomed that the urban areas would resist
any effort by the state to repeal the widely varying local sales
taxes and replace them with a uniform statewide tax offering
the cities less revenue than their local levies did. If representatives from the cities ever adopted this attitude, the state's last
major source of new revenue would be lost. "It is of the *utmost
importance* . . . that a statewide sales tax be enacted at this
winter's session of the General Assembly," wrote the Richmond
Times-Dispatch. "It may never be politically possible to enact
such a tax thereafter." [8]

[7] See *General Assembly Manual, 1966*, pp. 227–90.
[8] Richmond *Times-Dispatch*, Oct. 3, 1965.

Both Godwin and outgoing Governor Harrison realized the urgency of the situation. Harrison, in his farewell speech to the General Assembly, advocated the quick adoption of the tax at the state level and "the repeal and discontinuance of all local sales taxes." [9] Godwin pushed even further: "Clearly, the question before us is not whether to adopt a general retail state sales tax, but how it shall be imposed, and more specifically, how the proceeds shall be distributed." [10]

This last consideration prompted sharp debate. The myriad competing views on the distribution of revenue threatened to defeat whatever sales tax proposals might be advanced. Urban areas wished to retain the right to impose local levies on top of a state sales tax; they insisted also that the proceeds from a state sales tax should be distributed in large part on a point of collection or point of sale basis. [11] Richmond, Hampton Roads, northern Virginia, and other big shopping and trading centers of the state would thus receive the bulk of the revenue since the greatest volume of trade and general exchange took place there.

Rural representatives protested such suggestions. Distributing revenues on a point of sales basis, they argued, would increase the benefits to trading areas, not proportionately, but almost in geometric progression. Other county representatives claimed it was unfair to let each locality add a tax of its own, because country people often spent their money in the cities, and cities should not benefit from a tax on those sales. Rather the sales tax revenue should be distributed on the basis of school age population, since the state's foremost goal was better education and the greatest need within this field came from those poorer rural areas where retail sales were low but school age population was relatively high.

A third formula for the allocation of sales tax revenue had been devised by an expert statistician, Alan S. Donnahoe of Richmond Newspapers. This was an effort formula, an incentive plan under which both cities and counties could gain. The

[9] *Address to General Assembly,* Jan. 12, 1966.
[10] *Address to General Assembly,* Jan. 17, 1966.
[11] Richmond *Times-Dispatch,* Feb. 8, 1966.

Donnahoe plan advocated a 2 per cent sales tax to be levied by the state, with all counties and cities authorized to add another 1 per cent for their own use. A portion of the state tax, equal to the gross yield from a 1 per cent levy, would be distributed to counties and cities through a new Local Incentive Fund. This Local Incentive Fund would be determined as follows: For every cent of local funds appropriated for school operations per $100 of true values in real estate and public service property, the county or city would receive 80 cents for each child in average daily attendance.[12]

The Donnahoe plan received much favorable editorial comment across the state and provoked discussions on the sales tax during the 1965 gubernatorial campaign. It offered unique advantages. Of all the projected distribution schemes, it was the only one to take into account local effort for educational improvement. Donnahoe argued that present school grants from existing tax sources considered only local ability. Combining the ability factor of present school grants with the effort factor under his sales tax plan would give Virginia "a unique system of interaction and support among all of its governmental units, which might well serve as a model for the nation." [13] The Donnahoe proposal was the one which most encouraged localities to use funds from the state sales tax bonanza for local educational improvement instead of an excuse to reduce local taxes. Cities, it was contended, would benefit from the 1 per cent local option provision of the plan, while counties would benefit from the specifics of the incentive formula, since schools were the dominant expenditure in the counties, whereas many other functions were maintained at considerable cost by the cities.

It was Godwin's responsibility to extract from the differing factions a meaningful piece of legislation. If he did not move cautiously and provide a plan which attracted widespread support, his dream for a progressive Virginia could be seriously damaged. The Governor synthesized the various proposals in his quest for a politically viable bill. He took the basic outline

[12] Richmond *Times-Dispatch*, Oct. 3, 1965.   [13] *Ibid.*

of the Donnahoe plan and called for a 2 per cent state sales tax
with localities authorized to add another 1 per cent for their
own use.[14] The 2 per cent state sales tax, he reasoned, would
give Virginia sorely needed tax dollars, and the 1 per cent local
option tax would mollify those urban representatives who complained their local tax rights were being taken away. Donnahoe's effort formula had to be set aside as "politically
impossible." ° His Local Incentive Fund would pressure localities into a race for public school improvement at a far faster
and more competitive rate than many were prepared to go.
Godwin therefore proposed to return 1 per cent of the 2 per
cent state sales tax to localities on the basis of school age
population,[15] a move designed to attract support from rural
legislators.[16]

Godwin's bill was delicately balanced, and he braced himself to guide it through the legislature. Cries of anguish arose

[14] See *Acts of Assembly, 1966,* pp. 261, 277.

[15] *Acts of Assembly, 1966,* p. 276; New York *Times,* March 13, 1966.

[16] Several other provisions of the Godwin sales tax proposals assured the state
of an equitable portion of the sales tax funds. Localities had been guaranteed
the return of 1 per cent of the 2 per cent state sales tax plus the additional
proceeds of the 1 per cent local option taxes. The state thus was left with only
1 per cent of its 2 per cent sales tax and much of that amount was consumed in
costs of administration and compensation for the pending reduction of such
levies as the gross receipts tax on merchants. The state meanwhile was almost
solely responsible for complex highway improvement programs and many
additional services. The Governor proposed a separate but companion bill to
place a 2 per cent tax on automotive sales, a levy designed to produce about
$26 million annually with the proceeds earmarked for highway construction. He
further appended to his 2 per cent state sales tax bill a clause to hike the state
sales tax to 3 per cent by July 1, 1968, the extra 1 per cent to go to the state.
The Governor's final sales tax proposal thus emerged as follows:

To become effective September 1, 1966, (a) a 2 per cent state sales
tax—estimated annual yield of $85–$100 million—1 per cent retained by state
and 1 per cent returned to localities on the basis of school age population
(designed to appeal to rural representatives); (b) a 1 per cent optional local
sales tax—collected by state but returned to localities on point of collection basis
(designed to appeal to urban representatives); (c) a 2 per cent tax on
automotive sales—estimated annual yield of $26 million—proceeds earmarked
for highway construction.

To become effective July 1, 1968, an additional 1 per cent tax (raising
state sales tax to 3 per cent). This 1 per cent was to be retained by the state
(*Acts of Assembly, 1966,* pp. 258 ff. and 863–64; Richmond *Times-Dispatch,*
Jan.–Feb. 1966; New York *Times,* March 13, 1966).

from around the state. Urbanites were most vociferous. The Virginia Municipal League, not happy with the 1 per cent ceiling on local option taxes, unanimously resolved to oppose any reduction of the present taxing powers of municipalities. Mayor Morrill M. Crowe of Richmond registered a "strong protest" against the Godwin distribution formula which would "very materially deteriorate this capital city and place it in fiscal jeopardy." Crowe estimated that the Godwin school age population formula for the distribution of sales tax revenue would give back to Richmond "barely 20 per cent" of what the tax took from the city. Crowe's prediction that Richmond would be "plunged into a grave fiscal crisis" was echoed by other urban areas.[17] Spokesmen from Hampton Roads promised to oppose any legislation prohibiting counties, cities, and towns from imposing a local sales tax of more than 1 per cent.[18]

Urban spokesmen fought in committee and offered floor amendments and substitute bills to scrap the limitation on local sales taxes. They protested against school age population as the sole basis for revenue distribution of that part of the sales tax returned to the localities. Yet these efforts to change the sales tax bill were unsuccessful. "Whatever the cities wanted, the cities didn't get," wrote one reporter. "In vote after vote, the [House Finance] committee turned aside modifications that would have liberalized the revenue returns to cities and urban areas."[19]

Urban legislators were often not united in their search for a more congenial distribution formula. The Governor's sales tax bill, by allowing localities an optional 1 per cent tax, actually gave urban centers greater latitude than many had heretofore predicted.[20] Many urban legislators, realizing this, stuck with

[17] Richmond *Times-Dispatch*, Feb. 8, 12, 1966.
[18] Richmond *News Leader*, Feb. 8, 1966.   [19] *Ibid.*, Feb. 11, 1966.

[20] Though urbanites still complained, the provision for the 1 per cent local option levy was more favorable to urban areas than many of the previously discussed sales tax packages. Governor Harrison advocated in his farewell address "the discontinuance of all local sales taxes" and Godwin was initially inclined to go along with Harrison's suggestion. Although Harrison would have distributed 1 per cent of the state sales tax to localities on a slightly different basis (¼ point of collection, ¾ school age population), urban centers would still have received far less under this formula than under the final Godwin package.

the Governor in his proposals. Senator Ed Breeden, a deft and articulate legislator from Norfolk, managed Godwin's sales tax bill on the Senate floor and attracted substantial urban support for the Governor's proposals.[21] Godwin himself wheedled, traded, and cajoled to keep his measure intact. He commanded a winning coalition on every important vote.[22]

If there were significant differences as to the method of revenue distribution, the 1966 Virginia General Assembly was remarkably united in its willingness to pass a general retail sales tax. Considering the dismal fate of such measures in the past, it was remarkable that debate in the 1966 legislature centered not on whether to enact a general sales tax but on how best to distribute the proceeds. The fifteen municipalities which had enacted their own sales taxes jolted the state government into action before it was too late. But the sudden change in the legislative climate owed much to other causes. Mills Godwin had carefully prepared the state for a sales tax with his pronouncements over the past year. He had campaigned on a program of meeting state needs with additional revenue. Most important, he demonstrated sufficient legislative craftsmanship to guide a carefully conceived compromise package through an Assembly with divergent interests.[23]

The 1966 General Assembly went on record as the "sales tax session" of the Virginia legislature. There were, however, other important occurrences. For years rural legislators had thwarted attempts to raise the minimum driver's age in the state from fifteen to sixteen years. When freshman Delegate William M. ("Bullet Bill") Dudley of Lynchburg introduced a bill to that effect in the 1966 General Assembly session, most observers

[21] Richmond *Times-Dispatch*, Feb. 26, 1966.

[22] The closest vote came on an amendment to dump the 1 per cent increase in the sales tax scheduled for July 1968. The House voted 47 to 46 to abandon the increase; the Senate voted 23 to 17 to keep it. Friendly persuasion got the House to reconsider its initial position and restore the automatic increase. After this last struggle Godwin's proposal passed the legislature virtually unaltered. See Richmond *Times-Dispatch*, Feb. 25, 1966.

[23] The Godwin compromise can be best appreciated by a glance at the table in Appendix IX on the distribution of sales tax proceeds of December 1966.

expected it would meet the same fate as its predecessors. Rural representatives still voiced strong objections: Delegate C. W. ("Willie") Cleaton of Mecklenburg County explained that county school buses were driven by fifteen-year-olds, and Delegate Pope of Southampton pleaded that fifteen-year-old drivers were needed by the farmers to operate tractors.[24] The House, however, passed the bill over these protests by the overwhelming margin of 71 to 26,[25] and the measure likewise cleared the Senate. Urban forces savored a long-awaited victory.

Another urban-rural controversy arose over utility bills introduced by Senator FitzGerald Bemiss of Richmond. Many counties had long been fond of slapping stiff tax rates on utilities to ease the tax burden for citizens. The Bemiss bills professed to remedy the inequities.[26] The measures predictably sent Senator Ed McCue and his rural colleagues on a rampage. McCue vowed the Bemiss bills were the worst he had seen in his thirty-three years in the General Assembly. They gave the big corporations preferential treatment over "ordinary taxpayers." "The utility lawyers who wrote the bill should have their fees doubled," scowled McCue. The legislation only "turned loose . . . utilities" against good, honest, ordinary folk across the state.[27] McCue's objections failed to impress the Assembly.

[24] Richmond *News Leader,* Jan. 26, 1966.

[25] *Journal of House,* 1966, pp. 135–36.

[26] Many rural localities were classifying utility installations as personal property and taxing them at the personal property rate, which was much higher than the tax on real estate. A second favorite strategy of these localities was to assess nonutility real estate at a low rate and impose a high tax rate on the assessment. The utilities, however, all had to be assessed at a uniform 40 per cent rate by the State Corporation Commission. Then they had to pay the high local tax rate on the 40 per cent assessment.

The Bemiss bills set out to remedy these inequities. They required that all future public utility property be classified as real estate, not personal property, and further designated a twenty-year period during which localities had to reclassify certain present utility properties as real estate. All future additions to utility installations would be assessed at the local assessment ratio, not at the 40 per cent imposed by the State Corporation Commission. See *Acts of Assembly,* 1966, pp. 724–26; Richmond *Times-Dispatch,* March 5, 1966.

[27] Richmond *Times-Dispatch,* March 5, 1966.

The legislation passed 24 to 11, and the vote broke in large part along urban-rural lines.[28]

Many significant proposals of the urban legislators in the 1966 General Assembly never found their way to the statute books. Rural conservatives, who still dominated vital committees, sidetracked much progressive legislation long before it reached the floor. Yet in one crucial area, that of highway finance and pay-as-you-go policy, urban forces mustered unprecedented strength. They lost the skirmish in the 1966 session, but many observers believe they will soon succeed.

By 1964 pay-as-you-go and highway financing in general were drawing increasing fire from influential quarters.[29] The Byrd organization had always been more generous to farm-to-market roads than city streets in the distribution of highway revenue, and by 1964 the urban areas were in real difficulties. Urban Virginians had never been enamored of pay-as-you-go as a method of highway financing in the first place, and they were even less enchanted with the fund distribution formulas which the rural chieftains of the Byrd organization managed to concoct. Finally, with traffic volume soaring in the commonwealth's metropolitan areas, the 1964 General Assembly began to respond. The Road Acts of 1964 abandoned antique formulas for the distribution of highway revenue and assured Virginia cities of something more than a few financial crumbs. Under the new provisions the streets of cities and towns over 3,500 population were formally designated a separate highway system and were divorced from the primary system through which the allocation of funds had previously flowed. This urban system, was guaranteed a minimum of 14 per cent of all highway funds, exclusive of Interstate Federal Aid. The acts further established a flat rate of $10,000 per mile per year for

[28] Voting against were the following eleven senators, all of them representing rural districts: Ames of Accomack County; Barnes of Tazewell County; D. W. Bird, of Bland County; Campbell of Hanover County; Davis of Amherst County; Gray of Sussex County; Hagood of Halifax County; Hutcheson of Brunswick County; Long of Wise County; McCue of Charlottesville; Rawlings of Southampton County (*Journal of Senate*, 1966, p. 547).

[29] See Chapter 2 for a discussion of pay-as-you-go and highway finance under the Byrd organization.

primary route extensions through the cities and towns and of $800 per mile per year for other streets. In future financing of urban construction only 15 per cent would be required from a city or town in lieu of the 25 per cent previously demanded.[30]

The Road Acts of 1964 represented a giant step in the equitable distribution of pay-as-you-go funds, but urban areas were not overjoyed. The predominantly rural roads of the secondary system were still assured of 33 per cent of all highway funds, more than twice the amount guaranteed city streets.[31] A resolution from urban delegates in 1964 calling for further study of inequities in the distribution system was blocked by the state Senate, but Governor Harrison, mindful of the importance of the matter, directed the Virginia Advisory Legislative Council to undertake a comprehensive examination of the situation and report with further recommendations in two years.[32]

Further questioning of highway finances and pay-as-you-go came on the heels of a report by the State Highway Commission in 1965 showing that the gap between estimated revenue from existing tax sources and revenue actually needed to bring the highway system to "minimum tolerable conditions" by 1975 was a staggering $329,000,000.[33] The primary, secondary, and urban systems were all destined to be woefully short of funds unless there was a substantial increase in present taxes. The questions plaguing all legislators were whether sufficient additional revenue could be provided within the framework of the pay-as-you-go policy and whether pay-as-you-go was in fact

[30] See the report of the Highway Commission of Virginia, *A Program of Highway Improvement, 1966–1975* (Richmond, 1966), pp. 23–26, for a detailed analysis of the Road Acts of 1964.

[31] *Ibid.*, p. 24. Defenders of the "33 per cent" allocation formula for secondary roads make a cogent case. They point out that the secondary system contains approximately three-fourths of the total highway mileage of the state, that almost one-half of the secondary roads are still not hard-surfaced, and that the secondary road system includes not merely farm-to-market roads but important mileage in such big suburban counties as Fairfax, Chesterfield, and Roanoke. The Road Acts of 1964 represented a forward step in highway planning and administration, but they could not provide sufficient revenue for Virginia's soaring highway needs.

[32] See Virginia Advisory Legislative Council, *Urban Streets and Highways* (Richmond: Department of Purchases and Supply, 1966), pp. 5–6.

[33] Virginia Highway Commission, *Program of Highway Improvement*, p. 72.

the cheapest or quickest method of financing future highway needs.

During the 1965 gubernatorial campaign and throughout the 1966 session of the General Assembly, pay-as-you-go received rude treatment at the hands of the Virginia press. Editors sought to prove that this once-honored slogan was now more outmoded than the Model-T Ford. "We continue to build stretches of highway on a gradual, pay-as-we-go basis," noted the Roanoke *World News,* "avoiding bond issue costs incurred by other states. But unsafe roads will keep claiming lives un-necessarily—and the postponement of construction will only lead to higher land acquisition and building costs later on, thus sweeping away most if not all of the 'savings' from debt-free financing." [34] Most vitriolic in its opposition to pay-as-you-go was Hampton Roads. To improve roads, residents of this area had been forced to establish authorities to issue revenue bonds at high interest rates and build toll facilities to meet the bond requirements. "Taxpaying motorists who use these tunnels and bridges and roads pay the bill," claimed the Norfolk *Ledger-Dispatch.* "They not only pay, when, in most cases, they ought to ride free but, even embracing the toll approach, they pay a higher price than ought to be necessary. This is because the revenue bonds carry considerably higher interest rates than would bonds backed by the full credit of the state, pushing the cost of these projects literally millions of dollars higher." [35] The Suffolk *News-Herald* also argued that the quicker highway construction resulting from the issuance of bonds would bring profits to the state in the form of "business, industrial and residential growth as a result of better flow of commerce. . . . Too much has been said about the 'pay-as-you-go' policy keep-ing Virginia debt free," claimed its editor. "Nothing could be more false, for the localities are strapped with debt to their upper limits, in most instances." [36]

The 1966 General Assembly was under pressure to react to growing disillusionment with pay-as-you-go and to cope with Virginia's mounting highway needs. It enacted a 2 per cent tax on automobile sales, the proceeds of which would accrue to the

[34] Oct. 22, 1965.   [35] Feb. 17, 1966.   [36] Jan. 29, 1966.

state's highways. Cities obtained a much needed increase of $200 per mile per year for the maintenance of city streets. But the most significant resolution of the session was the one that did not pass.

State Senator William Hopkins of Roanoke expected he would pick up five or six co-patrons when he began passing around a little resolution last week to loosen the State's pay-as-you-go fiscal policy, [noted the Norfolk *Virginian-Pilot*]. But he raised the estimate to nine or ten, and then stopped estimating as the signatures kept pouring in, and the bill wound up with eighteen sponsors. Next day three more Democrats said they would support the bill if the committee reported it, and the four Republicans said they would have been happy to sign if somebody had thought to ask them. So in the 40-member State Senate, formerly the citadel of obdurate reaction in fiscal matters, 25 members are urging a departure from the State's cash-and-carry financing of its needs.[37]

Hopkin's resolution would have changed the Virginia constitution to allow the state to borrow up to 5 per cent of the assessed valuation of taxable real estate within its borders for highway construction and up to 10 per cent for other purposes.[38] It was remarkable, as more than one dumbfounded analyst observed, that "a majority of the Virginia Senate, the once unshakeable citadel of the Byrd organization's no-debt fiscal conservatism, was actually on the verge of relaxing pay-as-you-go." [39] But the relaxers were not strategically placed, and the resolution met sudden death in the Senate Finance Committee where Byrd conservatives still called the tune. The final committee vote was 11 to 7, and it fell along rural-urban lines.[40]

[37] Jan. 29, 1966.   [38] *Ibid.*
[39] Richmond *Times-Dispatch,* Jan. 27, 1966.
[40] The Senate Finance Committee vote was as follows: voting for the repealer were Senators Aldhizer of Harrisonburg, Baldwin and Breeden of Norfolk, Bateman of Newport News, Fenwick of Arlington, Fitzgerald of Fairfax, and Willey of Richmond. Voting against the resolution were Ames of Accomack, D. W. Bird, of Bland, L. C. Bird, of Chesterfield, Campbell of Hanover, Collins of Covington, Gray of Sussex, Hagood of Halifax, Hutcheson of Brunswick, Long of Wise, McCue of Charlottesville, and Wyatt of Danville (Norfolk *Virginian-Pilot,* Feb. 19, 1966).

The issue of highway financing and pay-as-you-go told much
of the story of the 1966 General Assembly. Vast strides were
made in the financing of state needs, but no floodgates were
opened, and few thought Virginia in any danger of going too
far, too fast. Rural conservatives were still the legislative traffic
cops. One reporter summed the session up this way:

There were signs—and ample ones—that the lawmakers who came
to town two months ago reflected the growing power of urban
voters. They seem capable of forcing even greater change in the
years ahead.

But they didn't take over this time.

Rurally oriented and traditional conservative Democrats still
were the ones that controlled major committees. They could—and
did—put to death many measures they thought were too moderate,
too progressive, too new for Virginia.

There was pressure to repeal the hallowed pay-as-you-go. A
committee killed off attempts at modification there. There was
considerable effort to change the state's bottle-only liquor laws; a
committee took care of that effort.

.   .   .   .   .

Committees killed all poll tax repeal legislation. They killed even
the proposals for a study of Virginia election laws. . . .

In committees death also came to such measures as a state
minimum wage bill, abolition of capital punishment, repeal of
tuition grants and statewide compulsory school attendance laws.[41]

The 1966 session of the Virginia General Assembly will,
however, be remembered far more for what it did than for
what it failed to do. Some rated it the "most productive and
progressive" session of the General Assembly since Governor
Harry Byrd pushed through his Program of Progress forty long
years before. Most judgments agreed that the session marked a
historic turning point in state fiscal policy. Virginia at last
became more concerned with quality education and improved
public services than with low taxes and budget balancing.
Godwin's basic plea for a general sales tax stirred up remarkably little opposition in or out of the General Assembly. When

[41] Richmond *News Leader,* March 14, 1966.

the Tuck tax program came up in 1948, editorial writers, business leaders, and citizens around the state joined in opposition. The Almond program of 1960 also stirred up animosity, and the 1960 temporary taxes on liquor and cigarettes were widely deplored. By contrast, the basic thrust of the Godwin program encountered little resistance. There were the differences over the distribution of revenue, but the climate of acceptance of new taxes was totally different than it had been in the past. John Warren Cooke, floor leader of the Democratic majority, commented, "At this session, instead of getting mad at you for voting more taxes, people got mad at you for not voting more taxes." "It's a quiet revolution," said C. F. Hicks, counsel for the Virginia Association of Counties. "The General Assembly at last has caught up with the people." [42]

The 1966 General Assembly "put laws on the statute books which will enable the Old Dominion to move ahead purposefully and in tune with the modern age," Virginius Dabney remarked in the Richmond *Times-Dispatch*. "Many of us have dreamed that the day would come when Virginia would finally face up to its responsibilities in all fields of government service and take those steps which would bring us to the forefront in the South," declared Dr. Robert F. Williams, executive secretary of the Virginia Education Association. "Our dream seems at last to be coming true." [43]

And in fact it was. Appropriations for public education for 1966–68 increased 37.5 per cent over the last biennium. Summer schools received a $1,500,000 appropriation for the first time. Kindergartens and educational TV were incorporated into the state educational effort for the first time. Minimum salary scales for teachers were hiked by $700, and the minimum increment for a master's degree for teachers was increased from $200 to $500. Basic salaries of school superintendents were raised $200. The legislature established a statewide textbook rental system with an appropriation of $2,000,000 or $2.00 per child. The 1 per cent of the state sales tax returned to localities had an estimated yield of $33,600,000 in 1966–67 and

---

[42] Richmond *Times-Dispatch*, March 20, 1966.
[43] *Ibid.*, March 14, 15, 1966.

$47,000,000 in 1967–68, all of which was earmarked for education. Over and above all, the accumulating surplus from preceding years and the new sales tax revenue were to finance an extensive system of two-year community colleges to accommodate those unable or unwilling to enroll in one of the state's four-year institutions.[44]

Always pushing the offensive was Governor Godwin. "His unmistakable mark of leadership was visible on virtually every piece of major legislation that cleared the Assembly during its arduous 60-day session," wrote one reporter.[45] Another toasted Godwin as a "master persuader, a master in the field of political healing arts." [46]

On October 5, 1966, the Governor called together educational, political, and business leaders from around the state in a mass meeting to further the state's educational effort:

I have not asked you here in order that we might engage in mutual congratulations over what already has been done, impressive though that record is.

.   .   .   .   .

For what we do in these two years will largely be a catching up with our sister states. There will still be too few that we can say we have passed by.

.   .   .   .   .

For I would not deceive you. I would not lull you into the benign belief that all is now serene in education.

There will still be pockets of procrastination across our land, where Virginia children, short-changed in their public schooling, will cast an accusing shadow upon our collective conscience.

Proper expectations of the rewards of higher learning will still go unfulfilled.

But we have begun, and the excitement of that striving has captured the imagination of our people. We would do well to read the signs of their enthusiasm before it sours into discontent.

.   .   .   .   .

[44] See *Acts of Assembly, 1966*, pp. 1494–1502, for breakdown of public school appropriations for 1966–1968 biennium.
[45] Richmond *Times-Dispatch*, March 14, 1966.
[46] Richmond *News Leader*, March 14, 1966.

Already in Virginia we have condensed a century of progress into a decade, and still, relentlessly, the pace of change increases. Precedents and concepts we thought unshakeable, have been overturned or washed away.

However mightily we may wish it were not so, it is time to shed the comfortable arguments, the warm and familiar excuses, the pleasant encumbrances of the old ways—for we know in our hearts they will not—they cannot—serve us now.[47]

Godwin pushed back "the pleasant encumbrances of the old ways" in areas other than education. He keynoted the annual convention of the AFL-CIO amid wails from conservatives that his presence was making organized labor respectable in Virginia. He denounced the Ku Klux Klan and offered rewards for information leading to the arrest of those burning crosses.

But what of Godwin and the organization captained by Senator Harry Flood Byrd? Godwin considered himself a product of the Byrd organization, and his Byrd background was indeed typical. Yet during his gubernatorial campaign and his first year in office the classic maxims of the Byrd organization were replaced by a wholly new set of concerns within Virginia. The rhetoric of race and massive resistance, the dread of deficit, the attacks on organized labor, and the blind reverence of Virginia's past were deliberately set aside by the new Mills Godwin. Godwin gave receptive Virginians a new campaign dialogue, a hard-nosed appraisal of present and future needs, and, most important, the taxes to help meet these needs. He swept to victory behind a coalition of Byrd and anti-Byrd elements and fused a dynamic consensus of these elements when in office. He served notice that Democrats in Virginia would respect their ties with the national party.

Every clue to Virginia politics, moreover, augured further change, further upheaval. A more urban legislature would batter at the remaining vestiges of Harry Byrd's Virginia. Pay-as-you-go, bottle-only liquor laws, the poll tax, had been granted only for the moment the executioner's stay. Furthermore, greater opportunities beckoned greater numbers in the Vir-

[47] *Address at the Governor's Conference on Education,* Oct. 5, 1966 (Richmond: Department of Purchases and Supply, 1966).

ginia of the future. That future Virginia Godwin had helped to inaugurate. Into that future some form of Democratic organization would extend. Yet if the organization was already so transformed from what it had been, should its name still read Byrd?

Chapter 12

The 1966 Democratic Primary

Nᴏᴛ all parts of the Byrd machine had been remodeled. Senator Byrd, embedded in earlier verities, viewed with dismay the errant course of younger leaders. While Byrd kept silence, Godwin rode the Lady Bird Special. To the end Byrd disdained leftward influences in Virginia; Godwin courted their support. An uncommon schizophrenia thus pervaded the organization by 1965. Younger and more urban leaders boldly took fresh views while the patriarch still solemnly steered his accustomed course.

The Senator held around him a corporal's guard of lifelong conservatives who still played prominent roles in the commonwealth's politics. Senator Robertson, Congressmen Abbitt, Tuck, and Smith, state legislators Gray, Moore, and Byrd, Jr., formed the hard-core element of the old Byrd organization which clung to the orthodoxies of Byrd conservatism in spite of change. This element had systematically alienated certain social, economic, and political forces throughout Virginia. The Tuck labor wars, the massive resistance program, the Young Turk struggle, and fiscal deprivations under pay-as-you-go had turned labor, Negroes, and many young and urban Virginians against the machine. These forces, when first alienated, were somewhat anemic, but by 1966 they had become dragon slayers and caused several of Byrd's chief lieutenants abruptly to reach the end of a long political road.

Retirement came first for Byrd himself. Guy Friddell wrote:

In the spring [1965], Byrd had a series of luncheons for fellow senators, Berryville neighbors, and friends from around Virginia. On the broad, pillared porch overlooking the orchards, a hundred or so gathered at the final party, liberal Northeastern senators chatting with Deep South conservatives, Midwest Republicans talking with West Coast Democrats.

Midway, Byrd left the porch and came out, unseen, onto a small second-story balcony and looked down at the throng. Gradually, the guests became aware of his watching them. The talk stilled, some men raised their glasses to him, the women clapped, a rippling of applause, and then, in the intense silence, before he turned and clumped off the balcony, Byrd said, softly, "Finest people I ever saw." [1]

Shortly afterward he began to fade. Few knew the will he had to exert to preside over his committee. Talking once to Mrs. Elizabeth Springer, clerk of the Finance Committee, Byrd clenched his teeth and spoke of his arthritic knee. "Elizabeth," he said, "it hurts me so, I don't believe I can stand it." [2] On November 11, 1965, Harry Byrd retired.

Senatorial courtesy flowed bounteously for the courtly Southerner. President Johnson termed the Virginian "one of the authentic giants" of the United States Senate. "He is a man of sincere convictions, always a gentleman and ever a patriot," remarked Hubert Humphrey. "A tower of strength in the Senate," observed senior Republican George Aiken of Vermont, and other colleagues, Democrats and Republicans, liberals and conservatives, voiced their respect. [3]

Others, however, were not so encomium-minded. For more than thirty years Byrd had opposed the spending plans, welfare proposals, and civil rights measures of the executive branch. He "voted nay to the very movement of history," observed one editor, [4] while columnist Kenneth Crawford likened Byrd's record to a "mark left by tenaciously sustained foot dragging." [5] "His resignation at the age of 78 marks the end of

---

[1] Friddell, p. 77.   [2] *Newsweek*, Nov. 22, 1965.
[3] Washington *Post*, Nov. 12, 13, 1965.   [4] *America*, Nov. 27, 1965, p. 664.
[5] *Newsweek*, Nov. 29, 1965, p. 34.

an epoch in Democratic Politics in Virginia and reduces the southern provincial power in the Senate," reported the London *Times*.[6] Calling Byrd a "gentle obstructionist," the Washington *Post* dutifully marked the passing of one who for three decades had been "a national symbol of fiscal, racial, and social welfare conservatism." [7]

Predictions abounded on the future of Byrd's organization in Virginia. "It [the retirement] may have been the Byrd dynasty's swan song," conjectured *Time*,[8] and the New York *Times* wrote that "the survival of the Byrd organization without the active presence of the stern, apple-cheeked senior Senator from Virginia at its head was regarded as questionable." [9] The *New Republic* focused on the heritage of Byrd's organization:

Although a champion of states' rights, he [Byrd] never showed any interest in state responsibilities. His machine let Virginia's educational system deteriorate into one of the nation's worst. While holding up Virginia's pay-as-you-go system as a model of fiscal purity, he conveniently ignored the parsimony that made it possible; nor did he care that towns and cities went deeply into debt financing services the state wouldn't. Courtly, courteous, well liked by his congressional confreres, Byrd foisted on his people the most iniquitous policy devised by any Southern state to combat school desegregation.[10]

The timing of Byrd's retirement did not go unnoticed amid the varying verdicts on his long career. Byrd stepped down after Godwin's election on November 2 but before he took office in early January. He did not unsettle the 1965 campaign scene, and he spared Godwin the delicate matter of a senatorial appointment. It was unlikely that the divergent elements of the Godwin coalition could have agreed on a new senator, and Godwin's legislative proposals might have been seriously endangered by a controversial appointment. The matter, therefore, conveniently went to Byrd's trusted friend, outgoing Gov-

[6] Nov. 12, 1965.   [7] Nov. 12, 1965.   [8] Nov. 19, 1965, p. 43a.
[9] Nov. 12, 1965.
[10] *New Republic*, Nov. 27, 1965, p. 9. (Reprinted by permission of *The New Republic*, © 1965, Harrison-Blaine of New Jersey, Inc.)

ernor Albertis Harrison, and Harrison, to no one's great surprise, appointed Harry Flood Byrd, Jr., to his father's seat.

Although it surprised no one, there were many the Byrd, Jr., appointment did not please. Truman's old quip about "too many Byrds in the Congress" came back to life. *Time* claimed Byrd, Jr., was "in some ways more rigidly conservative" [11] than Byrd, Sr., and the *New Republic* dubbed him a "more arrogant, less imposing, but otherwise faithful copy of his father." [12] "It took all I had to go for Godwin," moaned one northern Virginia Democrat. "Little Harry is just too much." [13] "These are the times for political giants, not the shadows of once great men," Robert Corber, Republican state chairman, exclaimed.[14] Recalling that he had campaigned for Godwin, Armistead Boothe nonetheless observed: "I just can't take young Harry." [15]

The career of Harry Byrd, Jr., was calculated to outrage most moderate Virginians. "From his earliest days," wrote the Washington *Post,* "he emulated his father and his walk, his speech and his philosophy. He even has the apple-cheeked glow that bespeaks hours spent outdoors and marks him, not as just a chip off the old block, but as an extension of the original." [16] He married Gretchen Bigelow Thomson, the 1937 Queen Shenandoah XIV of the annual Shenandoah Apple Blossom Festival in Winchester. Like his father, Byrd, Jr., had been a newspaper editor and publisher, an apple orchardist, and a member of the Virginia Senate. His eighteen-year-career in that body had been undeviatingly conservative. In the early fifties he championed the Byrd tax reduction act, the effect of which was to return "excess" state funds to the taxpayers rather than devote them to public services. When Armistead Boothe led the Young Turk revolt in 1954 to appropriate these surplus funds for public education, Byrd, Jr., stoutly insisted on returning them to the taxpayers.[17] He was a principal architect and supporter of the massive resistance program from 1956 to 1958,[18] and in 1960 he successfully killed the Almond sales tax proposals but failed to trim the state budget by some

[11] Nov. 19, 1965, p. 43a.   [12] Nov. 27, 1965, pp. 9–10.
[13] Washington *Post,* Nov. 14, 1965.   [14] *Ibid.,* Nov. 13, 1965.
[15] *Ibid.,* Nov. 12, 1965.   [16] *Ibid.,* Nov. 13, 1965.   [17] See Chapter 4.
[18] See Chapter 5.

$23,000,000.[19] In presidential elections when Senator Byrd, Sr., maintained golden silence, Harry Byrd, Jr., was similarly hushed.

Harry Byrd, Jr., however, faced real difficulty in the 1966 election for the four remaining years of the senior Byrd's term. *Time* surmised that "Little Harry . . . might find himself in an unaccustomed spot for a Byrd—on the outside looking in," [20] and the *New Republic* gloated that "for the first time in a generation, the election of a Byrd in Virginia will not be automatic." [21] To be sure, the loyalists of the organization quickly closed ranks behind the younger Byrd. Bill Tuck declared him "ideally equipped and suited" for his new job.[22] Yet the united support of the Byrd organization had long since ceased to frighten eligible challengers, and already Congressman Pat Jennings stated he would "in all probability" be a candidate for the Senate in 1966. Other Virginians outside the organization, including Armistead Boothe and state Senators William Spong, Henry Howell, and William Hopkins weighed the possibility of making the race.

There was another complicating factor in the politics of Virginia for 1966. Senator A. Willis Robertson's term expired that year, and he was expected to seek re-election. Robertson's political life had been as long as that of the Byrd organization. He came to the Virginia Senate in 1916, the same year as Byrd, became commonwealth's attorney of Rockbridge County, 1922–26, Commissioner of Game and Inland Fisheries, 1926–33, and congressman, 1932–46, and entered the United States Senate on the death of Carter Glass in 1946, where he had served for the next twenty years. At seventy-nine years of age Robertson still appeared to one reporter as "an enviable physical specimen of manhood, raw-boned, hard as nails, and not more than ounces off his college-day weight. In 1906 and 1907 he played every minute of every game at tackle on the Spider [University of Richmond] football team—and looks as if he could repeat the feat this season." [23] More important, however, was Robertson's seniority: he was chairman of the Senate

[19] Washington *Post*, Nov. 13, 1965.   [20] Nov. 19, 1965, p. 43a.
[21] Nov. 27, 1965, p. 10.   [22] Washington *Post*, Nov. 12, 1965.
[23] Houston, "Smith and Robertson," p. 31.

Banking and Currency Committee and the sixth ranking member of Appropriations. With Byrd retired, Robertson's position was even more significant.

Although Robertson had been as conservative as Senator Byrd, Sr., had been as shocked as his colleague at the growing national debt, and had regularly supported the organization's stands, he had never been close personally to Harry Byrd. Robertson never sat in the organization's inner sanctum, and his influence on state policy never ranked with that of Combs, Prieur, Tuck, Moore, Smith, Kellam, Gray, Abbitt, and other top organization leaders. He had been involved in an off-again, on-again friction with the organization which both sides had taken care to mask from public view. Key reported that "in the 1946 Democratic convention to nominate a successor to fill the unexpired senatorial term of Carter Glass, it was believed in some quarters that Senator Byrd desired the nomination of Representative Howard Smith, of Alexandria, who was even more extreme than the Senator in his dislike of the New Deal. But the convention was not well managed and the high command acquiesced in the nomination of Willis Robertson. The delegates believed that Robertson could be elected with less outcry from the antiorganization element." [24] Friddell remarked that Robertson "flourished oak-like in politics without the semblance of a machine, only a host of friends and admirers. Indeed, when the Organization tried to purge him in 1952, Senator Robertson, riding with a newsman on an evening's journey, was moved to tell him how every time he received a letter or a telephone call of support, all of them spontaneous and unsolicited, he took a pin and marked his backer's residence on the wall map in his office. 'You'd be surprised,' he said, 'at the pins on that map.' " [25]

Willis Robertson had lived long in the shadow of Harry Byrd. A conservative with a deep sense of pride, it hurt him to be known as "Virginia's other Senator." As late as age seventy-eight and after twenty years of service, he was still the junior Senator from Virginia. Privately Robertson spoke of Senator Byrd as a great Virginian—but also one who lacked a sense of

[24] Page 24.   [25] Page 72.

party loyalty, who too often sided with Republicans on purely partisan issues, and who was not in as good standing in the Senate's inner circle as was popularly supposed. By the middle fifties and early sixties, however, Robertson and the Byrd organization had made peace. They were both conservative; Robertson was too entrenched to be budged, and the organization had more fundamental problems about which to fret. Nonetheless, when Byrd finally retired, Robertson saw a long-awaited chance to come fully into his own.

There were others, however, who wanted to ease Robertson out. Shortly after the appointment of Byrd, Jr., several top leaders of the organization gathered at the Waldorf-Astoria after an annual Chamber of Commerce meeting in New York. There the possibilities of replacing Robertson were discussed. Of the top spokesmen at the meeting—Harrison, Godwin, Byrd, Jr., and Kellam—Kellam was believed to have urged a trial balloon for Congressman Tom Downing of the First District.° He had strong reasons for supporting the move. An organization ticket of Byrd, Jr., and Robertson was felt to be too conservative. It would be difficult to attract the moderate support necessary for a comfortable Democratic primary victory. Since both Byrd, Jr., and Robertson came from rural areas in the Shenandoah Valley in western Virginia, the friends 'n neighbors vote would be too concentrated. Furthermore, Robertson, at seventy-nine seemed too old and the organization badly needed a rejuvenated image. What Kellam urged was a move toward Downing as a follow-up to the Godwin victory of 1965. Downing was young, forty-eight, held the congressional seat in the more urban First District in eastern Virginia, and was a good organization man (a devoted Kellam disciple), yet his moderate votes in Congress would draw progressive Virginians to the organization's aid. If the Downing seat were vacated, moreover, Kellam might be able to put his brother, then a state senator from Virginia Beach, into that place.°

The main hitch in the plan was Robertson's refusal to move over. Despite frequent pressurings, Robertson made clear his intention to run "regardless of the number of my opponents." [26]

[26] Richmond *News Leader,* March 3, 1966.

Downing hovered on the edge of the race, then decided not to run when the persistent though cloaked attempts by the organization to push Robertson aside began to anger the Senator's friends and supporters. Byrd, Jr., and Robertson were thus thrown together for the coming election. Charles McDowell termed their personal relations "distant, if courteous" and remarked that each seemed to think the other might pull him down in the primary on July 12. "Robertson has long been outside the councils of the political organization headed for more than 30 years by Senator Byrd, Jr.'s father," continued McDowell. "Robertson is a Byrd organization candidate because there is no other." [27]

On the eve of the 1966 primary campaign the Byrd organization presented a divided image, symbolized on the one hand by Godwin's 1965 campaign and the 1966 General Assembly session and on the other by the old-style conservatism of Harry Byrd, Jr., and Willis Robertson. To the Washington *Post* the organization seemed "caught between past and present— bound to hereditary succession with dynastic overtones while reaching out to a new streamlined brand of consensus politics that could assure its longevity among a changing, more urban electorate." The 1966 elections were to test the holding power of the older element of the Virginia machine and "the selling power of the Byrd name itself." [28]

While the organization struggled to smooth out differences and to present at least an ostensibly united front, a group of potent challengers jockeyed for the chance to oppose the two conservatives. Whereas the organization finally settled on the most conservative of all possible combinations, the opposing camp put forward two men with whom they hoped to gain middle-of-the-road support. The most liberal of the potential candidates, state Senator Howell of Norfolk and Congressman Jennings of the Ninth District, withdrew in favor of the more moderate Armistead Boothe of Alexandria and state Senator William B. Spong of Portsmouth. Boothe would oppose Byrd, Jr., while Spong was to run for Robertson's seat.

[27] Richmond *Times-Dispatch*, April 20, 1966.   [28] Nov. 14, 1965.

The challengers came from the Washington suburbs and Hampton Roads, the two urban areas of Virginia where feeling against the Byrd organization ran highest. Both challengers, moreover, had been members of the Young Turk movement in 1954, and since that time the hard core of the Byrd organization had neither changed its course of action nor welcomed these two Turks to its inner councils. For fifteen years Boothe had been a formidable opponent of the organization. In his early years in the General Assembly under Governors Tuck and Battle he urged desegregation of public transportation and more equitable apportionment of the state legislature. In 1954 he personally led the Young Turk revolt for additional revenue for public schools.[29] He urged compliance with, not defiance of, the Supreme Court's decision throughout the massive resistance era.[30] When Boothe opposed Godwin in 1961 for lieutenant governor, he ran a very creditable race.[31] Yet when the latter moderated in 1965, Boothe strongly backed his gubernatorial bid. But Boothe had little in common with Byrd, Jr.[32]

William B. Spong of Portsmouth had been less adamant and less vocal in his opposition to the Byrd organization. He came to the House of Delegates in 1954 and sided with Boothe during the Young Turk revolt, though, as a freshman, he never captained the rebellious forces. During massive resistance he voted steadily for local option measures but was careful not to pose as a champion of desegregation. His first real opportunity came when Governor Almond appointed him chairman of the Commission on Public Education "to make a thorough study and report upon the public school system of Virginia." The result was a firm but tactful statement suggesting the progressive steps necessary to alleviate teacher shortages and inferior standards in many of Virginia's public schools.[33] The Spong Report, more thorough than inspirational, served as Spong's major credential for his projected statewide candidacy. He challenged Robertson in 1966 without the benefit of Boothe's widespread exposure and fervent following, but also with few, if any, personal enemies.

[29] See Chapter 4.   [30] See Chapter 5.   [31] See Chapter 9.
[32] Washington *Post*, Nov. 12, 1965.
[33] See Va. Commission on Public Education, *Va. Schools in Space Age.*

The senatorial campaigns were not the only political treat in store for Virginians in the summer of 1966. Eighty-three year old Howard Smith, seeking his nineteenth term in Congress from Virginia's Eighth District, faced the most serious opposition of his fifty-year political career. Judge Smith had been a power not only in the Byrd organization but on the national scene as well. He was the heart, at least in the House of Representatives, of the coalition of Republicans and southern Democrats that had been a thorn in the flesh of the Truman, Eisenhower, Kennedy, and Johnson administrations. Smith, as chairman of the House Rules Committee, directed the coalition's operations. Long a close adviser of Byrd, Howard Smith seemed to be safely secluded from the winds of change in his sprawling rural district in central, piedmont Virginia. The district, however, was grievously underpopulated, and the Supreme Court in *Wesberry* v. *Sanders*, February 17, 1964, had ruled there was "no excuse for ignoring our Constitution's plain objective of making equal representation for equal numbers of people the fundamental goal for the House of Representatives."[34] The 1965 special session of the General Assembly was compelled to dump a large sector of Fairfax County in Virginia's Washington suburbs into Smith's district. This pocket of moderate suburbanites formed a tempting political base from which to challenge the incumbent, and Delegate George C. Rawlings, Jr., of Fredericksburg announced for Smith's congressional seat. "The times demand representatives capable of recognizing 20th-century problems and able to offer 20th-century solutions," Rawlings insisted, and to this young liberal Howard Smith seemed little more than a political dinosaur.[35]

By late April campaigning was brisk across Virginia. "After so many years when so many Virginia senatorial campaigns have been placid and predictable, not to say somnolent, the current Democratic doubleheader has a promise of liveliness that is downright un-Virginian," wrote McDowell. He noted the candidates "working the fish-fries and shad-plankings,

[34] *Wesberry* v. *Sanders* 376 U.S. 1 (1964).
[35] Richmond *News Leader*, March 28, 1966.

shaking hands, testing their rhetoric, and picking up the rhythm of a grand enterprise." [36]

The Byrd, Jr.–Boothe race offered a clear-cut struggle on a whole range of issues between old adversaries. It will be "his record against mine," declared Boothe. "I hope the contrast will be clear." [37] Boothe was, as always, a dangerous opponent. Stylish and poised, he spoke and moved with easy grace and flair. Always attacking, he jabbed Byrd with tart wit. All he ever wanted to do, Boothe professed, was to prove to parents that "their children can be elected senators from Virginia even though their fathers were not themselves United States Senators." He merely hoped that the children could be chosen "by the four million of the state where appointments are not available to them from the four hundred." [38] As for Harry Byrd, Jr., he was "not a chip, or even a splinter, off the old block and . . . hardly a feather off the old Byrd." [39] His record was "thin and insipid . . . minus and negative . . . irrelevant." [40] "He once refused," said Boothe, "to vote for the Virginia state budget because he was mad at Governor Almond. He walked out of the Senate floor because he wanted his own way." [41] Alas, Boothe was afraid that Little Harry had not changed his ways, even in this modern day and age. "It is unbelievable that he has not grown educationally or intellectually in the last 10 years," Boothe remarked on one occasion.[42] When Byrd termed himself a progressive, Boothe chuckled that if it were so, "then a progressive would make a snail look like Brer Rabbit." [43]

Boothe took Byrd to task on massive resistance. "The issue," said Boothe, "is not dead as Byrd would like for us to think, especially for those whose education and lives were delayed because of it." [44] "If Harry Byrd, Jr. had had his way," Boothe reiterated, "the public schools of Virginia would have been

[36] Richmond *Times-Dispatch*, April 24, 1966.
[37] Richmond *News Leader*, March 28, 1966.
[38] Richmond *Times-Dispatch*, April 13, 1966.
[39] Richmond *News Leader*, May 12, 1966.
[40] Richmond *Times-Dispatch*, May 17, 1966.   [41] *Ibid.*, May 10, 1966.
[42] Richmond *News Leader*, June 17, 1966.
[43] Richmond *Times-Dispatch*, May 8, 1966.   [44] *Ibid.*

closed. It is entirely possible that we might not have a public school system in Virginia today at all. . . . To this day he has not expressed one word of regret for his effort to close the schools of Virginia. But Little Harry says, 'This is passé.' He falls back on a French word to cloak his sin with respectability." [45]

Armistead Boothe wholeheartedly supported bills that appalled conservative Virginians. Because he came from Alexandria, Boothe knew the plight of urban areas which were underrepresented in state legislatures. He pledged his support to the Supreme Court's "one man, one vote" principle and promised to oppose any congressional move to modify it. "I want you to send me to the Senate," he explained, "so I can convince Senator Dirksen we want no referendum, that we need no referendum in Virginia on the right of a man to vote." [46] Boothe openly endorsed Medicare and federal aid to depressed areas, called federal aid to education a "settled issue," and urged Virginia to work for its share. [47] His suggestion that the United States consider recognizing Red China brought a sharp rejoinder from Byrd's campaign manager, W. C. ("Dan") Daniel. Daniel reminded Virginians that China was providing the weapons to kill Americans in Vietnam and continued by exclaiming: "If there's one thing the United States has had enough of, it is information about China." [48]

Armistead Boothe would not, however, commit political suicide. Out of a sense either of conviction or political reality, he supported Virginia's right-to-work law, opposed the open housing bill before Congress, and stood against any withdrawal in Vietnam. Nonetheless, Boothe could not escape being branded a liberal by many Virginians seeking a fitting denunciation of his "wild-eyed" course. "To show you how liberal . . . I was," Boothe remarked, somewhat amused at this dreaded label, "I was promoting [in the General Assembly] some things other states had done 30 years before." [49]

Harry Byrd, Jr., campaigned very differently. The classic

[45] Richmond *News Leader*, May 18, 1966.   [46] *Ibid.*, April 23, 1966.
[47] *Ibid.*, May 26, 1966.   [48] *Ibid.*, June 28, 1966.
[49] *Ibid.*, July 8, 1966.

style of the senior Byrd had always been to ignore his opponent. Byrd, Jr., pleasantly but firmly reminded reporters that he would not reply to charges from the opposition. Instead he concentrated on a steady reiteration of basic Virginia verities. "Where Virginia is concerned, I have a crusading spirit," Byrd proclaimed,[50] and he promised to defend Virginia virtues and individual liberties with such fervor that Boothe chided him not to "just sing praise to our Constitution, which we all love and revere." [51]

The younger Byrd was probably the most exuberant and genuinely affable man on the campaign circuit that summer. More open than his father, Byrd, Jr., was called by the normally hostile Washington *Post* an "amiable, charming, courteous, and gracious Virginia gentleman." [52] Like his father, Byrd, Jr., had a ruddy, almost cherubic glow to his face and a quick, dancing twinkle in his eye. Whereas the elder Byrd's campaign dress was a striking double-breasted, white linen suit and blue shirt, Harry, Jr., wore a "well-tailored, dark slate-blue suit of nubby silk, white shirt and red-black-gray striped tie." [53] A trim and eager campaigner, he was often restless and nervous beneath his beaming exterior. If he was a choppy, somewhat hesitant speaker, he nonetheless had a story which would invariably produce laughter and applause on his courthouse tours. He explained that in flying to Franklin, Virginia, his pilot had mistakenly landed at Franklin, North Carolina. After that experience, Byrd concluded, not the flying machine, but the Byrd machine was still the most reliable one around.[54]

The newly appointed senator selected a limited range of controversial issues and hammered them home. He rotated between attacks on the Supreme Court for "abetting criminals," occasional lamentation about the state of the national debt, and persistent criticism of America's allies for failing to aid our Vietnam war effort and for trading with North Vietnam. "One reason they would like to see me eliminated as a Senator, they say, is because as a member of the Virginia

---

[50] Richmond *Times-Dispatch,* June 20, 1966.
[51] Richmond *News Leader,* May 21, 1966.   [52] Nov. 16, 1965.
[53] Richmond *Times-Dispatch,* June 20, 1966.   [54] *Ibid.*

Senate I didn't introduce very many bills. That is correct. I think we have too many laws on the statute books as it is." Later in the speech Byrd ended an explanation of his "no" votes in the United States Senate by discussing the open housing bill: "When the vote is taken on the right of an individual property owner to dispose of his property as he sees fit, I shall again vote 'NO.' " [55] The audience, a gathering of conservatives from Goochland, Fluvanna, Louisa, and Powhatan counties, gave the newest Byrd their latest version of an ancient approbation.

The Robertson-Spong race did not seem to present so clear an ideological contrast as that between Byrd and Boothe. Strategists in both the Byrd and Boothe camps felt that victory depended on obtaining from their respective conservative and liberal followings every possible vote. Neither Robertson nor Spong saw himself irrevocably identified with a machine or antimachine label. Each hoped to cut into the other's support. Spong sensed an opportunity to draw away moderate conservatives or organization voters who thought that Robertson was too old to run for another six-year term. Robertson judged his Senate seniority and history of political independence valuable assets in wooing urban and even Negro votes. As a result, the political and philosophical issues often were obfuscated by a campaign dialogue on age, seniority, campaign finances, and similar topics. Yet a sharp philosophical cleavage persisted, and on election day it was more than clear that the voters recognized this.

Spong ran as a realist and a modernist. His campaign billboards proclaimed him the MAN OF TODAY. "The problems of our time cannot be comprehended and will not be solved by status quo thinking," said Spong. "We must not be led by those who would march backward into a comfortable past that no longer exists and cannot be disinterred." [56] He claimed a perspective geared "to the latter third of the twentieth century"; Robertson's, he believed, was molded in the nineteenth.[57] He attacked the incumbent's votes against measures designed to

[55] *Ibid.*, May 14, 1966.   [56] Richmond *News Leader,* July 7, 1966.
[57] Richmond *Times-Dispatch,* June 30, 1966.

cope with twentieth-century needs. "[Senator Robertson] hasn't voted for a major education bill in the last 20 years," the young challenger asserted.[58] In a tour through the Ninth District he recalled Robertson's vote against the Appalachia bill to "provide many miles of highways in Southwest Virginia." [59] The Higher Education Act (1965), the Water Pollution Control Act (1965), the Urban Mass Transit Act (1963–64), the Nuclear Test Ban Treaty (1963), pay reform for federal workers (1962)—on all these measures, the nay votes of the elderly senator were sharply criticized.[60]

Spong entered the campaign the least familiar of the four candidates. For three months his major problem was simply to become known. With a smaller campaign fund than the other three candidates,[61] Spong met the voters the hard way, not on a television screen, but through personal encounters. One reporter wrote:

He estimates he has shaken 60,000 hands; he has moved into virtually every city and county of Virginia; he has made enough speeches to give his voice a built-in hoarseness.

He has stood in broiling sun outside industrial plants, shaking hands with workers. He has plunged into supermarkets, variety stores, barber shops and street crowds with his "Hi! I'm Bill Spong and I'd like to have your support."

He has flown by commercial and private aircraft. He has ridden in scores of autos; he has wondered where the next clean shirt was coming from; he has shaved when he could grab the chance, and wolfed down dinners in 15 minutes.

He wants very much to be a United States Senator.[62]

Spong's background was urban, and the success of his candidacy rested primarily on an urban appeal. Virginia's urban centers had long lacked a statewide leader, and Spong's home area of Hampton Roads had been excluded from statewide

---

[58] Richmond *News Leader,* April 11, 1966.

[59] Richmond *Times-Dispatch,* May 22, 1966.   [60] *Ibid.,* June 7, 1966.

[61] Financial statements filed with the State Board of Elections showed Robertson's reported expenditures at $253,831.79, Byrd's at $228,553.41, Boothe's at $179,455.49, and Spong's at $132,150.78.

[62] Richmond *News Leader,* July 7, 1966.

office since the early 1940's when Colgate Darden of Norfolk was governor. Byrd, Jr., and Robertson both were "mountain" senators; they came from the Shenandoah Valley in northwestern Virginia. Spong's hometown of Portsmouth lay in the southeastern tip of the state; there the sea, not the mountains, was the basic fact of life. Spong thus had to appeal subtly to the urban and coastal sections of eastern Virginia without alienating the voters of the highlands.

A less subtle appeal could be directed at Virginia youth. Spong was the youngest of the senatorial quartet. He argued that his election would mean that the generation of Virginians who left colleges and universities to serve in World War II would be represented for the first time in major public service.[63] The Byrd organization had aged and had neglected its opportunity to incorporate youth in its inner councils. Two former Young Turks were now running against it, and Spong meant to tell young Virginians that waiting one's turn for Harry Byrd's nod was nonsense. "We have a young group at work on our campaign," Spong noted. "My campaign manager, Bill Battle, and I, at 45, are the oldest ones. All the rest are younger, and all are unpaid volunteers except two." [64] He deplored the fact that too often in Virginia "potential new leaders have been made to stand and wait." [65] Virginia's glorious past had never condoned such a thing, and Spong was fond of recounting how Patrick Henry was governor of Virginia at forty, Thomas Jefferson drafted the Declaration of Independence at thirty-three, James Monroe went to the Senate at thirty-two, and John Marshall became Chief Justice at forty-five.[66]

Absalom Willis Robertson belied his years. On the campaign trail he kept farmer's hours—up at 5:30, to bed by 9:00. Despite his age he hit the hustings determined to retain his seat. He was, said one reporter, "an old oak in deep woods—tall, gnarled, and plenty tough." [67] Long hours in the July sun at barbecues and catfish fries—Robertson faced them all in the toughest fight of his fifty-year political career.

[63] *Ibid.*   [64] Richmond *Times-Dispatch,* June 30, 1966.
[65] *Ibid.,* July 10, 1966.   [66] Richmond *News Leader,* July 7, 1966.
[67] *Ibid.*

Robertson was in every way a fundamentalist. He personified Spartan discipline, pioneer individualism, Puritan and Calvinist morality. For Robertson it was "important to preserve basic principles. . . . There are eternal truths." [68] He salted his rhetoric with quotations from Jonathan Edwards, Shakespeare, and the Bible; he warned of Ahab and his vineyard, spoke of millenniums and Gabriel's horn. On the stump he could be fearsome, peering down on his audience with a ruddy, weatherbeaten face and thick, bushy eyebrows. This country was "born of the brain and purchased with the blood" of our forefathers, he reminded his listeners. It was important always to retain "the kind of principles Virginia has endorsed in the past." [69]

What mattered most to Robertson was his self-respect. For fifty years he had survived in Virginia politics, often with the help of the Byrd organization, but always able to go it alone. The Senator had slowly accumulated a large personal following, and throughout Virginia he could name friends, relatives, and political cronies in abundance. He enjoyed with his friends an endless diet of rustic humor; he felt in his blood the concerns of the farmer, small-town folk, and the mountaineer.

But Robertson had also to campaign in modern, urban, and politically competitive Virginia. The lack of a ready-made political organization hurt him as no other candidate. In rural Virginia, Byrd was often six deep in campaign personnel in counties where Robertson still scurried to find a local manager. In much of urban Virginia the elderly conservative desperately needed an organization to counter Spong's appeal to moderate and liberal elements. State Senator Edward Willey, Robertson's campaign manager, spent hours trying to construct a campaign team from scratch. It was fortunate that in many areas of the state the Byrd organization comanaged local vote drives for both Byrd and Robertson. Yet its primary allegiance was generally to Byrd.

Although Robertson was a moving stump speaker, a grand extemporizer, he little sensed how his orations would appear in the cold ink of tomorrow's newspaper. Innocent remarks often

[68] *Ibid.,* June 27, 1966.   [69] *Ibid.*

afforded the opposition valuable ammunition. Robertson often brought this on himself. He bragged that he was "physically fit," and once he pledged to serve vigorously for another six-year term, "if God lets me live." [70] "It's not pleasant to have to enter deliberately into a campaign against an elderly man," Bill Battle, Spong's campaign manager, remarked. "We hadn't planned to campaign on the issue of age. We were not going to refer to it. But Senator Robertson has mentioned it at every meeting he's attended." [71]

Robertson brought his seniority into the campaign at the beginning. His brochures announced him as Virginia's "bread 'n butter" Senator; his billboards read ROBERTSON—GETS RE-SULTS. His chairmanship of the Banking and Currency Committee and ranking seat on Appropriations could get Virginia far more than a mere freshman such as Spong. For Roanoke, Robertson hoped to get several million dollars for a proposed civic center; in Richmond he would do the same for the projected coliseum and Gathright Dam; Portsmouth might be assured that its naval yard would be protected; federal largesse would rain upon Virginia. Spong thought it interesting that "Santa Claus comes only at election time" [72] and charged hypocrisy at Robertson's policy of voting against nearly all federal spending programs while seeking pork for Virginia. The Senator also ran into trouble on a $2,000,000 peanut research laboratory recently constructed in Georgia. Robertson had worked earnestly to locate it in peanut-producing southside Virginia, but the combined seniority of Georgia Senators Russell and Talmadge secured the project for the Peach State. The Spong camp made political capital out of the loss to Virginia. State Senator William V. Rawlings declared, "Robertson with all his seniority failed to block that measure which deprived the Virginia-Carolina area of the laboratory. . . . In spite of his seniority and alleged power he provided totally ineffective support for our peanut producers." [73]

The big issue, however, was campaign finances. It shot

[70] *Ibid.*, June 10, 1966.   [71] *Ibid.*, April 23, 1966.
[72] Richmond *Times-Dispatch*, July 5, 1966.
[73] Richmond *News Leader*, July 7, 1966.

Spong to the headlines of the state's newspapers and gave him quantities of free publicity. It was Robertson, however, who touched the whole thing off. On a campaign swing through southside Virginia the Senator intimated that his opponent's campaign was heavily financed by big labor, while casually acknowledging that the banking industry was "kicking in a few thin dimes" in his behalf.[74] Spong made the speech the basis of a carefully plotted and cleverly sustained sequence of moves designed to portray Robertson as a pawn of big bankers both inside and outside Virginia. On June 13 Spong swore under oath that his own campaign contributions contained no more than $300 from organized labor.[75] In the meantime one of the challenger's close friends, Dr. Russell Cox, resigned as a member of the advisory board of the Portsmouth branch of the Bank of Virginia claiming he was "shocked to the point of amazement" by the "coercion and arm-twisting tactics" used by the bank to raise money for the Robertson campaign. Cox further claimed that a senior officer of the Bank of Virginia said each of the officers in the Portsmouth branch would be expected to contribute to the Robertson campaign and that the officer replied to Cox's objections, "Doctor, I certainly do intend to twist their arms as hard as necessary, I'll tell you that." [76]

The support of the banking industry for Robertson was not surprising. As chairman of the Banking and Currency Committee, the Senator had successfully passed a number of banking law reforms friendly to the industry. Were Robertson defeated, the chairmanship would in turn devolve on Senator Sparkman of Alabama, Douglas of Illinois, and Proxmire of Wisconsin, the first of whom bankers regarded with indifference, the third with suspicion, and the second with unmitigated horror. The extent of Robertson's banking support caught the fancy of reporters and columnists everywhere and it received far more

[74] Richmond *Times-Dispatch,* June 11, 1966.

[75] This statement naturally would not include whatever funds organized labor spent for Spong's campaign independently of the candidate's knowledge; labor does most of its work on a candidate's behalf independently of that candidate's official campaign organization. This fact, not recalled by the general public, did not detract from the campaign value of Spong's fund disclosure.

[76] Richmond *News Leader,* June 13, 1966.

attention than any other matter in the campaign. The Spong forces accused Robertson of hiring a former bank lobbyist for his staff, of receiving extravagant financial help from the vaults of New York and Wall Street, and generally of conducting a gilt-edged campaign with extensive television time and an unending splotch of billboards across the state. "I cannot help but agree that this activity goes beyond tolerable limits," Spong professed, as national columnists Evans and Novak deplored "the blatant arm-twisting that is going on in the highest reaches of the banking industry." [77] The banking fracas changed few if any committed votes but it gave Spong as much free publicity as the incumbent received from all his bank-backed advertisements. As such, it was the turning point in Spong's campaign.

The bitterest of the 1966 contests was between Smith and Rawlings. Their campaign left a residue of animosity which influenced events long after the primary votes were counted. Rawlings and columnist Drew Pearson joined hands in impugning Smith's integrity by pointing to his role in the Rules Committee in blocking a bill to place the Financial General Corporation under the control of the Federal Reserve Board. The Financial General Corporation, they said, owned stock in twenty-six banks, among them the Alexandria National Bank of which Smith was the chairman. Never in his life had his integrity been so questioned, Smith replied. "If you don't believe in me, turn me out. . . . I'm not going to stand up here and answer all the charges being put up against me." [78]

Rawlings played politics with no holds barred. He attacked with a gusto that recalled Francis Pickens Miller's charges against the senior Byrd in 1952. Rawlings was interested more in winning than in being termed a Virginia gentleman. "It grates on my nerves and gnaws at my soul," he said, "that in the present system of Virginia politics, one must be called upon by someone higher up in the political structure in order to run for office. The people, not the incumbent, should name the next candidate." Calling Smith a "reactionary," Raw-

[77] Richmond *Times-Dispatch*, June 21, 1966.   [78] *Ibid.*, July 13, 1966.

lings promised to be "constructive, not obstructive—I give you my progressive record as my credentials." [79]

Smith did not regret his record. He urged the voters to resist change "just for the sake of change," complaining that the United States had "too much change already," and it was his duty "to slow it down." [80] Reminded that he had been criticized for voting against two-thirds of the administration's bills, the eighty-three-year-old congressman added, "And I wonder if I should apologize for voting for the other one-third." [81]

None of the three organization candidates stood any chance of gaining union endorsement and only Robertson thought it possible to win a segment of the Negro vote. His supporters made discreet overtures to Moses Riddick, the founder and executive secretary of the Virginia Independent Voter's League which controlled most of the Negro vote in the Hampton Roads area. Riddick, however, was rudely overturned in the VIVL convention, and the Negro delegates passed a resolution endorsing Spong and Boothe and repudiating Robertson and Byrd for "a long history of rejection of modern day social and civil rights legislation." [82] Robertson, who had counted on Riddick to control the convention, was stunned when he heard the news. Meetings with top campaign advisers in the next several days persuaded him to pitch his closing campaign theme less on seniority and more on the old Byrd style of conservatism in an effort to win with a big rural vote.

One segment of the New Dominion was not neglected by any candidate. Although Byrd and Robertson were forced to abandon hope for the Negro vote, they did not let Virginia's rapidly growing Washington suburbs go unattended. There were too many votes here for any candidate to ignore. "The good people of Northern Virginia," wrote McDowell, "have long contended that the rest of the state did not pay any attention to them, particularly in politics. In the current double-barreled campaign for two Senate seats, however, they have had endless attention paid to them. The four candidates

[79] *Ibid.*, April 30, 1966.   [80] Richmond *Times-Dispatch*, July 13, 1966
[81] Houston, p. 28,   [82] Richmond *Times-Dispatch*, June 19, 1966,

have spent much more time up here than anywhere else, and they have stalked the voters relentlessly and ingeniously." Boothe looked to this progressive, hometown area for his largest support. Spong "knocked on doors in dozens of neighborhoods, visited community swimming pools, and dropped into back yards by helicopter to speak to wide-eyed householders as comfortably and earnestly as if nothing dramatic had happened." Robertson was never too busy with his Senate duties to take a quick jaunt to the Washington suburbs to speak to his constituency there. Byrd, whose home town of Winchester was somewhat removed from this area, nonetheless cordially addressed the suburbanites as "fellow Northern Virginians." [83] Boothe, in fact, accused his opponent of carrying on "the most frantic courtship since Romeo courted Juliet" in his effort to win the votes of the Second, Ninth, and Tenth Districts. "I am here," said Boothe, "to save Juliet from a fate worse than death and to enable all men and women of all districts to rally around a moderate Virginian." [84]

The activity in the Washington suburbs did not delight rural conservatives in the Southside. The Virginia Conservative party, through some reasoning process which many bravely sought to unravel, decided that both Byrd and Robertson had succumbed to liberal dogma and were in imminent danger of surrendering to the Great Society. The party nominated its own candidates for the general election in November and urged its followers to refrain from voting in the Democratic primary. Nominated to oppose the winner of the Byrd-Boothe race was John Carter, one of the party's guiding spirits and the Conservative candidate for attorney general in the fall of 1965. "We got out of this foul and filthy [Democratic] party," snorted Carter, "but Byrd and Robertson stayed in it. Therefore they don't deserve Conservative support." [85] Reid T. Putney, chairman of the Virginia Conservative party, warned his followers that "a vote cast in this primary regardless for whom it is cast is a vote in the support of Lyndon Johnson, Hubert Humphrey, and Orville Freeman and their welfare programs." [86]

[83] *Ibid.*, July 10, 1966.   [84] Richmond *News Leader*, July 7, 1966.
[85] *Ibid.*, May 23, 1966.   [86] *Ibid.*, July 6, 1966.

The Conservative party posed a problem for Byrd and Robertson. They had somehow to convince the more than 75,000 Virginians who voted the Conservative ticket in the fall of 1965 as a protest to Godwin that they were to the right of the present governor's political philosophy. If that could be done, there still remained a legal obstacle to returning the wayward Southsiders of last fall to their traditional Byrd Democratic fold. By law and by loyalty oath those who voted for another party's candidate in the last general election were not eligible to enter the Democratic primary the following year. This law, however, was rarely enforced. It was, in fact, almost impossible to enforce so long as the secret ballot remained a part of American democracy. Enforcement or even mention of the law was the last thing Byrd and Robertson wanted. They worked desperately to woo last year's Conservative supporters into the 1966 Democratic primary. "I personally am not going to discourage anybody from voting," Byrd emphasized. "The larger the number of individuals who vote, the better it is for Virginia and the nation." [87] It was interesting, people remarked, how a Byrd was now urging an expanded electorate.

To make matters worse for Byrd and Robertson, the Republican party now turned fickle. In previous years when elections got sticky for the organization, Republicans would surge loyally into the polls to give it a hand. Republican leaders openly exhorted their followers to bail out John Battle in the 1949 Democratic primary. Now, however, the Republican party was very much an independent political force, and its leaders pointedly urged all Republicans to stay out of the Democratic primary. The Third District chairman, Art Brinkley, insisted Republicans were "legally and morally obliged" to refrain from voting in the Democratic primary.[88] This decision presented a gloomy prospect for the organization.

Despite the urgings of their party leaders, the organization continued to serenade Conservative and Republican voters in hopes of luring them into the primary. "They [Republicans-Conservatives] don't holler for us to come help them run their

[87] Richmond *Times-Dispatch*, July 1, 1966.   [88] *Ibid.*, July 11, 1966.

conventions or nominate their candidates," protested Boothe, "and they don't believe they should take part in our primary to nominate our candidates." [89] The Byrd organization, however, had never taken such a strict view of party structure. If too many Republicans and Conservatives stayed out of the primary and too many Negroes, union workers, and the "wrong kind" of urbanites came in, the curtains would close on a long hegemony. It was decided in the last weeks of the campaign to give liberal influences in Virginia a last drubbing in the hope of arousing Democratic, Republican, and Conservative conservatives to enter the primary.

"The real issue in this campaign," Robertson told his southside audience, "is not what I may be expected to do in the next six years, but what would be the record of one who might enter the Senate next January beholden to labor unions on the one hand and Robert F. Kennedy on the other." [90] The Senator repeatedly linked Spong's candidacy to his AFL-CIO supporters and to the junior senator from New York. This linkage derived from the fact that Spong's campaign manager, William Battle, had managed John F. Kennedy's presidential campaign in Virginia in 1960. Robertson's campaign manager charged repeatedly that Spong voted against a measure in the 1954 General Assembly to "put the teeth into the 'right-to-work' law." Spong's AFL-CIO endorsement, Willey said, "puts the union label squarely on Spong's candidacy and links him to a closed shop despite any protests to the contrary." [91] Former Governor Harrison thought it "most significant" that Robertson was opposed by "the professional bosses of the Virginia AFL-CIO and of some of the more militant Negro political organizations." [92]

Few alluded openly to the race issue. Such a course was too hazardous. Yet there were oblique ways of reminding southside whites that Negro-endorsed candidates were strongly competing for election. In opposing federal aid to education one was conveniently opposing federal desegregation guidelines as well. In talking of organized "pressure groups," it was

[89] *Ibid.*, July 6, 1966.   [90] Richmond *News Leader,* June 11, 1966.
[91] *Ibid.*, June 8, 1966.   [92] Richmond *Times-Dispatch,* July 6, 1966.

not difficult to discern exactly what a "pressure group" might mean. Thus when Byrd, his campaign manager Daniel, and Fourth District Congressman Abbitt traveled through southside Virginia in the closing days of the campaign, no one had any illusions as to their purpose. "I'm in favor of every Virginian qualified to cast a vote to do so," Byrd began. "I don't believe in restricting the electorate. I would like to see it expanded." A light primary vote, continued Byrd, "would mean that the vote could be controlled by small pressure groups." Abbitt was more emphatic: "When the special interest groups arouse people and the average citizen such as you stays home, the result can only be bad." [93]

The 1966 Democratic primary deserved a heated finish. But on July 8, 1966, Byrd, Jr., canceled his day's campaign plans and hurried to the bedside of his father at Berryville, who was in a deep coma and in considerable danger of death. Robertson announced that should Byrd die, he, Robertson, would end his campaign "to be with . . . [Byrd's] family and host of friends." [94] The next day Boothe canceled all his remaining public campaign appearances, and the lively Virginia political scene fell silent.

Election day, July 12, 1966, saw politics resume its preoccupation with the present. All day the candidates listened eagerly for scraps of news and gossip. At 5 P.M. Robertson flew into Richmond to join his son, campaign staff, and capital city supporters. The Senator was worried; even in his home town of Lexington folks had not been going to the polls, and a light vote throughout the Shenandoah Valley meant trouble, deep trouble, both for Byrd and for himself. He had heard that the Negroes were voting heavily in Richmond, but not so heavily, he was told, as they had in the municipal elections a month before. He grimaced at news of big turnouts in Hampton Roads and northern Virginia, then shifted comfortably back in his seat at reports of a slow pace in the southwest. Ah well— nothing to do but wait. The old gentleman checked into a room at the Hotel Richmond West, flicked on the radio long enough

[93] Richmond *News Leader*, July 2, 1966.   [94] *Ibid.*, July 8, 1966.

to learn he was faring well in Roanoke, then shuffled out to the Captain's Grill for a good meal. He would return, he said, when the votes really started pouring in.

Like most primary nights in Virginia, July 12, 1966, was unrelentingly muggy. Armistead Boothe escaped the heat by retiring into the paneled study of his home in Alexandria to follow the returns. From the first he seemed quiet and calmly skeptical although he was ahead in the early counting. "I don't like what I have heard from the Roanoke area. The only report I have from the Ninth District is not too encouraging," Boothe said softly to a reporter on the telephone a few minutes before 9 P.M. "But it's neck and neck. It really is terribly close, isn't it?" [95] Meanwhile, in Boothe's backyard, hundreds of northern Virginia campaign workers gathered to watch the returns on big, lighted boards. By 10 P.M. the crowd had grown to perhaps seven hundred people under the old trees, and it was a quiet, tense crowd, not satisfied to be close.

July 12, 1966, was unlike most other primary nights in the Byrd hometown of Winchester. A crowd gathered early in the Winchester Hotel for the inevitable victory celebration, for what else could there be for a Byrd in Virginia? But this night seemed somehow different. "People here are confused," said one of Byrd's staff shortly before 9 P.M. when more than half of the precincts were in and the computer said Byrd and Boothe were practically even.

Senator Harry F. Byrd, Jr., followed the returns at home. Long election nights by his father's side had taught him the voting habits of every hill and hamlet in Virginia. From the outset he knew that the enormous victories of his father would not be his—at least not on this night. He was steadily on the phone calling around the state to friends who might tell him more than he learned from the growing totals. "We are still optimistic," said a staff man shortly before 9 P.M. But he said it wistfully. Not since 1925, when Harry Byrd, Sr., was elected governor of Virginia had a candidate named Byrd run behind in a statewide race, even in the early returns. The staff man

---

[95] See Richmond *Times-Dispatch*, July 13, 1966, especially article by Charles McDowell, for details of election night at Byrd and Boothe headquarters.

described Byrd, Jr., as outwardly calm "but inwardly somewhat tense . . . wouldn't you be?"

At the Winchester Hotel the band played valiantly. The
crowd received new results with alternating gasps and little
eddies of applause. By 10 P.M. Byrd began to inch ahead—
slowly, waveringly, but ahead. "We think we've got it by a
very, very slim margin," the staff man permitted himself to say.
"That's my estimate, but I'm not sure of anything if you really
want to know."

At 11:50 P.M. when almost complete unofficial figures
showed him leading Boothe by 8,000 votes, the younger Byrd
joined his several hundred supporters at a victory party in the
Winchester Hotel. "I'm sorry I kept you waiting so long," he
told the cheering crowd that sung "For He's a Jolly Good
Fellow" as he walked slowly through the ballroom. "I am grateful to the people of Virginia tonight for the vote they have
given me. The only way I know to repay this debt . . . is to
dedicate myself and redouble my efforts to serve all the people
of Virginia." There was the familiar victory statement. What
they had just gone through—all the waiting—perhaps it was
just a very bad dream.

July 12, 1966, made William B. Spong a United States senator. It had been a long night, even for a young man, and
toward the end Spong removed his glasses, very deliberately,
and rubbed his bleary eyes. He had stayed in Portsmouth that
night. Why drive to Richmond for a victory celebration, only to
learn half way there that you had lost, and return—numbly—to
your home town? By 1 A.M. the Spong margin teetered between 142 and 800—back and forth, like the finger of a scale
jiggling slowly to rest. When it stopped (and it never seemed
to), Spong would not be regarded as a political lightweight.

The Spong margin was averaging slightly better than one-
tenth of a vote per precinct, but his Richmond headquarters
acted as if there were untold thousands of ballots to be frit-
tered away. There was much gaiety among the seventy-five
college boys and girls and loose cracks about Landslide Spong.
Campaign manager Battle was a good-natured father trying to
keep order in a very rowdy house. "Please," he shouted, lifting

both hands for silence, "We've heard from the . . . district. And it's virtually assured that it's in the bag for our boy." [96]

On July 12, 1966, Howard Smith's political career came to a close. No one believed it, of course. The mass gathering at the Winter Garden on the Hotel Richmond's ninth floor at first watched the senatorial races far more intently than Smith's congressional struggle. Early returns might show Smith behind, but conservatives confidently predicted that the Judge was biding his time like an old experienced race horse who would leave his opponent in the dust at the home stretch. The home stretch came, but Smith's expected pull away did not. Even late returns from conservative Hanover County still left him slightly behind Rawling's total. "This is a terrible loss to Congress," liberal congressman and Rules Committee member James J. Delaney was to say the next day. "No matter what you think of his politics—he is a great man." "He was the most skilled legislative obstructionist in the Rules Committee," liberal Democrat Richard Bolling would declare.[97]

"They don't believe any 70-year-old man can do the job," said Robertson. "They—the voters—can't believe I have the stamina to carry on." [98] The old senator sat quietly in his campaign headquarters on the fourth floor of the Hotel Richmond. In a back room staff members still listened intently to the radio for mistakes in the tabulations, for several unreported precincts in friendly Montgomery County. In the choked, clogged lobbies outside supporters pushed, pleaded for news that their man would pull it out. Only the Senator seemed philosophical. He had run hard—for fifty years he stuck stoutly by his beliefs and principles, and now, suddenly, it all was over. Let his friends stay on and wait for further dribblings of late news. He was going to bed. Head unbowed, he walked slowly from the room past a train of supporters, suddenly quieted. In a characteristic gesture some five months later he resigned his Senate seat early so that William B. Spong could more quickly take office and Virginia might have the added seniority.

[96] Richmond *News Leader,* July 13, 1966.
[97] Richmond *Times-Dispatch,* July 14, 1966.
[98] Richmond *News Leader,* July 13, 1966.

The Byrd organization was shaken to its cornerstones. The defeats of Senator Robertson and Congressman Smith constituted the first major electoral setbacks for a powerful Democratic organization which had dominated Virginia politics since 1925. The senior Byrd was gone. His son had emerged with at best a pyrrhic victory. The organization had often been scared but never before beaten. Yet within a year the fabled Byrd machine had lost its progenitor, two of its top conservative spokesmen, and a century of seniority in Congress. Its prestige had been tarnished, and its omnipotent image destroyed. Its future, if it had one, lay on a course far different from its past.

The vote was, of course, the culmination of the trends developing in the commonwealth's politics for the past twenty years. Officially the final vote read as follows:

Senator—Four-year term

Harry F. Byrd, Jr.	221,221	50.9%
Armistead L. Boothe	212,996	49.1%
	434,217	

Senator—Six-year term

William B. Spong, Jr.	216,885	50.1%
A. Willis Robertson	216,274	49.9%
	433,159	

Congressman—8th District

George C. Rawlings, Jr.	27,115	50.6%
Howard W. Smith	26,470	49.4%
	53,585	

The turnout, 434,217, was the largest ever recorded in a Democratic primary in Virginia. The previous high for a primary was the Harrison-Stephens race in 1961 when over 350,000 persons voted. Contributing to the large 1966 primary vote was the excitement generated by the two Senate contests, each of which appeared extremely close. For the first time, many who opposed the organization believed they had a real chance for victory.

The second major factor which contributed to the large turnout was the absence of the poll tax as a prerequisite for voting. Although the Twenty-Fourth Amendment to the United States Constitution had banned poll tax payment as a requirement for voting in federal elections in January, 1964, the Democratic senatorial primary of 1966 was the first Virginia primary where the political effects of poll tax repeal could be observed. [99]

Poll tax repeal and the excitement of the senatorial race increased voter participation 23 per cent over the 1961 primary total, but to many the turnout was disappointingly low. The percentage increase in votes between the 1961 and 1966 Democratic primaries was less than the increase in the presidential vote from 1960 to 1964. Many had forecast a total vote in excess of 500,000. "In terms of the turnout," Professor Ralph Eisenberg wrote, "the victory by Senator Byrd was even less impressive. Assuming that a larger turnout in urban areas would have been to the political advantage of his opponent, the fact that Senator Byrd won by a very small margin with a relatively small turnout suggests that a larger turnout, reaching the 500,000 figure anticipated by the opposition, might have been fatal to his candidacy." [100]

Predictably there was a high coincidence in areas supporting Byrd and Robertson and those supporting Boothe and Spong. Only seven of Virginia's ninety-six counties and five of its thirty-five cities did not pair their majorities either for Byrd and Robertson or for Boothe and Spong. It was the regional breakdown of the vote which was most significant.

Boothe and Spong derived their major support from the urban areas (see Table 24). Boothe won majorities in each of the nine largest cities in Virginia and Spong carried seven of these, losing only Roanoke and Hampton.[101] Byrd and Robert-

[99] Poll tax payment is no longer required as a prerequisite to voting in state elections as a result of the U.S. Supreme Court decision in *Harper* v. *Virginia Board of Elections,* 383 U.S. 663 (1966).

[100] "1966 Politics in Virginia: The Democratic Senatorial Primary," *University of Virginia News Letter,* Jan. 15, 1967.

[101] Spong lost Roanoke partially because of a "friend 'n neighbors" vote for Robertson whose home town of Lexington is nearby and whose relatives were

Table 24   Urban Support for Boothe and Spong

Area	Percentage of vote received		Percentage of total vote cast *
	Boothe	Spong	
The urban corridor †	54.8	56.2	59.2
Virginia's nine largest cities ‡	57.8	58.7	33.0
All cities, regardless of size §	54.0	55.3	44.7
Virginia's immediate Washington suburbs ‖	65.8	67.5	14.2
Six large Tidewater cities—Hampton Roads #	59.0	61.0	21.4

* The percentage of total vote cast was computed for the Byrd-Boothe race. In this respect differences between the two Senate races are negligible.
† The urban corridor included in 1966 the cities of Alexandria, Chesapeake, Colonial Heights, Fairfax, Falls Church, Fredericksburg, Hampton, Hopewell, Newport News, Norfolk, Petersburg, Portsmouth, Richmond, Virginia Beach, and Williamsburg and the counties of Arlington, Caroline, Charles City, Chesterfield, Clarke, Dinwiddie, Fairfax, Fauquier, Hanover, Henrico, James City, Loudoun, New Kent, Prince George, Prince William, Spotsylvania, Stafford, and York.
‡ Virginia's nine largest cities were Alexandria, Chesapeake, Hampton, Newport News, Norfolk, Portsmouth, Richmond, Roanoke, and Virginia Beach.
§ This included all of the thirty-five independent cities in Virginia at the time of the election.
‖ The immediate Washington suburbs included the cities of Alexandria, Fairfax, and Falls Church and the counties of Arlington and Fairfax.
The six large Tidewater cities comprising Hampton Roads were Chesapeake, Hampton, Newport News, Norfolk, Portsmouth, and Virginia Beach.

son generally won only smaller cities situated in the midst of largely rural areas or traditionally conservative cities in or near the Southside such as Danville or Lynchburg. Of the entire vote of cities regardless of size, Spong won 55.3 per cent and Boothe 54.0 per cent.

The two counties and three cities in Virginia's Washington suburbs gave Spong a majority of 20,815 and Boothe a margin

active in Roanoke politics. In the cities of Hampton and Newport News, Spong's candidacy ran into a different kind of trouble. The economy of Newport News–Hampton rests greatly on a private shipyard, whereas Spong's hometown of Portsmouth thrived on a shipyard run by the federal government. Despite his protests, many in Newport News–Hampton thought Spong, as a U.S. senator, would give preference to the needs of the Portsmouth shipyard. This issue was responsible for the fact that Spong lost Hampton 5,335 to 5,229 and only carried Newport News by 6,484 to 6,313. Boothe ran substantially better in both cities.

of 19,459, 67.5 and 65.8 per cent of the vote respectively.[102] In
the six large cities of Hampton Roads (Norfolk, Portsmouth,
Virginia Beach, Chesapeake, Newport News, and Hampton)
the two challengers won heavy support. Boothe carried them
all and Spong lost only Hampton and that by only 106 votes.
Together these cities provided Spong with a majority of 20,815
and 61 per cent of the vote and Boothe with a 16,706 majority
and 59 per cent of the vote.[103] The Boothe-Spong performance
in the Hampton Roads and Washington suburb areas demonstrated how effectively the organization could be challenged
with a limited regional base.

The urban support for Boothe and Spong also was evident in
the voting results from Virginia's urban corridor.[104] In this strip
Spong received 56.2 per cent of the vote and Boothe 54.8 per
cent. This showing was especially significant because the corridor included conservative Richmond suburbs and several semirural areas which voted heavily for Byrd, Jr., and Robertson.
Most important, the corridor now contributed over 59 per cent
of the total statewide primary vote as compared with 40 per
cent in the late 1940's. Since population was continuing to
grow much faster in the urban corridor than elsewhere, it
would probably contribute an even greater share of the vote in
the years ahead.

Urban growth was the major factor in the defeat of Howard
Smith. Smith carried thirteen of the twenty counties in his
district, many by substantial percentages. Rawlings, however,
swept his own House of Delegates district of Fredericksburg
city and Stafford and Spotsylvania counties; he also carried a
cluster of small counties (Charles City, King and Queen, New
Kent, and Caroline) where Negroes comprised over 50 per
cent of the population. The critical factor in the race was that
part of Fairfax County which the 1965 special session of the
Virginia General Assembly had placed in Smith's district in

[102] See Chapter 7, Part A, for an account of the Washington suburbs'
complaints against the Byrd organization.
[103] See Chapter 7, Part C, for an account of Hampton Road's complaints
against the Byrd organization.
[104] See Chapter 7, Part D, for a discussion of the urban corridor.

order to boost its population.[105] It cast almost three times as many votes as the second-heaviest-voting county, Prince William. It cast 23.5 per cent of the total vote in the district. George Rawlings had 8,104 ballots to Smith's 4,485 or 64.4 per cent of the vote.[106] Fairfax County provided 30 per cent of Rawlings' total vote and his margin there was five and a half times his margin of victory in the district as a whole. Moreover, of eight voting units which Rawlings carried, seven were in the urban corridor; of the thirteen which Smith carried, four were in the urban corridor. Howard Smith did not fare well in urban Virginia.

Byrd and Robertson were relying for victory on a heavy rural vote to be supplied by seasoned organization troops in the courthouses across Virginia. The rural base of the Byrd-Robertson candidacies was apparent not only in the large number of counties they won but also in their proportionate share of the vote in those counties. In the twenty-five counties and seven cities in predominantly rural southside Virginia, Byrd led Boothe 49,474 to 29,169, gaining 62.9 per cent of the vote. The Southside cast 18.1 per cent of the total primary vote. A second bastion of organization support lay in the Shenandoah Valley from Frederick to Rockbridge counties. The Shenandoah was home territory for both Byrd and Robertson, and both candidates ran consistently over 60 per cent in this area, with some counties and small cities producing well over 70 per cent. Counties in central Virginia gave the organization substantial majorities ranging from 60 to 80 per cent. In the counties of the Northern Neck and middle peninsula the organization's majorities were more erratic. The only rural support for Boothe and Spong was in southwest Virginia, particularly in the Ninth District, where majorities of 4,526 for Boothe and 5,300 for Spong emerged.

The Byrd and Robertson majorities generally were less than

[105] In that same session the Assembly had to take from Smith's district the friendly rural counties of Albemarle, Culpeper, Fluvanna, Greene, and Orange and the city of Charlottesville in order to place them in the rural Seventh District, which also needed additional population.

[106] In 1960 Fairfax County was only 5.4 per cent Negro; the antiorganization vote in the Washington suburbs was not due to the Negro vote.

60 per cent in counties where spillover urban growth had occurred. Prince William, Loudoun, and Fauquier, where rural life was receding before the expanding Washington suburbs, gave Byrd 55, 58, and 58 per cent of their respective votes. Suburban Roanoke County gave Byrd 57 per cent of its vote, and the Northern Neck counties bordering the Potomac River and the counties in the Hampton Roads region all exhibited smaller Byrd and Robertson percentages than the rural counties of the Southside, central Virginia, and the Shenandoah Valley. The organization fared magnificently, however, in the cities and suburbs of Danville and Lynchburg, whose voting habits stemmed from their location in or near the Southside. The Richmond suburbs, traditionally conservative, also gave Byrd and Robertson large margins. With the important exceptions of the suburbs of Richmond, Danville, and Lynchburg, however, those counties experiencing advancing urban growth showed declining organization majorities.

The Negro vote in the 1966 primary totaled approximately 75,000,[107] and it went heavily against Byrd and Robertson.[108] Negro votes in the 1966 primary exceeded the total cast in the 1965 gubernatorial election but fell far short of the number cast in the 1964 presidential race. Only 49.5 per cent of the voters in the precincts listed in Appendix X voted in the 1966 primary compared with the total number who voted in the 1964 general elections.[109] The potential Negro vote against the Byrd organization was not fully realized in 1966. Boothe captured 95.8 per cent of the vote in thirty-seven predominantly Negro precincts (see Appendix X), and Spong was able to win 91.7 per cent of their vote. Professor Eisenberg concluded that the "consistency of the Boothe-Spong share of the vote in the 37 precincts suggests the pattern of Negro voting elsewhere in the state." [110]

---

[107] Best available estimate from James Latimer and Allen Jones, political reporters of the Richmond *Times-Dispatch,* and George Kelley, political reporter of the Norfolk *Virginian-Pilot,* in the wake of the 1966 primary election.
  [108] See Appendix X.   [109] "1966 Politics in Va.," p. 2.
  [110] *Ibid.,* p. 4. Several qualifications to this statement must be added. First, 35 of the 37 precincts were selected from the Richmond and Hampton Roads area, the two sections of the state where Negro voting is heaviest and best organized. It is difficult to determine whether Negro voting in, for example,

It is evident that the Negro vote hurt Howard Smith also. He lost each of the four counties in his district (Caroline, Charles City, King and Queen, New Kent) where the Negro population exceeded 50 per cent. His opponent waged a vigorous drive to register Negro voters and get them to the polls, and the effort paid off handsomely.

The Virginia Conservative party ironically played a part in crippling Byrd conservatism. An estimated 15,000 to 20,000 Conservatives refrained from voting in the 1966 Democratic primary,[111] and their abstinence undoubtedly caused Robertson's and probably Smith's defeat. Most Conservative defections were in the Southside. Byrd collected fewer actual votes from this region than Harrison did in the 1961 Democratic primary, though the 1966 statewide vote was 23.3 per cent above the 1961 total. Due primarily to the Conservative defections and the growing power of the Negro vote, Byrd's percentage in the Southside shrank to 62.9 compared with Harrison's 71.4 just five years before. The advent of the Virginia Conservative party helped to defeat one conservative United States Senator and to give another the scare of his life.

Other important factors in the 1966 primary do not yield to exact analysis. The refusal of many Republicans to enter the primary, the vote of organized labor, and the disgruntlement of youth with the Byrd organization undoubtedly played significant parts in the election which cannot, however, be statistically pinpointed.

Why Robertson lost and Byrd won is a difficult question. Many observers felt that the senior Byrd's illness in the last days of the campaign aroused sympathy for his son and that it hurt Robertson by dramatizing the health hazards of an elderly

---

Roanoke, Petersburg, Fredericksburg, or the rural counties in the Southside, Piedmont, and Northern Neck was quite so monolithic. Returns from precincts in Charlottesville and Lynchburg (the two precincts not in the Richmond or Hampton Roads area) showed slightly lower percentages for Boothe and Spong. Negro voting, however, was seldom below 80 per cent for the challengers and in most cases was considerably higher. It was undoubtedly a major factor in Spong's victory and Boothe's near-victory.

[111] Best available estimate from James Latimer, Allen Jones, and George Kelley.

man. The AFL-CIO claimed that "Boothe would have won the election except for the capitalizing on the critical illness of former Senator Harry F. Byrd, Sr. by the opposition forces." The *Virginia Observer,* the official organ of the state AFL-CIO, commented:

Senator Byrd resigned his Senate seat last November "for reasons of health." His son, Harry, Jr. was appointed in his stead. In March it was discovered the elder Byrd had a tumor—but this fact was reported only a week before his son was to be judged by the people in the primary election.

The younger Byrd cancelled his campaign after the release "to be with" his father. Everyday until the election, reports were carried about the elder's condition. The last prominent coverage by the big newspapers ceased the day after the primary election—when the son won the election by less than 1% of the vote.

And after the election, the junior Byrd went back to Washington, and left the bedside vigil, or so the Washington *Post* reported.

Senator Byrd, Sr. was a political leader, but his illness is tragic.

It is most unfortunate for both the family and the people to have had this personal tragedy to be implicated in politics. But it was indeed. Someone someday will have to answer for this intrusion of sacred sorrow.[112]

Professor Eisenberg offers other reasons for the Byrd victory and the Robertson defeat:

The marginal factor may have been the age issue—the fact that Senator Robertson at age 79 was seeking another 6 year Senate term. Certainly the defection of some Organization support on this issue occurred and may have made the difference. But if this issue was the decisive one, it was operative only above and beyond the basic divisiveness between the pairs of candidates. Similarly the attraction of the family name and its place in Virginia political history both aided and hurt Senator Byrd's campaign although in the close race it may well have been decisive. These factors may have accounted for Boothe's general lag behind Spong vote totals, not extensively in any one area, but generally throughout most of

[112] July 22, 1966.

the state. It suggests that the small amount of Organization support that Spong captured from a Robertson who was never clearly very close to the Organization's hierarchy, was decisive.[113]

To this must be added Spong's more moderate image, his direct appeal to youth, and his clever handling of the banking matter.

Both Harry F. Byrd, Jr., and William B. Spong went on to win in the November elections. Spong's margin was noticeably larger than Byrd's because of Negro, labor, and urban support. The Conservative party's vote shrank noticeably.

United States Senate 1966 — General Elections

William B. Spong, Jr. (Dem.)	429,855	58.6%
James P. Ould, Jr. (Rep.)	245,681	33.5
F. Lee Hawthorne (Cons.)	58,251	7.9
Harry F. Byrd, Jr. (Dem.)	389,028	53.3%
Lawrence M. Traylor (Rep.)	272,804	37.4
John W. Carter (Cons.)	57,692	7.9
J. B. Brayman (Soc.)	10,180	1.4

At the congressional level conservatism carried the day, though not the old-style Byrd conservatism. Two Republicans, William L. Scott and William C. Wampler, defeated two of the state's most liberal Democrats, George Rawlings and Pat Jennings, in closely fought congressional contests in the Eighth and Ninth Districts. In both races it was the defection of Byrd Democrats to the Republicans which determined the winner. The Republicans, who for years had helped to rescue Byrd Democrats in close primaries, now saw the Byrd Democrats, no longer all powerful, return the favor. Of Virginia's ten congressional seats, the Republicans now held four and promised to press for further gains in each new election.[114]

By the end of 1966 Virginia's political life displayed a

[113] "1966 Politics in Va.," p. 4.
[114] Republican incumbents Poff and Broyhill retained their Sixth and Tenth District congressional seats, to which were added the victories in the Eighth and Ninth Districts.

healthy variation. Urban, Negro, youthful, and Republican political forces seemed to be on the upswing and together they
brought an end to Byrd's Virginia. Not that conservatism was
or would be dead in Virginia; both the state's major parties
retained strong conservative strains, especially at the national
level. Yet both parties showed a willingness to shape their
philosophies and programs to the needs of modern Virginia.
After forty years in control, the Byrd machine gave way to a
Democratic organization whose future lay with a brand of
Godwin progressivism which could attract the support of
urban Virginia. Each of the major prospects for the 1969 Democratic gubernatorial nomination, William C. Battle, Armistead
L. Boothe, Thomas N. Downing, T. Marshall Hahn, Jr., Henry
E. Howell, and Fred G. Pollard, has taken a position looking in
this direction.

Chapter 13

Conclusion

THE Byrd machine was for many years the least flamboyant but most entrenched institution of southern politics. To Huey Long, Gene Talmadge, and other old-time southern spellbinders it quietly conceded the headlines, but it deferred to no one in its record of electoral success. The durable machine seemed destined to defy all marks of mortality in life and politics; it sought to remain a changeless isle amid surrounding seas of political flux.

The Byrd organization worked itself into Virginia's psychology; it mirrored the "Virginia virtues" of honesty, gentility, and whisper worship of the past. The Byrd name bespoke an almost mystic communion with the state's folklore; the machine reflected a pleasant provincialism which maintained that the genteel life exempted the Old Dominion from statistical scrutiny and the tyranny of fact.

More than mystique motored the machine. Harry Flood Byrd, the Virginia gentleman, was a grand master in the techniques of practical politics. The unbroken successes of his organization stand as quiet testimony to his political genius. Both patronage and policy for years catered to the loyal following of farmers, small-town merchants, and courthouse chieftains in the Virginia countryside.

By 1967 Byrd had died; two conservative consorts met defeat. Godwin took a moderate course while southside Virginia

defected. The poll tax was repealed and the legislature reapportioned. Massive resistance had been abandoned; golden
silence had been broken. Key personnel had aged and retired.
Virginia was shedding its outmoded fiscal policies. The Byrd
organization, a gateway to culture and guardian of caste in the
old Southland, had of a sudden been battered down.

The forces toppling the Byrd organization were active in the
rest of the South as well. Once many agreed with state Senator
Charles Moses of Appomattox, who said, quite frankly, that the
reins of government ought to rest in the hands of those who
turned the sod and fed the hogs.[1] In the 1960's, however, the
agrarian South retreated before what C. Vann Woodward
termed the "Bulldozer Revolution." [2] The revolution encom-
passed five major demographic shifts in the eleven former
Confederate states: (1) accelerated urban, metropolitan, and
industrial growth, (2) drastic declines in agricultural employment and rural farm population, (3) an exodus of Negroes
from the South, (4) an influx of young families to southern
suburbs, and (5) a migration of Negroes from rural areas to
urban cores forsaken by people who moved out to the suburbs.

In Virginia the urban revolution brought higher levels of
education and income, generated expanded public services
both in state and city governments, compelled the adoption of
a state sales tax, offered greater political participation to Negro
citizens, refused massive resistance, undermined the traditional supremacy of the Southside, produced moderate leaders
with national as well as regional commitments, and gave the
Republican party beachheads of suburban strength. The urban
revolution was the factor most responsible for the demise of
Harry Byrd's Virginia.

The decline of Harry Byrd's Virginia eclipsed the traditional
divisions and conflicts of southern politics. No longer pre-emi-
nent were battles of planter and highlander, or even Negro and
white. The South was now more than the storied struggles of
the Delta and the Hills. Though often clouded, many of the

[1] Friddell, p. 50.
[2] C. Vann Woodward, *The Burden of Southern History* (New York: Random
House, 1960), p. 6.

major underlying differences in Virginia since World War II were rural-urban ones. The conflicts on the financing of schools and roads, on local discretion on the race issue, legislative apportionment, pay-as-you-go, bottle-only liquor laws, sales tax distribution formulas, and positions of statewide leadership were in essence rural-urban clashes, results of the growing pains of the New Dominion. Most of the major reforming impulses in Virginia politics—the Young Turks, the antiresistance forces, the breakers of golden silence, Richmond Forward, the Crusade for Voters, Virginia Independent Voters' League, and the like—had roots in or drew the bulk of their support from urban areas and most met resistance from the rurally based Byrd machine.

"The race issue . . . ," wrote Key, "must be considered as the number one problem on the southern agenda. Lacking a solution for it, all else fails." [3] Race made of the South a much maligned region and threw it on the defensive. Politicians exploited the issue as no other, and the dogma of white supremacy stymied economic progress and clouded debate on solutions for basic southern needs. The decline of Harry Byrd's Virginia saw power and influence move from the black belt and Southside to the urban corridor, an area far less hostile to the Negro cause. Respect for urban voting power and attention to urban growing problems helped emancipate Virginia from racial obsessions during the Harrison and Godwin years. The exodus of Negroes from Virginia and the South and adjustments to integration less terrifying in practice than in prediction stood as hopeful signs of future racial harmony. Negro voting power made politicians cautious if not congenial, and the anguished aftermath of the Brown decision gave way in Virginia to a period of gradual, peaceful Negro gains.

The racial issue proved unable to obscure the rural-urban cleavage in Virginia; race simply lost its traditional potency as a unifying cry. Massive resistance worked for a time, but the urban corridor increasingly soured on the policy. As early as 1960, massive resistance was more burden than benefit. God-

[3] Page 675.

win hurriedly unhooked himself from the resister train, and by the 1966 primary even Harry Byrd, Jr., was quick to assure audiences that the issue was "passé."

That it was passé was due in large part to the Negro himself. In the late 1950's the Negro graduated from a pliant, and at times purchasable, object in Virginia politics to a purposeful voter and participant. Leaders in the Crusade for Voters in Richmond and the Virginia Independent Voters' League in the Tidewater dealt equally with the most sophisticated Virginia whites. Much the same awakening of Negro leadership occurred throughout the South.[4] The American assimilative process has generally required minorities to acquire political leverage before forging to other gains. The Negro in the 1960's was at last able to assume a respected role within the southern political process—a necessary prerequisite to other achievements.

By the middle of the 1960's the Negro was surpassing southside Virginia as the state's most powerful political bloc. In 1964 Negroes provided Johnson's margin of victory in Virginia; in 1965 they did the same for Godwin; and in 1966 they made the difference in the primary victories of Rawlings and Spong. Southside whites objected in varying degrees to each of these candidates. Many backed Goldwater in 1964, deserted Godwin for the Conservative party in 1965, and opposed Spong in the Democratic primary of 1966. In each of these elections, Negro votes thwarted the aims of southside segregationists.

Negroes provided balance-of-power ballots elsewhere in the South. In the eleven states of the old Confederacy, Negro registration increased from 2,174,200 in 1964 to an estimated 2,671,514 in the fall of 1966. Voting studies of the 1966 general election indicated that the Negro vote was clearly the margin of victory in the election of Senator Hollings of South Carolina, Governor Winthrop Rockefeller of Arkansas, and two United States congressmen—one from North Carolina, the other from Tennessee. Twenty Negroes were elected to southern legisla-

---

[4] See C. Vann Woodward, "From the First Reconstruction to the Second," *Harper's Magazine,* CCXXX (April 1965), 127–33.

tures, and Negroes provided swing votes in dozens of other local contests.[5]

National power pierced the magnolia curtain with mounting frequency after World War II. To the Byrd organization the intrusions proved annihilative. Harry Byrd's Virginia was above all a creature of region, a product of Reconstruction and the Civil War. Political parties ossified in their Civil War molds; Virginia's dread of deficit can be traced to its Reconstruction struggle to repay a staggering Civil War debt. The poll tax and segregation statutes had been enacted at the turn of the twentieth century to reverse the Negro's Reconstruction "gains." Byrd's mentality was thoroughly southern. His organization exemplified southern integrity, and it echoed the Virginia tradition of the planter oligarchy. When southern practices were threatened, Byrd and his fellow southern senators almost instinctively drew the traditional battlelines below the Potomac. They succeeded in stalling federal action in the legislative branch, but they fell before judicial decree. Public school integration, legislative reapportionment, congressional redistricting, and poll tax repeal all followed Court decisions, and all damaged the organization's position. Increasingly after World War II a national consciousness competed with the regional tone of the Byrd organization. In-migration to the Washington suburbs and Hampton Roads, the emergence of a new generation in Virginia, urban growth, and the national transportation and communication revolution fostered the growth of a national perspective. The Young Turks, the halters of massive resistance, the breakers of golden silence, were all people less chained to the balanced budget, segregated schools, state political parties, and other partial outgrowths of the Civil War and Reconstruction period than were the old Byrd leaders. "The Commonwealth we love will always be Virginia," proclaimed Mills Godwin, "but Virginia . . . is of the nation, and it is by the nation's standards that we are now called upon to judge her." [6]

The history of the Byrd organization demonstrated the hy-

[5] New York *Times*, Nov. 27, 1966.   [6] *Inaugural Address, Jan. 15, 1966.*

pocrisy and sterility of the strict states' rights ethic. The machine's states' rights views conflicted with other conservative commandments. Under such practices and policies as the State Compensation Board, the circuit judge, massive resistance, and state bottle-only liquor laws, local powers and initiatives were severely undermined. The organization under its states' rights banner minimized opportunities for Negroes, labor, urbanites, Republicans, and other dissident elements. Far from destroying conservative tenets, national intervention actually aided in establishing them. In providing integrated schools, poll tax repeal, and a reapportioned legislature, the Court equalized rather than erased competitive opportunities. It gave to Virginia's underprivileged and underrepresented elements the incentive which the Byrd machine had repressed.

The power and policies of the national party structure seriously threatened the solidarity of the Democratic South. In Virginia the more conservative appeal of the Republican party and Republican presidential candidates, the racial alienation of the Southside from the national Democratic party, the disillusionment of business and professional men in the Richmond area with New Deal economics, the influx of outsiders to the Washington suburbs and urban corridor, general suburban and metropolitan growth, the appearance of a new generation, and the resulting erosion of the Civil War as a determinant of party behavior—all jeopardized the Democratic *status quo*.

Similar hopes for the Republican party abounded in most southern states. One noted professor explained that in the South "Republicans benefited from the white migration into the region, the increase in the number of professional people and college graduates, the expanding middle class, and the rapid urbanization." [7] By 1967 the Republicans claimed two governors, three United States senators, and twenty-three representatives in the eleven former Confederate states. Ordinarily conservative, the Republican party in the South maintained more moderate branches in Arkansas, Virginia, and Tennessee. The new Republican challenge foreshadowed the end of Byrd's fond Republican–southern Democratic coalition. It forced on

[7] Grantham, "The South and the Reconstruction of American Politics," p. 235.

Democrats the new sense of responsibility toward the national party manifest in Virginia in the 1964 Democratic convention and presidential election. In the last analysis, the Republican party was more a result than a cause of the changing South. The new political and economic diversity made a safe Democratic consensus increasingly difficult in Virginia. The New South would be too multiform for one-party monopoly.

It is, however, unwise to speak of the New South. The New South has been expected for so long that new calls for its arrival run the risk of seeming unrealistic. Yet if the fall of the Byrd machine has not dawned the day of a New Dominion, it, at least, has inaugurated in Virginia and the South a period quite different from those before.

Yet even the most progressive Southerner might view with some misgivings the changes in his region. The new urban and industrial growth threatens to subsume the South in a national identity, to make of the once-unique region an indistinguishable slice of American modernism. With his agrarian and racial traditions routed, the Southerner groped for a new and more enduring identity.

Woodward suggested that the South possessed a "unique" sense of history. In many respects the history of Virginia and the South had been quite "un-American." In his essay, "The Search for Southern Identity," Woodward delineated those traits in the southern heritage which separated the region from the general American experience. In an America of abundance, success, innocence, freedom, and mobility, the South had not fully belonged. Its history had a darker lining with the specter of military defeat and subsequent impoverishment always looming large. Slavery and racial caste struck shadows of guilt across the South, leaving the region a tortured conscience and a defensive exterior. Then, too, the Southerner enjoyed a sense of place—the feeling of being located and contained. But in the American story of might and mobility, in the ethos of abundance and unending success, there had been all too little room for the South.[8]

America, however, needed the South's experience to save it

---

[8] Woodward, *The Burden of Southern History*, pp. 3–25.

from the recklessness of untempered optimism, the arrogance of assumed innocence, the shallowness of a past planted primarily on the sunny side of life. To the vanquished lay the role of restraining the victor, of reminding the "people of plenty" that history often leaves a bitter taste.[9]

Southerners claimed a uniqueness of humanity as well as of history. Thomas G. Wicker, grappling with the South's future identity, best struck the chord of a southern humanity:

the chastened and rooted South with its love of earth, its continuity, its humor, its patience, and its humanism can call upon those qualities of mind and heart and experience to light the way for a nation that has all too few of them. For as the age of technology, of electronics, of instant communications, of mass and regimented man slouches toward Bethlehem to be born, might we not be called upon to exalt again the idea of natural man in his natural environment?

        .   .   .   .   .

What a marvelously ironic notion! The reviled, beaten, recalcitrant, mean, and indolent South become the new Athens of a century of unimaginable dullness, mediocrity, apathy, materialism, ease, and conformity. But is it so strange an idea? . . .

I think it is not so strange a notion. For as technology and government combine to ease the ancient struggles for food, shelter, and security, Americans—including Southerners—surely face new battles against new and insidious dangers to humanity itself, and a new and sweeping reconstruction of the conditions of life.

And where else but in the South have Americans learned so well to fight such wars—to make do with what is left to them, to cling to their identity, to cherish their individuality, to live with themselves in their surroundings?[10]

Harry Byrd and his organization were rich and valuable parts of any southern uniqueness of history and humanity. Byrd was born of the somber side of southern history. His organization, notwithstanding its faults, was truly coined from

[9] See *ibid.*

[10] Address at annual meeting of the Southern Regional Education Board in Miami, June 1966 (printed in Richmond *Times-Dispatch*, June 26, 1966).

the mint of its time. If it was parsimonious, it emerged from a period when Virginia had little of which to give. If it feared deficits, it remembered the state's staggering Reconstruction debts. If it was oligarchic, it was so by reason of long inheritance. If it was regionally oriented, it bore still the scarred tissue of the Civil War. If it was rurally flavored, it respected the power of the farmer's franchise and the state's agrarian heritage. If it was slow—too slow—to change, Virginia had long been changeless.

There are those who end life feeling the future will nourish their cause. There are those also whose causes pass with themselves. Harry Byrd's political cause belonged to the latter category. In the nation a more positive role for federal government was fast becoming an American political axiom; likewise, Harry Byrd's Virginia would soon seem but yesteryear's quaint and curious memento. But Byrd's personal cause—his honesty, courtesy, in short, his humanity—was not tied to time. The greatest men have often urged dated or debatable specifics. George Washington warned against foreign alliances; Thomas Jefferson dreamed of an agrarian utopia; Woodrow Wilson warred against bigness in American life; Robert E. Lee struggled valiantly for a divided nation. History values men as much for what they are as for what they espouse. Let not its view of balanced budgets determine its judgment of Harry Byrd.

Appendixes, Bibliography and Index

Appendix I

Traditional Form of County Government in Virginia *

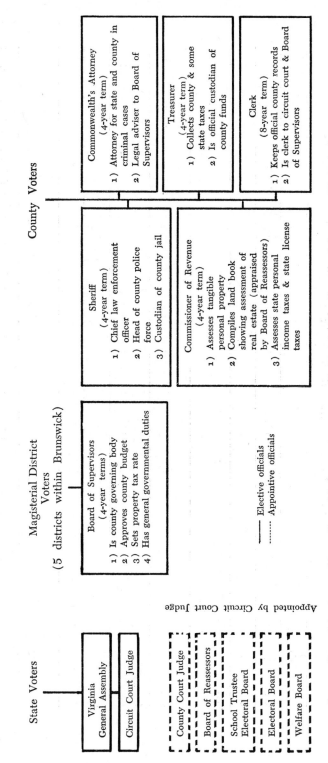

State Voters

Virginia General Assembly

Circuit Court Judge

Appointed by Circuit Court Judge

County Court Judge

Board of Reassessors

School Trustee Electoral Board

Electoral Board

Welfare Board

Magisterial District Voters
(5 districts within Brunswick)

Board of Supervisors
(4-year terms)
1) Is county governing body
2) Approves county budget
3) Sets property tax rate
4) Has general governmental duties

Sheriff
(4-year term)
1) Chief law enforcement officer
2) Head of county police force
3) Custodian of county jail

Commissioner of Revenue
(4-year term)
1) Assesses tangible personal property
2) Compiles land book showing assessment of real estate (appraised by Board of Reassessors)
3) Assesses state personal income taxes & state license taxes

County Voters

Commonwealth's Attorney
(4-year term)
1) Attorney for state and county in criminal cases
2) Legal adviser to Board of Supervisors

Treasurer
(4-year term)
1) Collects county & some state taxes
2) Is official custodian of county funds

Clerk
(8-year term)
1) Keeps official county records
2) Is clerk to circuit court & Board of Supervisors

———— Elective officials
·········· Appointive officials

Sources: Personal inquiry on visits to Brunswick County, Aug. 1–3, 1966; Virginia State State Chamber of Commerce, *Virginia's Government*, pp. 98–104.

* This chart has been simplified for clarity. It in no way pretends to describe the full operation of county government but only to sketch its major functions.

Appendix II

Paths to Leadership in the Byrd Organization

Office	Tuck	Battle	Stanley	Almond	Harrison	Godwin	Robertson
Governor	1946–50	1950–54	1954–58	1958–62	1962–66	1966–	
U.S. Senator							1946–66
Lieutenant Governor	1942–46					1962–66	
Attorney General				1948–57	1958–62		
U.S. Representative			1946–53	1946–48			1933–46
State Senator		1934–50			1948–58	1952–62	1916–22
State Delegate		1930–33	1930–46			1948–52	
County or City Office *	1932–42			1933–45 †	1932–48 ‡		1922–28 §

Years served in lower appointive and elective offices before reaching governor's chair or U.S. Senate were as follows: Tuck, 22; Battle, 20; Stanley, 24; Almond, 25; Harrison, 30; Godwin, 18; Robertson, 30.

† Almond was judge of the hustings court in the city of Roanoke.

‡ Harrison was commonwealth's attorney of Brunswick County.

§ Robertson was commonwealth's attorney for Rockbridge County; from 1926 to 1932 he served as chairman of the Commission of Game and Inland Fisheries.

* Offices below the rank of county constitutional officer are not included (for example, Almond's three years as assistant commonwealth's attorney of Roanoke).

Appendix III

Platform of Moss A. Plunkett in 1945 Democratic Primary

"Virginia has lagged behind all of the States in the Union in suffrage, education, health, welfare and crime prevention." [1]

Suffrage—Repeal of the poll tax as a prerequisite to voting. Adoption of a reasonable literacy test as a qualification for registration and voting, bearing in mind that it is the interest of the individual and not of a political machine which must be served. Creation of truly bipartisan electoral boards. Revision of the absentee voter law and other election laws to simplify Democratic processes and eliminate corruption.

Judiciary—Immediate divorce of judiciary from politics by relieving the judges of all political appointments.

Taxation—A revision of the tax laws of the State to correct the evils of the tax segregation system, which has enriched the State and pauperized the localities, to insure uniformity of taxes on the various classes of property and to distribute the remainder of the tax burden, including new taxes necessary for education, health and welfare on the basis of ability to pay. The proposed sales tax would violate the sound principle last stated and is opposed for that reason.

Agriculture—Housing of all agricultural agencies in Richmond in one new building. Full cooperation with the localities and the Federal government in all conservation and development programs beneficial to agriculture, the largest business in the State.

Industry—Encouragement of new and diverse industries, properly located, so that our numerous resources may be utilized and a stable economy established.

Labor—Recognition and protection of labor's rights to bargain collectively and to decent wages and working conditions. Improvement of

[1] Platform is reprinted from the Richmond *Times-Dispatch,* July 12, 1945.

laws relating to unemployment and workmen's compensation. Upon the buying power of those who labor depends the fortunes of those who produce, distribute and sell.

Civil Service—A progressive, non-political Civil Service system for all State employees.

Housing and Public Works—Encouragement of slum clearance and modern housing programs by all localities including full cooperation with local welfare agencies. . . .

Education—Immediate minimum appropriation of $100 per annum for each child in average daily attendance in the public schools. This is essential to competent instruction, adequate courses, necessary equipment, free textbooks, public transportation and other services. Emphasis must be placed upon steadily increasing salaries and adequate retirement provisions for teachers.

Health—Assurance of medical care for every person in Virginia by establishing county or district health departments and ample hospital centers throughout the State with suitable provisions for those unable to pay.

Welfare—Increased appropriations for those requiring public assistance to an amount per person at least equal to the average in other States.

Crime Prevention—An immediate comprehensive study to ascertain why Virginia's crime rate is four times that of the nation as a whole. Prompt application of the lesson learned.

Roads—Immediate planning for a comprehensive development of the entire system of highways including farm-to-market and school roads to be launched in cooperation with the Federal government at the end of the war.

Appendix IV

Investigation of State Compensation Board

In its investigation of the Board the Richmond *News-Leader* determined the total allowances granted by the Board to officials in each county and city in Virginia. This actual allowance was then compared to a par value, i.e., the allowances that local officials ought to receive solely on the basis of their work load. Finally, all areas were assigned a Byrd loyalty rating on the basis of their support for Senator Byrd in his fight against Francis Pickens Miller in the 1952 Democratic primary. By comparison of the loyalty rating with the percentage of "par" of actual official allowances, it was possible to determine whether officials' salaries had any relation to their devotion to the organization. Excerpts from the findings follow:

County or city	Total allowances	Total par	Per cent of par *	Byrd loyalty † rating
Albemarle	$ 90,593	$ 64,010	141	76.7
Buchanan	74,661	68,714	109	33.8
Carroll	53,100	56,456	94	38.7
Dickenson	66,362	46,422	143	26.8
Fauquier	56,613	52,864	107	83.7
Frederick	35,562	44,374	80	84.2
Hanover	40,304	53,230	76	68.7
Lee	51,110	62,437	82	30.2
Pittsylvania	97,027	126,640	77	68.8
Scott	67,171	53,020	127	34.3
Alexandria	216,370	155,035	139	53.9
Norfolk	396,999	433,631	91	55.4
Newport News	138,238	103,676	133	48.5
Richmond	455,515	564,062	81	63.2

Source: Richmond *News Leader*, Aug. 12, 1955.

* If per cent of par is over 100, officials in a county are relatively overpaid. If per cent of par is under 100, they are relatively underpaid.

† Compare Columns C and D to find relation between salary scales and Byrd support. Notice that some anti-Byrd localities such as Buchanan, Dickenson, and Scott have relatively overpaid officials, while some loyal Byrd counties such as Frederick and Pittsylvania have underpaid officials. The reverse situation also exists.

Appendix V

Apportionment of the Virginia Legislature (1956)

Congressional District	Population (1950)	Rural population	Vote for Byrd in 1952 Primary	Delegates *	Senators	Ratio of state representatives to inhabitants †
		%	%			
1	307,144	47.1	60.6	9.5	4	1/22,751
2	408,923	5.8	50.3	10	4	1/28,852
3	334,127	17.9	63.2	10	3.5	1/24,750
4	338,514	74.2	70.1	11.5	5	1/20,516
5	316,734	75.6	65.4	10	4	1/22,624
6	337,947	44.1	62.6	10	3.5	1/25,033
7	289,598	71.8	77.6	10.5	4.5	1/19,307
8	296,985	84.6	72.9	9.5	4	1/21,999
9	390,380	83.8	47.2	13	4.5	1/22,307
10	303,328	23.6	53.2	6	3	1/33,703
State	3,318,680	53.0	62.7	100.0	40.0	1/23,705

Sources: U.S. Census, *County and City Data Book, 1956*, p. 512; official election returns, 1952 Democratic primary; *General Assembly Manual, 1956.*

* Delegates representing constituencies in two congressional districts are counted as one-half for each district.

† A strict population standard leaves much to be desired as a measurement of the equity of traditional apportionment schemes in the South. One must take into account that Negroes, especially in rural areas, had very little say in the political process and their inclusion in apportionment charts giving ratios of representatives to total inhabitants distorts the results. Whites in rural districts with large numbers of Negroes (such as the 1st, 4th, 5th, and 8th Districts) were even more overrepresented than this table indicates.

Appendix VI

Votes of Virginia's 1965 Congressional Delegation

A. Conservative coalition scores — Percentage of 1965 votes (51, House; 61, Senate) cast with and against the conservative coalition when the majority of voting Republicans and the majority of voting southern Democrats, forming a "conservative coalition," opposed the stand taken by the majority of voting northern Democrats. (Failure to vote lowers both scores.) Mississippi, South Carolina, and North Carolina were the only delegations supporting the conservative coalition more frequently than Virginia.

Virginia congressmen	Votes supporting conservative coalition	Votes opposing conservative coalition
	%	%
John O. Marsh (Dem., 7th District)	100	0
Richard H. Poff (Rep., 6th District)	100	0
David E. Satterfield, III (Dem., 3rd District)	100	0
Howard W. Smith (Dem., 8th District)	100	0
Watkins M. Abbitt (Dem., 4th District)	98	0
William M. Tuck (Dem., 5th District)	98	0
Joel T. Broyhill (Rep., 10th District)	94	4
Thomas N. Downing (Dem., 1st District)	86	10
Porter Hardy, Jr. (Dem., 2nd District)	53	14
W. Pat Jennings (Dem., 9th District)	57	37
Virginia senators		
Harry Flood Byrd (Dem.)	52 *	2
A. Willis Robertson (Dem.)	77	8

Source for sections A, B, C: *Congressional Quarterly Almanac, 1965*, pp. 1092–94, 1101–4, 1115–17.

* Byrd's arthritis kept him away from several votes in 1965 and consequently lowered his scores.

B. *Support for or opposition to Johnson* — Percentage of 1965 votes (112, House; 162, Senate) in which representative agrees or disagrees with President Johnson's position. (Failure to vote lowers both scores.) Mississippi was the only state to disagree with Johnson more often than Virginia.

Virginia congressmen and senators	Votes in agreement with Johnson	Votes in disagreement with Johnson
	%	%
Tuck	31	60
Poff	34	66
Abbitt	35	55
Marsh	38	62
Satterfield	38	62
Smith	38	56
Broyhill	42	51
Downing	54	41
Hardy	54	28
Jennings	70	23
Byrd	15	35
Robertson	31	51

C. *Support for larger federal role* — Number of key 1965 roll call votes (13, House; 12, Senate) on which representative favored or opposed larger federal role. Votes include crucial "Great Society" issues such as Rent Subsidies, Medicare, Aid to Education. Mississippi was the only state to oppose a larger federal role more often than Virginia.

Virginia congressmen and senators	Votes for larger federal role	Votes against larger federal role
Poff	1	12
Abbitt	1	11
Marsh	2	11
Satterfield	2	11
Smith	2	11
Tuck	2	11
Broyhill	3	10
Downing	4	9
Hardy	5	8
Jennings	12	1
Byrd	1	10
Robertson	0	12

Appendix VII

Virginia's School Enrollment (1950 and 1960)

School population by age	1950			1960		
	National average	Virginia	Virginia's rank *	National average	Virginia	Virginia's rank †
	%	%		%	%	
5–29 years	49.4	45.1	48th	—	—	—
16 and 17	74.4	63.9	46th	80.9	72.8	49th
18 and 19	32.2	25.0	47th	42.1	36.2	48th
20 and 21	—	—	—	21.1	15.5	50th
22 to 24	—	—	—	10.2	6.7	49th
20 to 24	12.9	9.3	48th	—	—	—
Median school years completed (persons 25 years & over)	9.3	8.5	40th	10.6	8.8	48th

Sources: U.S. Bureau of the Census, *Population, 1950*, II, A, *U.S. Summary*, and *Population, 1960*, I, A, *U.S. Summary*.
* Survey includes 48 states and District of Columbia.
† Survey includes 50 states and District of Columbia.

Appendix VIII

Richmond's Negro Precinct 64: Voting in 1966 Council Election

Candidate	Votes received
Marsh III (Negro) *	1,015
Cephas (Negro) *,†	957
Mundle (Negro) *,†	876
Carwile *	813
Bagley *,†	688
House *	479
Covey *	444
Sheppard †	437
Crowe †	343
Wheat †	261
Miller †	238
Habenicht †	223
R. T. Marsh †	213
Throckmorton	159
Bradley	94
Holt	68

Source: Richmond *News Leader*, June 15, 1966.
* Endorsed by Crusade for Voters.
† Endorsed by Richmond Forward.

Appendix IX

Distribution of Proceeds of State Sales Tax
December 1966

The following table gives a sampling of sales tax proceeds distributed in December 1966. It will be noted that the rural counties in southside and southwest Virginia received substantially more from the 1 per cent of the state sales tax distributed to localities on the basis of school age population than from their 1 per cent local option taxes. These counties had large school age populations with a clear need for improved educational systems. They would be hard pressed to finance the improvements solely on the basis of revenue from local sales.

On the other hand, such cities and suburban counties as Richmond, Norfolk, Arlington, and Henrico gained far more from the 1 per cent local option taxes. Sales in these localities were brisk, and these areas claimed that the bulk of the revenue should be returned to the trading centers from whence it came. In the 1 per cent local option provision, the claim was honored; under the school age population formula the big metropolitan areas might help to bolster less fortunate school systems in the rest of the state.

Locality	Description	Proceeds from state tax returned on school age population basis	Proceeds from 1% local option tax
Brunswick Co.	Rural-southside Va.	$ 16,526.00	$ 7,714.00
Buchanan Co.	Rural-southwest Va.	46,541.00	18,018.00
Mecklenburg Co.	Rural-southside Va.	31,821.00	21,945.00
Arlington Co.	Washington suburbs	117,196.00	181,857.00
Henrico Co.	Richmond suburbs	125,224.00	158,039.00
Norfolk City		220,172.00	338,230.00
Richmond City		141,894.00	350,889.00

Source: Official accounts of distribution of sales tax revenue in Comptroller's Office, State Finance Building, Richmond, Va.

Appendix X

Voting for United States Senator in Selected Predominantly Negro Precincts in Virginia (1966 Primary)*

City	Precinct	Spong	Per cent	Robertson	Per cent	Total	Boothe	Per cent	Byrd	Per cent	Total
Charlottesville	Firehouse	263	79.2	69	20.8	332	275	83.1	56	16.9	331
Lynchburg	1-1	206	77.4	60	22.6	266	210	77.8	60	22.2	270
Norfolk	1	473	88.7	60	11.3	533	485	93.4	34	6.6	519
Norfolk	2	598	92.6	48	7.4	646	610	97.8	14	2.2	624
Norfolk	4	1,117	95.9	48	4.1	1,165	1,118	98.2	20	1.8	1,138
Norfolk	5	499	92.9	38	7.1	537	514	98.8	6	1.2	520
Norfolk	6	339	93.9	22	6.1	361	345	98.0	7	2.0	352
Norfolk	7	536	94.9	29	5.1	565	544	98.4	9	1.6	553
Norfolk	8	856	90.4	91	9.6	947	873	97.7	21	2.3	894
Norfolk	9	176	93.1	13	6.9	189	178	96.7	6	3.3	184
Norfolk	17	375	85.8	62	14.2	437	384	91.9	34	8.1	418
Norfolk	42	691	97.2	20	2.8	711	699	99.3	5	.7	704
Virginia Beach	Seatack	228	67.1	112	32.9	340	239	72.2	92	27.8	331
Portsmouth	Stuart-8d	1,390	96.0	58	4.0	1,448	1,298	98.2	24	1.8	1,322
Hampton	Kecoughtan	547	96.1	22	3.9	569	548	97.0	17	3.0	565
Hampton	Pembroke	600	95.2	30	4.8	630	618	97.6	15	2.4	633
Newport News	2-1	371	71.6	147	28.4	518	445	90.4	47	9.6	492
Newport News	2-2	441	88.2	59	11.8	500	476	96.6	17	3.4	493
Newport News	2-3	398	90.2	43	9.8	441	419	97.0	13	3.0	432
Newport News	3-2	337	79.7	86	20.3	423	369	90.0	41	10.0	410
Newport News	3-5	582	86.4	92	13.6	674	622	95.5	29	4.5	651
Newport News	Jeff. Park	489	89.6	57	10.4	546	516	97.0	16	3.0	532

Appendix X (continued)

City	Precinct	Spong	Per cent	Robert-son	Per cent	Total	Boothe	Per cent	Byrd	Per cent	Total
Richmond	1	293	95.4	14	4.6	307	305	98.4	5	1.6	310
Richmond	4	495	93.2	36	6.8	531	513	97.3	14	2.7	527
Richmond	5	146	81.1	34	18.9	180	159	85.0	28	15.0	187
Richmond	6	260	86.7	40	13.3	300	257	86.5	40	13.5	297
Richmond	18	751	97.2	22	2.8	773	772	98.6	11	1.4	783
Richmond	19	477	92.3	40	7.7	517	467	93.0	35	7.0	502
Richmond	24	665	93.3	48	6.7	713	682	94.7	38	5.3	720
Richmond	46	729	94.6	42	5.4	771	744	97.1	22	2.9	766
Richmond	55	618	95.4	30	4.6	648	623	97.2	18	2.8	641
Richmond	62	891	94.9	48	5.1	939	913	97.6	22	2.4	935
Richmond	63	175	90.2	19	9.8	194	178	93.7	12	6.3	190
Richmond	64	860	96.3	33	3.7	893	884	99.5	4	.5	888
Richmond	65	495	93.2	36	6.8	531	511	97.0	16	3.0	527
Richmond	66	593	95.0	31	5.0	624	599	97.9	13	2.1	612
Richmond	67	724	94.9	39	5.1	763	735	97.7	17	2.3	752
Totals		19,684	91.7	1,778	8.3	21,462	20,127	95.8	878	4.2	21,005

Source: Taken from Ralph Eisenberg, "1966 Politics in Virginia: The Democratic Senatorial Primary," *University of Virginia News Letter*, Jan. 15, 1967, p. 3.
* Based on preliminary voting returns.

Appendix XI

Voting Studies, 1945–1964

THE following is a brief analysis of the decline of the Byrd organization as shown on voting maps of eight important statewide elections from 1945 to 1966. It supplements election data in the text.

App. Map I illustrates the overwhelming victory scored by Tuck over Plunkett in the 1945 Democratic primary. From 1925 to 1945 the organization had been winning statewide elections easily, often with 70 per cent or more of the total vote. Tuck's was the last of these landslide victories. As the map illustrates, Tuck won primarily on the basis of widely dispersed rural strength. He carried 96 of Virginia's 100 counties, took 76.7 per cent of the total county vote, and carried 60 per cent of all counties by margins of better than 3 to 1 (75 per cent). The organization was still strong in areas which later came to plague it (i.e., southwest Virginia, Washington suburbs, and Hampton Roads). Although Virginia's larger cities (Richmond, Norfolk, Roanoke, Newport News, and Alexandria) were not so enthusiastic about Tuck as the counties, their vote was irrelevant in the face of one-sided county returns.

With the Byrd-Hutchinson race of 1946 (App. Map II) emerged a more clearly discernible urban-rural split. The rural majorities of the organization still held up, especially in the Shenandoah Valley and the Piedmont, but the organization sagged noticeably in urban and suburban areas and in far southwest Virginia. Byrd lost the suburban counties of Henrico, Chesterfield, and Norfolk and ran well below his statewide percentage in Elizabeth City, Warwick, Arlington, Fairfax, and Roanoke. Only Lynchburg, among the commonwealth's largest cities, gave Byrd good support. (See Chapter 4 for a description and general analysis of the 1949 Democratic primary.)

Byrd's 1952 race against Miller (App. Map III) shows the development of several trends which eventually caused the organization's decline. Southwest Virginia, as in the 1949 Democratic primary, went against the organization, primarily in response to Byrd's refusal to support national Democratic tickets. Byrd lost many of the counties in the area by wide margins and only narrowly won several others. Several light-voting counties in the urban corridor (Prince William, Stafford, Spotsylvania) also gave diminished percentages of their vote to Byrd. The organization had not substantially improved its standing with the urban community, and urban areas were casting increasing shares of the total vote (see Chapter 7, Part D).

App. Maps II and III demonstrate that Byrd polled his highest percentages in the Shenandoah Valley (Frederick to Rockbridge counties), and the northern Piedmont (Loudoun to Albemarle). This picture varied somewhat for the organization's candidates for governor (see App. Maps I, IV, V, VI), most of whom ran strongest in the Southside. This slight variation in relative strengths of the different candidates is an interesting comment on "friends 'n neighbors" voting in Virginia. Regional appeals and identifications (such as Byrd was able to strike with the Shenandoah Valley and northern Piedmont, and Tuck, Stanley, and Harrison struck with the Southside) generally made a difference of 5 to 10 per cent of a county's vote. That the fluctuation was so small testifies to the entrenched positions of the Byrd organization across the state. The relative predictability of the vote in each county regardless of the particular candidate was almost unique in the South. In each of the eight Appendix maps the homes of the candidates are marked. Note that many antiorganization candidates failed to carry areas adjacent to their homes (see Plunkett in App. Map I, Miller in App. Map III, Stephens in App. Map VI). Localism and "friends 'n neighbors" voting were negligible in comparison with such voting in most other southern states.

The Stanley-Dalton race of 1953 (App. Map IV) was the first in a series of three elections where southside Virginia spearheaded the organization's victory. The value of the Southside was its handsome support of the organization both in Democratic primaries and in general elections. (The Shenandoah Valley, on the other hand, though reliable territory for the machine in the primary, often had Republican proclivities in November.) Stanley garnered well over 70 per cent of the vote in all but a few southside counties and ran over 60 per cent in most other counties in the eastern two-thirds of the state. Republican Dalton was generally stronger in western Virginia, particularly in the traditionally Republican mountain counties from Botetourt to Smyth. In the east Dalton's inroads into normal Democratic strength came mainly in suburban counties (Arlington, Fairfax, Henrico) and cities (Norfolk, Hampton, Richmond, Newport News). Traditional Democratic allegiances in the rural areas generally held fast.

In the massive resistance campaign (App. Map V), Dalton was badly beaten. Almond's support predictably varied with the percentage of Negroes in the population (see Chapter 5, Map II). The more Negroes in a county, the more segregationist the white attitudes, and the more support for Almond. He thus ran best in the Southside, where Negroes were most numerous, well in the Northern Neck and Middle Peninsula,[1] where Negro population percentages were still high, and only slightly less well in the central and northern Piedmont, where Negro population tapered off a bit. In the Shenandoah Valley and Southwest, where Negroes were few, Almond's percentages were much less impressive. The organization picked up considerable support in the Hampton Roads and Richmond area. Massive resistance thus gave the machine swollen majorities in the eastern part of the state to cancel any disaffection in the western third and the more moderate Washington suburbs.

By 1961 massive resistance was over, and the areas which had long been disgruntled with the Byrd organization were in full-scale revolt. The organization reached its lowest ebb in the Southwest in the Harrison-Stephens race: Harrison collected but 29 per cent of the vote. The Washington suburbs gave Stephens almost 70 per cent of the vote for his attacks on the organization, and Hampton Roads also went against the machine, though the Harrison losses there were of manageable proportions. As expected, the Southside gave Harrison runaway margins, and the organization also ran well in the Valley, Piedmont, and Middle Peninsula. A big boost for the Harrison camp came from the increasingly conservative Richmond area. Henrico County gave Harrison 77 per cent of the vote. (App. Map VI; see Chapter 10 for an analysis of the 1965 general election.)

The 1966 primary is discussed in Chapter 12. The two principal reasons for Robertson's loss and Byrd's near loss were the growth of the Negro vote (see Appendix X) and the fatal weaknesses of the organization in urban and metropolitan areas. As App. Map VII demonstrates, Byrd, Jr., lost almost every large city (Alexandria, Chesapeake, Hampton, Newport News, Norfolk, Portsmouth, Richmond, Roanoke, and Virginia Beach). Significantly the organization also lost smaller cities which had once been reliable territory. Boothe carried Charlottesville, Fredericksburg, and Petersburg. Rarely had any of these cities deserted the organization in previous elections, but the growing Negro vote in Petersburg and Negro, academic and urban influences in Charlottesville and Fredericksburg were causing shifts in these three localities.

What App. Map VII demonstrates (and the analysis in Chapter 12 does not bring this out) is the weakening situation of the hard-core organization, even in the counties. Its urban weaknesses had long been apparent, but Byrd, Jr., did not approximate the margins of earlier

---

[1] Middle Peninsula includes Essex, Gloucester, King and Queen, King William, Mathews, and Middlesex counties.

organization candidates in rural and semirural areas. The organization fared somewhat better in the Southwest than in the 1961 Democratic primary, but that was virtually the only improvement in its rural position. On both the eastern and western tips of the Southside, the Byrd organization was slumping. It lost Patrick County for the first time and Byrd, Jr., carried Henry and Franklin Counties by 53 and 56 per cent respectively. These two counties, however, had long been trending against the machine. Robertson actually lost the city of Martinsville. On the eastern fringe of the Southside, the spillover of Hampton Roads influences and the growing Negro vote cut into the organization's majorities. Both Byrd, Jr., and Robertson were soundly beaten in Nansemond County; and such counties as Greenville, Isle of Wight, Surry, and Prince George showed less enthusiasm for the organization than in times past.

Another area of growing weakness was in the northeastern portion of the state. The invasion from the Washington suburbs cut into the machine's margins in Loudoun, Fauquier, and Prince William. Growth along the urban corridor, Negro voting, and energetic work by Byrd opponents such as George Rawlings eliminated the organization's margins in Stafford, Spotsylvania, Caroline, and King and Queen. Even the upper tier of counties in the Northern Neck (King George, Westmoreland, Northumberland) all gave Byrd, Jr., under 55 per cent of the vote. The organization's strength in the counties was far less formidable than in the past.

App. Map VIII merely illustrates how Spong successfully challenged the Byrd organization from a limited regional base. His only pocket of rural strength was in the Southwest, but the urban majorities outlined in Chapter 12 were sufficient to edge out Robertson for the first statewide defeat that the Byrd organization had suffered since its inception in 1925.

App. Map I. Democratic Primary for Governor, Tuck v. Plunkett (1945)

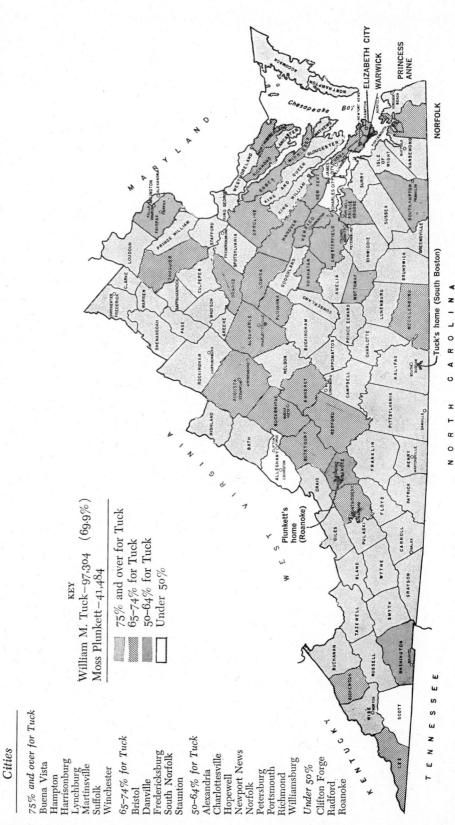

KEY

William M. Tuck—97,304   (69.9%)
Moss Plunkett—41,484

75% and over for Tuck
65–74% for Tuck
50–64% for Tuck
Under 50%

Cities

75% and over for Tuck
Buena Vista
Hampton
Harrisonburg
Lynchburg
Martinsville
Suffolk
Winchester

65–74% for Tuck
Bristol
Danville
Fredericksburg
South Norfolk
Staunton

50–64% for Tuck
Alexandria
Charlottesville
Hopewell
Newport News
Norfolk
Petersburg
Portsmouth
Richmond
Williamsburg

Under 50%
Clifton Forge
Radford
Roanoke

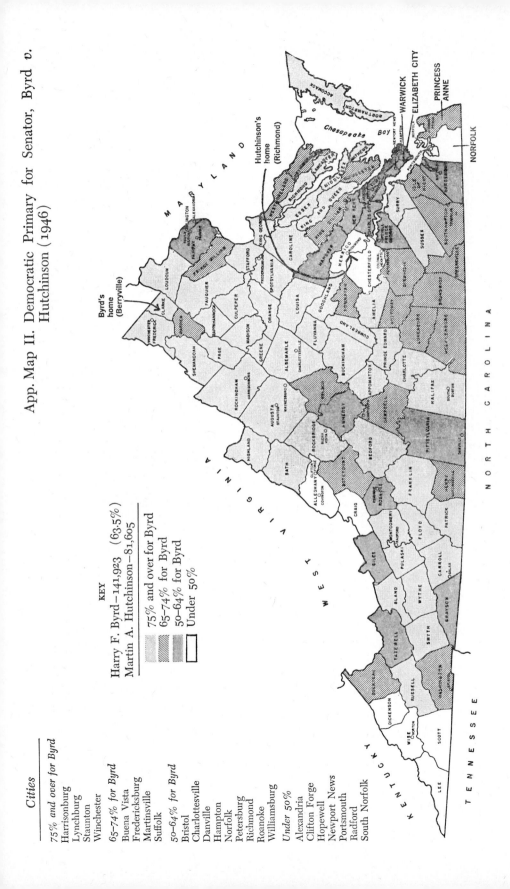

App. Map II. Democratic Primary for Senator, Byrd *v.* Hutchinson (1946)

KEY

Harry F. Byrd—141,923 (63.5%)
Martin A. Hutchinson—81,605

75% and over for Byrd
65–74% for Byrd
50–64% for Byrd
Under 50%

Cities

75% and over for Byrd
Harrisonburg
Lynchburg
Staunton
Winchester

65–74% for Byrd
Buena Vista
Fredericksburg
Martinsville
Suffolk

50–64% for Byrd
Bristol
Charlottesville
Danville
Hampton
Norfolk
Petersburg
Richmond
Roanoke
Williamsburg

Under 50%
Alexandria
Clifton Forge
Hopewell
Newport News
Portsmouth
Radford
South Norfolk

Byrd's home (Berryville)

Hutchinson's home (Richmond)

App. Map III. Democratic Primary for Senator, Byrd v. Miller (1952)

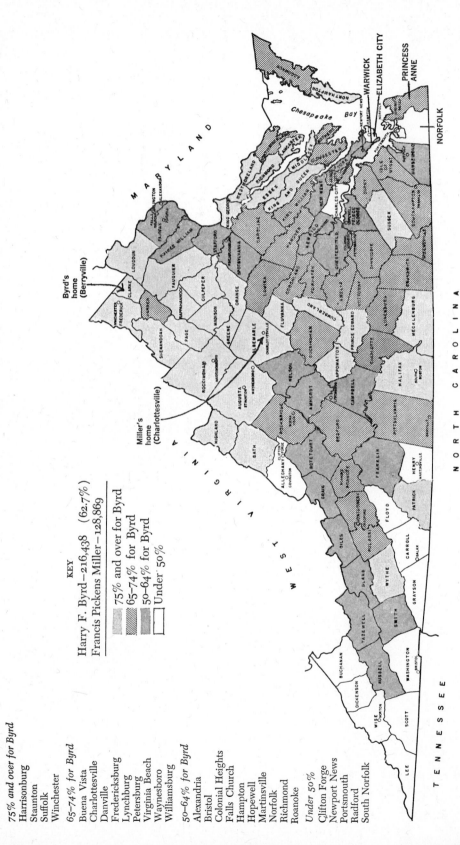

Cities

75% and over for Byrd
Harrisonburg
Staunton
Suffolk
Winchester

65–74% for Byrd
Buena Vista
Charlottesville
Danville
Fredericksburg
Lynchburg
Petersburg
Virginia Beach
Waynesboro
Williamsburg

50–64% for Byrd
Alexandria
Bristol
Colonial Heights
Falls Church
Hampton
Hopewell
Martinsville
Norfolk
Richmond
Roanoke

Under 50%
Clifton Forge
Newport News
Portsmouth
Radford
South Norfolk

KEY

Harry F. Byrd—216,438   (62.7%)
Francis Pickens Miller—128,869

75% and over for Byrd
65–74% for Byrd
50–64% for Byrd
Under 50%

Byrd's
home
(Berryville)

Miller's
home
(Charlottesville)

MARYLAND

VIRGINIA

WEST VIRGINIA

NORTH CAROLINA

TENNESSEE

Chesapeake Bay

NORFOLK

WARWICK
ELIZABETH CITY
PRINCESS ANNE

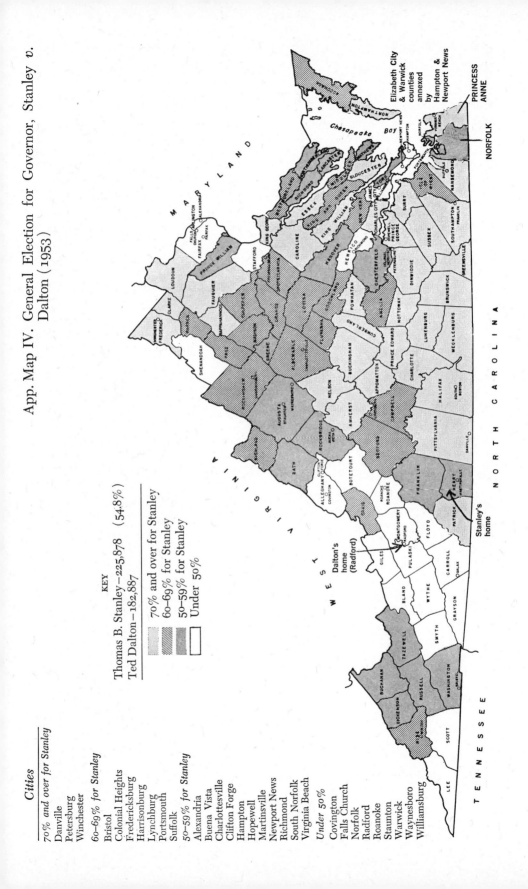

App. Map IV. General Election for Governor, Stanley v. Dalton (1953)

Cities

70% and over for Stanley
Danville
Petersburg
Winchester

60–69% for Stanley
Bristol
Colonial Heights
Fredericksburg
Harrisonburg
Lynchburg
Portsmouth
Suffolk

50–59% for Stanley
Alexandria
Buena Vista
Charlottesville
Clifton Forge
Hampton
Hopewell
Martinsville
Newport News
Richmond
South Norfolk
Virginia Beach

Under 50%
Covington
Falls Church
Norfolk
Radford
Roanoke
Staunton
Warwick
Waynesboro
Williamsburg

KEY

Thomas B. Stanley—225,878   (54.8%)
Ted Dalton—182,887

70% and over for Stanley
60–69% for Stanley
50–59% for Stanley
Under 50%

App. Map V. General Election for Governor, Almond *v.* Dalton (1957)

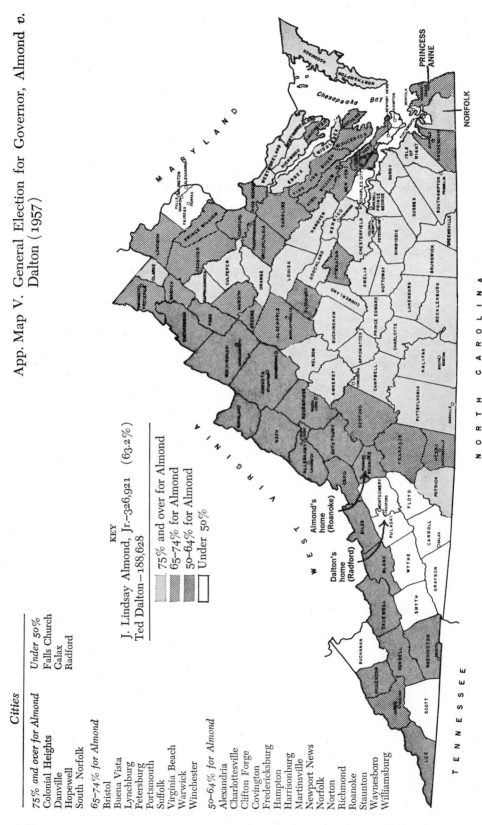

Cities

75% and over for Almond
Colonial Heights
Danville
Hopewell
South Norfolk

65–74% for Almond
Bristol
Buena Vista
Lynchburg
Petersburg
Portsmouth
Suffolk
Virginia Beach
Warwick
Winchester

50–64% for Almond
Alexandria
Charlottesville
Clifton Forge
Covington
Fredericksburg
Hampton
Harrisonburg
Martinsville
Newport News
Norfolk
Norton
Richmond
Roanoke
Staunton
Waynesboro
Williamsburg

Under 50%
Falls Church
Galax
Radford

KEY

J. Lindsay Almond, Jr.–326,921 (63.2%)
Ted Dalton–188,628

75% and over for Almond
65–74% for Almond
50–64% for Almond
Under 50%

App. Map VI. Democratic Primary for Governor, Harrison v. Stephens (1961)

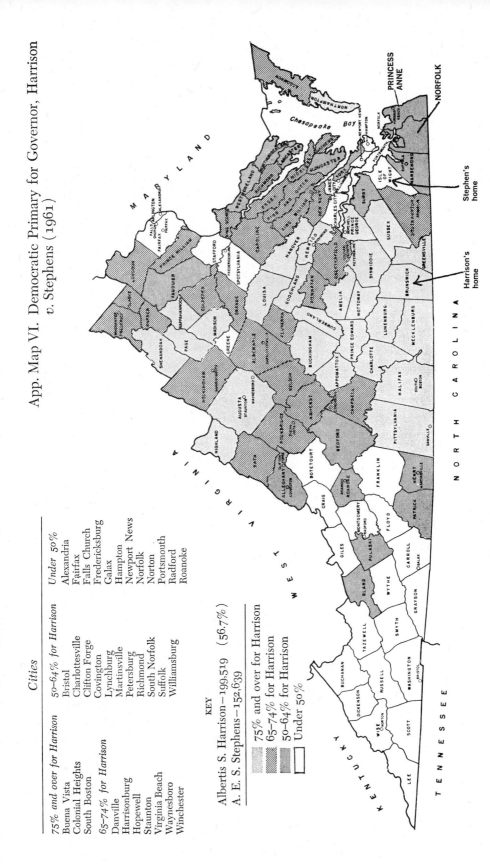

Cities

75% and over for Harrison
Buena Vista
Colonial Heights
South Boston

65–74% for Harrison
Danville
Harrisonburg
Hopewell
Staunton
Virginia Beach
Waynesboro
Winchester

50–64% for Harrison
Bristol
Charlottesville
Clifton Forge
Covington
Lynchburg
Martinsville
Petersburg
Richmond
South Norfolk
Suffolk
Williamsburg

Under 50%
Alexandria
Fairfax
Falls Church
Fredericksburg
Galax
Hampton
Newport News
Norfolk
Norton
Portsmouth
Radford
Roanoke

KEY

Albertis S. Harrison—199,519 (56.7%)
A. E. S. Stephens—152,639

75% and over for Harrison
65–74% for Harrison
50–64% for Harrison
Under 50%

App. Map VII. Democratic Primary for Senator, Byrd, Jr., *v.* Boothe (1966)

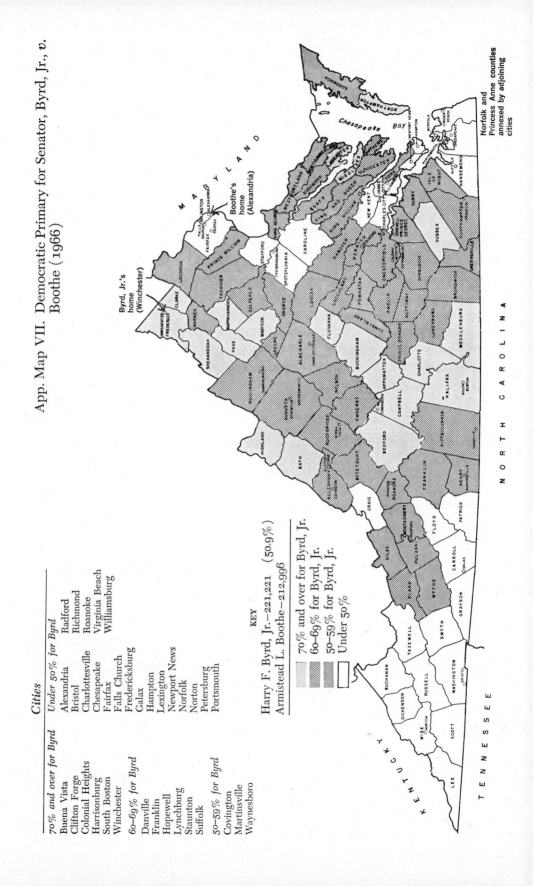

Cities

70% and over for Byrd
Buena Vista
Clifton Forge
Colonial Heights
Harrisonburg
South Boston
Winchester

60–69% for Byrd
Danville
Franklin
Hopewell
Lynchburg
Staunton
Suffolk

50–59% for Byrd
Covington
Martinsville
Waynesboro

Under 50% for Byrd
Alexandria   Radford
Bristol   Richmond
Charlottesville   Roanoke
Chesapeake   Virginia Beach
Fairfax   Williamsburg
Falls Church
Fredericksburg
Galax
Hampton
Lexington
Newport News
Norfolk
Norton
Petersburg
Portsmouth

KEY

Harry F. Byrd, Jr.—221,221   (50.9%)
Armistead L. Boothe—212,996

70% and over for Byrd, Jr.
60–69% for Byrd, Jr.
50–59% for Byrd, Jr.
Under 50%

Norfolk and Princess Anne counties annexed by adjoining cities

App. Map VIII. Democratic Primary for Senator, Spong *v.*
Robertson (1966)

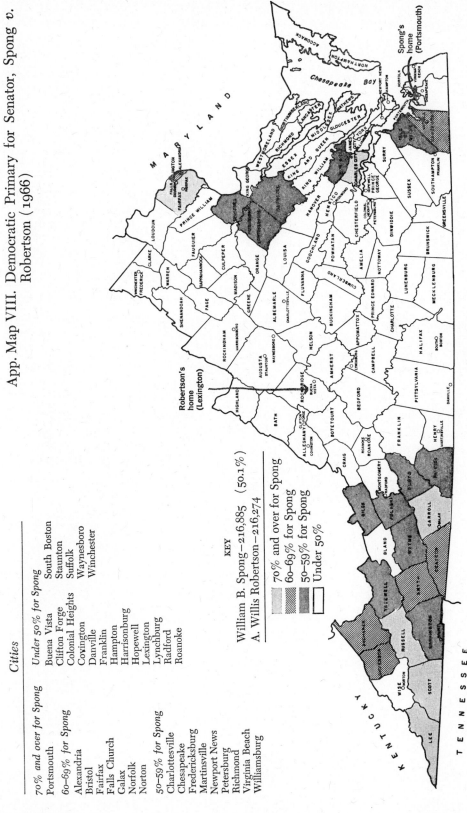

Cities

70% and over for Spong
Portsmouth

60–69% for Spong
Alexandria
Bristol
Fairfax
Falls Church
Galax
Norfolk
Norton

50–59% for Spong
Charlottesville
Chesapeake
Fredericksburg
Martinsville
Newport News
Petersburg
Richmond
Virginia Beach
Williamsburg

Under 50% for Spong
Buena Vista
Clifton Forge
Colonial Heights
Covington
Danville
Franklin
Hampton
Harrisonburg
Hopewell
Lexington
Lynchburg
Radford
Roanoke

South Boston
Staunton
Suffolk
Waynesboro
Winchester

KEY

William B. Spong—216,885 (50.1%)
A. Willis Robertson—216,274

70% and over for Spong
60–69% for Spong
50–59% for Spong
Under 50%

Bibliography

Manuscripts

Correspondence

Almond, J. Lindsay, Jr. Executive Papers, 1958–1962, Virginia State Library, Richmond.

Battle, John Stewart. Executive Papers, 1950–1954, Virginia State Library, Richmond.

Harrison, Albertis S. Executive Papers, 1962–1966, Virginia State Library, Richmond.

Hutchinson, Martin A. Personal Papers, Alderman Library, University of Virginia.

Stanley, Thomas B. Executive Papers, 1954–1958, Virginia State Library, Richmond.

Tuck, William M. Executive Papers, 1946–1950, Virginia State Library, Richmond.

Whitehead, Robert. Personal Papers, Alderman Library, University of Virginia.

Unpublished Reports, Special Studies, and Other Manuscript Materials

Clerks of the Circuit Court, Brunswick County. "Brunswick County Election Returns 1945–1955." Available in the Brunswick County Clerk's Office, Lawrenceville, Va.

Harris, W. Gibson, Jr. "J. Lindsay Almond and the Politics of School Desegregation in Virginia, 1954–1959." MS, Yale University, 1966.

Howard, Arthur D. "The Byrd Organization." MS, University of Richmond, May 1954.

Kilpatrick, James Jackson (ed.). "The Precinct Book: Voting in Richmond and Henrico County Precincts." Unpublished handbook in the offices of the Richmond *News Leader;* continually updated.

——. "Public Office in Richmond, Virginia, 1900–1964." Unpublished handbook in the offices of the Richmond *News Leader.*

Latimer, James. "Virginia Politics, 1950–1960." Unpublished MS, Richmond, 1961. Notes on Virginia politics by the chief political reporter for the Richmond *Times-Dispatch.*

Lilley, William. "The Southern Democracy in the Fair Deal, 1949–1950." Unpublished MS, Department of American Studies, Yale University, 1962.

Miller, Francis Pickens. "The Struggle for Democracy in Virginia." MS dated Feb. 1, 1956. In Hutchinson Papers, Alderman Library, University of Virginia.

Report of the Comptroller on Distribution of Sales Tax Proceeds, December 1966. Available at the State Finance Building, Richmond.

Reports on Campaign Expenditures. Filed by candidates at State Board of Elections, Richmond, 1953–66.

State Board of Elections. "Official Records of Voter Registration in Counties and Cities of Virginia 1950–1966." Mimeographed copies available at State Board of Elections, Richmond.

Thompson, Lorin A. "Income Payments by Cities and Counties, 1945 and 1947." University of Virginia Bureau of Population and Economic Research, Charlottesville.

Public Documents, State

Acts of the General Assembly of the Commonwealth of Virginia, 1946[–1966]. Richmond: Division of Purchase and Printing, 1946[–1966].

Bureau of Population and Economic Research, University of Virginia, *Estimates of the Population of the Counties and Cities of Virginia as of July 1, 1965.* Charlottesville, 1966.

Commission on Public Education. *Virginia's Schools in the Space Age—A Continued Evaluation of the Curriculum, Teacher Training, and Related Matters.* Richmond: Department of Purchases and Supply, 1961.

Constitution of Virginia, 1902. (The most up-to-date and best indexed version will be found in the most recent *Manual of the*

Virginia General Assembly. The constitution of 1902 is still in effect in Virginia, although it has often been amended.)

Division of Industrial Development and Planning. *Manufacturing Plants in Virginia Established Since 1950*. Richmond, 1966.

———. *The Virginia Economy in 1965*. Richmond, 1965.

Governors of Virginia. *Addresses to the People and General Assemblies of Virginia, 1946–1966*. Richmond: Division of Purchase and Printing, 1946–1966. (Individual speeches are available at the Virginia State Library, Richmond.)

Highway Commission of Virginia. *A Program of Highway Improvement, 1966–1975*. Richmond, 1966.

———. *Report, 1949–1950*. Richmond: Division of Purchase and Printing, 1950.

Journal of the House of Delegates of the Commonwealth of Virginia, 1946[–1966]. Richmond: Division of Purchase and Printing, 1946[–1966].

Journal of the Senate of Virginia, 1946[–1966]. Richmond: Division of Purchase and Printing, 1946[–1966].

Manuals of the Senate and the House of Delegates, 1946[–1966]. Richmond: Division of Purchase and Printing, 1946[–1966].

Report[s] of the Secretary of the Commonwealth to the Governor and General Assembly of Virginia, 1925[–1966]. Richmond: Division of Purchase and Printing, 1925[–1966].

Report of the Superintendent of Public Instruction, 1948–1949. Richmond: Division of Purchase and Printing, 1949.

State Board of Elections. *Official Statements of the Vote*. (Races for President, U.S. Senator, Governor, Lieutenant Governor, Attorney-General, U.S. Representative, and Member of the Virginia General Assembly, in Virginia General Elections and Democratic Primaries, 1945[–1966].) Richmond: Division of Purchase and Printing, 1945[–1966].

Virginia Advisory Legislative Council. *Urban Streets and Highways*. Richmond: Department of Purchases and Supply, 1966.

Virginia Election Laws in Effect as of July 1, 1966. Richmond: Department of Purchases and Supply, 1966.

Public Documents, National

The Book of the States, 1952[, 1954, 1966]. Chicago: Council of State Governments, 1952[, 1954, 1966].

Congress and the Nation, 1945–1964. Washington: Congressional Quarterly Service, 1965.

Congressional Quarterly Almanac. Vol. XI[, XVII, XXI]. Washington: Congressional Quarterly Service, 1955[, 1961, 1966].

Congressional Record (80th Congress, 1st Session), XCIII, Pt. 7, July 15, 1947.

U.S. Bureau of the Census. *Census of Population: 1950.* Vol. II, *Characteristics of the Population,* Pt. 1, *United States Summary.* Washington, 1953.

——. *Census of Population: 1950.* Vol. II, *Characteristics of the Population,* Pt. 46, *Virginia.* Washington, 1952.

——. *Census of Population: 1960.* Vol. I, *Characteristics of the Population,* Pt. 1, *United States Summary.* Washington, 1964.

——. *Census of Population: 1960.* Vol. I, *Characteristics of the Population,* Pt. 48, *Virginia.* Washington, 1963.

——. *Congressional District Data Book.* (*Districts of the 88th Congress*). Washington, 1963.

——. *County and City Data Book 1956.* Washington, 1956.

——. *State Government Finances in 1951.* Washington, 1951.

——. *State Tax Collections in 1962.* Washington, 1962.

Court Cases

Brown v. *Board of Education of Topeka,* 347 U.S. 483 (1954).
Harper v. *State Board of Elections,* 383 U.S. 663 (1966).
Harrison v. *Day,* 106 S.E. 2nd 636 (1959).
James v. *Almond,* 170 F. Supp. 342 (1959).
Reynolds v. *Sims,* 377 U.S. 533 (1964).
Wesberry v. *Sanders,* 376 U.S. 1 (1964).

Newspapers Consulted or Quoted

Charlottesville *Daily Progress.*
Lynchburg *News.*
New York *Times.*
Norfolk *Ledger-Dispatch.*
Norfolk *Virginian-Pilot.*
Richmond *Afro-American.*
Richmond *News Leader.*
Richmond *Times-Dispatch.*

Roanoke *Times.*
Roanoke *World News.*
Southern School News.
Suffolk *News-Herald.*
The Times (London).
The Virginia Observer.
The Wall Street Journal.
Washington *Post.*

Periodical Articles and Columns

Bennet, J. Gordon. "County Debt in Virginia," *University of Virginia News Letter,* May 15, 1957.

Blackford, Frank R. "Sidney Severn Kellam," *Virginia Record,* LXXXVII (March 1965).

Cope, Richard. "The Frustration of Harry Byrd," *Reporter,* Nov. 21, 1958.

Crawford, Kenneth. "Extinct Byrd," *Newsweek,* Nov. 29, 1965.

Dabney, Virginius. "What We Think of Senator Byrd's Machine," *Saturday Evening Post,* Jan. 7, 1950.

Egger, Rowland A. "Putting Our Financial House in Order," *Virginia Municipal Review,* XXXIV (Oct. 1957).

Eisenberg, Ralph. "The 1964 Presidential Election in Virginia: A Political Omen?" *University of Virginia News Letter,* April 15, 1965.

——. "1966 Politics in Virginia: The Democratic Senatorial Primary," *University of Virginia News Letter,* Jan. 15, 1967.

——. "Virginia Votes for President: Patterns and Prospects," *University of Virginia News Letter,* Sept. 15, 1964.

Forberg, F. C. "Assessment: Recent Developments in Virginia," *University of Virginia News Letter,* Dec. 15, 1960.

Grantham, Dewey W. "The South and the Reconstruction of American Politics," *Journal of American History,* LIV (Sept. 1966).

Holm, Edwin E. "The Changing Virginia Economy," *Virginia Economic Review,* XIV (Aug. 1962).

——. "The Importance of Education in the Economic Development of Virginia," *Virginia Economic Review,* XIV (July 1963).

——. "Virginia Grows Metropolitan," *Virginia Economic Review,* XIV (Jan. 1961).

Houston, Charles. "Smith and Robertson," *Commonwealth,* XXXIII (Oct. 1966).

Knapp, John L. "New Plants in Virginia," *Virginia Economic Review,* XV (Sept. 1963).

Lowance, Carter O. "The Governor of Virginia," *University of Virginia News Letter,* Feb. 15, 1960.

Makielski, S. J., Jr. "State Authorities: Virginia's Governmental Paradox," *University of Virginia News Letter,* July 15, 1965.

Manchester, William. "The Byrd Machine," *Harper's Magazine,* Nov. 1952.

Muse, Benjamin. "The Durability of Harry Flood Byrd," *Reporter,*
    Oct. 3, 1957.
Patterson, James T. "A Conservative Coalition Forms in Congress,
    1933–1939," *Journal of American History,* LII (March 1966).
Phillips, Cabell. "New Rumblings in the Old Dominion," *New York
    Times Magazine,* June 19, 1949.
———. "Virginia—The State and the State of Mind," *New York Times
    Magazine,* July 28, 1957.
Ragan, Allen E. "Virginia's Judicial System: Organization and Im-
    provement," *University of Virginia News Letter,* April 15, 1963.
Robinson, James A. "The Role of the Rules Committee in Arranging
    the Program of the U.S. House of Representatives," *Western
    Political Quarterly,* XII (Sept. 1959).
Snavely, Tipton R. "The Sales and Use Tax," *University of Virginia
    News Letter,* Nov. 15, 1955.
Spicer, George W. "Gubernatorial Leadership in Virginia," *Public
    Administration Review,* I (Autumn 1941).
Sutherland, M. M. "State Spending: Trends in the General Fund
    Budget," *University of Virginia News Letter,* Jan. 1, 1959.
Thompson, Lorin A. "Recent Population Changes in Virginia," *Uni-
    versity of Virginia News Letter,* Feb. 15, 1961.
———. "Virginia Population Changes: Age and Color 1960 and 1970,"
    University of Virginia News Letter, June 15, 1961.
Wicker, Thomas G. "The Role of the South in a Future America."
    Address delivered to the annual meeting of the Southern Re-
    gional Education Board in Miami, June 1966 (Printed in Rich-
    mond *Times-Dispatch,* June 26, 1966).
Woodward, C. Vann. "From the First Reconstruction to the Sec-
    ond," *Harper's Magazine,* CCXXX (April 1965).

Materials in the following periodicals are also cited: *America;
Congressional Digest; New Republic; Newsweek; Race Relations
Law Reporter; Time; United States News and World Report.*

Books

Bell, Edith Rathbun, and William Lightfoot Heartwell, Jr. *Bruns-
    wick Story: A History of Brunswick County.* Lawrenceville, Va.:
    Brunswick *Times-Gazette,* 1957.
Block, Maxine (ed.). *Current Biography 1942.* New York: H. W.
    Wilson Co., 1942.

Bolling, Richard. *House Out of Order.* New York: Dutton, 1965.

Clark, Thomas D. *The Emerging South.* New York: Oxford University Press, 1961.

Dabney, Virginius. *Dry Messiah.* New York: Alfred A. Knopf, 1949.

David, Paul T., and Ralph Eisenberg. *Devaluation of the Urban and Suburban Vote.* Charlottesville: University of Virginia Press, 1961.

——, Malcolm Moos, and Ralph M. Goldman. *Presidential Nominating Politics in 1952—The South.* Baltimore: Johns Hopkins Press, 1954.

Fishwick, Marshall W. *Virginia: A New Look at the Old Dominion.* New York: Harper and Brothers, 1959.

Friddell, Guy. *What Is It about Virginia?* Richmond: Dietz Press, 1966.

Gates, Robbins L. *The Making of Massive Resistance: Virginia's Politics of Public School Desegregation, 1954–1956.* Chapel Hill, N.C.: University of North Carolina Press, 1962.

Glueck, Sheldon (ed.). *The Welfare State and Our National Welfare.* Cambridge, Mass.: Addison Wesley Press, 1952.

Goldman, Eric R. *The Crucial Decade—and After.* New York: Random House, 1960.

Gottmann, Jean. *Virginia at Mid-Century.* New York: Holt, 1955.

Heard, Alexander. *A Two-Party South?* Chapel Hill, N.C.: University of North Carolina Press, 1952.

Hemphill, William Edwin, Marvin Wilson Schlegel, and Sadie Ethel Engelberg. *Cavalier Commonwealth.* New York: McGraw-Hill, 1957.

Houston, Charles. *Virginians in Congress.* Richmond: Richmond Newspapers, 1966.

Jacob, Herbert, and Kenneth N. Vines (eds.). *Politics in the American States.* Boston: Little, Brown and Co., 1965.

Key, V. O., Jr. *Southern Politics.* New York: Alfred A. Knopf, 1949.

Kilpatrick, James Jackson. *The Southern Case for School Segregation.* New York: Crowell-Collier Press, 1962.

Long, Huey. *Every Man a King: The Autobiography of Huey P. Long.* New Orleans: National Book Co., 1933.

Maclachlan, John M., and Joe S. Floyd, Jr. *This Changing South.* Gainesville, Fla.: University of Florida Press, 1956.

Muse, Benjamin. *Virginia's Massive Resistance.* Bloomington, Ind.: Indiana University Press, 1961.

National Education Association of the United States. *Educational Differences among the States, March 1954.* Washington, 1954.

——. *Rankings of the States, 1957[, 1963].* Washington, 1957[, 1963].

Reichley, James. *States in Crisis.* Chapel Hill, N.C.: University of North Carolina Press, 1964.

Richmond Chamber of Commerce. *Why the Richmond Chamber of Commerce Favors the City Manager Plan for Richmond.* Richmond: 1947.

Virginia State Chamber of Commerce. *Virginia's Government.* Richmond: Whittet and Shepperson, 1964.

White, William S. *Citadel.* New York: Harper and Brothers, 1956.

Woodward, C. Vann. *Origins of the New South, 1877–1913.* Baton Rouge, La.: Louisiana State University Press, 1951.

——. *The Burden of Southern History.* New York: Random House, 1960.

Wright, Jim. *You and Your Congressman.* New York: Coward-McCann, 1965.

Index

Harry Byrd
and the Changing Face
of Virginia Politics

was composed, printed, and bound by Kingsport Press, Inc., Kingsport, Tennessee. The paper is Glatfelter's GM, and the types are Caledonia and Bell. Design is by Edward G. Foss.